CRIMINAL PROCEDURE
FOR THE CRIMINAL JUSTICE PROFESSIONAL

FOURTH EDITION

CRIMINAL PROCEDURE

FOR THE CRIMINAL JUSTICE PROFESSIONAL

FOURTH EDITION

John N. Ferdico, J.D.
Member of the Maine Bar

Former Assistant Attorney General
and Director of Law Enforcement Education
for the State of Maine

WEST PUBLISHING CO.
St. Paul • New York • Los Angeles • San Francisco

Copy editing: Cheryl Drivdahl
Composition: Rolin Graphics
Cover Art: "Street Scene" 1959. Oil on panel, 16¼ x 20½ inches by Lennart Anderson.
Private collection.

Lennart Anderson studied at the Art Institute of Chicago (BFA), Cranbrook Academy (MFA), and Art Students League. He has received many awards including a Guggenheim Fellowship, 1983. The Museum of Fine Arts, Boston and the Whitney Museum of American Art, New York are only two of the museums that own Anderson's work. He is currently Distinguished Professor of Art at Brooklyn College, New York, and is represented by Davis & Langdale Company, New York.

COPYRIGHT © 1975,
1979, 1985   By WEST PUBLISHING COMPANY
COPYRIGHT © 1989 By WEST PUBLISHING COMPANY
50 W. Kellogg Boulevard
P.O. Box 64526
St. Paul, MN 55164-1003

Printed in the United States of America

96 95 94 93 92 91 90 89   8 7 6 5 4 3 2 1 0

Library of Congress Cataloging-in-Publication Data

Ferdico, John N.
  Criminal procedure for the criminal justice professional/John N. Ferdico.—4th ed.
    p.   cm.
  Includes index.
  ISBN 0–314–47350–5
  1. Criminal procedure—United States.   I. Title.
KF9619.F47   1989
345.73'05—dc19
[347.3055]   88–34660
          CIP

Preface

The fourth edition of *Criminal Procedure for the Criminal Justice Professional* is a complete revision and update of the third edition, which was published in 1985. This new edition covers all major developments in the law since the last revision, through September 30, 1988, with emphasis on decisions of the United States Supreme Court. Also, many of the older lower court cases discussed in the former edition have been replaced by more recent cases in an effort to keep the book relevant to current legal trends.

The book is directed toward providing guidelines for the law enforcement officer on the legal aspects of his or her daily duties while, at the same time, instilling an understanding of the reasons behind the rules. This approach is designed to make the book equally valuable to the criminal justice student, whatever career in the criminal justice system he or she chooses, and to the law enforcement officer on the beat, who can use the book as a practical field guide.

Review and discussion questions are provided at the end of each chapter. The questions are designed to encourage the reader to think about the implications and applications of the material presented in the text and do not merely call for a recital of memorized material. In developing the questions, an effort was made to stimulate the reader to apply his or her knowledge to fact situations other than those presented in the text and to consider the interrelationships of different topics in the criminal procedure area.

In closing, I would like to repeat two paragraphs from the preface to the first edition of *Criminal Procedure for the Law Enforcement Officer*, because I believe they continue to express the purpose and spirit behind the writing of this book.

"The law of criminal procedure is not only complex, but is constantly changing. The law enforcement officer is expected to understand these complexities and keep abreast of the changes. More importantly, he is required to apply the law to diverse situations which do not always neatly conform to the principles set out to guide him. To compound the law enforcement officer's problem, most court opinions on criminal procedure are written in a rambling, legalistic style that even lawyers and judges have trouble understanding. The result is a gap of communication and understanding between those who make the rules (judges) and those who must enforce them (law enforcement officers). Violation of rights of citizens by officers who are unaware or ignorant of court-imposed limitations on their activities is one of the main causes of the failure of many prosecutions and the reversal of many convictions.

"This book is an attempt to bridge the gap of communication and understanding between judges and law enforcement officers. I believe that law enforcement officers need understandable guidelines for conducting arrests, searches and seizures, interrogations, and lineups. I also believe that law enforcement officers should be familiar with the language and reasoning of the courts in

these areas. Officers, however, should not be expected to read through long involved opinions of every state and federal case that affects them and to extract
principles of law to guide them in the execution of their duties. They already
carry a heavy enough burden. Reading and interpreting the law is the job of an
attorney. Therefore, I have tried in this book to reduce the complexity of the law
of criminal procedure into simple straight-forward advice illustrated with examples of actual cases. I have also used quotations from cases, when I believed
they were written in clear, understandable language."

I hope that *Criminal Procedure for the Criminal Justice Professional* fulfills the
purpose of bridging the gap between judges and law enforcement officers and
that it proves to be a valuable and informative resource for students and other
professionals in the criminal justice system. I welcome any comments and suggestions for the improvement of future editions.

Finally, I would like to thank the staff of the Maine State Law Library in Au-
gusta for their able and friendly assistance throughout the preparation of the
manuscript of this book. And I would like to acknowledge everyone at West
Publishing Company who participated in the publication and promotion of the
book for their competence and their congenial professionalism.

John N. Ferdico

Summary of Contents

Table of Contents

PART FOUR
CONFESSIONS, IDENTIFICATION, AND ELECTRONIC SURVEILLANCE

Chapter 13.   Admissions and Confessions 295

PART ONE
A Framework for the Study of Criminal Procedure

CHAPTER 1
Individual Rights under the United States Constitution

INTRODUCTION

The law of criminal procedure can be described as the rules governing the balancing of the conflicting governmental functions of maintaining law and order and protecting the rights of citizens. These functions, common to every government that is not totally authoritarian or anarchistic, are necessarily conflicting because an increased emphasis on maintaining law and order will necessarily involve increased intrusions on individual rights. And, conversely, an increased emphasis on protecting individual rights will necessarily hamper the efficient maintenance of law and order. For example, an overprotective policy toward preserving individual rights is likely to result in an atmosphere conducive to increased violation of and disrespect for the law. Potential criminals will perceive that restrictions on police authority to arrest, detain, search, and question will decrease the likelihood of their getting caught and that complex and technical procedural safeguards designed to ensure the fairness of court proceedings will enable them to avoid punishment if they do get caught. The ultimate result, it is argued, is a society in which people do not feel secure in their homes or communities, and in which illegal activity abounds in government, business, and other aspects of daily life, to the detriment of everyone.

On the other hand, enforcement of the criminal laws would be much easier if persons suspected of crime were presumed guilty, if they had no privilege against self-incrimination, if their bodies, vehicles, and homes could be searched at will, and if they could be detained for long periods of time without a hearing. Life in many totalitarian countries today is characterized by such governmental abuses, and the citizenry of these countries lives in daily fear of official intrusion into the home, the disappearance of a loved one, or tighter restrictions on movement, speech, or association.

Because the United States was founded as a direct response to British abuses against the early colonists—although those abuses were certainly not as severe as the abuses under presentday dictatorships—our form of government has, from the beginning, reflected a strong commitment to the protection of individual rights from governmental abuse. This commitment was embodied in the original Constitution of 1788 and in the Bill of Rights, which was adopted shortly thereafter. This discussion of individual rights begins with a brief history of events leading to the adoption of the Constitution.

HISTORY

On September 17, 1787, a convention of delegates from all the original thirteen states except Rhode Island proposed a new Constitution to the Continental Congress and the States for ratification. The rights expressed and protected by this Constitution, and by the amendments adopted four years later, were not new. Some had roots in the societies of ancient Rome and Greece, and all were nurtured during almost six hundred years of English history since the signing of the Magna Carta.

As colonists under English rule, Americans before the Revolution were familiar with the ideas that government should be limited in power, and that the law was superior to any government, even the king. As the Declaration of Independence shows, the colonists rebelled because the English king and Parliament refused to allow them their historic rights as free English citizens. In September 1774, delegates from twelve colonies met in the First Continental Congress to petition England for their rights "to life, liberty, and property" and to trial by jury; "for a right peaceably to assemble, consideration of their grievances, and petition the King;" and for other rights that they had been denied. The petition was ignored, and soon afterward fighting broke out at Lexington and Concord. Meanwhile, citizens in Mecklenburg County, North Carolina, declared the laws of Parliament to be null and void and instituted their own form of local government with the adoption of the Mecklenburg Resolves in May 1775. In June 1776, a resolution was introduced in the Continental Congress, and a month later, on July 4, 1776, the Thirteen United Colonies declared themselves free and independent. Their announcement was truly revolutionary. They listed a large number of abuses they had suffered, and justified their independence in the historic words: "We hold these truths to be self-evident, that all men are created equal, that they are endowed by their Creator with certain Inalienable Rights, that among these are Life, Liberty and the pursuit of Happiness."

Two years later, in July 1778, the newly independent states joined in a united government under the Articles of Confederation, which was our nation's first Constitution. But it soon became clear that the Articles of Confederation did not adequately provide for a working, efficient government. Among their other weaknesses, the Articles gave Congress no authority to levy taxes or to regulate foreign or interstate commerce. In May 1787, a convention of delegates, meeting in Philadelphia with the approval of Congress, began to consider amendments to the Articles. But the delegates realized that a new system of government was necessary. After much debate, and several heated arguments, a compromise Constitution was agreed upon.

Although we now honor the wisdom of the delegates, they themselves had a different opinion of their work. Many were dissatisfied, and a few even thought a new Constitution should be written. No delegate from Rhode Island attended the convention nor signed the document on September 17, 1787, when the proposed Constitution was announced. Delaware was the first state to accept this Constitution, ratifying it on December 7, 1787, by a unanimous vote. Not all states were as pleased, and in some states the vote was extremely close. For a while it was not certain that a sufficient number of states would ratify. A major argument against ratification was the absence of a Bill of Rights. Only after it became generally agreed that the first order of business of the new government would be to propose amendments for a Bill of Rights was acceptance of the Constitution obtained by a sufficient number of states. On June 21, 1788, New Hampshire became the ninth state to sign on, and ratification of the new Constitution was completed. By the end of July 1788, the important states of Virginia and New York had joined New Hampshire.

On September 25, 1789, Congress proposed the first ten amendments to the new Constitution—the Bill of Rights. With the proposal of these guarantees, the states of North Carolina and Rhode Island, the last of the thirteen original colonies, ratified the Constitution. Ratification of the Bill of Rights was completed on December 15, 1791. Since that date, the Bill of Rights has served as our nation's testimony to its belief in the basic and inalienable rights of the people, and in the limitations on the power of government. Together with provisions of the original Constitution, it protects that great body of liberties that belong to every citizen.

For ease of discussion, the remainder of this chapter treats the original Constitution separately from the Bill of Rights and later amendments.

THE ORIGINAL CONSTITUTION

The Constitution of 1789 has served as the fundamental instrument of our government for almost all of our country's history as an independent nation. Drawn at a time when there were only thirteen original states, dotted with small towns, small farms, and small industry, the Constitution has provided a durable and viable instrument of government despite enormous changes in the political, social, and economic environment.

From serving a weak country on the Atlantic seaboard to serving a continental nation of fifty states with over 230 million people producing goods and services at a rate thousands of times faster than in 1789, the framework for democratic government set out in the Constitution has remained workable and progressive. Similarly, the individual rights listed in the Constitution and its twenty-six amendments have also retained an extraordinary vitality despite their being applied to problems and situations that could not have been envisioned by the Founding Fathers. Freedom of the press, for example, could have been understood only in the context of the small, still primitive printing presses of the late eighteenth century. Yet today that freedom applies not only to modern presses but to radio, television, and motion pictures—all products of the twentieth century.

It is the purpose of this chapter to explain how these basic rights have been applied and to develop a sensitivity to them as a prelude to the study of criminal procedure, in which these rights will confront the contervailing demands of society for the enforcement of the law and the detection and prevention of crime.

Each branch of the government—legislative, judicial, and executive—is charged by the Constitution with the protection of individual liberties. Within this framework, the judicial branch has assumed perhaps the largest role. Chief Justice John Marshall, speaking for the Supreme Court in the early case of Marbury v. Madison, 5 U.S. (1 Cranch) 137, 2 L.Ed. 60 (1803), declared that it was the duty of the judiciary to say what the law is, and that this duty included expounding and interpreting the law. Marshall stated that the law contained in the Constitution was paramount and that other laws that were repugnant to its provisions must-fall. It was the province of the courts, he concluded, to decide when other laws were in violation of the basic law of the Constitution and, where this was found to occur, to declare those laws null and void. This is the doctrine known as *judicial review*, which became the basis for the application of constitutional guarantees by courts in cases brought before them.

The Congress has played an important role in the protection of constitutional rights by enacting legislation designed to guarantee and apply those rights in specific contexts. Laws that guarantee the rights of Native Americans, afford due process to military service personnel, and give effective right to counsel to poor defendants are examples of the legislative role.

Finally, the executive branch, which is charged with implementing the laws enacted by Congress, contributes to the protection of individual rights by devising its own regulations and procedures for administering the law without intruding upon constitutional guarantees.

To properly understand the scope of constitutional rights, one must realize that, because of our federal system, an American lives under two governments rather than one: the federal government and the government of the state in which that person lives. The authority of the federal government is limited by the Constitution to the powers specified in the Constitution; the remainder of governmental powers is reserved to the states. The federal government is authorized, for example, to settle disputes between states, to conduct relations with foreign governments, and to act in certain matters of common national concern. States, on the other hand, retain the remainder of governmental power to be exercised within their respective boundaries.

THE BILL OF RIGHTS

Only a few individual rights were specified in the Constitution when it was adopted in 1788. Shortly after its adoption, however, ten amendments—called the Bill of Rights—were added to the Constitution to guarantee basic individual liberties. These liberties include freedom of speech, freedom of the press, freedom of religion, and freedom to assemble and petition the government.

The guarantees of the Bill of Rights originally applied only to actions of the federal government and did not prevent state and local governments from taking action that might threaten civil liberty. As a practical matter, states had their own constitutions, some containing their own bills of rights that guaranteed the same rights as or similar rights to those guaranteed by the Bill of Rights against federal intrusion. These rights, however, were not guaranteed by all the states; if they did exist, they were subject to varying interpretations. In short, citizens were protected only to the extent that the states themselves recognized their basic rights.

In 1868, the Fourteenth Amendment was added to the Constitution. In part it provides that no state shall "deprive any person of life, liberty, or property without due process of law." Not until 1925, in the case of Gitlow v. New York, 268 U.S. 652, 45 S.Ct. 625, 69 L.Ed. 1138, did the Supreme Court interpret the phrase "due process of law" to mean, in effect, "without abridgement of certain of the rights guaranteed by the Bill of Rights." Since that decision, the Supreme Court has ruled that a denial by a state of certain of the rights contained in the Bill of Rights represents a denial of due process of law. The Court has not ruled that all rights in the Bill of Rights are contained in the notion of due process, nor is that notion limited only to such rights as are enumerated in the Bill of Rights. The Court has simply found that there are concepts in the Bill of Rights so fundamental to the American scheme of justice that they must be recognized as part of due process of law and made applicable to the states as well as to the federal government.

At present, the following guarantees of the Bill of Rights have been applied to the states under the terms of the Fourteenth Amendment: Amendments I, IV, and VI; the self-incrimination, double jeopardy, and just compensation clauses of Amendment V; and the guarantee against cruel and unusual punishment of Amendment VIII. Only the right to indictment by grand jury in Amendment V, the right to jury trial in a civil suit in Amendment VII, and the prohibition against excessive bail or fines in Amendment VIII have not been applied to the states.

To place these rights in a broader perspective, one should realize that they make up only the core of what are considered to be *civil rights*—the privileges and freedoms that are accorded all Americans by virtue of their citizenship. There are many other civil rights that are not specifically mentioned in the Constitution but that nonetheless have been recognized by the courts, have often been guaranteed by statute, and are embedded in our democratic traditions. The right to buy, sell, own, and bequeath property; the right to enter into contracts; the right to marry and have children; the right to live and work where one desires; and the right to participate in the political, social, and cultural processes of the society in which one lives are a few of the rights that must be considered to be as fundamental to a democratic society as those specified by the Constitution.

Despite the inherent nature of the rights of American citizenship, the rights guaranteed by the Constitution or otherwise are not absolute rights in the sense that they entitle citizens to act in any way they please. Rather, to be protected by the law, people must exercise their rights in such a way that the rights of others are not denied. Thus, as Mr. Justice Oliver Wendell Holmes has pointed out, "Protection of free speech would not protect a man falsely shouting 'Fire' in a theater and causing a panic." Nor does freedom of speech and press sanction the publication of libel and obscenity. Similarly, the rights of free speech and free assembly do not permit one to knowingly engage in conspiracies to overthrow by force the government of the United States. Civil liberties thus carry with them an obligation on the part of all Americans to exercise their rights within a framework of law and mutual respect for the rights of their fellow citizens.

This obligation implies not only a restraint on the part of those exercising these rights but a tolerance on the part of those who are affected. Thus, citizens may on occasion be subjected to annoying political tirades, or disagreeable entertainment, or noisy demonstrations of protest. They may feel annoyed when a defendant refuses to testify, or when they see a seemingly guilty defendant go free because certain evidence was not admissible in court. But these annoyances or inconveniences are a small price to pay for the freedom one enjoys. If the rights of one are suppressed, it is, in the final analysis, the freedom of all that is jeopardized. Ultimately, a free society is a dynamic society, where thoughts and ideas are forever challenging and being challenged. Such a society is not without the risk that the wrong voice will be listened to or the wrong plan pursued. But a free society is one that learns by its mistakes and can freely pursue the happiness of its citizens.

INDIVIDUAL RIGHTS IN THE ORIGINAL CONSTITUTION

Article I, Section 9, Clause 2

The Privilege of the Writ of Habeas Corpus shall not be suspended, unless when in Cases of Rebellion or Invasion the public Safety may require it.

This guarantee enables a person whose freedom has been restrained in some way to petition a federal court for a writ of habeas corpus, to test whether the restraint was imposed in violation of the Constitution or laws of the United States. This right under the Constitution applies to all cases in which a person is confined by government authority. It can be suspended only when the president, pursuant to congressional authorization, declares that a national emergency requires its suspension and probably only when the courts are physically unable to function because of war, invasion, or rebellion. Habeas corpus is an important safeguard to prevent unlawful imprisonment and is discussed in further detail in Chapter 2.

Article I, Section 9, Clause 3

No Bill of Attainder . . . shall be passed [by the federal government].

Article I, Section 10, Clause 1

No State shall . . . pass any Bill of Attainder . . . .

Historically, a bill of attainder is a special act of a legislature that declares that a person or group of persons has committed a crime and that imposes punishment without a trial by court. Under our system of separation of powers, only courts may try a person for a crime or impose punishment for violation of the law. Section 9 restrains Congress from passing bills of attainder, and section 10 restrains the states.

Article I, Section 9, Clause 3

No . . . ex post facto Law shall be passed [by the federal government].

Article I, Section 10, Clause 1

No state shall . . . pass any . . . ex post facto Law. . . .

These two clauses prohibit the states and the federal government from enacting any criminal or penal law that makes unlawful any act that was not a crime when it was committed. They also prevent the imposition of a greater penalty for a crime than that in effect when the crime was committed. However, laws that retroactively determine how a person is to be tried for a crime may be changed so long as the substantial rights of the accused are not curtailed. Laws are not ex post facto if they make punishment less severe than it was when the crime was committed.

Article III, Sections 1 and 2

(Article III, Sections 1 and 2, of the Constitution deal with the judicial system of the United States and for purposes of this book are too long to be reproduced.)

Article III, Section 1, of the Constitution outlines the structure and power of our federal court system and establishes a federal judiciary that helps maintain the rights of American citizens. Article III, Section 2, also contains a guarantee that the trial of all federal crimes, except that of impeachment, shall be by jury. The Supreme Court has interpreted this guarantee as containing exceptions for "trials of petty offenses," cases rightfully tried before a court martial or other military tribunal, and some cases in which the defendant has voluntarily relinquished the right to jury.

Section 2 also requires that a federal criminal trial be held in a federal court sitting in the state where the crime was committed. Thus, a person is given protection against being tried without his or her consent in some part of the United States far distant from the place where the alleged violation of federal laws occurred.

Article III, Section 3

Treason against the United States, shall consist only in levying War against them, or in adhering to their Enemies, giving them Aid and Comfort. No Person shall be convicted of Treason unless on the Testimony of two Witnesses to the same overt Act, or on Confession in open Court.

> *The Congress shall have power to declare the Punishment of Treason, but no Attainder of Treason shall work Corruption of Blood, or Forfeiture except during the Life of the Person attained.*

Treason is the only crime defined by the Constitution. The precise description of this offense reflects an awareness by our forefathers of the danger that unpopular views might be branded as traitorous. Recent experience in other countries with prosecutions for conduct loosely labeled treason confirms the wisdom of the authors of the Constitution in expressly stating what constitutes this crime and how it shall be proved.

Article VI, Clause 3

> *[N]o religious Test shall ever be required as a Qualification to any Office or public Trust under the United States.*

Together with the First Amendment, this guarantee expresses the principle that church and government are to remain separate, and that religious beliefs are no indication of patriotism, ability, or the right to serve this country. Thus, a citizen need not fear that religious affiliations or convictions may legally bar him or her from holding office in the United States.

INDIVIDUAL RIGHTS IN THE BILL OF RIGHTS

Amendment 1

> *Congress shall make no law respecting an establishment of religion, or prohibiting the free exercise thereof; or abridging the freedom of speech, or of the press; or the right of the people peaceably to assemble, and to petition the Government for a redress of grievances.*

Religion

Two express guarantees are given to the individual citizen with respect to religious freedom. First, neither Congress, nor a state legislature because of the Fourteenth Amendment, may "make any law respecting an establishment of religion." This means no law may be passed that establishes an official church that all Americans must accept and support or to whose tenets all must subscribe, or that favors one church over another. Second, no law is constitutional if it "prohibits the free exercise" of religion. Citizens are guaranteed the freedom to worship in the way they choose.

The Supreme Court described the establishment clause as providing a "wall of separation between church and state." Everson v. Board of Education, 330 U.S. 1, 16, 67 S.Ct. 504, 512, 91 L.Ed. 711, 723 (1947). Governmental activity that leads to "excessive entanglement" with the church or its related institutions and practices has been ruled unconstitutional. Thus, the Court held that a state may not require prayer in the public schools, nor may it supplement or reimburse parochial schools for teachers' salaries and textbooks. To permit or authorize such activities would constitute governmental support of the religious organization affected. On the other hand, the Court held that it is permissible for public schools to release students at the students' own request, from an hour of classwork in order that those students may attend their own churches for religious instruction; or for a state to provide free bus transportation to children attending church or parochial schools if transportation is also furnished to children in the public schools. Furthermore, the Court upheld the tax-exempt status of church property used exclusively for worship purposes, and has sanctioned federal aid programs for new construction at church-related universities. It also held that the establishment clause does not prevent a state from designating Sunday as a day of rest.

Freedom to worship, as interpreted by the Supreme Court, must not conflict with otherwise valid government enactments. For example, a man may not have two wives and escape conviction for bigamy by attributing his conduct to his religious beliefs. Nor could a person commit an indecent act or engage in immoral conduct and then validly justify the actions on grounds of religious freedom. The Supreme Court also declared that it is an unconstitutional invasion of religious freedom to exclude from public schools children who, because of their religious beliefs, refuse to salute the American flag. The Court further ruled that requiring children of the Amish religious sect to attend public schools beyond the eighth grade was an impairment of the free exercise clause since such attendance prevented education in the traditional Amish framework.

Speech

As a general rule, citizens may freely speak out on any subject they choose. In addition, they may join organizations, wear buttons, buy books, and carry signs that represent their views. And they may take their cases to court when they feel they have been wronged.

The Supreme Court ruled, however, that the protections afforded by the First Amendment do not extend to all forms of expression. Highly inflammatory remarks that are spoken to a crowd and that advocate violence and clearly threaten the peace and safety of the community, or present a "clear and present danger" to the continued existence of the government, are not protected. Obscenity, too, has been judged unprotected by the First Amendment, although the Court has held that the mere possession of obscene materials in the home may not be punished.

Courts have also recognized that "symbolic speech," which involves more tangible forms of expression, falls within the protection of the First Amendment. Wearing buttons or clothing with political slogans, or displaying a sign or a flag, are examples of symbolic speech. The wearing of black arm bands by secondary school students in protest against the Vietnam War has been ruled protected by the First Amendment, so long as the activity was not disruptive or injurious to the rights of other students. The display of a black flag in protest to organized government has also been protected. On the other hand, burning draft cards in protest against the Vietnam War has not been protected, since it could be shown to disrupt or undermine the operation of the Selective Service System. Courts have also been reluctant to overturn hair and dress codes of public schools when the schools could show that the codes were designed to prevent disruption or distraction of classes.

Finally, censorship imposed by requiring official approval or a license in advance for speaking has been condemned frequently by the courts. Nevertheless, although a citizen is free to make speeches on the public streets, he or she may be prevented from doing so when using a loud and raucous amplifier in a hospital zone or when the location chosen is such that the address is likely to interfere with the movement of traffic.

Press

Freedom of the press is a further guarantee of the right to express oneself, in this case by writing or publishing one's views on a particular subject. The Founding Fathers recognized the importance of a free interplay of ideas in a democratic society and sought to guarantee the right of all citizens to speak or publish their views, even if those views were contrary to the views of the government or the society as a whole. Accordingly, the First Amendment generally forbids censorship or other restraint upon speech or the printed word. Thus, a school board's dismissal of a teacher who had protested school board activities in a letter to the editor of the local newspaper was held to infringe upon the teacher's First Amendment rights. And a state court order, issued in anticipation of the trial of an accused mass murderer, restraining the press and broadcasting media from reporting any confessions or incriminating statements made by the defendant or from reporting other facts "strongly implicative" of the defendant, was similarly struck down.

As with speech, however, freedom to write or publish is not an absolute right of expression. The sale of obscene materials is not protected, nor are printed materials that are libelous. The Supreme Court ruled, however, that public figures cannot sue for defamation unless the alleged libelous remarks were printed with knowledge of their falsity or with a reckless disregard for the truth.

The Court also ruled that the publication of a secret study into the origins of the United States' involvement in the Vietnam War could not be prevented owing to the First Amendment guarantee. The Court indicated, however, that freedom of the press may not extend to other similar matters that could be shown to have a more direct and substantial bearing on national security.

Finally, broadcasting, including radio, television, and motion pictures, receives the protections of the free press guarantee, and is subject to its limitations.

Assembly and Petition

American citizens, whether they are meeting for political activity, religious services, or other purposes, have the right to assemble peaceably. Public authorities cannot impose unreasonable restrictions on such assemblies, but they can impose limitations reasonably designed to prevent fire, hazard to health, or a traffic obstruction. The Supreme Court emphasized that freedom of assembly is just as fundamental as freedom of speech and press. Thus, while no law may legitimately prohibit demonstrations, there may be laws or other governmental actions that legitimately restrict demonstrations to certain areas or prohibit the obstruction and occupation of public buildings.

Picketing is also protected under the free speech guarantee. It may, however, be reasonably regulated to prevent pickets from obstructing movement onto and from the property involved. Picketing on private property has been upheld, but only where the property is open to the public and the picketing relates to the business being conducted on the property. Thus, the distribution of antiwar handbills on the premises of a privately owned shopping center has been held to be unprotected.

The right of petition is designed to enable citizens to communicate with their government without obstruction. When citizens exercise their First Amendment freedom to write or speak to their senator or member of Congress, they partake of "the healthy essence of the democratic process."

Amendment II

A well regulated Militia, being necessary to the security of a free State, the right of the people to keep and bear Arms, shall not be infringed.

The Second Amendment provides for the freedom of citizens to protect themselves against both disorder in the community and attack from foreign enemies. This right to bear arms has become much less important in recent decades as well-trained military and police forces have been developed to protect the citizenry. No longer do people usually need to place reliance on having their own weapons available. Furthermore, the Supreme Court held that the state and federal governments may pass laws prohibiting the carrying of concealed weapons, requiring the registration of firearms, and limiting the sale of firearms for other than military uses.

Amendment III

No Soldier shall, in time of peace be quartered in any house, without the consent of the Owner, nor in time of war, but in a manner to be prescribed by law.

Before the Revolution, American colonists had, against their will, frequently been required to provide lodging and food for British soldiers. The Third Amendment prohibited the continuation of this practice.

Amendment IV

The right of the people to be secure in their persons, houses, papers, and effects, against unreasonable searches and seizures, shall not be violated, and no Warrants shall issue, but upon probable cause, supported by Oath or affirmation, and particularly describing the place to be searched, and the persons or things to be seized.

In some countries, even today, police officers may invade a citizen's home, seize the citizen's property, or arrest the citizen whenever they see fit. In the United States, on the other hand, the Fourth Amendment protects the individual and his or her property from unreasonable search and seizure by officers of the law. In general, although there are many exceptions to the rule, a police officer may not search the home of a private citizen, seize any of the citizen's property, or arrest the citizen without first obtaining a court order called a warrant.

Before the warrant will be issued, the police officer must convince a magistrate that there is *probable cause*—good reason—to believe either that the person involved has committed a crime or that evidence of a crime is in a particularly described place.

Since the major portion of this book deals with the topics of arrest, search and seizure, and probable cause, further discussion of the Fourth Amendment appears in the chapters dealing with those topics.

Amendment V

No person shall be held to answer for a capital, or otherwise infamous crime, unless on a presentment or indictment of a Grand Jury, except in cases arising in the land or naval forces, or in the Militia, when in actual service in time of War or public danger; nor shall any person be subject for the same offense to be twice put in jeopardy of life or limb; nor shall be compelled in any criminal case to be a witness against himself, nor be deprived of life, liberty, or property, without due process of law; nor shall private property be taken for public use, without just compensation.

Grand Jury

The Fifth Amendment requires that before a person is tried in federal court for an infamous crime, he or she must first be indicted by a grand jury. The grand jury's duty is to make sure that there is probable cause to believe that the accused person is guilty. This provision prevents a person from being subjected to a trial when there is not enough proof that he or she has committed a crime.

An *infamous* crime is a felony (a crime for which a sentence of more than one year's imprisonment can be given) or a lesser offense that can be punished by confinement in a penitentiary or at hard labor. An indictment is not required for a trial by court martial or by other military tribunal. Furthermore, the constitutional requirement of grand jury indictment does not apply to trials in state courts. However, where states do use grand juries in their criminal proceedings, the Supreme Court has ruled that the grand juries must be free of racial bias.

Double Jeopardy

The Fifth Amendment also guarantees the individual that he or she will not be placed in double jeopardy—that is, will not be tried before a federal or state court more than once for the same crime. The Supreme Court held that, under the due process safeguard of the Fourteenth Amendment, state courts may not harass defendants by successive prosecutions for the same act of misconduct.

A defendant is considered to be in jeopardy at a criminal trial when the jury is empaneled and sworn. Double jeopardy occurs when a second trial is for the same offense as the first. A second trial for the same offense may occur, however, when the first trial results in a mistrial, as when the jury cannot agree on a verdict, or when a second trial is ordered by an appellate court.

Double jeopardy does not arise when a single act violates both federal and state laws and the defendant is exposed to prosecution in both federal and state courts. Nor does a criminal prosecution in either a state court or a federal court exempt the defendant from being sued for damages by anyone who is harmed by his or her criminal act. Furthermore, a defendant may be prosecuted more than once for the same conduct if that conduct involves the commission of more than one crime. For instance, a person who kills three victims at the same time and place can be tried separately for each killing.

Self-incrimination

The right of every person not to be compelled in any criminal case to be a witness against himself or herself applies to federal proceedings and to state proceedings through the Fourteenth Amendment, and signifies that no one is obliged to provide answers to questions tending to convict him or her of a crime. Questions directed toward eliciting incriminating information may be asked at a the very earliest stages of the investigation of a crime; thus, the Supreme Court ruled that when an individual is interrogated while in the custody of the police, or while deprived of freedom of action in any significant way, the guarantees of the Fifth Amendment apply.

To ensure that the right against self-incrimination is protected, the Court ruled, in the case of Miranda v. Arizona, 384 U.S. 436, 86 S.Ct. 1602, 16 L.Ed.2d 694 (1966), that before custodial interrogation, citizens must be warned of their right to remain silent, that what they say may be used against them in court, and that they have a right to counsel, which will be furnished them free of charge if they are unable to afford counsel. Failure to give these warnings results in any statements obtained by the questioning being inadmissible in later criminal proceedings.

Fifth Amendment rights may be waived, but the accused must do so knowingly and voluntarily. Any confession obtained by use of force, threat, or other form of coercion will be excluded from the evidence presented at the trial, whether or not the *Miranda* warnings have been given. (The entire subject of admissions and confessions, *Miranda* warnings, and voluntariness is discussed in detail later in this book.)

Courts have ruled that the guarantee against self-incrimination applies only to testimonial actions. Thus, it has been held that handwriting samples, blood tests, and confrontations with witnesses for identification purposes do not violate the Fifth Amendment.

Courts have also ruled that the Fifth Amendment prohibits both federal and state prosecutors and judges from commenting on the refusal of a defendant to take the witness stand in his or her own defense. The refusal of witnesses to testify to matters that could subject them to criminal prosecutions at a later date has also been upheld. The Courts recognize, however, a limited right of the government to question employees about the performance of official duties, and have upheld the dismissals of such employees for their refusal to answer the questions.

Government regulations requiring the registration of items such as highly dangerous weapons or narcotics for which possession is a crime have also been invalidated on the grounds that they require information that may be used in a criminal prosecution against the person who registers.

Due Process

The words "due process of law" express the fundamental ideas of American justice. A due process clause is found in both the Fifth and Fourteenth Amendments as a restraint upon both the federal and state governments. The due process clause affords protection against arbitrary and unfair procedures in judicial or administrative proceedings that could affect the personal and property rights of a citizen. Notice of a hearing or trial that is timely and that adequately informs the accused of the charges against him or her is a basic concept included in due process. The opportunities to present evidence in one's own behalf before an impartial judge or jury, to be presumed innocent until proven guilty by legally obtained evidence, and to have the verdict supported by the evidence presented are other rights repeatedly recognized within the protection of the due process clause.

The due process clauses of the Fifth and Fourteenth Amendments also provide other basic protections whereby the state and federal governments are prevented from adopting arbitrary and unreasonable legislation or other measures that would violate individual rights. Thus, constitutional limitations are imposed on governmental interference with important individual liberties—such as the freedom to enter into contracts, to engage in a lawful occupation, to marry, and to move without unnecessary restraints. To be valid, governmental restrictions placed on one's liberties must be reasonable and consistent with due process.

Just Compensation

The Fifth Amendment requires that whenever the government takes a person's property, the property acquired must be taken for public use and its full value must be paid to the owner. Thus, property cannot be taken by the federal government from one person simply to be given to another. However, the Supreme Court has held that it is permissible to take private property for such purposes as urban renewal, even though ultimately the property taken will be returned to private ownership, since the taking is for the benefit of the community as a whole. To qualify for just compensation, property does not have to be physically taken from the owner. If governmental action leads to a lower value of private property, that action may constitute a "taking" and therefore require payment of compensation. Thus, the Supreme Court held that the disturbance of the egg-laying habits of chickens on a man's poultry farm, caused by the noise of low-level flights by military aircraft from a nearby airbase, lessened the value of that farm and that, accordingly, the landowner was entitled to receive compensation equal to his loss.

Amendment VI

In all criminal prosecutions, the accused shall enjoy the right to a speedy and public trial, by an impartial jury of the State and district wherein the crime shall have been committed, which district shall have been previously ascertained by law, and to be informed of the nature and cause of the accusation; to be confronted with the witnesses against him; to have compulsory process for obtaining witnesses in his favor, and to have the Assistance of Counsel for his defence.

This amendment sets forth specific rights guaranteed to persons facing criminal prosecution. Its guarantees apply to both the federal courts and the state courts by virtue of the Fourteenth Amendment.

The right to a speedy and public trial requires that the accused be brought to trial without unnecessary delay, and that the trial be open to the public. Intentional or negligent delay by the prosecution that prejudices the defendant's right to defend himself or herself has been held to be grounds for dismissal of the charges. For example, the Supreme Court ruled that delay in prosecution was not justified by the defendant's confinement on an earlier conviction because the defendant should have been temporarily released for purposes of trial on the later charge.

Trial by an impartial jury supplements the earlier guarantee contained in Article III of the Constitution. The requirements that the jury have twelve members and that the jury reach a unanimous verdict were derived from the common law and are not specifically accorded by the Constitution. The Supreme Court ruled that state juries need not necessarily be composed of twelve members and has approved a state statutory scheme providing for only six. Moreover, the Court has ruled that jury verdicts in state courts need not necessarily be unanimous. The right to jury trial does not apply to trials for petty offenses, which the Supreme Court has suggested are offenses punishable by six months' confinement or less. In all trials in which a jury is used, that jury must be impartially selected, and no one can be excluded from jury service merely because of race, class, or sex.

The Sixth Amendment requirement that a person "be informed of the nature and cause of the accusation" means that an accused person must be given notice in what respects it is claimed he or she has broken the law, to provide the person with an opportunity to prepare a defense. This also means that the crime must be established by statute beforehand so that all persons are aware of what is illegal before they act. The statute must not be so vague or unclear that it does not inform people of the exact nature of the crime. Generally, the accused is entitled to have all witnesses against him or her present their evidence orally in court; subject to certain exceptions, hearsay evidence cannot be used in federal criminal trials. Moreover, the accused is entitled to the aid of the court in having issued compulsory process—usually a subpoena—which will order into court as witnesses persons whose testimonies are desired at the trial.

Finally, the Sixth Amendment provides a right to be represented by counsel. For many years, this was interpreted to mean only that defendants had a right to be represented by a lawyer if they could afford one. In the case of Gideon v. Wainwright, 372 U.S. 335, 83 S.Ct. 792, 9 L.Ed.2d 799 (1963), however, the Supreme Court held that the amendment imposed an affirmative obligation on the part of the federal and state governments to provide at public expense legal counsel for those who could not afford it, in order that their cases could be adequately represented to the court. The Supreme Court held that this right extends even to cases involving petty offenses if there is a chance that a jail sentence might result. The indigent are entitled to counsel at any "critical stage of the adjudicatory process." Thus, courts have accorded this right at custodial interrogations, at police lineups conducted at or after the initiation of adversary judicial criminal proceedings, and at all stages of the trial process. In addition, indigents were given the right to a free copy of their trial transcript for purposes of appeal of their conviction. Congress enacted the Criminal Justice Acts of 1964 and 1970 to implement this right to counsel by establishing a federal defender system to represent defendants who could not afford legal counsel. Most state legislatures have enacted similar measures.

Amendment VII

In suits at common law, where the value in controversy shall exceed twenty dollars, the right of trial by jury shall be preserved, and no fact tried by a jury, shall be otherwise re-examined in any Court of the United States, than according to the rules of the common law.

The Seventh Amendment applies only to federal civil trials and not to civil suits in state courts. Except as provided by local federal court rules, if a case is brought in a federal court and a money judgment is sought that exceeds twenty dollars, the party bringing the suit and the defendant are entitled to have the controversy decided by the unanimous verdict of a jury of twelve people.

Amendment VIII

Excessive bail shall not be required, nor excessive fines imposed, nor cruel and unusual punishments inflicted.

Bail

Bail has traditionally meant payment by the accused of an amount specified by the court to ensure the presence of the accused at trial. Accused persons who are released from custody and subsequently fail to appear for trial forfeit their bail to the court.

The Eighth Amendment does not specifically provide that all citizens have a *right* to bail, but only that bail will not be excessive. A right to bail has, however, been recognized in common law and in statute since 1791. In 1966, Congress enacted the Bail Reform Act to provide for pretrial release of persons accused of noncapital crimes. Congress thus sought to end pretrial imprisonment of indigent defendants who could not afford to post money bail and who were, in effect, confined only because of their poverty. The act also discouraged the traditional use of money bail by requiring the judge to seek other means as likely to ensure that the defendant would appear when the trial was held.

The Bail Reform Act of 1984 substantially changed the 1966 act to allow a judicial officer, in determining pretrial release, to consider the defendant's danger to individuals or the community. This change marked a significant departure from the basic philosophy of the 1966 act, which was that the only purpose of bail laws must be to ensure the defendant's appearance at judicial proceedings. The 1984 act also eliminated the presumption in favor of bail pending appeal.

The lack of a specific constitutional guarantee of the right to bail has indirectly contributed to legislative enactments that have modified the availability of bail. In 1970, Congress provided for a system of pretrial detention in the District of Columbia for defendants considered to be dangerous and likely to commit additional crimes if released before trial. The law was highly controversial and is considered by many to be a violation of the right to bail implied in the Eighth Amendment.

Whether bail, where it is available, is excessive or not will depend upon the facts of each particular case. Bail is excessive in violation of the Eighth Amendment when it is set at a figure higher than an amount reasonably calculated to ensure that the accused will stand trial and submit to sentence if found guilty. In a few instances, as when a capital offense such as murder is charged, bail may be denied altogether.

Cruel and Unusual Punishment

Whether fines or periods of confinement are cruel and unusual must be determined on the facts of each particular case. Clearly excessive practices, such as torture, are prohibited. The Supreme Court has found that the penalty of death for deliberate murder is not per se cruel and unusual, but that mandatory death statutes leaving the jury or trial judge no discretion to consider the individual defendant and his or her crime are cruel and unusual, and that standards and procedures may be established for the imposition of death that would remove or mitigate the arbitrariness and irrationality characteristic of many death penalty laws.

In addition to excessive forms of punishment, the clause has also been applied to the imposition of punishment for a condition that the "criminal" had no power to change. Thus, a law making the status of narcotics addiction illegal was struck down by the Supreme Court as cruel and unusual since it punished a condition beyond the control of the accused. Some courts have held that laws punishing public drunkenness were cruel and unusual when applied to homeless alcoholics since it was impossible for homeless alcoholics to avoid public places.

Amendment IX

The enumeration in the Constitution, of certain rights, shall not be construed to deny or disparage others retained by the people.

The Ninth Amendment emphasizes the view of the Founding Fathers that powers of government are limited by the rights of the people, and that it was not intended, by expressly guaranteeing in the Constitution certain rights of the people, to grant the government unlimited power to invade other rights of the people.

The Supreme Court has on at least one occasion suggested that this amendment is a justification for recognizing certain rights not specifically mentioned in the Constitution, or for broadly interpreting those that are. The case involving the Ninth Amendment was Griswold v. Connecticut, 381 U.S. 479, 85 S.Ct. 1678, 14 L.Ed.2d 510 (1965). At issue was whether the right to privacy was a constitutional right and, if so, whether the right was one reserved to the people under the Ninth Amendment or was only derived from other rights specifically mentioned in the Constitution.

Courts have long recognized particular rights to privacy that are part of the First and Fourth Amendments. As the Court in *Griswold* said, "the specific guarantees in the Bill of Rights have penumbras, formed by emanations from those guarantees that help give them life and substance." 381 U.S. at 484, 85 S.Ct. at 1681, 14 L.Ed.2d at 514. Thus, freedom of expression guarantees freedom of association and the related right to be silent and free from official inquiry into such associations. It also includes the right not to be intimidated by government for the expression of one's views. The Fourth Amendment's guarantee against unreasonable search and seizure confers a right to privacy because its safeguards prohibit unauthorized entry onto one's property and tampering with one's person, property, or possessions.

The court in *Griswold* ruled that the Third and Fifth Amendments, in addition to the First and Fourth, created "zones of privacy" safe from governmental intrusion and, without resting its decision upon any one of these or on the Ninth Amendment itself, simply held that the right of privacy was guaranteed by the Constitution.

Amendment X

The powers not delegated to the United States by the Constitution, nor prohibited by it to the States, are reserved to the States respectively, or to the people.

The Tenth Amendment embodies the principle of federalism, which reserves for the states the residue of powers not granted to the federal government or withheld from the states.

LATER AMENDMENTS DEALING WITH INDIVIDUAL RIGHTS

Amendment XIII

Section 1.   Neither slavery nor involuntary servitude, except as a punishment for crime whereof the party shall have been duly convicted, shall exist within the United States, or any place subject to their jurisdiction.

Section 2.   Congress shall have power to enforce this article by appropriate legislation.

The amendment prohibits slavery in the United States. It has been held that certain state laws were in violation of this amendment because they had the effect of jailing a debtor who did not perform his or her financial obligations. The Supreme Court has ruled that selective service laws, which authorize the draft for military duty, are not prohibited by this amendment.

The courts have also justified certain civil rights legislation that condemned purely private acts of discrimination but that did not constitute "state action," on the basis of the authority granted in Section 2 of this amendment and Section 5 of the Fourteenth Amendment, which is similar. An example is the civil rights legislation of 1866 and 1964 designed to end discrimination in the sale or rental of real or personal property. These discriminatory practices were seen as "badges of servitude," which the Thirteenth Amendment was intended to abolish.

Amendment XIV

Section 1.   All persons born or naturalized in the United States, and subject to the jurisdiction thereof, are citizens of the United States and of the State wherein they reside. No State shall make or enforce any law which shall abridge the privileges or immunities of citizens of the United States; nor shall any State deprive any person of life, liberty, or property, without due process of law; nor deny to any person within its jurisdiction the equal protection of the laws. . . .

Section 5.   The Congress shall have power to enforce, by appropriate legislation, the provisions of this article.

Due Process

The Fourteenth Amendment limits the states from infringing upon the rights of individuals. The Bill of Rights—the first ten amendments—does not specifically refer to actions by the states, but applies only to actions by the federal government. Through judicial interpretation of the phrase "due process of law" in the Fourteenth Amendment, many of the Bill of Rights guarantees have been made applicable to actions by state governments and their subdivisions, such as counties, municipalities, and cities. Under this principle, certain rights and freedoms are deemed so basic to the people in a free and democratic society that state governments may not violate them, even though states are not specifically barred from doing so by the Constitution

The Fifth Amendment, discussed earlier, also contains a due process clause that applies to actions of the federal government.

Equal Protection

In addition to containing the due process clause, the Fourteenth Amendment also prohibits denial of the "equal protection of the laws." This requirement prevents the state from making unreasonable, arbitrary distinctions between different persons as to their rights and privileges. Therefore, since "all people are created equal," no law could deny red-haired men the right to drive an automobile. The state does, however, remain free make reasonable classifications. Therefore, the law can deny minors the right to drive.

Some classifications, such as those based on race, religion, and national origin, have been held to be patently unreasonable. Thus, racial segregation in public schools and other public places, laws that prohibit the sale or use of property to certain races or minority groups, and laws that prohibit interracial marriage have been struck down. Furthermore, the Supreme Court held that purely private acts of discrimination can be in violation of the equal protection clause if they are customarily enforced throughout the state, whether or not there is a specific law or other explicit manifestation of action by the state.

The equal protection clause has been interpreted to mean that a citizen may not arbitrarily be deprived of the right to vote and that every citizen's vote must be given equal weight to the extent possible. Thus, the Supreme Court held that state legislatures and local governments must be apportioned strictly in terms of their populations in such a way as to accord one person one vote.

Section 5 of this amendment provided the authority for much of the civil rights legislation passed by Congress in the 1960s.

Amendment XV

Section 1.   The right of citizens of the United States to vote shall not be denied or abridged by the United States or by any State on account of race, color, or previous condition of servitude.

Section 2.   The Congress shall have power to enforce this article by appropriate legislation.

Amendment XIX

Section 1.   The right of citizens of the United States to vote shall not be denied or abridged by the United States or by any State on account of sex.

Section 2.   Congress shall have power to enforce this article by appropriate legislation.

Amendment XXVI

Section 1.   The right of citizens of the United States, who are eighteen years or older, to vote shall not be denied or abridged by the United States or any State on account of age.

Section 2.   The Congress shall have power to enforce this article by appropriate legislation.

The intent and purpose of these three amendments are clear. The right to vote, which is the keystone of our democratic society, may not be denied any citizen over the age of eighteen because of race, color, previous condition of servitude, or sex. The Twenty-sixth Amendment, which lowered the voting age for all elections from twenty-one to eighteen years of age, became law on July 1, 1971. These amendments, together with the Fifth and Fourteenth, prohibit any arbitrary attempt to disenfranchise any American citizen.

Amendment XXIV

Section 1.   The right of citizens of the United States to vote in any primary or other election for President or Vice President, for electors for President or Vice President, or for Senator or Representative in Congress,

*shall not be denied or abridged by the United States or any State by reason
of failure to pay any poll tax or other tax.*
  *Section 2.   The Congress shall have power to enforce this article by
appropriate legislation.*

The Twenty-fourth Amendment prohibits denial of the right to vote for federal officials because a person has not paid a tax. This amendment was designed to abolish the requirement of a poll tax, which, at the time of its ratification, five states imposed as a condition to voting. The Supreme Court subsequently held that poll taxes were unconstitutional under the equal protection clause of the Fourteenth Amendment on the basis that the right to vote should not be conditioned on one's ability to pay a tax. Accordingly, poll taxes in any election, state or federal, have been prohibited.

CONCLUSION

In addition to the specific constitutional rights outlined in this chapter, certain safeguards for the individual are inherent in the structure of American government. The separation of powers between legislative, executive, and judicial branches of government is the basis for a system of checks and balances— which prevents excessive concentration of power, with the inevitable threat to individual liberties that accompanies such concentration. With respect to the legislative power itself, the existence of two houses of Congress—each chosen by a different process—is itself a protection against ill-advised laws that might threaten constitutional rights. Similarly, our federal system, which divides authority between the national government and the governments of the various states, has provided a fertile soil for the nourishment of constitutional rights.

No matter how well a constitution may be written, the rights it guarantees have little meaning unless there is popular support for those rights and for that constitution. Fortunately, that support has existed in the United States. Indeed, in this country the most fundamental protection of personal liberty rests in the well-established American traditions of constitutional government, obedience to the rule of law, and respect for the individual. These traditions provide the groundwork for the entire body of law dealing with criminal procedure and should be foremost in the minds of students of and participants in our criminal justice system. The remainder of this book shows how the criminal justice system operates to achieve a balance between the protection of individual rights guaranteed by the Constitution and the maintenance of the rule of law and public order in our society.

REVIEW AND DISCUSSION QUESTIONS

  1. How has the Constitution been able to remain a durable and viable instrument of government despite the enormous changes that have occurred in our society since its adoption? Discuss this issue in terms of specific changes.
  2. Discuss generally the most important roles and functions under the Constitution of each of the following: the three branches of the federal government,

the state governments, the average citizen, the law enforcement officer. Explain some of the interrelationships among those roles and functions.

3. The Constitution speaks predominantly in terms of the protection of individual rights from governmental abuse or abridgment. What corresponding obligations and burdens must each citizen undertake or bear to ensure that everyone remains free to exercise these rights to their full extent?

4. Name three constitutional sources for the protection of the right to privacy, and explain how they differ.

5. If a state legislature passed a law requiring all bookstores that have, in the last six months, sold or advertised for sale pictures of the Pope to be immediately closed down and their owners immediately arrested and jailed, what provisions of the Constitution might be violated?

6. If a terminally ill cancer patient wishes to refuse medical treatment and die a "natural" death because of her religious beliefs, can that person be required under state law to undergo treatment? What if the person's wish to die is not based on a religious belief, but the person is a minor or is mentally incompetent? What if the person's cancer was caused by exposure to radiation and the person wishes her death to be a political statement on the dangers of nuclear power and nuclear war?

7. Discuss the constitutional issues involved in compelling a newsperson to reveal a confidential source of information when the source would be useful to the government in a criminal investigation or helpful to a criminal defendant at trial. Should the government be able to obtain a search warrant to look into files, audit tapes, or view films in the possession of the news media to find evidence of crime?

8. Should members of the news media have greater access than that of members of the general public to court proceedings and court records? What about greater access to prisons to interview prisoners? What about greater access to police investigative files?

9. Would the Fifth Amendment privilege against self-incrimination prohibit the government from any of the following: requiring all participants in a lineup to speak certain words; requiring a person to produce income tax records; threatening a person with a reduction in pay in his government job if he does not make testimonial incriminating admissions about a non-job-related matter?

10. What does the phrase "checks and balances" mean? What aspects of the Constitution other than separation of powers help fulfill the purposes of checks and balances?

CHAPTER 2
An Overview of the Criminal Court System

Most of the law enforcement officer's daily law-related duties involve the enforcement of the laws, the keeping of the public peace, and the investigation and prevention of crime. To properly perform these duties, officers must be sensitive to the constitutional rights of all persons, as discussed in Chapter 1; must be familiar with the criminal laws of their states; and must understand the law dealing with arrest, search and seizure, confessions, and pre-trial identifications, with which most of the remainder of this book is concerned.

Most law enforcement officers are not as familiar with the rules and procedures that govern the course of a prosecution beyond the investigatory stage. Law enforcement officers play an important role in this process, often as chief witnesses for the prosecution in their cases. Nevertheless, outside their roles as witnesses, officers are often ignored as their cases move through pleadings, motions, jury selection, trial, and appeal. To many officers, the entire process may look like a complex legal jumble involving the prosecuting attorney, the defense attorney, and the judge. Since law enforcement officers are an integral part of the criminal justice system, and since their actions early on in a case vitally affect the outcome of the case at nearly all stages of the prosecution, they should have a basic understanding of what happens to their case when it reaches the prosecutor and the courts, and why.

Other criminal justice professionals are usually less involved in a criminal case than are law enforcement officers. Nevertheless, whatever their level of participation in the criminal justice process, a general knowledge of the criminal court system can help them to function effectively within that system.

Criminal court procedure in most states is governed by court rules and statutes designed for use by judges and attorneys to ensure the just and efficient processing of criminal offenders. Many of the rules and statutes are quite complex and do not directly concern law enforcement officers or other criminal justice professionals. Therefore, this chapter highlights pertinent court procedures and legal terms in order to provide a comprehensive view of how the system works, without dwelling too heavily on details that are of little direct concern to the criminal justice professional.

So far as possible, this chapter presents the different stages of criminal court procedure in chronological order, following a criminal case from beginning to end. The discussion is limited to court procedures for serious offenses and does not cover procedures for traffic offenses and other petty misdemeanors. Wherever certain aspects of criminal court procedure are covered in another chapter, reference is made to that chapter. Because the information in this chapter is general, and because criminal court procedure differs by state, do not take the information presented here as a final authority; be sure to consult your own state's pertinent statutes or rules.

STRUCTURE OF THE COURT SYSTEM

Before discussing the preliminary proceedings in a criminal case, this chapter first briefly outlines the basic structure of the federal court system and of a typical state court system, and briefly describes the criminal trial jurisdiction of the different courts. As used here, the term *jurisdiction* simply means the authority of a court to deal with a particular case.

The federal court system is larger and more complex than any state court system, but the basic structures of the two court systems are similar. Both the federal system and the state system consist of courts that have original jurisdiction over criminal matters and courts that have appellate jurisdiction. *Original jurisdiction* means the authority to deal with a case from the beginning, to try the case, and to pass judgment upon the facts and the law. *Appellate jurisdiction* means the authority to deal with a case, not in its initial stages, but only after it has been finally decided by an inferior court, and then only to revise or correct the proceedings in the inferior court.

The federal court system is divided into ninety-seven judicial districts, each served by a U.S. district court. Each state has at least one district within it. The district courts have original jurisdiction over criminal cases, and the great majority of federal criminal cases begin in the district courts.

The U.S. courts of appeals and the U.S. Supreme Court both have appellate jurisdiction in criminal matters. The court of appeals is an intermediate appellate court because its decision can be further appealed to the U.S. Supreme Court. There are twelve divisions or circuits of the U.S. court of appeals throughout the country. A thirteenth federal circuit court, the U.S. Court of Appeals for the Federal Circuit, was recently created to hear patent and customs appeals from across the country. The U.S. Supreme Court is the appellate court of last resort, meaning that it is a court from which there is no appeal.

The U.S. Supreme Court has original jurisdiction in certain limited areas, but its greatest work load is to review the decisions of the lower federal courts and the highest state courts. The most common way in which the Supreme Court exercises its appellate jurisdiction is through the granting of a *writ of certiorari*.

The granting of a writ of certiorari means that the Supreme Court, upon petition of a party, agrees to review a case decided by one of the circuit courts of appeals or by the highest court of a state. Certiorari is granted at the Court's discretion when a case presents questions whose resolution will have an immediate impact and import beyond the particular facts of the case. Some cases may also reach the U.S. Supreme Court by direct appeal—for example, when a state court declares a statute unconstitutional or a federal court finds that the provisions of a state statute are contrary to the treaties, laws, or Constitution of the United States. In addition, a few cases may reach the U.S. Supreme Court upon a certification from a U.S. court of appeals requesting instructions on procedure with respect to a particular point of law.

Besides the courts mentioned, the federal court system also includes a number of specialized courts that have been established to hear particular classes of cases. Examples are the U.S. Court of International Trade, the U.S. Court of Military Appeals, and the U.S. Tax Court. In addition, there are quasi-judicial boards or commissions, which have special and limited jurisdiction under specific federal statutes.

A typical state court system has the same basic structure as the federal system. Courts of original jurisdiction are usually divided into (1) courts that try only misdemeanor cases and (2) higher courts that try both misdemeanors and felonies. The courts that try only misdemeanor cases are usually established on a local level and may be called municipal courts, traffic courts, minor criminal courts, district courts, or something similar. For purposes of this chapter, these courts are called local courts. The courts with original jurisdiction over both misdemeanors and felonies are usually established on a county or regional level and may be called county courts, district courts, superior courts, or something similar. Generally the more serious criminal cases will be instituted in these courts. In some states these courts may also exercise a limited appellate jurisdiction over certain cases appealed from the local courts. For purposes of this chapter, these country, regional, or district courts are called county courts.

From the county court level, a case may proceed through one or more intermediate appellate courts until it reaches the highest court (or the court of last resort) of the state, usually called the state supreme court. If a case involves important constitutional issues, it may finally reach the U.S. Supreme Court for review. Generally the state supreme court also has the power to prescribe rules of pleading, practice, and procedure before itself and the other lower courts of the state.

PRELIMINARY PROCEEDINGS

The Complaint

A criminal process against a defendant formally begins with a complaint. The word *formally* is used here because persons can be arrested for an offense before a complaint is filed or a warrant is issued. Such an arrest would be considered the beginning of the criminal process. However, since an arrest without a warrant is considered an exception to the basic warrant requirement, the complaint is still considered the formal beginning of proceedings.

The complaint can serve a dual purpose in a criminal proceeding. If the defendant has been arrested without a warrant, the complaint is prepared, signed, and filed at the defendant's initial appearance before the magistrate. The complaint serves as the charging document upon which the preliminary examination will be held. If the defendant has not been arrested, and is not before the court, the complaint serves as the basis for determining whether there is probable cause to justify the issuance of a warrant for his or her arrest.

The complaint must be made on oath or affirmation, must state the essential facts of the offense being charged, must be in writing, and must be made before a judicial officer authorized to issue process in criminal cases. This officer is usually called a magistrate. The information in the complaint does not have to be derived from personal observation or experience, but may be based upon information from others or upon circumstantial evidence. Nevertheless, the evidence put forth in the complaint must be strong enough to convince the magistrate that there is probable cause to believe that an offense has been committed and that the defendant committed it. Probable cause is discussed in Chapters 3 and 6.

Affidavits

Information that is not contained in the complaint or that comes from witnesses other than the complainant may be brought to the court's attention in the form of an affidavit. An *affidavit* is a sworn written statement of the facts relied upon in seeking the issuance of a warrant. An affidavit need not be prepared with any particular formality. It is filed with the complaint and together these documents can provide a sufficient written record for a reviewing court to examine in determining whether probable cause existed for the issuance of a warrant.

Warrant or Summons Issued on the Complaint

Once the magistrate has determined from the complaint and accompanying affidavits that there is probable cause to believe that an offense has been committed and that the defendant committed it, the magistrate will issue either a summons or a warrant for the defendant's arrest. If the defendant is already before the court, no summons or warrant is necessary.

Once the summons or warrant is issued, the law enforcement officer must serve the summons or execute the warrant by arresting the defendant and bringing the defendant before a judicial officer as commanded in the warrant. A detailed discussion of arrest warrant procedure appears in Chapter 4.

Proceedings before the Magistrate

Once a person has been arrested, either with or without a warrant, he or she is required by statute to be brought before a magistrate "without unnecessary delay," or "forthwith," depending upon statutory language. The details of this procedure are also discussed in Chapter 4.

The purpose of bringing an arrested person before a magistrate without unnecessary delay is to inform the person of the

1. charge;
2. right to retain counsel; and
3. right to have a preliminary examination.

Under some statutes, defendants must be informed that they are not required to make a statement, and that any statement made by them may be used against them. In addition, some statutes require that a defendant be informed of the right to request the assistance of free counsel in case of indigency. The defendant is then given reasonable time and opportunity to consult an attorney and is admitted to bail where appropriate.

Preliminary Examination

At the preliminary examination (also called the preliminary hearing), the magistrate must determine whether there is probable cause to believe that an offense was committed and that the defendant committed it. The purpose of the preliminary examination is to provide another judicial determination of the existence of probable cause and to protect the defendant from a totally baseless prosecution. Nevertheless, many defendants waive the preliminary examination, allowing their cases to go directly to the grand jury.

The preliminary examination consists mainly of the presentation of evidence against the defendant by the prosecuting attorney. The defense attorney may cross-examine witnesses against the defendant as well as introduce evidence in the defendant's behalf. If probable cause to believe that the defendant committed the offense is found, the defendant will be held to answer to the grand jury in the county where the trial is to be held. This is often called binding the defendant over to the grand jury. The magistrate may admit the defendant to bail at the preliminary examination or may continue, increase, or decrease the original bail. If no probable cause is found, the magistrate will dismiss the complaint and discharge the defendant.

INDICTMENT AND INFORMATION

The indictment and the information are the documents that charge the defendant with an offense and upon which the defendant is brought to trial. The indictment and the information are very similar in nature and content. Each is a concise and definite written statement of the essential facts constituting the offense charged. The main difference between the indictment and the information is that the indictment is issued by a grand jury and signed by the foreperson of the grand jury. The information is signed and sworn to by the prosecuting attorney without the approval or intervention of the grand jury. Laws governing when the indictment or the information is used differ from state to state.

A variety of somewhat technical state statutes and rules deal with drafting, amending, and joining indictments or informations and with joining offenses or defendants for trial together. These provisions are of direct concern only to judges and attorneys, and are not discussed here.

An example of a typical indictment appears on page 31.

Grand Jury

The grand jury usually consists of from twelve to twenty-three jurors, selected from their communities according to law to serve during the criminal term of the appropriate court. The duty of the grand jury is to receive complaints in criminal cases, hear the evidence put forth by the state, and find an indictment when they are satisfied that there is probable cause that the defendant has committed an offense. The concurrence of a specified number of grand jurors is required in order to find an indictment.

Grand jury proceedings are traditionally kept secret. During deliberations or voting, no one other than the jurors is allowed to be present. When the grand jury is taking evidence, however, the attorneys for the state, the witnesses under examination, and an official court reporter may be present. Matters occurring before the grand jury, other than the deliberations or the votes of any juror, may be disclosed to the prosecuting attorney for use in performing his or her duties. Otherwise, these matters are to be kept secret, unless the court orders that they be disclosed.

The reasons for keeping grand jury proceedings secret can be summarized as follows:

1. To prevent an escape from jurisdiction of someone who is not yet in custody but whose indictment may be contemplated

2. To provide the utmost freedom for the grand jury in its deliberations and to protect jury members from outside influences

3. To prevent tampering with witnesses who may testify before the grand jury and later appear at the trial of those indicted

4. To encourage the free and unrestrained disclosure of information by persons who have information on the commission of crimes

5. To protect innocent persons who are exonerated of charges from disclosure of the fact that they were under grand jury investigation

Waiver of Indictment

In some states, a defendant who does not wish to be prosecuted by indictment may waive the indictment and be prosecuted by information. The waiver of an indictment procedure is of great advantage to a defendant who wishes to plead guilty or *nolo contendere*. (These pleas are discussed in further detail in this chapter.) In effect, the waiver of indictment procedure enables a defendant to begin serving a sentence immediately instead of having to wait for a grand jury, which sits only during the criminal term of court. The defendant can thereby secure release from custody at an earlier date than by going through the indictment procedure

---

STATE OF MAINE

Superior Court

Knox _____ , ss

SUPERIOR COURT
CR– 120–88 _____

STATE OF MAINE

Vs.

INDICTMENT FOR VIOLATION
17-A OF M.R.S.A. SECTION 353

_____ Miles Prower _____

(_____ THEFT Class B _____)

THE GRAND JURY CHARGES:

that Miles Prower of Camden, in the County of Knox and State of Maine, on the second day of February, 1987, in the Town of Warren, County of Knox and State of Maine, did commit theft by obtaining or exercising control over the property of Roy L. Paine, to wit, one Realistic stereo receiver of the value of fifty dollars; one Winchester single shot, .22 rifle of the value of fifty dollars; one Zenith 19-inch color TV of the value of three hundred dollars; one table lamp of the value of fifteen dollars; one CB radio converter of the value of thirty dollars; and one pepper mill of the value of five dollars, all of the aggregate value of four hundred and fifty dollars, with intent to deprive said Roy L. Paine thereof.

A True Bill.

Date: July 5, 1988 _____

_____ Clay Potts _____
Foreman

CR-18

Warrant or Summons Issued on the Indictment

An indictment may sometimes be found against a defendant before the defendant has been taken into custody and brought before the court. In these cases, upon the request of the attorney for the state, or by direction of the court, the clerk shall issue a summons or a warrant for the arrest of each defendant named in the indictment. This process indicates no change of procedure for law enforcement officers, who are required to execute the warrant or serve the summons in the same way as they would any other warrant or summons. Procedures for executing an arrest warrant or serving a summons appear in Chapter 4.

ARRAIGNMENT AND PREPARATION FOR TRIAL

The next step in the criminal proceeding, after an indictment or information is found, is the arraignment. The meaning of the term *arraignment* is often confused with the initial appearance before a magistrate by a defendant who has been arrested. Part of the reason for the confusion is that in misdemeanor proceedings in many local courts, the two procedures are combined. The essence of the arraignment is that the defendant is *called upon to plead* to the charge after the magistrate reads the substance of the charge. In local court misdemeanor proceedings, if there is no requirement of prosecution by indictment or information, the *complaint* is read to the defendant and the plea is made to the complaint. However, in courts in which prosecution must be by indictment or information, the *indictment* or *information* is read to the defendant and the plea is made to the indictment or information. Therefore, in courts that require prosecution by indictment or information, the arraignment proceeding must be separate from the initial appearance before the magistrate.

Pleas

In general, the pleas available to the defendant differ from state to state. Three of the most common pleas are as follows:

1. Not guilty
2. Guilty
3. *Nolo contendere* (no contest)

A plea of not guilty puts in issue all the material facts alleged in the indictment, information, or complaint. A defendant has a right to refuse to plead at all, in which case the court must enter a plea of not guilty.

To plead guilty or *nolo contendere*, the defendant must obtain the consent of the court. Both these pleas have the same effect on the defendant, with one exception. They simply mean that the defendant does not wish to contest the charge but will submit to the judgment of the court. The exception is that a guilty plea may constitute an admission of guilt by the defendant and may be used against him or her in a *civil* action based on the same facts. A plea of *nolo contendere* is not an admission and cannot be used against the defendant in a civil action. The court may not accept a plea of guilty or *nolo contendere* in a felony proceeding unless the court is satisfied, after inquiry, that the defendant committed the crime charged and that the plea is made voluntarily with an understanding of the nature of the charge.

In some states, a plea of not guilty by reason of insanity may be entered. This plea is required if the defendant intends to raise the defense of insanity. A defendant may plead not guilty and not guilty by reason of insanity to the same charge. When a plea of not guilty by reason of insanity is entered, the court may, on petition, order the defendant committed to an appropriate institution for the mentally ill for examination. The insanity plea is rarely raised in a misdemeanor proceeding.

Motions

Before trial, there are many contentions and requests that the defendant may put forth by way of motions. These motions are heard by the court and may result in various forms of relief ranging from amending or curing a defect in the complaint, indictment, or information to discharging the defendant. Most motions are primarily of concern to judges and attorneys, and are not discussed in detail here. Two pre-trial motions are, however, of direct concern to the law enforcement officer: (1) the motion to suppress evidence and (2) the motion to suppress a confession. These motions are made by defendants who believe they are aggrieved by either an unlawful search and seizure or an unlawfully obtained admission or confession. Some states do not allow one or both of these motions to be made before trial.

The purpose of a motion to suppress is twofold:

1. To enable the defendant to invoke the exclusionary rule and prevent the use of illegally obtained evidence at trial

2. To enable the court to resolve the issue of the legality of a search and seizure or confession without interrupting the trial

The hearing on the motion to suppress is often the point in the proceedings at which a law enforcement officer's performance in a case is carefully scrutinized by the court. If the defendant is able to prove that evidence was illegally obtained by an officer and if the evidence is essential to the prosecution's case, suppression of the evidence is likely to result in a dismissal of charges or the granting of a motion for judgment of acquittal. Therefore, law enforcement officers must know the law not only at the time they conduct a search and seizure or obtain a confession, but also when they may be called upon to justify their actions at a hearing on a motion to suppress.

Depositions

When a witness is unable to attend a criminal trial, and it is shown that the witness's testimony is material to a just determination of the case, the court may order that a deposition of the witness be taken at any time after the filing of an indictment or information. Obtaining a deposition involves taking the testimony of a witness out of court and preserving that testimony in writing for later use in court. A deposition is used only in exceptional circumstances and not for the mere convenience of a witness or party. It may be requested by either the state or the defendant, and the opposing party may attend the taking of the deposition.

A deposition, or a part of a deposition, may be used at a trial or hearing if it appears that any of the following circumstances exist:

1. The witness who gave the deposition is dead.

2. The witness is out of the state (unless the party offering the deposition caused the witness's absence).

3. The witness is unable to attend or testify because of sickness or infirmity.

4. The party offering the deposition is unable to procure the attendance of the witness by subpoena.

Furthermore, depositions may be used even if the witness does testify at the trial, but only for the purposes of contradicting or impeaching the witness's testimony.

Discovery

Discovery is a procedure whereby the defendant or the prosecution is enabled to inspect, examine, copy, or photograph items in the possession of the other party. Among the items subject to discovery are tangible objects, tape recordings, books, and papers, including written or recorded statements made by the defendants or witnesses, and the results or reports of physical examinations and scientific tests, experiments, and comparisons. The general purpose of discovery is to make the criminal trial a fairer search for the truth.

Ordinarily, to obtain the right to discovery, a party must make a motion before the court and must show that the specific items sought may be material to the preparation of its case and that its request is reasonable. Nevertheless, states differ considerably with respect to the conditions under which discovery is allowed and the items that are subject to discovery. Some states do not allow discovery at all. Other states allow discovery only for the defendant, in an effort to correct the imbalance between the investigative resources of the state and the defendant, thereby enabling the defendant to more adequately prepare a defense. A recent development is automatic informal discovery for certain types of evidence, without the necessity for motions and court orders. The state of the law governing discovery is constantly changing, but the trend appears to be in favor of broadening the right of discovery for both the defense and the prosecution.

Subpoena

The term *subpoena* describes the process used to secure the attendance of witnesses or the production of books, papers, documents, or other objects at a criminal proceeding. The subpoena is issued by a judicial officer and it commands the person to whom it is directed to attend a trial, hearing, or deposition for the purpose of testifying at the proceeding or bringing a named document or object. A subpoena can be served by a law enforcement officer or any other adult person who is not a party to the proceedings.

VENUE

One final pretrial matter to be considered is venue. Venue is often confused with jurisdiction. *Jurisdiction* refers to the authority of the court to deal with a particular case. For instance, a municipal court may have jurisdiction over misdemeanor offenses. *Venue*, on the other hand, merely refers to the place at which the authority of the court should be exercised. For example, some statutes require that the trial of certain types of cases be held in the geographic division of the court in which the offense was committed.

Most states have special rules relating to the proper venue for an offense that is committed on a boundary of two counties or an offense part of which is committed in one county and part of which is committed in another county. These technicalities are not discussed here.

Change of Venue

Sometimes, because of heavy publicity or intense community feeling, a defendant may wish to have his or her case tried in a different place than the one authorized by statute. A procedure is therefore provided for a defendant to make a motion for a change of venue. The motion usually must be made before the jury is impaneled or, in cases in which there is no jury, before any evidence is received. The defendant must give adequate reasons in support of the motion. Typical grounds for granting a motion for change of venue are as follows:

1. There is such prejudice in the county where the case is to be tried that the defendant cannot obtain a fair and impartial trial there.

2. Another location is much more convenient for the parties and witnesses than the intended place of trial, and the interests of justice require a transfer of location.

THE TRIAL

The U.S. Constitution and most state constitutions guarantee a defendant in a criminal prosecution a speedy, public, and impartial trial by jury. This guarantee means that a defendant must be provided a jury trial in all criminal prosecutions except those for petty offenses. Defendants who do not wish to be tried by a jury may, however, with the approval of the court, waive in writing their right to a jury trial.

Trial without a Jury

When a case is tried without a jury, the judge must perform the jury's functions of weighing the evidence, determining the credibility of witnesses, and finding the facts, in addition to performing his or her regular duties as judge. The judge must also make a finding as to the guilt or innocence of the defendant based upon the evidence presented. Outside the performance of these jury functions in a nonjury trial, the judge's other regular duties are essentially the same in either a jury or a nonjury trial. Therefore, the remainder of this chapter is concerned primarily with jury trials.

Selection of Jurors

Once it has been determined that the trial will be by jury, the next step in the criminal proceeding is the selection of the jurors. The jurors will perform the crucial tasks of finding the facts, determining the credibility of witnesses, weighing the evidence, and ultimately issuing a verdict of guilty or not guilty. Because of the importance of the jury's function, there are detailed rules governing the selection of jurors. These rules are designed to protect the state or the defendant from having a person who is prejudiced against its cause sitting as a member of the jury during the trial of the case.

The selection of the jury is accomplished by the court through an examination of prospective jurors on the jury panel or venire. The *jury panel* is a list of members of the community considered fit for jury service. The list is compiled by local officials, often according to statute. It must be indiscriminately drawn and must not *systematically* exclude any class of persons.

The examination of prospective jurors on the panel is commonly referred to as *voir dire*. The usual method of examination is to question the prospective jurors with regard to their feelings and views on various matters. The parties or their attorneys may conduct the examination unless the court elects to conduct the initial examination itself. If the court conducts the initial examination, the court must allow the parties or their attorneys to address additional questions to the prospective jurors on any subject that has not been fully covered and that is relevant to the juror's qualifications.

The purpose of the examination or *voir dire* is to determine whether any prospective juror is prejudiced about the case in any way. Typical questions asked relate to whether prospective jurors know the defendant, the attorneys, or any of the witnesses; whether they have read about the case in the newspapers; and whether they have formed any opinions on the case.

If either attorney wishes to have a prospective juror dismissed on the basis of these questions or for any other reason, the attorney may issue a challenge to that juror. Two types of challenges are available. One is a *challenge for cause* and is directed toward the qualifications of a juror. Most states have statutes setting out the permissible grounds for a challenge for cause. Typical grounds are as follows:

1. The juror is related to one of the parties.
2. The juror has given or formed an opinion in the case.
3. The juror has a bias, prejudice, or particular interest in the case.

Each party has an unlimited number of challenges for cause available to it, assuming that the grounds for such a challenge can be established to the satisfaction of the judge.

The other form of challenge is known as the *peremptory challenge*. Peremptory challenges are available to each party as a means for dismissing prospective jurors who may be qualified, but who for some other reason are felt to be undesirable by one party's attorney. No reason need be given for a peremptory challenge. Peremptory challenges have to be exercised with great care. It is often difficult to determine from a few questions whether a prospective juror will be receptive or antagonistic to a party's position. Furthermore, the number of peremptory challenges available to each side is limited in number.

Once all the challenges available to both the prosecution and the defense are exercised, a jury of twelve is chosen and is sworn in by the judge to try the case. In some cases, additional jurors are selected as alternates, who sit in on the case but who do not enter deliberations unless one of the regular twelve jurors becomes ill or dies, or is unable to serve for some other reason. The parties may agree, with the approval of the court, to a jury of less than twelve. This is rarely done, however, except in cases in which a juror dies during trial and there is no alternate available. After administering an oath to the jurors, the judge admonishes the jurors to discuss the case with no one until the jury goes into deliberations to decide the case after hearing all the evidence.

Presentation of Evidence

Once the jury has been impaneled, the presentation of evidence begins with the opening statement of the prosecuting attorney. The prosecuting attorney gives an outline of what the state intends to prove by the evidence to be presented. Following this, the defense counsel makes an opening statement to the jury outlining what the defense intends to prove. Sometimes, however, the defense counsel will wait until the prosecutor has presented the state's evidence before giving an opening statement, thereby concealing the course of the defense until the government has disclosed its proof.

After the opening statement or statements are given, the prosecutor begins the introduction of the state's proof. The state is entitled to present its evidence first in a criminal case because it is the plaintiff and therefore has the burden of proof. The burden of proof means the duty to establish the truth of facts alleged in support of every element of the offense charged against the defendant. The burden of proof is upon the prosecution from the beginning to the end of the trial because of the presumption that the accused is innocent. Furthermore, the prosecution is required to prove the defendant's guilt *beyond a reasonable doubt*. *Reasonable doubt* is a term requiring little interpretation although various courts have attempted to formulate somewhat involved definitions that add little beyond its plain meaning. Suffice it to say that proof beyond a reasonable doubt requires that the guilt of the defendant be established to a reasonable, but not absolute or mathematical, certainty. Probability of guilt is not sufficient.

Rules of Evidence

The rules of evidence govern which evidence will be admissible in court and which will be excluded. These rules are designed to ensure that only trustworthy, competent, and relevant information is presented to the jury. A discussion of the rules of evidence is beyond the scope of this book.

Order of Presentation of Evidence

The order of presentation of evidence begins with the *direct examination* or *examination in chief* of the prosecution's first witness. This witness will be someone the prosecution has called and will be expected to give evidence favorable to the state's position. The examination of the witness is designed to produce evidence that will prove the state's case against the defendant. A law enforcement officer is usually involved as a witness for the prosecution, sometimes as its only witness.

When the prosecutor is through questioning the prosecution's witness, the defense counsel has a right to question the same witness. This is known as *cross-examination*. Its purpose is either to discredit information given by the witness or to impeach the person's credibility as a witness. In some states, the defense attorney on cross-examination is limited to questioning the witness on matters raised by the prosecutor during direct examination. In other states, the defense attorney is not so limited, and the witness may be cross-examined concerning any matter that is relevant and material to an issue in question. The judge determines what is relevant and material.

After cross-examination, the prosecutor may wish to reexamine the prosecution's witness in order to rehabilitate him or her in the eyes of the jury. This is called *redirect* examination. Unlike cross-examination, the scope of redirect examination is limited to the matters brought out in the previous examination by the adverse party. This same rule applies if the defense counsel wishes to conduct a recross-examination. This order of presenting evidence by direct examination, cross-examination, redirect, and recross is followed for all the prosecutor's witnesses until all the state's evidence has been presented.

Motion for Acquittal

After the prosecutor has presented the state's evidence, the defense counsel may move for a judgment of acquittal. A judgment of acquittal will be granted in cases in which the evidence is insufficient to sustain a conviction on the offense or offenses charged. This will usually mean the judge has decided that reasonable persons could not conclude that guilt has been proven beyond a reasonable doubt. If the motion is not granted at the close of the state's evidence, the defense may then offer its evidence. The motion for acquittal may be renewed at the close of all the evidence, or, at the judge's discretion, it may be renewed after the jury returns a verdict or is discharged without having returned a verdict.

The Defendant's Evidence

Assuming that the court does not grant a motion for judgment of acquittal at the close of the prosecution's evidence, the defense counsel then has an opportunity to present evidence. The defense may put forth one or more of several possible defenses to refute the proof offered by the state. Among the defenses available to the defendant are alibi, insanity, self-defense, and entrapment. In presenting any of these defenses, the defense counsel may call witnesses on direct examination. The prosecutor has a right to cross-examine each of the defense witnesses, just as the defense counsel had a right to cross-examine the state's witnesses.

Defendants may or may not choose to testify in their own behalf. There is an absolute constitutional right to *not* testify. Defendants who do testify are treated much like any other witness. If a defendant does not choose to testify, the prosecuting attorney is not permitted to comment to the jury upon the failure to testify. The basis for this principle is the constitutional privilege that protects a person from self-incrimination.

Rebuttal by the Prosecution

Assuming that a motion for judgment of acquittal is not granted at the close of defendant's evidence, the prosecution is entitled to present rebuttal proof at this time. Rebuttal proof is designed to controvert evidence presented by the defense and to rebut any special defenses raised. Rebuttal proof is limited to new matter brought out in the defendant's presentation of evidence. Law enforcement officers may be called as witnesses again at this stage of the prosecution to correct any errors or misleading impressions that might be left after the defendant's presentation of evidence.

Closing Arguments

After all the evidence has been presented, both the prosecutor and the defense attorney are allotted certain amounts of time, usually specified by statute or rule, for final argument. In the final argument, attorneys for each side attempt to convince the jury (or in nonjury cases, the judge) of the correctness of their positions. The prosecutor presents the state's argument first and is followed by the attorney for the defense. The prosecutor is then allowed to present a short rebuttal. Much leeway is given for the attorneys for both sides to use their wit and imagination to win the jury over to their respective positions. However, the attorneys are required to confine themselves to a discussion of the evidence presented and of reasonable inferences to be derived from that evidence.

Instructions to the Jury

After the final arguments and before the jury retires for deliberations, the judge must give instructions to the jury regarding the law of the case. Attorneys for both sides are given an opportunity to submit written requests to the judge for particular instructions that they wish to be given. In a typical case, the instructions will cover such matters as the respective responsibilities of the court and the jury, the presumption of innocence and the burden of proof, various evidentiary problems, a definition of the offense or offenses charged, additional clarification of the critical elements of those offenses, any defenses that are available in the case, and the procedures to be followed in the jury room. The exact content of the instructions is a matter for the judge's discretion, but the attorneys are given an opportunity to object to any portion of the charge or any omission therefrom.

The judge may summarize the evidence for the jury, help them recall details, and attempt to resolve the complicated evidence into its simplest elements. However, the judge may not express any opinion on any issue of fact in the case nor favor either side in summarizing the evidence.

Verdict

After receiving instructions, the jury retires to the jury room to begin deliberations on a verdict. The *verdict* is the decision of the jury as to the defendant's guilt or innocence, and it must be unanimous. If the jurors are unable to agree on a verdict, a hung jury results. The jurors are then dismissed and the case must be either retried or dropped. If, however, an agreement is reached, the jurors return to courtroom and the verdict is read in open court by the jury foreperson. Any party, or the court itself, may then request a *poll* of the jury. This simply involves asking each individual juror if he or she concurs in the verdict. The purpose of polling the jury is to make sure that the verdict was not reached as a result of the coercion or domination of one juror by others or as a result of sheer mental or physical exhaustion of a juror. If, during the poll, it is found that any juror did not concur in the verdict, the whole jury may be directed to retire for further deliberations or may be discharged by the judge.

SENTENCE AND JUDGMENT

After the defendant's guilt or innocence has been determined, either by verdict of the jury or by a judge without a jury, the judge must enter a judgment in the case. The judgment is merely the written evidence of the final disposition of the case by the court. If the defendant is found not guilty or for some other reason is entitled to be discharged, the judgment is entered accordingly, and the defendant is free forever from any further prosecution for the crime for which he or she was tried. If the defendant is found guilty, the judge must pass sentence on the defendant before entering judgment.

The determination of the sentence is perhaps the most sensitive and difficult decision the judge has to make because of the effect it will have on the defendant's life. For this reason, most states have laws directing and guiding the judge in this determination. A typical provision requires the judge to impose sentence without unreasonable delay. This protects the defendant from a prolonged period of uncertainty about the future. In addition, before imposing sentence, the judge is usually required to address the defendant personally and ask if the defendant desires to be heard before the imposition of sentence. The defendant may be heard personally or by counsel or both. The purpose of this provision is to enable the defendant to present any information that may be of assistance to the court in determining punishment.

Another typical statutory provision that is designed to assist the court in fixing sentence allows the court, in its discretion, to direct the state probation and parole board to make a pre-sentence investigation and report to the court before the imposition of sentence. This report will contain any prior criminal record of the defendant and such other information on personal characteristics, financial condition, and the circumstances affecting the defendant's behavior as may be helpful to the court in reaching its decision.

The court has a number of alternatives open to it with respect to sentencing, depending largely on individual state criminal statutes. Some criminal statutes have mandatory sentences, some have fixed maximum sentences, some have fixed minimum sentences, and others leave the matter of sentencing to the judge. Therefore, depending upon the offense for which the defendant has been convicted, the court may have very broad discretion in fixing sentence, or no discretion whatsoever. In a few states, the jury has the power to fix the sentence as well as to determine guilt or innocence.

Probation

The court also has the power to place a defendant on probation provided the conviction was not for an offense punishable by life imprisonment. Probation is usually controlled by statute. It is a procedure by which a person found guilty of an offense is released by the court, subject to conditions imposed by the court, without being committed to a state penal or correctional institution.

Probation of a defendant is usually effected in one of two ways. The court may sentence the defendant, suspend the execution of the sentence, and place the defendant on probation, or the court may continue the matter for sentencing for a period of not more than two years and during that period place the defendant on probation. A defendant placed on probation is under the control and supervision of the state probation and parole board, although still under the jurisdiction of the court.

In some states, a different type of probation may be imposed by the court for cases that involve the violation of any statutes concerning controlled or illegal drugs or narcotics. In these cases, the court may impose sentence, place the defendant on probation, and require as a condition of probation that the defendant participate in programs at an approved drug treatment facility.

POST-TRIAL MOTIONS

After judgment has been entered, several motions are still available to the defendant to challenge the decision of the court. One of these is the motion for judgment of acquittal, sometimes called a motion for "judgment notwithstanding the verdict." The statutes or rules in some states provide that this motion can be made after the jury has been discharged as long as it is made within a specified time after the discharge. Courts will usually not grant such a motion unless

1. the state's evidence was insufficient or nonexistent on a vital element of the offense charged; or

2. the indictment or information did not state a criminal offense under state law.

Another motion open to the defendant is the motion for a new trial. This motion may be made in addition to a motion for acquittal. When it is made alone, it is sometimes deemed to include a motion for judgment or acquittal. In the latter case, if the defendant moves for a new trial, the court in granting it may either enter a final judgment of acquittal or grant a new trial. A new trial may be granted by the court if it is required in the interest of justice. The usual ground for granting a new trial is the insufficiency of the evidence to support the verdict. Some courts have also considered errors of law and improper conduct of trial participants during the trial under the motion.

Another ground for granting a motion for a new trial is the discovery of new evidence, which carries with it a difference in procedure. The procedural difference is an extended time period during which a motion for a new trial may be made based on the ground of newly discovered evidence. The time period varies from state to state but is usually longer than the period for a motion based on any other ground. This longer period allows a reasonable amount of time for the discovery of new evidence. To justify the granting of a motion for a new trial on the ground of newly discovered evidence, it must be shown that the new evidence will probably change the result of the trial, that it could not have been discovered before the trial by the exercise of due diligence, that it is material to the issue, and that it is not merely cumulative or impeaching.

Either by motion of the defendant or by motion of the court, the defendant may obtain a revision or correction of sentence. The power to revise a sentence is granted to enable the trial court to change a sentence that is inappropriate in a particular case, even though the sentence may be legal and was imposed in a legal manner. This power to revise a sentence includes the power to increase as well as to reduce the sentence.

In contrast with the power to revise, the power to correct a sentence is granted to enable the court to change a sentence because the sentence either was illegal or was imposed in an illegal manner. An illegal sentence might be one that was in excess of the statutory maximum. An illegally *imposed* sentence might be one in which the defendant was not personally addressed by the judge and given an opportunity to be heard before sentencing, where such a procedure is required by statute. The court must exercise both its power to revise and its power to correct a sentence within specific time periods or the powers are lost.

REMEDIES AFTER CONVICTION

There are two major forms of relief for a defendant after being convicted of a crime: *appeal* and *habeas corpus*. Each is discussed separately here.

Appeal

A defendant has a right to appeal after being convicted of a crime and after all post-trial motions have been denied by the trial judge. The appeal procedure varies from state to state and is not detailed here. It involves, among other things, the filing of a notice of appeal, the designation of the parts of the trial record to be considered on appeal, the filing of a statement of points on appeal, the filing of briefs, and the arguing of the briefs before the appellate court. If a defendant is unable to afford a lawyer to handle the appeal, provision is made by state statute or state court rule for a lawyer to be appointed by the court free of charge.

In some states, by statute, the prosecution is also given a right to appeal adverse decisions of the trial court. The prosecution's right to appeal, however, is usually much more limited than the defendant's right. Typical state statutes allow appeal by the prosecution of adverse rulings made *before* the jury hears the case or in cases in which the defendant has appealed. The procedure for appeal by the prosecution is essentially the same as it is for appeal by the defendant.

Remember that the appeal procedure is *not* a retrial of the case, nor is it ordinarily a reexamination of factual issues. The determination of factual issues is the function of the jury or, in a nonjury case, of the lower court judge. The function of the appellate court in an appeal is primarily to review the *legal* issues involved in the case. The following example illustrates this point.

Suppose a law enforcement officer obtained a confession from a defendant but forgot to give the *Miranda* warnings before a custodial interrogation. During the trial of the case, the trial judge erroneously permitted the officer who obtained the confession to read it to the jury over the objection of the defense.

The jury convicted the defendant. On appeal, the defendant argues that the trial judge committed an error of law in allowing the jury to hear the confession.

The appellate court would very likely reverse the conviction on the basis of the error of law made by the trial judge. Along with reversal, the usual procedure is to remand the case (send it to the trial court for a new trial) with instructions to exclude the confession from the jury in the new trial. A different jury would then hear the evidence in the case, without the illegally obtained confession, and render another verdict. Therefore, even though a conviction is reversed on appeal, it does not necessarily mean that the defendant is acquitted and can go free. It usually means simply that the defendant has won the right to be tried again.

If the appellate court finds that the trial court committed no errors of law, it will affirm the defendant's conviction. The defendant may, however, still have a chance for further appeal. If the appeal was heard in an intermediate appellate court, there is the possibility of an additional appeal to the highest appellate court in the state. If the defendant's appeal was heard in the highest appellate court in the state, an appeal may be made to the U.S. Supreme Court. Note that the U.S. Supreme Court and the highest appellate courts of some states have discretionary jurisdiction and may select the cases they will hear. Defendants have no right to insist upon having their appeal heard by such a court.

Appeals may be taken only from cases that have come to a final judgment. This means that an appellate court will not decide any legal issues nor will it review the denial of any motions until the case has been finally disposed of by the trial court. The reason for this rule is to prevent unnecessary delays in the conduct of trials that would result if the parties could appeal issues during the course of a trial. There are some minor exceptions to the final judgment rule, but they are not discussed here.

When an appellate court decides a case, it delivers a written opinion to explain and justify its decision. In this way the higher court explains the trial judge's errors and also informs the party losing the appeal that it has lost, and why. The decisions of the appellate courts are compiled and published in books of reported court decisions, which can be found in law libraries. These reported decisions are used by attorneys and judges as authorities for arguing and deciding future cases that raise issues similar to those already decided.

Habeas Corpus

FEDERAL HABEAS CORPUS FOR STATE PRISONERS. State prisoners may challenge their state convictions on constitutional grounds by means of a petition for a writ of habeas corpus in federal court. The federal statute governing the remedy is 28 U.S.C. § 2254. Initially, the constitutional grounds for which habeas corpus relief could be granted were limited to those relating to the jurisdiction of the state court, but the U.S. Supreme Court extended the scope of the writ to all constitutional challenges by its decision in Fay v. Noia, 372 U.S. 391, 83 S.Ct. 822, 9 L.Ed.2d 837 (1963).

In 1976, the U.S. Supreme Court again limited federal habeas corpus review of state prisoners' claims of violations of federal constitutional rights, holding that "where the State has provided an opportunity for full and fair litigation of a Fourth Amendment claim, a state prisoner may not be granted federal habeas corpus relief on the ground that evidence obtained in an unconstitutional search or seizure was introduced at his trial." Stone v. Powell, 428 U.S. 465, 494, 96 S.Ct. 3037, 3052, 49 L.Ed.2d 1067, 1088 (1976). With that limitation, however, other constitutional claims of state prisoners may be heard in a federal habeas corpus proceeding even though the claims have been fully adjudicated by a state court. Townsend v. Sain, 372 U.S. 293, 83 S.Ct. 745, 9 L.Ed.2d 770 (1963). In addition, constitutional claims that were not adjudicated in a state court because the prisoner forfeited the remedy by failing to observe state procedural rules may nevertheless still be considered on habeas corpus by a federal court.

Defendants may forfeit their right to federal habeas corpus review of a constitutional claim if they *deliberately* fail to comply with valid state procedural requirements for enforcing that claim. Fay v. Noia, supra. Federal habeas corpus review may likewise be barred if a defendant is unable to show cause for noncompliance with a state procedural rule and show some actual prejudice resulting from the alleged constitutional violation. Wainwright v. Sykes, 433 U.S. 72, 97 S.Ct. 2497, 53 L.Ed.2d 594 (1977).

Prisoners must exhaust available state remedies before a federal court will consider their claim on habeas corpus. This means that, if an appeal or other procedure to hear a claim is still available by right in the state court system, the prisoner must pursue that procedure before a federal habeas corpus application will be considered.

POST-CONVICTION RELIEF FOR FEDERAL PRISONERS. In 1948, Congress enacted a statute (28 U.S.C. § 2255) that was designed to serve as a substitute for habeas corpus for federal prisoners. The primary purpose of the statute was to shift the jurisdictions of the courts hearing habeas corpus applications. The basic scope of the remedy that had been available to federal prisoners by habeas corpus was not changed by the statute.

Section 2255 provides, in part, as follows:

> A prisoner in custody under sentence of a court established by Act of Congress claiming the right to be released upon the ground that the sentence was imposed in violation of the Constitution or laws of the United States, or that the court was without jurisdiction to impose such sentence, or that the sentence was in excess of the maximum authorized by law, or is otherwise subject to collateral attack, may move the court which imposed the sentence to vacate, set aside or correct the sentence. . . .
>
> An application for a writ of habeas corpus in behalf of a prisoner who is authorized to apply for relief by motion pursuant to this section, shall not be entertained if it appears that the applicant has failed to apply for relief, by motion, to the court which sentenced him, or that such court has denied him relief, unless it also appears that the remedy by motion is inadequate or ineffective to test the legality of his detention.

The Section 2255 remedy is similar to the habeas corpus remedy for state prisoners, discussed earlier. Although there are some significant distinctions between the two remedies, they are beyond the scope of this book and are not discussed here.

STATE POST-CONVICTION RELIEF. Almost all states have post-conviction procedures permitting prisoners to challenge constitutional violations. These procedures may derive from statutes, court rules, or the common law. Many of these state remedies are as extensive in scope as federal habeas corpus for state prisoners. Other states provide much narrower remedies. The differences in post-conviction remedies among the states are also beyond the scope of this book and are not discussed here.

SUMMARY

The purpose of this chapter is to provide law enforcement officers and other criminal justice professionals with a better understanding of some of the legal terms and procedures involved in a criminal case from the initial report of a crime through an appeal to the U.S. Supreme Court. Although much of the information does not bear directly on the criminal justice professional's daily duties, it can help enhance the criminal justice professional's perception of his or her role in the entire criminal justice system and the importance of the proper performance of that role to the effective and just operation of the system.

REVIEW AND DISCUSSION QUESTIONS

1. Draw a diagram of the hierarchy of federal and state courts with criminal jurisdiction in your state. Indicate whether each court has original or appellate criminal jurisdiction, and explain any peculiarities in the jurisdiction of each court (e.g., whether it handles only misdemeanors, or whether it has a limited appellate jurisdiction).

2. Draw a diagram of the progress of a state felony case from warrantless arrest through appeal to the U.S. Supreme Court. Assume that, at each stage of the proceedings, the decision is adverse to the defendant, who then seeks relief at the next highest tribunal.

3. Discuss the differences and similarities among a complaint, an affidavit, an indictment, and an information.

4. Why is the arraignment sometimes confused with the initial appearance before the magistrate?

5. What is the grand jury, and what is its function?

6. What pleas are available to a person charged with a crime, and what is the effect of each?

7. What is the difference between *jurisdiction* and *venue*, and between a *challenge for cause* and a *peremptory challenge*?

8. Why is a motion to suppress important to a law enforcement officer?

9. Explain the meaning of *burden of proof* in a criminal case. In your explanation, discuss the standard of proof in a criminal case.

10. Name and briefly describe three ways in which a defendant can obtain relief from the courts after a verdict of guilty.

CHAPTER 3
Basic Underlying Concepts

Before discussing in detail the law of arrest, search and seizure, admissions and confessions, and pre-trial identification, it is helpful to lay some further groundwork by presenting three basic concepts that underlie much of what is to follow. The concepts discussed here are the exclusionary rule, privacy, and probable cause. Later in the book these concepts are developed in greater detail and are clarified by examples. Because these concepts are so pervasive and so essential to an understanding of criminal procedure, treating them at the outset should make the later chapters more meaningful.

EXCLUSIONARY RULE

The exclusionary rule requires that any evidence obtained by police using methods that violate a person's constitutional rights be excluded from being used in a criminal prosecution against that person. This rule is of rather recent vintage in the development of our legal system. Under the common law, the seizure of evidence by illegal means did not affect its admissibility in court. Any evidence, however obtained, was allowed as long as it satisfied other criteria for admissibility, such as relevance and trustworthiness. The exclusionary rule was first developed in 1914 in the case of Weeks v. United States, 232 U.S. 383, 34 S.Ct. 341, 58 L.Ed. 652, and was limited to a prohibition on the use of evidence illegally obtained by federal law enforcement officers. Not until 1949, in the case of Wolf v. Colorado, 338 U.S. 25, 27–28, 69 S.Ct. 1359, 1361, 93 L.Ed. 1782, 1785, did the U.S. Supreme Court rule that the Fourth Amendment was applicable to the states through the due process clause of the Fourteenth Amendment:

> The security of one's privacy against arbitrary intrusion by the police—which is at the core of the Fourth Amendment—is basic to a free society. It is therefore implicit in the "concept of ordered liberty" and as such enforceable against the States through the Due Process Clause.

The Court did not, however, go so far as to require that the Fourth Amendment be enforced against state law enforcement officials by excluding illegally seized evidence in court. That decision did not come until 1961, in the landmark decision of Mapp v. Ohio, 367 U.S. 643, 655, 81 S.Ct. 1684, 1691, 6 L.Ed.2d 1081, 1090, in which the Court said:

> Since the Fourth Amendment's right of privacy has been declared enforceable against the States through the Due Process Clause of the Fourteenth, it is enforceable against them by the same sanction of exclusion as is used against the Federal Government. Were it otherwise then just as without the Weeks rule the assurance against unreasonable federal searches and seizures would be "a form of words," valueless and undeserving of mention in a perpetual charter of inestimable human liberties, so too, without that rule the freedom from state invasions of privacy would be so ephemeral and so neatly severed from its conceptual nexus with the freedom from all brutish means of coercing evidence as not to merit this Court's high regard as a freedom "implicit in 'the concept of ordered liberty.'"

The *Mapp* decision reflects the Court's belief that alternative measures, such as the prosecution of law enforcement officers, the administrative disciplining of officers, or the bringing of civil actions against officers, were not sufficiently effective methods of enforcing the Fourth Amendment and that the exclusionary rule was the only effective method.

The U.S. Supreme Court has made other constitutional amendments in the Bill of Rights applicable to the states through the due process clause of the Fourteenth Amendment. For example, the Fifth Amendment privilege against self-incrimination was made applicable to the states in Malloy v. Hogan, 378 U.S. 1, 84 S.Ct. 1489, 12 L.Ed.2d 653 (1964). Likewise, the Sixth Amendment right to counsel was made applicable to the states in Gideon v. Wainwright, 372 U.S. 335, 83 S.Ct. 792, 9 L.Ed.2d 799 (1963). The manner in which the exclusionary rule is used to enforce the rights guaranteed in these amendments and others is discussed in detail in later chapters of this book.

The U.S. Supreme Court has also invoked the exclusionary rule to protect certain "due process of law" rights that are not specifically contained in the Constitution or its amendments. For example, a confession that has been coerced and is therefore involuntary will be excluded from evidence, not because of the privilege against self-incrimination, but because a coerced confession is a violation of due process of law. Similarly, pre-trial identification procedures that are not fairly administered may be violations of due process of law.

The purposes of the exclusionary rule are to deter official misconduct and to preserve the integrity of the judicial system. It follows that evidence illegally obtained by persons other than government officials will not be rendered inadmissible in court. In Burdeau v. McDowell, 256 U.S. 465, 41 S.Ct. 574, 65 L.Ed. 1048 (1921), a private citizen illegally seized certain papers from another private citizen and turned them over to the government. The Court said, "The papers having come into the possession of the government without a violation of petitioner's right by governmental authority, we see no reason why the fact that individuals, unconnected with the government, may have wrongfully taken them, should prevent them from being held for use in prosecuting an offense where the documents are of an incriminatory character." 256 U.S. at 476, 41

S.Ct. at 576, 65 L.Ed. at 1051. If, however, police instigate, encourage, or participate in an illegal search or other constitutional violation, and the private citizen acts with the intent of assisting the police, the individual will be considered an agent of the government. The individual's actions will be subject to the exclusionary rule in the same way as those of a governmental official. United States v. Lambert, 771 F.2d 83, 89 (6th Cir. 1985).

Federal-State Conflict

Mapp v. Ohio did not require the states to follow all interpretations of federal courts in the area of criminal procedure, but only interpretations dealing with constitutional guarantees. Some of the rulings handed down by the U.S. Supreme Court are based on the Court's statutory authority to promulgate rules for the supervision of federal law enforcement. These rulings apply only in federal courts. In Ker v. California, 374 U.S. 23, 83 S.Ct. 1623, 10 L.Ed.2d 726 (1963), the Court explicitly stated that *Mapp* established no assumption by the Supreme Court of supervisory authority over state courts, and therefore implied no total obliteration of state laws relating to arrests and searches in favor of federal law. The Court went on to say that "[t]he States are not thereby precluded from developing workable rules governing arrests, searches and seizures to meet 'the practical demands of effective criminal investigation and law enforcement' in the States, provided that those rules do not violate the constitutional proscription of unreasonable searches and seizures and the concomitant command that evidence so seized is inadmissible against one who has standing to complain." 374 U.S. at 34, 83 S.Ct. at 1630, 10 L.Ed.2d at 738.

The practice of state courts affording the accused greater protection under state law than that required by the federal Constitution is sometimes called the *new federalism*. It is derived from the well-established rule that state court decisions based upon "adequate and independent state grounds" are immune to federal review. Murdock v. Memphis, 87 U.S. (20 Wall.) 590, 22 L.Ed. 429 (1875). Under this rule, state courts are free, as a matter of state constitutional, statutory, or case law, to expand individual rights by imposing greater restrictions on police than those imposed under federal constitutional law. State courts may not, however, decrease individual rights below the level established by the federal Constitution. Nor may state courts impose greater restrictions on police activity as a matter of federal constitutional law when the U.S. Supreme Court specifically refrains from imposing such restrictions. Oregon v. Hass, 420 U.S. 714, 95 S.Ct. 1215, 43 L.Ed.2d 570 (1975).

A state court has several options in responding to a U.S. Supreme Court decision raising issues of federal law:

1. Apply the ruling as it thinks the Supreme Court would. This might include adopting the ruling as a matter of state law.

2. Factually distinguish the case before it from the Supreme Court case, whereupon the decision would be subject to reversal by the Supreme Court.

3. Reject the Supreme Court ruling on adequate and independent state grounds by interpreting the state constitution or state statutes to provide rights unavailable under the federal Constitution as interpreted by the U.S. Supreme

Court. This approach clearly expresses disapproval of the Supreme Court ruling and insulates the state court decision from Supreme Court review.

In recent years, many state courts, reacting against the Burger Court's reluctant and sparing approach to protecting the rights of the accused, have resorted to the third listed option to keep alive the Warren Court's active commitment to the protection and expansion of individual rights. This trend can be expected to continue under the Rehnquist Court.

One example of this trend is the case of South Dakota v. Opperman, 428 U.S. 364, 96 S.Ct. 3092, 49 L.Ed.2d 1000 (1976). In that case, the South Dakota Supreme Court ruled that an automobile inventory conducted by South Dakota law enforcement officers violated the Fourth Amendment, but the U.S. Supreme Court reversed the decision, holding that the police conduct was reasonable. On remand, the South Dakota Supreme Court, in State v. Opperman, 247 N.W.2d 673 (S.D. 1976), decided that the police inventory procedure violated the South Dakota Constitution and held that the evidence seized was inadmissible. This South Dakota court's decision is noteworthy because the search and seizure provision of the South Dakota Constitution is essentially similar to the Fourth Amendment of the U.S. Constitution and because neither the prosecution nor the defense in the case had raised the issue of the state constitution. Other examples of the new federalism are presented in later chapters dealing with particular areas of conflict.

Criticism of the Exclusionary Rule

The exclusionary rule has, throughout its existence, been the object of criticism and attempted reform. In recent years, no less a public authority than the chief justice of the U.S. Supreme Court has complained of the ineffectiveness of the exclusionary rule to achieve its purpose—the deterrence of police misconduct. In his dissent in the case of Bivens v. Six Unknown Named Agents of the Federal Bureau of Narcotics, 403 U.S. 388, 416–18, 91 S.Ct. 1999, 2015, 29 L.Ed.2d 619, 638–39 (1971), Chief Justice Warren E. Burger said:

> The rule does not apply any direct sanction to the individual official whose illegal conduct results in the exclusion of evidence in a criminal trial. . . . The immediate sanction triggered by application of the rule is visited upon the prosecutor whose case against a criminal is either weakened or destroyed. The doctrine deprives the police in no real sense; except that apprehending wrongdoers is their business, police have no more stake in successful prosecutions than prosecutors or the public. The suppression doctrine vaguely assumes that law enforcement is a monolithic governmental enterprise. . . . But the prosecutor who loses his case because of police misconduct is not an official in the police department; he can rarely set in motion any corrective action or administrative penalties. Moreover, he does not have control or direction over police procedures or police actions that lead to the exclusion of evidence. It is the rare exception when a prosecutor takes part in arrests, searches, or seizures so that he can guide police action. Whatever educational effect the rule conceivably might have in theory is greatly diminished in fact by the realities of law enforcement work. Policemen do not have the time, inclination, or training to read and grasp the nuances of the appellate opinions that ultimately define the standards of conduct they are to follow. . . . Nor can judges, in all candor, forget that

opinions sometimes lack helpful clarity. The presumed educational effect of judicial opinions is also reduced by the long time lapse—often several years—between the original police action and its final judicial evaluation. Given a policeman's pressing responsibilities, it would be surprising if he ever becomes aware of the final result after such a delay. Finally, the exclusionary rule's deterrent impact is diluted by the fact that there are large areas of police activity that do not result in criminal prosecutions—hence the rule has virtually no applicability and no effect in such situations.

The criticism and attempts at reform of the exclusionary rule have resulted in limitations on the application of the rule and refusals to further extend the application of the rule. For example, in United States v. Calandra, 414 U.S. 338, 94 S.Ct. 613, 38 L.Ed.2d 561 (1974), the Supreme Court held that the Fourth Amendment did not prevent the use of illegally obtained evidence by a grand jury. In United States v. Janis, 428 U.S. 433, 96 S.Ct. 3021, 49 L.Ed.2d 1046 (1976), the Court held that illegally obtained evidence need not be suppressed at trial in a civil case brought by the United States. And in Stone v. Powell, 428 U.S. 465, 494, 96 S.Ct. 3037, 3052, 49 L.Ed.2d 1067, 1088 (1976), the Court held that "where the State has provided an opportunity for full and fair litigation of a Fourth Amendment claim, a state prisoner may not be granted federal habeas corpus relief on the ground that evidence obtained in an unconstitutional search or seizure was introduced at his trial." The *Stone v. Powell* decision is noteworthy not only because it limited the application of the exclusionary rule, but also because it strengthened the authority of state courts in interpreting the Fourth Amendment.

Despite the U.S. Supreme Court's cutting back on certain applications of the exclusionary rule in recent years, the basic holding of *Mapp v. Ohio* remains good law and the basic tenets of the exclusionary rule remain valid legal doctrine. Any further limitations or changes in the exclusionary rule will depend largely on the makeup of the Supreme Court and the opportunities presented to the Court in the cases brought before it.

Fruit of the Poisonous Tree Doctrine

The exclusionary rule is not limited to evidence that is the direct product of illegal police behavior, such as a coerced confession or the items seized as a result of an illegal search. The rule also requires exclusion of evidence that is obtained indirectly as a result of a violation of one's constitutional rights. This type of evidence is sometimes call *derivative* or *secondary* evidence.

In Silverthorne Lumber Co. v. United States, 251 U.S. 385, 392, 40 S.Ct. 182, 183, 64 L.Ed. 319, 321 (1920), the Court invalidated a subpoena that had been issued on the basis of information obtained through an illegal search. The Court said:

> The essence of a provision forbidding the acquisition of evidence in a certain way is that not merely evidence so acquired shall not be used before the Court but that it shall not be used at all. Of course this does not mean that the facts thus obtained become sacred and inaccessible. If knowledge of them is gained from an independent source they may be proved like any others, but the knowledge gained by the Government's own wrong cannot be used by it in the way proposed.

Thus, the prosecution may not use in court evidence obtained directly or indirectly from an unconstitutional search. The prohibition against using this derivative or secondary evidence is often called the rule against admission of "fruit of the poisonous tree," the tree being the illegal search and the fruit being the evidence obtained as an indirect result of that search. The fruit, or the evidence indirectly obtained, is sometimes referred to as *tainted* evidence. Although the rule against the admission of fruit of the poisonous tree was originally developed in applying the exclusionary rule to unconstitutional searches, it has been applied equally to evidence obtained as the indirect result of other constitutional violations. Thus, evidence may be inadmissible if it is acquired indirectly as a result of an illegal arrest, an illegal identification procedure, or an involuntary confession.

The fruit of the poisonous tree doctrine applies only when a person's constitutional rights have been violated and does not apply when a violation of rights is not of constitutional dimensions, such as when *Miranda* procedures are violated. As stated by the U.S. Supreme Court, "If errors are made by law enforcement officers in administering the prophylactic *Miranda* procedures, they should not breed the same irremediable consequences as police infringement of the Fifth Amendment itself." Oregon v. Elstad, 470 U.S. 298, 309, 105 S.Ct. 1285, 1293, 84 L.Ed.2d 222, 232 (1985).

INDEPENDENT SOURCE.   There are several recognized exceptions to the fruit of the poisonous tree doctrine, allowing the admission of tainted evidence under certain conditions. One exception already referred to, is the *independent source exception*. This exception allows the admission of tainted evidence if that evidence was also obtained through a source wholly independent of the primary constitutional violation. The independent source exception is compatible with the underlying rationale of the exclusionary rule: the deterrence of police misconduct. As stated by the U.S. Supreme Court, "The independent source doctrine teaches us that the interest of society in deterring unlawful police conduct and the public interest in having juries receive all probative evidence of a crime are properly balanced by putting the police in the same, not a *worse*, position than they would have been in if no police error or misconduct had occurred." Nix v. Williams, 467 U.S. 431, 443, 104 S.Ct. 2501, 2509, 81 L.Ed.2d 377, 387 (1984).

In a case applying the independent source doctrine, law enforcement officers illegally entered an apartment, secured it, and then remained for about nineteen hours until a search warrant arrived. Despite the illegal entry, the U.S. Supreme Court admitted the evidence found during the execution of the warrant. The Court found an independent source for the tainted evidence because the information on which the warrant was based came from sources entirely separate from the illegal entry and was known to the officers well before that entry. The Court held that "[w]hether the initial entry was legal or not is irrelevant to the admissibility for the challenged evidence because there was an independent source for the warrant under which that evidence was seized." Segura v. United States, 468 U.S. 796, 813–814, 104 S.Ct. 3380, 3390, 82 L.Ed.2d 599, 614 (1984).

ATTENUATION. Another exception to the fruit of the poisonous tree doctrine was first established in Nardone v. United States, 308 U.S. 338, 60 S.Ct. 266, 84 L.Ed. 307 (1939), and is referred to as the *attenuation doctrine*. This doctrine states that, even where the tainted evidence would not have been discovered except through the constitutional violation, there being no independent source, the evidence may still be admissible if the means of obtaining the evidence were sufficiently remote from and distinguishable from the primary illegality. The key question, as posed in Wong Sun v. United States, 371 U.S. 471, 488, 83 S.Ct. 407, 417, 9 L.Ed.2d 441, 455 (1963), is "whether granting establishment of the primary illegality, the evidence to which instant objection is made has been come at by exploitation of that illegality or instead by means sufficiently distinguishable to be purged of the primary taint." If the tainted evidence is obtained by means sufficiently distinguishable from the primary illegality, the causal connection between the primary illegality and the evidence indirectly derived from it is said to be attenuated, and the evidence is admissible even though tainted. The rationale behind this exception is that the deterrent purpose of the exclusionary rule is not served where an officer could not have been aware of the possible benefit to be derived from his or her illegal actions at the time of taking those actions.

In the *Wong Sun* case, narcotics agents illegally broke into Toy's laundry and followed Toy into his living quarters where he was arrested and handcuffed. Almost immediately thereafter, Toy told the agents that Yee had been selling narcotics. The agents subsequently seized heroin from Yee, who told them that it had been brought to him by Toy and Wong Sun. Wong Sun was illegally arrested, arraigned, and released on his own recognizance. Several days later, Wong Sun returned voluntarily and made an oral confession to a narcotics agent.

Toy argued that his statement and the heroin later seized from Yee were fruit of the illegal entry into his dwelling and his illegal arrest. The Court agreed and held both inadmissible. Wong Sun claimed that his statement was the fruit of his illegal arrest. The Court disagreed:

> We have no occasion to disagree with the finding of the Court of Appeals that his arrest, also, was without probable cause or reasonable grounds. At all events no evidentiary consequences turn upon that question. For Wong Sun's unsigned confession was not the fruit of that arrest, and was therefore properly admitted at trial. On the evidence that Wong Sun had been released on his own recognizance after a lawful arraignment, and had returned voluntarily several days later to make the statement, we hold that the connection between the arrest and the statement has "become so attenuated as to dissipate the taint." 371 U.S. at 491, 83 S.Ct. at 419, 9 L.Ed.2d at 457.

In determining whether the connection between the primary illegality and the resulting evidence has sufficiently attenuated, courts look for an intervening independent act between the two, such as Wong Sun's voluntary return to make a statement. In the words of the Supreme Court of California, "That degree of 'attenuation' which suffices to remove the taint from evidence obtained directly as a result of unlawful police conduct requires at least an intervening independent act by the defendant or a third party which breaks the causal chain linking the illegality and evidence in such a way that the evidence is not in fact obtained 'by exploitation of the illegality.'" People v. Superior Court (Casebeer) 71 Cal.2d 265, 271–72, 78 Cal.Rptr. 210, 215, 455 P.2d 146, 151 (Cal. 1969).

Courts applying the attenuation doctrine make a distinction between physical and verbal evidence. In United States v. Ceccolini, 435 U.S. 268, 98 S.Ct. 1054, 55 L.Ed.2d 268 (1978), the Supreme Court held that because of the cost to the truth-finding process of disqualifying knowledgeable witnesses, the exclusionary rule should be invoked with much greater reluctance when the fruit of the poisonous tree is the testimony of a live witness rather than an inanimate object. Therefore, a court will not exclude the testimony of a witness discovered as the result of a constitutional violation, unless the court finds a more direct link between the discovery and the violation than is required to exclude physical evidence. Furthermore, the court must find that the constitutional violation is the kind that will be deterred by application of the exclusionary rule. In a case illustrating the kind of constitutional violation that should be deterred, police obtained an involuntary statement from the defendant for the very purpose of discovering the defendant's crimes and witnesses to testify to those crimes. The court held that legitimate concerns for the deterrence of police misconduct compelled the application of the exclusionary rule to the testimony of sexually abused children who were revealed through the defendant's coerced statement. Commonwealth v. Lahti, 501 N.E.2d 511 (Mass. 1986).

INEVITABLE DISCOVERY. Another exception to the fruit of the poisonous tree doctrine is the *inevitable discovery doctrine*. This doctrine is a variation of the independent source exception. Whereas the independent source exception allows the admission of tainted evidence if the tainted evidence was also obtained from an independent source, the inevitable discovery doctrine allows admission of the evidence if it would inevitably have been discovered in the normal course of events. Under this exception, the prosecution must establish by a preponderance of the evidence that, even though the evidence was actually discovered as the indirect result of a constitutional violation, the evidence would ultimately or inevitably have been discovered by lawful means—for example, as the result of the predictable and routine behavior of a law enforcement agency, some other agency, or a private person.

The U.S. Supreme Court specifically adopted the inevitable discovery exception in Nix v. Williams, 467 U.S. 431, 104 S.Ct. 2501, 81 L.Ed.2d 377 (1984). In that case, police initiated a search for a ten-year-old girl who had disappeared. While the search was going on, the defendant was arrested and, in response to illegal questioning, led police to the girl's body. The search was called off, but the girl's body was found in a place that was essentially within the area to be searched. Although the defendant's illegally obtained statements, leading to the discovery of the body, rendered evidence relating to the body inadmissible, the Court allowed the admission of the evidence under the inevitable discovery doctrine. The Court found that the volunteer search parties were approaching the actual location of the body, that they would have resumed the search had the defendant not earlier led the police to the body, and that the body would inevitably have been found.

The Court justified its adoption of the inevitable discovery doctrine using the rationale underlying the independent source exception. The Court said:

> [I]f the government can prove that the evidence would have been obtained inevitably and, therefore, would have been admitted regardless of any overreaching by the police, there is no rational basis to keep that evidence from the jury in order to ensure the fairness of the trial proceedings. In that situation, the State has gained no advantage at trial and the defendant has suffered no prejudice. Indeed, suppression of the evidence would operate to undermine the adversary system by putting the State in a *worse* position than it would have occupied without any police misconduct. 467 U.S. at 447, 104 S.Ct. at 2511, 81 L.Ed.2d at 389–90.

Furthermore, in response to the defendant's contention that the prosecution must prove the absence of bad faith on the part of the police, the Court said that such a requirement "would place courts in the position of withholding from juries relevant and undoubted truth that would have been available to police absent any unlawful police activity. Of course, that view would put the police in a *worse* position than they would have been in if no unlawful conduct had transpired. And, of equal importance, it wholly fails to take into account the enormous societal cost of excluding truth in the search for truth in the administration of justice." 467 U.S. at 445, 104 S.Ct. at 2510, 81 L.Ed.2d at 388. Finally, the Court dismissed arguments that the inevitable discovery exception will promote police misconduct. A police officer who is faced with an opportunity to obtain evidence illegally will rarely, if ever, be in a position to calculate whether the evidence sought would inevitably be discovered. Even when an officer is aware that evidence will inevitably be discovered, there will be little to gain from taking dubious shortcuts to obtain the evidence. Other significant disincentives to obtaining evidence illegally include the possibility of departmental discipline and civil liability.

Lower courts have been careful to scrutinize claims of inevitable discovery. For example, in United States v. Satterfield, 743 F.2d 827 (11th Cir. 1984), the court stated that "[t]o qualify for admissibility, there must be a reasonable probability that the evidence in question would have been discovered by lawful means, and the prosecution must demonstrate that the lawful means which made discovery inevitable were possessed by the police and were being actively pursued *prior* to the occurrence of the illegal conduct." 743 F.2d at 846. In the Satterfield case, despite the claim by police that they would have undoubtedly found a shotgun during a search of the defendant's home, no warrant was sought until several hours after an illegal search that uncovered the weapon. Therefore, the police did not *before* the illegal action possess the legal means that would have led to the discovery of the shotgun. The shotgun was ruled inadmissible.

Occasionally, courts will find inevitable discovery based not on the behavior of law enforcement officers, but on the behavior of ordinary civilians. In State v. Miller, 680 P.2d 676 (Or. 1984), after obtaining, in violation of *Miranda*, the defendant's statement that he had "hurt someone" in his hotel room, a law enforcement officer conducted a warrantless search of the hotel room and discovered a dead body. The Court held that evidence of the discovery of the body was admissible despite the *Miranda* violation, because the maid would inevitably have discovered the body and would normally be expected to come forward and cooperate with police authorities.

Good Faith Exception

In United States v. Leon, 468 U.S. 897, 104 S.Ct. 3405, 82 L.Ed.2d 677 (1984), the U.S. Supreme Court adopted another exception to the exclusionary rule: the *good faith exception* for searches conducted pursuant to a warrant. Under this exception, whenever a law enforcement officer acting with objective good faith has obtained a search warrant from a detached and neutral judge or magistrate had has acted within its scope, evidence seized pursuant to the warrant will not be excluded, even though the warrant is later determined to be invalid. The Court reasoned that excluding such evidence would not further the purposes of the exclusionary rule—deterrence of police misconduct–since the officer is acting as a reasonable officer would and should act under the circumstances. In determining what is good faith on the part of an officer, the Court said:

> [O]ur good-faith inquiry is confined to the objectively ascertainable question whether a reasonably well-trained officer would have known that the search was illegal despite the magistrate's authorization. In making this determination, all of the circumstances—including whether the warrant application has previously been rejected by a different magistrate—may be considered. 468 U.S. at 922–23, n. 23, 104 S.Ct. at 3421, n. 23, 82 L.Ed.2d at 698, n. 23.

The Court described several circumstances under which an officer would *not* have reasonable grounds for believing that a warrant was properly issued:

— In issuing the warrant, the magistrate or judge was misled by information in an affidavit that the affiant knew was false or would have known was false except for a reckless disregard of the truth.

— The issuing magistrate wholly abandoned a neutral and detached judicial role and acted either as a "rubber stamp" or as an arm of the prosecution.

— The warrant was based on an affidavit so lacking in indicia of probable cause as to render official belief in its existence entirely unreasonable (see Chapter 6).

— The warrant was so facially deficient—in failing to particularize the place to be searched or the things to be seized—that the executing officers could not reasonably presume it to be valid (see Chapter 5).

Under such circumstances, not only would the warrant be declared invalid, but any evidence seized pursuant to the warrant would be ruled inadmissible.

The U.S. Supreme Court cited an example of good faith behavior in Massachusetts v. Sheppard, the companion case to United States v. Leon:

> The officers in this case took every step that could reasonably be expected of them. Detective O'Malley prepared an affidavit which was reviewed and approved by the District Attorney. He presented that affidavit to a neutral judge. The judge concluded that the affidavit established probable cause to search Sheppard's residence . . . and informed O'Malley that he would authorize the search as requested. O'Malley then produced the warrant form and informed

the judge that it might need to be changed. He was told by the judge that the necessary changes would be made. He then observed the judge make some changes and received the warrant and the affidavit. At this point, a reasonable police officer would have concluded, as O'Malley did, that the warrant authorized a search for the materials outlined in the affidavit. 468 U.S. 981, 989, 104 S.Ct. 3424, 3428, 82 L.Ed.2d 737, 744 (1984).

In Illinois v. Krull, 480 U.S. 340, 107 S.Ct. 1160, 94 L.Ed.2d 364 (1987), the U.S. Supreme Court extended the good faith exception to the exclusionary rule, holding that the exclusionary rule does not apply to evidence obtained by police who acted in objectively reasonable reliance upon a statute that authorized warrantless administrative searches, but which was subsequently found to violate the Fourth Amendment. Following the approach used in the *Leon* case, the Court said that application of the exclusionary rule in this situation would have as little deterrent effect on an officer's actions as would the exclusion of evidence when an officer acts in objectively reasonable reliance on a warrant.

> Unless a statute is clearly unconstitutional, an officer cannot be expected to question the judgment of the legislature that passed the law. If the statute is subsequently declared unconstitutional, excluding evidence obtained pursuant to it prior to such judicial declaration will not deter future Fourth Amendment violations by an officer who has simply fulfilled his responsibility to enforce the statute as written. 480 U.S. at 349–50, 107 S.Ct. at 1167, 94 L.Ed.2d at 375.

The discussion of the exceptions to the exclusionary rule serves to highlight an important feature of the rule: The exclusionary rule does not necessarily bar or stop a prosecution. At most, it will cause the suppression of evidence obtained as the direct or indirect result of a constitutional violation. If that evidence is essential to the prosecution's case against a defendant, the prosecution may decide that it is futile to go on with the prosecution. If, however, the prosecution has sufficient other evidence, either legally obtained or falling within one of the exceptions to the exclusionary rule, the prosecution may go forward despite the illegal police conduct.

Standing

To invoke the exclusionary rule to challenge the admissibility of evidence, a defendant must have *standing*. A defendant has standing when his or her own constitutional rights have been violated.

> "Fourth Amendment rights are personal rights which, like some other constitutional rights, may not be vicariously asserted." . . . A person who is aggrieved by an illegal search and seizure only through the introduction of damaging evidence secured by a search of a third person's premises or property has not had any of his Fourth Amendment rights infringed. . . . And since the exclusionary rule is an attempt to effectuate the guarantees of the Fourth Amendment, . . . it is proper to permit only defendants whose Fourth Amendment rights have been violated to benefit from the rule's protections. Rakas v. Illinois, 439 U.S. 128, 133–34, 99 S.Ct. 421, 425, 58 L.Ed.2d 387, 394–95 (1978).

In determining whether a defendant's Fourth Amendment rights have been violated, courts will analyze whether the defendant had a reasonable expectation of privacy in the area searched or the item seized. The topic of privacy is discussed in the following section.

PRIVACY

In a criminal case, for the Fourth Amendment to be applicable to a particular fact situation, there must be a search and a seizure accompanied by an attempt by the prosecution to introduce what was seized as evidence in court. Whether there was a search and seizure within the meaning of the Fourth Amendment and, if so, whether the search and seizure violated someone's constitutional rights depends on the nature of the interest that the Fourth Amendment protects. Under the common law, it was clear that the security of one's property was a sacred right and protection of that right was a primary purpose of government. In an early English case, the court said:

> The great end for which men entered into society was to secure their property. That right is preserved sacred and incommunicable in all instances where it has not been taken away or abridged by some public law for the good of the whole.... By the laws of England, every invasion of private property, be it ever so minute, is a trespass. No man can set foot upon my ground without my license but he is liable to an action though the damage be nothing.... Entick v. Carrington, 19 Howell's State Trials 1029, 1035, 95 Eng.Rep. 807, 817–18 (1765).

The protection of property interests as the basis of the Fourth Amendment was adopted by the U.S. Supreme Court, and until relatively recently, analysis of Fourth Amendment issues centered around whether there was an intrusion into a "constitutionally protected area." Three cases involving electronic surveillance illustrate this approach. In Olmstead v. United States, 277 U.S. 438, 48 S.Ct. 564, 72 L.Ed. 944 (1928), one reason for the Court's holding that wiretapping was not covered by the Fourth Amendment was that there had been no physical invasion of the defendant's premises. The Court said:

> The evidence was secured by the use of the sense of hearing and that only. There was no entry of the houses or offices of the defendants.... The intervening wires are not part of his house or office.... 277 U.S. at 464–65, 48 S.Ct. at 568, 72 L.Ed. at 950.

In Silverman v. United States, 365 U.S. 505, 81 S.Ct. 679, 5 L.Ed.2d 734 (1961), however, a spike mike was pushed through a party wall until it hit a heating duct, and the Court held that the electronic surveillance was an illegal search and seizure. And in Clinton v. Virginia, 377 U.S. 158, 84 S.Ct. 1186, 12 L.Ed.2d 213 (1964), the Court ruled as inadmissible evidence obtained by means of a mechanical listening device stuck into the wall of an apartment adjoining the defendant's. The rationale for the *Silverman* and *Clinton* cases was that the listening devices had actually physically invaded the target premises, even though the invasion was slight.

This emphasis on property concepts in interpreting the Fourth Amendment began to lose favor in the 1960s. Justice William O. Douglas, concurring in the *Silverman* case, said that "our sole concern should be with whether the privacy of the home was invaded." 365 U.S. at 513, 81 S.Ct. at 683, 5 L.Ed.2d at 740. In a later case, the Court said:

> The premise that property interests control the right of the Government to search and seize has been discredited.... We have recognized that the princi-

pal object of the Fourth Amendment is the protection of privacy rather than property, and have increasingly discarded fictional and procedural barriers rested on property concepts. Warden v. Hayden, 387 U.S. 294, 304, 87 S.Ct. 1642, 1648, 18 L.Ed.2d 782, 790 (1967).

Finally, in Katz v. United States, 389 U.S. 347, 88 S.Ct. 507, 19 L.Ed.2d 576 (1967), another electronic surveillance case, the Court dispensed with the requirement of an actual physical trespass in applying the Fourth Amendment. The issue was the admissibility of telephone conversations overhead by FBI agents who had attached an electronic listening and recording device to the outside of a public telephone booth. The Court said:

> [T]his effort to decide whether or not a given "area," viewed in the abstract, is "constitutionally protected" deflects attention from the problem presented by this case. For the Fourth Amendment protects people, not places. What a person knowingly exposes to the public, even in his own home or office, is not a subject of Fourth Amendment protection. . . . But what he seeks to preserve as private, even in an area accessible to the public may be constitutionally protected. 389 U.S. at 351–52, 88 S.Ct. at 511, 19 L.Ed.2d at 582.

The Court held that the government's activities in electronically listening to and recording the defendant's words violated the privacy upon which the defendant justifiably relied while using the telephone booth and thus constituted a search and seizure within the meaning of the Fourth Amendment. The Court added: "The fact that the electronic device employed to achieve that end did not happen to penetrate the wall of the booth can have no constitutional significance." 389 U.S. at 353, 88 S.Ct. at 512, 19 L.Ed.2d at 583.

The *Katz* case signaled a major shift in the interpretation of the Fourth Amendment away from a property approach toward a privacy approach. Court decisions since the *Katz* case no longer focus on whether there has been an intrusion into a constitutionally protected area. Now the formula for analysis of Fourth Amendment problems is that "wherever an individual may harbor a reasonable 'expectation of privacy,' . . . he is entitled to be free from unreasonable governmental intrusion." Terry v. Ohio, 392 U.S. 1, 9, 88 S.Ct. 1868, 1873, 20 L.Ed.2d 889, 899 (1968). It would seem that such a sweeping change in approach in interpreting the Fourth Amendment would result in a large-scale overturning of earlier decisions. Yet, as Justice John Marshall Harlan noted in his concurring opinion in the *Katz* case, the determination of what protection the Fourth Amendment affords to people requires reference to a "place." Therefore, many of the pre-*Katz* decisions are not necessarily changed or overruled by the *Katz* decision. These cases should, however, be evaluated not only in terms of the reasoning employed in them, but also in terms of the new standard announced in *Katz*. In later chapters of this book discussing the Fourth Amendment, both pre-*Katz* and post-*Katz* cases are discussed, to help you gain as complete an understanding as possible of this continually developing area of the law.

In analyzing Fourth Amendment issues, many courts take the approach suggested by Justice Harlan in his concurring opinion in the *Katz* case. Justice Harlan said that "there is a twofold requirement, first that a person have exhibited an actual (subjective) expectation of privacy and, second, that the expectation be one that society is prepared to recognize as 'reasonable.'" 389 U.S. at

361, 88 S.Ct. at 516, 19 L.Ed.2d at 588. If these requirements are satisfied, any governmental intrusion upon the expectation of privacy is a search for purposes of the Fourth Amendment. Reflecting Justice Harlan's approach, the U.S. Supreme Court defined the terms *search* and *seizure* as follows:

> A "search" occurs when an expectation of privacy that society is prepared to consider reasonable is infringed. A "seizure" of property occurs when there is some meaningful interference with an individual's possessory interests in that property. United States v. Jacobsen, 466 U.S. 109, 113, 104 S.Ct. 1652, 1656, 80 L.Ed.2d 85, 94 (1984).

The case of Maryland v. Macon, 472 U.S. 463, 105 S.Ct. 2778, 86 L.Ed.2d 370 (1985), illustrates the application of these definitions. A county police detective, who was not in uniform, entered an adult bookstore. After browsing for several minutes, the detective purchased two magazines from a salesclerk, paying for them with a marked fifty-dollar bill. The detective then left the store and showed the magazines to his fellow officers, who were waiting nearby. The officers concluded that the magazines were obscene, reentered the store, and arrested the salesclerk. They also retrieved the marked fifty-dollar bill from the cash register, but neglected to return the change received at the time of the purchase.

In determining whether there was a search, the Court said:

> [R]espondent did not have any reasonable expectation of privacy in areas of the store where the public was invited to enter and to transact business. . . . The mere expectation that the possibly illegal nature of product will not come to the attention of the authorities, whether because a customer will not complain or because undercover officers will not transact business with the store, is not one that society is prepared to recognize as reasonable. The officer's action in entering the bookstore and examining the wares that were intentionally exposed to all who frequent the place of business did not infringe a legitimate expectation of privacy and hence did not constitute a search within the meaning of the Fourth Amendment. 472 U.S. at 469, 105 S.Ct. at 2782, 86 L.Ed.2d at 376–77.

In determining whether there was a seizure, the Court said:

> [R]espondent voluntarily transferred any possessory interest he may have had in the magazines to the purchaser upon the receipt of the funds. . . . Thereafter, whatever possessory interest the seller had was in the funds, not the magazines. At the time of the sale the officer did not "interfere" with any interest of the seller; he took only that which was intended as a necessary part of the exchange. 472 U.S. at 469, 105 S.Ct. at 2782, 86 L.Ed.2d at 377.

Therefore, no seizure occurred for the purposes of the Fourth Amendment.

In this book, the primary concern is with governmental actions that are sufficiently intrusive as to be considered searches and seizures, and with the legality of those actions. Generally, to be legal, a search or seizure must be conducted under the authority of a valid warrant, or must fall within a recognized exception to the warrant requirement. Parts two and three of the book deal with the search warrant requirement and its exceptions.

Note that privacy, as one of the basic rights guaranteed to individuals in our society, encompasses much more than the protections offered by the Fourth

Amendment, even as interpreted under the *Katz* formula. This point is perhaps best stated in the *Katz* decision itself:

> [T]he Fourth Amendment cannot be translated into a general constitutional "right to privacy." That Amendment protects individual privacy against certain kinds of governmental intrusion, buts its protections go further, and often have nothing to do with privacy at all. Other provisions of the Constitution protect personal privacy from other forms of governmental invasion. But the protection of a person's general right to privacy—his right to be let alone by other people—is, like the protection of his property and of his very life, left largely to the law of individual States. 389 U.S. at 350–51, 88 S.Ct. at 510–11, 19 L.Ed.2d at 581.

PROBABLE CAUSE

The Fourth Amendment to the U.S. Constitution provides an introduction to the concept of probable cause: "The right of the people to be secure in their persons, houses, papers, and effects, against unreasonable searches and seizures, shall not be violated, and no Warrants shall issue, but upon probable cause, supported by Oath or affirmation, and particularly describing the place to be searched, and the persons or things to be seized." From this language, it is apparent that probable cause is necessary for the issuance of an arrest or search warrant.

To explain what probable cause means, it is helpful to start with the U.S. Supreme Court's often-cited definition of probable cause to arrest set forth in Brinegar v. United States: "Probable cause exists where 'the facts and circumstances within their [the arresting officers'] knowledge and of which they had reasonably trustworthy information [are] sufficient in themselves to warrant a man of reasonable caution in the belief that' an offense has been or is being committed [by the person to be arrested]." 338 U.S. 160, 175–76, 69 S.Ct. 1302, 1310–11, 93 L.Ed.1879, 1890 (1949). The Court noted that probable cause has come to mean more than bare suspicion. Other courts have held that absolute certainty or "evidence beyond a reasonable doubt" is not required to establish probable cause. In this regard, the Wisconsin Supreme Court said:

> Probable cause to arrest refers to the quantum of evidence which would lead a reasonable man to believe that the defendant probably committed a crime. While the standard is objective . . . it is not necessary that the evidence be sufficient to prove ultimate guilt beyond a reasonable doubt or even that it be sufficient to prove that guilt is more probable than not. It is only necessary that the information lead a reasonable officer to believe that guilt is more than a possibility. Browne v. State, 129 N.W.2d 175, 180 (Wis. 1964).

Note that, although this discussion has focused on probable cause to arrest, the same quantum of evidence is required to establish probable cause to search. Probable cause to search, however, requires a belief that certain items are contraband or fruits, instrumentalities, or evidence of crime and are in a particular place or on a particular person, rather than a belief that a particular person has committed or is committing a crime.

As discussed in detail in later chapters, many arrests and searches are conducted without a warrant. The quantum of evidence required to establish probable cause for a warrantless arrest or search is somewhat greater than that required under authority of a warrant. The reason why a greater degree of probable cause may be required in the warrantless situation is that the Supreme Court has expressed a strong preference for arrest warrants (Beck v. Ohio, 379 U.S. 89, 85 S.Ct. 223, 13 L.Ed.2d 142 [1964]) and for search warrants (United States v. Ventresca, 380 U.S. 102, 85 S.Ct. 741, 13 L.Ed.2d 684 [1965]). This preference is so strong that less persuasive evidence will justify the issuance of a warrant than would justify a warrantless search or warrantless arrest. In Aguilar v. Texas, the U.S. Supreme Court said that "when a search is based upon a magistrate's, rather than a police officer's determination of probable cause, the reviewing courts will accept evidence of a less 'judicially competent or persuasive character than would have justified an officer in acting on his own without a warrant,' . . . and will sustain the judicial determination so long as 'there was a substantial basis for [the magistrate] to conclude that [seizable evidence was] probably present. . . .'" 378 U.S. 108, 111, 84 S.Ct. 1509, 1512, 12 L.Ed.2d 723, 726 (1964).

The warrant procedure is preferred because it places responsibility for deciding the delicate question of probable cause with a neutral and detached judicial officer. Thereby, law enforcement is served, because law enforcement officers are enabled to search certain places and seize certain persons or things when the officers can show reasonable grounds that those persons, places, or things are significantly connected with criminal activity. The Fourth Amendment rights of citizens are also served by the warrant procedure, because the decision to allow a search and seizure is removed from the sometimes hurried and overzealous judgment of law enforcement officers engaged in the competitive enterprise of investigating crime.

Whether law enforcement officers are applying for a warrant or are determining their authority to arrest or search without a warrant, they must have sufficient information to establish probable cause. Probable cause may arise through facts or information that an officer has personally observed or gathered. It may also be based upon apparently reliable information from third parties such as the victim, other police agencies, witnesses, reporters, and informants, or even on information from the defendant. Chapter 6 contains a detailed discussion of what information may and may not be considered in arriving at probable cause in addition to procedures to assist the law enforcement officer in establishing probable cause, both when the information comes from informants and when it does not.

Probable cause is evaluated by examining the collective information in the possession of the police at the time of the arrest or search, and not merely on the personal knowledge of the arresting or searching officer. Therefore, if the knowledge of the police is in its totality sufficient to establish probable cause, a law enforcement officer's actions in making a warrantless arrest or search upon orders to do so will be justified, even though that officer does not personally have all the information upon which probable cause is based. State v. Smith, 277 A.2d 481 (Me. 1971). Even if the collective knowledge of the police is not sufficient to establish probable cause, the officer arresting upon orders will be protected from civil and criminal liability. The arrest or search would be unlawful in these circumstances, because it was not based upon probable cause. Whiteley v. Warden, 401 U.S. 560, 91 S.Ct. 1031, 28 L.Ed.2d 306 (1971).

SUMMARY

This chapter is designed to round out your preparation for the detailed study of the law of criminal procedure. Chapter 1 introduced the Constitution, the well-spring from which flow all the rules and principles to follow. Emphasis was placed on the constitutional sources of individual rights, and the necessary conflict between the protection of individual rights and the maintenance of law and order was pointed out. Future chapters deal with specific instances of this conflict and show how the delicate balance between these competing interests is maintained.

Chapter 2 presented an overview of the criminal court system, the arena in which the balancing takes place and in which the reasonableness, appropriateness, and thoroughness of the law enforcement officer's activities are ultimately tested. Chapter 2 was designed to give an overall picture of the criminal justice system as a backdrop for a more integrated understanding of the law of criminal procedure.

Finally, this chapter introduces the basic concepts of the exclusionary rule, privacy, and probable cause, which wind through the following chapters of this book. The law enforcement officer or other criminal justice professional who knows the potentially devastating effects of the exclusionary rule, who is sensitive to the constitutional rights of all citizens, especially to their reasonable expectation of privacy, and who understands the meaning and importance of probable cause is well on the way to appreciating the constitutional restraints that characterize the operation of our criminal justice system. The remainder of this book provides the details of criminal procedure, the knowledge of which can enable a person to function effectively within that system.

REVIEW AND DISCUSSION QUESTIONS

1. Explain why the application of the exclusionary rule does not necessarily mean that the prosecution is ended and the defendant goes free.

2. Discuss the probable effectiveness in terms of deterring illegal police conduct of the following suggested alternatives to the exclusionary rule: criminal prosecution of law enforcement officers; administrative disciplining of officers; bringing of civil actions for damages against officers.

3. Explain why a state court may refuse to follow certain holdings of the U.S. Supreme Court.

4. Give three reasons in support of the exclusionary rule and three reasons it should be abolished.

5. Discuss three theories under which evidence may be admissible in court even though it is fruit of the poisonous tree.

6. What did Justice Harlan mean when he said, in his concurring opinion in *Katz v. United States*, that the answer to the question of what protection the Fourth Amendment affords to people requires reference to a place?

7. Should a person in a telephone booth be given the same degree of Fourth Amendment protection as a person in his or her bedroom? as a person in his or her garage? as a person in his or her automobile?

8. Although *Katz v. United States* dispensed with the requirement of an actual physical trespass to trigger the Fourth Amendment, is a physical trespass always an intrusion on a person's reasonable expectation of privacy?

9. Compare the standard of probable cause against the following statements of degree of certainty: absolutely positive; pretty sure; good possibility; beyond a reasonable doubt; reasonable suspicion; preponderance of the evidence; reasonable probability; strong belief; convinced.

10. Why do reviewing courts accept evidence of a "less judicially competent or persuasive character" to justify the issuance of a warrant than they would to justify officers acting on their own without a warrant?

PART TWO
Arrest, Search Warrants, and Probable Cause

CHAPTER 4
Arrest

The power of arrest is the most important power that a law enforcement officer possesses. It enables the officer to deprive a person of the freedom to carry out daily personal and business affairs, and it initiates against a person the processes of criminal justice, which may ultimately result in that person being fined or imprisoned. Since an arrest has a potentially great detrimental effect upon a person's life, liberty, and privacy, the law governing arrest provides many protections to ensure that a person will be arrested only when reasonable and necessary. These protections take the form of severe limitations and restrictions on the law enforcement officer's exercise of the power of arrest. The law governing arrest is based upon guarantees in the Fourth Amendment to the U.S. Constitution which provides as follows:

> The right of the people to be secure in their *persons* houses, papers, and effects, against unreasonable searches and seizures, shall not be violated and no Warrants shall issue, but upon probable cause, supported by Oath or affirmation, and particularly describing the place to be searched and the *persons* or things *to be seized*. (emphasis supplied) U.S.C.A.Const.Amend.IV.

There is a common misunderstanding that the Fourth Amendment applies only to searches and seizures of material things and not to people. The word *persons* has been emphasized in the preceding passage to indicate clearly that this amendment is not so restricted, but that it also protects individuals from illegal seizures of their persons.

With the Fourth Amendment as a backdrop, the discussion now turns to defining arrest and exploring the law enforcement officer's powers and duties with respect to arrest.

DEFINITION OF FORMAL ARREST

Arrest is a difficult term to define because it is used in different senses. In its narrow sense, sometimes called a formal or technical arrest, the term arrest "signifies the apprehension or detention of the person of another in order that he may be forthcoming to answer for an alleged or supposed crime." State v. MacKenzie, 210 A.2d 24, 32–33 (Me. 1965). In its broader sense, sometimes called a seizure tantamount to arrest or an arrest for constitutional purposes, the term arrest refers to any seizure of a person significant enough to resemble a formal arrest in important respects.

This chapter refers to the narrow sense as a formal arrest and to the broad sense as a seizure tantamount to arrest or simply an arrest. Seizures tantamount to arrest are discussed in the next section of the chapter.

The discussion of formal arrest begins here with a listing of the basic elements necessary for a formal arrest:

1. A purpose or intention of a law enforcement officer to effect an arrest under real or pretended authority

2. An actual or constructive seizure or detention of the person to be arrested by an officer having the present power to control the person

3. A communication by the arresting officer to the person to be arrested of the intention or purpose then and there to make the arrest

4. An understanding by the person to be arrested that it is the intention of the arresting officer then and there to arrest and detain him or her

Each of these elements is discussed separately in this section.

Intention to Arrest

To satisfy the first requirement of formal arrest, a law enforcement officer must have an intention to take a person into the custody of the law and to deprive that person of liberty and freedom of movement at the time the officer takes action. This intention of the arresting officer to take the person into the custody of the law is the basic element that distinguishes a formal arrest from lesser forms of detention. Examples of lesser forms of detention are as follows:

1. Restraining a person who is behaving in a manner that is dangerous either to self or others

2. Briefly stopping a person to seek information or render assistance

3. Serving a subpoena or other process such as a summons or notice to appear in court

4. Asking a suspect or witness to appear at the station for questioning

5. Briefly stopping a vehicle to inspect license, equipment, or load

Although this is not a complete list, it illustrates the type of situation in which there is no intention by the law enforcement officer to take the person into the custody of the law and therefore no formal arrest. Ways in which lesser forms of detention can develop into the constitutional equivalent of a formal arrest are discussed in the next section on seizures tantamount to arrest.

One further detention situation that deserves mention is that in which a police officer stops a person under suspicious circumstances and conducts a brief, general on-the-scene investigation about the possible commission of a crime. If, accompanying this brief detention of the person, there is a limited search of the person for possible weapons, the entire encounter would be commonly referred to as stop and frisk. Because a separate body of law has developed to govern such encounters, stop and frisk is discussed separately in Chapter 12. For purposes of this chapter, note that the ordinary stop and frisk situation does not involve an intention to arrest and therefore does not constitute a formal arrest.

A law enforcement officer's intention to arrest must be under real or pretended authority. Real authority is simply the legal right to make a formal arrest either with or without a warrant. That right may derive from the warrant itself or from the officer's having probable cause to believe that a particular person committed or was in the process of committing a particular crime. An example of pretended authority is an officer making a formal arrest without the legal right to do so, but erroneously assuming to have that right. The arrest is still technically a formal arrest despite the officer's error. This authority requirement distinguishes arrest from the situation in which a person is seized and detained without any type of authority being apparent or claimed. An example is a kidnapping, when a person is seized but no one claims any kind of authority to arrest.

Seizure or Detention

To be formally arrested, the arrested person must come within the actual custody and control of the law enforcement officer. Two kinds of seizure or detention will satisfy this requirement—actual and constructive.

An actual seizure or detention is the taking into custody of a person with the use of hands or with force, including the use of weapons. The ordinary situation would include the grabbing, holding, or handcuffing of a person to restrain freedom of action. However, the mere touching of the person is also considered to be an actual seizure and may constitute a formal arrest if the other elements of formal arrest are present. Childress v. State, 175 A.2d 18 (Md. 1961).

A constructive seizure may be accomplished when the person being arrested submits to the control of the law enforcement officer without any touching or physical force whatsoever being applied. This peaceable submission eliminates the need for physical action and satisfies the requirement of seizure or detention. State v. Donahue, 420 A.2d 936 (Me. 1980).

Merely telling a person "You are under arrest," without anything else, will not be sufficient to satisfy the seizure or detention element of formal arrest. There must be, in addition, an actual physical restraint or seizure of the person or a submission by the person to the officer's will and control. Furthermore, the seizure need be only momentary and if the other necessary elements of formal arrest are present, the formal arrest is completed, even if it is followed by an immediate escape. The person does not have to be permanently confined for the seizure or detention requirement to be satisfied.

Communication and Understanding

The final two elements of formal arrest can be considered together because they are two aspects of the same issue. Briefly stated, the law enforcement officer's actions in making an arrest must result in the arrested person's understanding that an arrest is being made. This understanding is ordinarily conveyed by the officer's notifying the person of the arrest. Surrounding circumstances, however, such as handcuffing or other physical restraint or confinement, may make the fact of arrest obvious to the arrested person. The officer may never say a word but the circumstances convey the idea. If the arrested person is unconscious, under the influence of drugs or alcohol, or mentally impaired, the requirement of understanding may be delayed or dispensed with.

Communication and understanding have been the subject of several court decisions in recent years. Problems concerning these issues arise when an encounter between the police and a person does not quite fit the description of a formal arrest, but the intrusion on the person's freedom of action is significantly greater than with an ordinary brief investigative detention or other minimal street encounter. The next section discusses such seizures, which, although not formal arrests, may be tantamount to arrests for purposes of the Fourth Amendment.

SEIZURES OF A PERSON TANTAMOUNT TO AN ARREST

A law enforcement officer investigating crime or otherwise enforcing the laws or keeping the public peace will have contact with members of the public in degrees of intensity varying from the briefest observation or questioning to a full-fledged formal arrest with the use of force. With respect to the most minimal of these police contacts with members of the public, the U.S. Supreme Court stated:

> [L]aw enforcement officers do not violate the Fourth Amendment by merely approaching an individual on the street or in another public place, by asking him if he is willing to answer some questions, by putting questions to him if the person is willing to listen, or by offering in evidence in a criminal prosecution his voluntary answers to such questions.... Nor would the fact that the officer identifies himself as a police officer, without more, convert the encounter into a seizure requiring some level of objective justifications.... The person approached, however, need not answer any question put to him; indeed, he may decline to listen to the questions at all and may go on his way.... He may not be detained even momentarily without reasonable, objective grounds for doing so; and his refusal to listen or answer does not, without more, furnish those grounds.... If there is no detention—no seizure within the meaning of the Fourth Amendment—then no constitutional rights have been infringed. Florida v. Royer, 460 U.S. at 497–98, 103 S.Ct. at 1324, 75 L.Ed.2d at 236 (1983).

Some encounters with members of the public, however, are more intense than those described in the previous paragraph and involve greater intrusions on a person's freedom of movement and privacy. An example is a so-called *Terry*-type investigative stop and frisk, which is a brief detention of a person for investigative purposes accompanied by a limited search. Officers may "stop" a person only if they have a reasonable suspicion that criminal activity is afoot. Officers may "frisk" a person only if they have reason to believe that they are dealing with an armed and dangerous individual. Both the stop and the frisk must be reasonable under the circumstances. (Stop and frisk is discussed in

Chapter 12, after the discussions of arrest and search and seizure, because it involves elements of both.)

At a still higher level of intensity are police contacts with members of the public involving a detention or temporary seizure of a person that is more intrusive on a person's freedom of action than is a brief investigatory stop, but that does not satisfy the four elements of a formal arrest (discussed earlier). In these instances, courts often hold that despite the lack of a formal arrest, the seizure is so similar to an arrest in important respects that it should be allowed only if supported by probable cause to believe a crime has been or is being committed. The leading case on this subject is the U.S. Supreme Court case of Dunaway v. New York, 442 U.S. 200, 99 S.Ct. 2248, 60 L.Ed.2d 824 (1979).

In the *Dunaway* case, the defendant was picked up at his neighbor's home by the police and taken to the police station for questioning about an attempted robbery and homicide. Although the defendant was not told that he was under arrest, he would have been physically restrained if he had attempted to leave. The police did not have probable cause to arrest the defendant. He was given *Miranda* warnings, waived his right to counsel, was questioned, and eventually made statements and drew sketches incriminating himself.

The U.S. Supreme Court examined the seizure of the defendant and held that the police violated his Fourth Amendment and Fourteenth Amendment rights. The seizure was much more intrusive than a traditional stop and frisk (see Chapter 12) and could not be justified on the mere grounds of "reasonable suspicion" of criminal activity. Whether or not technically characterized as a formal arrest, the seizure was in important respects indistinguishable from a formal arrest. Instead of being questioned briefly where he was found, the defendant was taken from a neighbor's home to a police car, transported to a police station, and placed in an interrogation room. He was never informed that he was free to go and would have been physically restrained if he had refused to accompany the officers or had tried to escape their custody. The mere facts that the defendant was not under formal arrest, was not booked, and would not have had an arrest record if the interrogation had proven fruitless did not make his seizure something less than an arrest for purposes of the protections of the Fourth Amendment. The seizure was, therefore, illegal because it was not supported by probable cause.

Therefore, even though an officer does not intend to formally arrest a person, a court may find that the officer's actions are tantamount to an arrest if they are indistinguishable from an arrest in important respects. If an officer seizes or detains a person significantly, beyond a mere stop and frisk or other minor investigatory detention, but does not comply with all the requirements of a formal arrest, the seizure or detention may nevertheless be considered an arrest for purposes of the Fourth Amendment. As such, the seizure or detention will be ruled illegal unless it is supported by probable cause.

In a case similar to *Dunaway*, in which police took a burglary-rape suspect against his will from his home to the police station for fingerprinting, the U.S. Supreme Court reiterated its principles regarding seizures tantamount to arrests: "[W]hen the police, without probable cause or a warrant, forcibly remove a person from his home or other place in which he is entitled to be and transport him to the police station, where he is detained, although briefly, for investigative purposes...such seizures, at least where not under judicial supervision, are sufficiently like arrests to invoke the traditional rule that arrests may constitutionally be made only on probable cause." Hayes v. Florida, 470 U.S. 811, 816, 105 S.Ct. 1643, 1647, 84 L.Ed.2d 705, 710 (1985).

The possibility of obtaining judicial authority for detaining suspects for further investigation was further discussed by the Court.

> We...do not abandon the suggestion in *Davis* and *Dunaway* that under circumscribed procedures, the Fourth Amendment might permit the judiciary to authorize the seizure of a person on less than probable cause and his removal to the police station for the purpose of fingerprinting....[S]ome States...have enacted procedures for judicially authorized seizures for the purpose of fingerprinting. The state courts are not in accord on the validity of these efforts to insulate investigative seizures from Fourth Amendment invalidation. 470 U.S. at 817, 105 S.Ct. at 1647, 705 L.Ed.2d at 711.

Many issues involving seizures tantamount to arrest arise as a result of investigative detentions of suspected drug law violators on the public concourses of airports. In one such case, Florida v. Royer, 460 U.S. 491, 103 S.Ct. 1319, 75 L.Ed.2d 229 (1983), the U.S. Supreme Court concluded that the detention of the defendant was tantamount to an arrest. In that case, narcotics agents had adequate grounds to suspect the defendant of carrying drugs, based on his traveling under an assumed name and his appearance and conduct fitting the "drug courier profile." The agents therefore had the right to temporarily detain the defendant, within the limits of the *Terry* case, in order to confirm or dispel their reasonable suspicions. The agents, however, not only asked the defendant for his identification and to accompany them to another room. They told him they were narcotics agents and had reason to believe he was carrying illegal drugs; they kept his identification and airline ticket; they took him to a small room where he found himself alone with two police officers; they retrieved his checked luggage from the airlines without his consent; they never informed him he was free to board his plane if he so chose; and they would not have allowed him to leave the interrogation room even if he had asked to do so. Under these circumstances, the Court held that the officers' conduct was more intrusive than necessary to effectuate an investigative detention authorized by the *Terry* case. The detention was, therefore, a seizure tantamount to an arrest, and since the officers did not have probable cause to arrest, it was an illegal seizure. The defendant's consent to a search of his luggage in the interrogation room was tainted by the illegal seizure, and therefore the search of the luggage was also illegal.

When a suspect is in a motor vehicle, police may have more leeway in stopping the suspect for investigation before the stop rises to the level of an arrest. In United States v. Jones, 759 F.2d 633 (8th Cir. 1985), the court found no seizure tantamount to arrest where two officers, acting on reasonable suspicion that a fleeing man was involved in a burglary, blocked the suspect's car with theirs, drew their guns, forcefully ordered the suspect out of his vehicle, and repeatedly demanded identification. Noting the danger inherent in the situation, the court said, "Blocking generally will be reasonable when the suspect is in a vehicle because of the chance that the suspect may flee upon the approach of police with resulting danger to the public as well as to the officers involved." 759 F.2d at 638.

ARREST AUTHORITY UNDER A WARRANT

Even though the authority of law enforcement officers to arrest without a warrant in proper circumstances has been recognized for a long time, arrests made under the authority of a warrant have always been preferred. The warrant procedure is favored because it places the sometimes delicate decision of determining whether there is probable cause to justify an arrest in the hands of an impartial judicial authority. The U.S. Supreme Court said that "'the informed and deliberate determinations of magistrates empowered to issue warrants...are to be preferred over the hurried action of officers.'" Aguilar v. Texas, 378 U.S. 108, 110–111, 84 S.Ct. 1509, 1512, 12 L.Ed.2d 723, 726 (1964). This preference for warrants attempts to avoid placing the responsibility for determining probable cause upon law enforcement officers who, in their eagerness to enforce the law and investigate crime, might be tempted to violate constitutional rights.

Although warrants are often considered a hindrance by law enforcement officers, they protect officers in an important way. If a warrant is proper on its face and the officer does not abuse authority in executing the arrest, the officer is protected against civil liability for false arrest or false imprisonment, even though it is later determined that the arrest was unjustified. The officer is not so protected when making warrantless arrests.

Arrest Warrant

The arrest warrant is a written order, issued by a proper judicial authority upon probable cause, directing the arrest of a particular person or persons. A typical form for an arrest warrant appears on page 76. The person issuing the arrest warrant could be a judge, a magistrate, a complaint justice, a justice of the peace, or a clerk of the court. Every jurisdiction authorizes different judicial officers to issue warrants. (For the remainder of this chapter, the term *magistrate* is used to designate the judicial officer authorized to issue arrest warrants.) The warrant is issued on the basis of a sworn statement, called the complaint, charging that a particularly described suspect has committed a described offense against the state or the United States. The person swearing out the complaint is often a law enforcement officer.

Complaint

The complaint must state the essential facts constituting the offense charged, including the time and place of the offense's commission and the name of the suspect or a reasonably definite description of the suspect if the name is not known. The complaint must be sworn to and signed by the person charging the offense (the complainant). A warrant issued upon an unsworn complaint is void, and any arrest made under such a warrant is illegal. A typical complaint form appears on page 77. (The complaint is discussed in further detail in Chapter 2.)

AO 442 (Rev. 12/85) Warrant for Arrest

United States District Court

_____ DISTRICT OF _____

UNITED STATES OF AMERICA
V.

WARRANT FOR ARREST

CASE NUMBER:

To: The United States Marshal
    and any Authorized United States Officer

YOU ARE HEREBY COMMANDED to arrest _____
                                                            Name

and bring him or her forthwith to the nearest magistrate to answer a(n)

☐ Indictment   ☐ Information   ☐ Complaint   ☐ Order of court   ☐ Violation Notice   ☐ Probation Violation Petition

charging him or her with (brief description of offense)

in violation of Title _____ United States Code, Section(s)_____

Name of Issuing Officer   Title of Issuing Officer

Signature of Issuing Officer   Date and Location

Bail fixed at $ _____ by_____
                                                       Name of Judicial Officer

RETURN
This warrant was received and executed with the arrest of the above-named defendant at _____

DATE RECEIVED	NAME AND TITLE OF ARRESTING OFFICER	SIGNATURE OF ARRESTING OFFICER
DATE OF ARREST		

Probable Cause

Before an arrest warrant can be issued, the magistrate must be satisfied from the complaint that there is probable cause to believe that the offense charged in the complaint was committed by the accused. (Probable cause is discussed briefly in Chapter 3 and in detail in Chapter 6.)

```
AO 91 (Rev. 5/85)  Criminal Complaint
```

United States District Court

———————————————— DISTRICT OF ————————————————

UNITED STATES OF AMERICA
V.

CRIMINAL COMPLAINT

CASE NUMBER:

(Name and Address of Defendant)

I, the undersigned complainant being duly sworn state the following is true and correct to the best of my

knowledge and belief. On or about _____ in _____ county, in the

_____ District of _____ defendant(s) did, (Track Statutory Language of Offense)

in violation of Title _____ United States Code, Section(s) _____.

I further state that I am a(n) _____ and that this complaint is based on the following
                                              Official Title

facts:

Continued on the attached sheet and made a part hereof: ☐ Yes   ☐ No

_____
Signature of Complainant

Sworn to before me and subscribed in my presence,

_____   at   _____
Date   City and State

_____   _____
Name & Title of Judicial Officer   Signature of Judicial Officer

If a complaint has insufficient space, a separate affidavit or affidavits setting forth in detail the facts and circumstances upon which probable cause is based may be filed with the complaint. An affidavit need not be prepared with any particular formality and may be merely a sworn statement of the facts upon which the complainant relies in seeking the issuance of a warrant. The magistrate may require additional affidavits of other persons having pertinent and reliable information bearing upon probable cause. All the information upon which probable cause is based must appear in the original complaint and in the affidavits attached to it. The reason for this requirement is to maintain a record of the evidence produced before the magistrate issuing the warrant in case the validity of the warrant is called into question at a later date.

Requirements of Arrest Warrant

The arrest warrant must conform to certain requirements. Although these requirements may differ from state to state, the following list is representative of what an arrest warrant must contain.

1. The caption of the court or division of the court from which the warrant issues.

2. The name of the person to be arrested, if known; if not known, any name or description by which the person can be identified with reasonable certainty. The warrant must show on its face that it is directed toward a particular individual in order to satisfy the Fourth Amendment requirement that a warrant particularly describe the person to be seized.

3. A description of the offense charged in the complaint. This description should be in the language of the appropriate statute or ordinance. The important consideration, however, is that the description be in words definite enough for the defendant to readily understand the charge. Stating that the defendant is charged merely with "a felony" or "a misdemeanor" is insufficient and will invalidate the warrant.

4. The date of issuance.

5. The officer or officers to whom the warrant is directed together with a command that the defendant be brought before the proper judicial official.

6. The signature of the issuing magistrate together with a statement of the magistrate's official title.

An officer to whom a warrant is directed should read the warrant carefully. If the warrant satisfies the requirements listed here, the officer may execute the warrant without fear of civil liability arising from a challenge to the validity of the warrant.

Summons

A magistrate may issue a summons instead of an arrest warrant in certain situations. The requirements for a summons are the same as those for a warrant except that a summons directs the defendant to appear before a court at a stated time and place rather than ordering the defendant's arrest. Court rules and statutes usually provide that if a defendant fails to appear in response to a summons, a warrant will be issued for his or her arrest. A typical summons form appears on pages 80 and 81.

The summons is usually used when the offense charged in a complaint is a violation of a municipal ordinance or some other misdemeanor or petty offense. If the offender is a citizen with "roots firmly established in the soil of the community," and thus can be easily found for service of a warrant if the summons is ignored, the summons procedure is a much easier and better way of inducing the defendant to appear in court than is arresting the defendant and taking him or her into custody.

The term *summons* may be confusing because it is often used to describe a citation, ticket, or notice to appear issued by a law enforcement officer, especially in traffic cases. Such a notice is *not* a summons in the legal sense because it is not issued by a magistrate on the basis of a complaint. A citation, ticket, or notice to appear merely gives notice to offenders that they may be arrested if they do not voluntarily appear in court to answer the charges against them.

ARREST AUTHORITY WITHOUT A WARRANT

Law enforcement officers are often faced with the decision of whether to apply for an arrest warrant or to arrest without a warrant. Since officers often have to make an immediate decision in this respect, they must have a clear working knowledge of the law governing arrest without a warrant.

Authority to arrest without a warrant depends on the difference between a felony and a misdemeanor. In most states, a felony is defined as any crime that is or may be punished by death or imprisonment in a state prison. Since most states do not provide for imprisonment in the state prison unless the term of the sentence is one year or more, a crime is probably not a felony unless the penalty is at least one year's incarceration. Note that it is the punishment that *may* be imposed that determines whether a crime is a felony or misdemeanor, not the penalty that finally *is* imposed. *Therefore, a felony can be defined as any crime for which the punishment could possibly be imprisonment for a term of one year or more. All crimes that do not amount to a felony are classified as misdemeanors.*

States differ greatly as to which specific crimes are classified as felonies and which are misdemeanors. Law enforcement officers must familiarize themselves with the classifications of crimes into felonies and misdemeanors in their states.

Misdemeanors

In most states, unless otherwise provided by statute, a law enforcement officer may arrest without a warrant for a misdemeanor only when the misdemeanor is "committed in the officer's presence." Ordinarily, this means that the officer must personally observe the misdemeanor being committed before making an arrest. However, sight is not the only means of perceiving the commission of a crime. Therefore, courts have generally held that a misdemeanor is committed in an officer's presence if the officer is able to perceive it through any of the five senses—sight, hearing, touch, taste, and smell. For example, an officer had authority to make a warrantless misdemeanor arrest when he heard, through a door, a person dial a telephone and accept a bet on a horse race. People v. Goldberg, 280 N.Y.S.2d 646, 227 N.E.2d 575 (N.Y. 1967). In another case, an officer's smelling of alcohol on a driver's breath justified a conclusion that a misdemeanor was being committed in the officer's presence. State v. Hines, 504 P.2d 946 (Ariz. App. 1973). Furthermore, an officer investigating crime may enhance his or her senses in various ways.

AO 83 (Rev. 12/85) Summons in a Criminal Case

United States District Court

DISTRICT OF _____

UNITED STATES OF AMERICA
V.

(Name and Address of Defendant)

SUMMONS IN A CRIMINAL CASE

CASE NUMBER:

YOU ARE HEREBY SUMMONED to appear before the United States District Court at the place, date and time set forth below.

Place	Room
	Date and Time
Before:	

To answer a(n)
☐ Indictment   ☐ Information   ☐ Complaint   ☐ Violation Notice   ☐ Probation Violation Petition

Charging you with a violation of Title _____ United States Code, Section(s) _____

Brief description of offense:

_____   _____
Signature of Issuing Officer   Date

_____
Name and Title of Issuing Officer

AO 83 (Rev. 12/85) Summons in a Criminal Case   ⊕

RETURN OF SERVICE

	Date
Service was made by me on:[1]	

Check one box below to indicate appropriate method of service

☐ Served personally upon the defendant at: _____
_____

☐ Left summons at the defendant's dwelling house or usual place of abode with a person of suitable age and
discretion then residing therein and mailed a copy of the summons to the defendant's last known address.
Name of person with whom the summons was left: _____
_____

☐ Returned unexecuted:_____
_____
_____
_____

      I declare under penalty of perjury under the laws of the United States of America that the foregoing
information contained in the Return of Service is true and correct.

Returned on _____   _____
                    Date   Name of United States Marshal

                                                _____
                                                    (by) Deputy United States Marshal

Remarks:

1) As to who may serve a summons see Rule 4 of the Federal Rules of Criminal Procedure.

Permissible techniques of surveillance include more than just the five senses of officers and their unaided physical abilities. Binoculars, dogs that track and sniff out contraband, search-lights, fluorescent powders, automobiles and airplanes, burglar alarms, radar devices, and bait money contribute to surveillance without violation of the Fourth Amendment in the usual case. United States v. Dubrofsky, 581 F.2d 208, 211 (9th Cir. 1978).

The "presence" requirement may even be satisfied by the defendant's admission of guilt. People v. Ward, 252 N.W.2d 514 (Mich. App.1977). But information from other witnesses may not be used to satisfy the presence requirement:

> When the basis of the officer's belief that the defendant has committed a misdemeanor is information imparted to him by, say, victims, witnesses or informers, he must present the evidence to a magistrate and seek an arrest warrant. He may not act on his own appraisal of the reasonableness of the information. People v. Dixon, 222 N.W.2d 749, 751 (Mich. 1974).

An officer must perceive the commission of a misdemeanor *before* arresting the offender. If the officer arrests on mere suspicion or chance that a misdemeanor is being committed, the arrest is illegal, even if later developments show that a crime did take place. In re Alonzo C., 151 Cal.Rptr. 192 (Cal. App. 1978).

An officer also has no authority to arrest without a warrant for a past or completed misdemeanor, even if the offender is still at the crime scene. If the misdemeanor was completed before the officer arrived, it could not have been committed in the officer's presence. In this situation, the officer has one of two choices:

1. Invite the offender to submit voluntarily to custody.
2. Identify the offender and apply for an arrest warrant.

MISDEMEANOR ARRESTS ON PROBABLE CAUSE. In recent years, some state legislatures have enacted laws making exceptions to the general rule that an arrest without a warrant for a misdemeanor is authorized only for offenses committed in an officer's presence. These laws authorize arrests on probable cause for certain types of misdemeanors, such as shoplifting, driving while intoxicated, fish and game violations, and liquor violations. Since the laws of each state are different, each law enforcement officer must determine for what misdemeanors, if any, state law allows warrantless arrests on probable cause.

PROMPTNESS OF ARREST. An arrest without a warrant for a misdemeanor committed in an officer's presence must be made promptly and without unnecessary delay. The officer must set out to make the arrest at the time the offense is perceived and must continue that effort until the arrest is accomplished or abandoned.

> The arrest for misdemeanors committed or attempted in the presence of officers must be made as quickly after commission of the offense as the circumstances will permit. After an officer has witnessed a misdemeanor, it is his duty to then and there arrest the offender. Under some circumstances, there may be

justification for delay, as for instance, when the interval between the commission of the offense and the actual arrest is spent by the officer in pursuing the offender, or in summoning assistance where such may reasonably appear to be necessary.... If, however, the officer witnesses the commission of an offense and does not arrest the offender, but departs on other business, or for other purposes, and afterwards returns, he cannot then arrest the offender without a warrant; for then the reasons for allowing the arrest to be made without a warrant have disappeared. Smith v. State, 87 So.2d 917, 919 (Miss. 1956).

Reasonable delay in making a warrantless misdemeanor arrest that is closely connected with the offense itself or with an attempted flight by the offender will usually not invalidate the arrest. Examples of reasonable delays are delays to summon assistance in making the arrest, to plan strategy to overcome resistance to arrest, to pursue a fleeing offender, or to take safety precautions. If an officer delays a warrantless misdemeanor arrest for reasons unconnected with the process of arrest, however, the arrest will be unlawful. Such delays require the officer to obtain a warrant and to arrest in accordance with the warrant.

Felonies

A law enforcement officer may make a warrantless public arrest for a felony if, at the time of arrest, the officer has probable cause to believe that a felony has been committed and that the person to be arrested is committing or has committed the felony. The U.S. Supreme Court said:

> Law enforcement officers may find it wise to seek arrest warrants where practicable to do so, and their judgments about probable cause may be more readily accepted where backed by a warrant issued by a magistrate.... But we decline to transform this judicial preference into a constitutional rule when the judgment of the Nation and Congress has for so long been to authorize warrantless public arrests on probable cause rather than to encumber criminal prosecutions with endless litigation with respect to the existence of exigent circumstances, whether it was practicable to get a warrant, whether the suspect was about to flee, and the like. United States v. Watson, 423 U.S. 411, 423–24, 96 S.Ct. 820, 827–28, 46 L.Ed.2d 598, 608–9 (1976).

Some states, however, either by statute or by court interpretation of the state constitution, place greater restrictions on the arrest authority of law enforcement officers. In People v. Hoinville, 553 P.2d 777 (Colo. 1976), the court held that a state statute providing that "[a]n arrest warrant should be obtained when practicable" required police officers to obtain a warrant whenever possible.

FELONY ARRESTS AND PROBABLE CAUSE. Assuming that most states allow warrantless felony arrests on probable cause, the key terms law enforcement officers must know to determine their authority are felony and probable cause. *Felony* was defined earlier in this chapter as any offense for which the punishment could possibly be imprisonment for a term of one year or more. *Probable cause* was defined in Chapter 3 and is discussed in detail in Chapter 6. For purposes of this discussion, note that before making a warrantless arrest, a law enforcement officer must have specific facts or information connecting the person to be arrested with a particular felony. If the officer is unable to later justify the arrest by articulating the facts and circumstances supporting probable cause, the arrest is likely to be declared illegal.

If an officer making an arrest has probable cause to believe that a felony has been committed and that the defendant committed it, it makes no difference whether the officer is right or wrong in making the arrest or whether the defendant will later be acquitted of the crime for which the arrest is made. The officer is still justified in making the arrest and it is a legal arrest. On the other hand, if the officer, on mere suspicion or chance, makes a warrantless arrest without probable cause, the arrest is illegal whether the defendant is guilty or not. Therefore, probable cause is the main consideration in determining the validity of an arrest.

PROMPTNESS OF ARREST. Unlike a warrantless arrest for a misdemeanor, which must be made immediately, a warrantless arrest for a felony may be delayed, whether or not the felony was committed in the officer's presence. United States v. Drake, 655 F.2d 1025 (10th Cir. 1981). Delay may be justified for a variety of reasons, so long as the delay is not designed to prejudice an offender's constitutional rights. Reasons justifying delay include an inability to locate the defendant, the need to complete additional undercover investigation, a desire to avoid alerting other potential offenders, and the need to protect the identity of undercover agents or informants.

> The police are not required to guess at their peril the precise moment at which they have probable cause to arrest a suspect, risking a violation of the Fourth Amendment if they act too soon, and a violation of the Sixth Amendment if they wait too long. Law enforcement officers are under no constitutional duty to call a halt to a criminal investigation the moment they have the minimum evidence to establish probable cause, a quantum of evidence which may fall far short of the amount necessary to support a criminal prosecution. Hoffa v. United States, 385 U.S. 293, 310, 87 S.Ct. 408, 417, 17 L.Ed.2d 374, 386 (1966).

Some courts hold that a person has no constitutional right to be arrested, suggesting that a warrantless felony arrest may be delayed indefinitely. United States v. Hudgens, 798 F.2d 1234 (9th Cir. 1986). The safer procedure for the law enforcement officer, however, is to arrest soon after a crime is committed unless there are good reasons for delay. "[A] point can be reached where the delay is so great that the prejudice to the defendant caused by it—due to faded memories of parties and witnesses, loss of contact with witnesses, and loss of documents—becomes so great that due process and fundamental fairness require that the charges be dismissed." People v. Hall, 729 P.2d 373, 375 (Colo. 1986).

EFFECTING A FORMAL ARREST

To effect a formal arrest, a law enforcement officer must satisfy the basic requirements of a formal arrest (discussed earlier in this chapter). Other aspects of effecting an arrest include notice, time of day, safety considerations, warrant requirements, assistance, and the use of discretion.

Notice

The notice required to be given by a law enforcement officer when making an arrest is usually governed by statute and differs from state to state. The following is a list of typical information to be included in that notice.

1. Notice that the person is under arrest. "The obvious purpose of informing the suspect he is under arrest is not to make the arrest legal but to indicate to the person being arrested that his detention is legal, so that he will not resist." Pullins v. State, 256 N.E.2d 553, 556 (Ind. 1970).

2. Notice of the officer's authority to arrest. This can be accomplished by the officer's announcing his or her identity as a law enforcement officer. This announcement is not necessary, however, if the officer's authority is already known to the defendant or is obvious from the display of a badge, uniform, or other indicia of authority. State v. Erdman, 292 N.W.2d 97 (S.D. 1980).

3. Notice of the cause of the arrest. An otherwise lawful arrest is not rendered unlawful, however, if the arresting officer states the offense inaccurately or imprecisely, particularly where the officer acts in good faith and the defendant is not prejudiced by the error. State Department of Public Safety v. Rice, 323 N.W.2d 74 (Minn. 1982).

An officer may dispense with giving any notice before making an arrest when one or more of the following are true:

1. It would endanger the officer to do so.

2. It would adversely affect the making of the arrested.

3. The offense is being committed in the officer's presence. Dillard v. State, 543 S.W.2d 925 (Ark. 1976).

4. The person to be arrested is fleeing the scene of the crime.

Time of Day

An arrest, with or without a warrant, may be made on any day of the week and at any time of the day or night, unless otherwise provided in the warrant or by statute. State v. Perez, 277 So.2d 778 (Fla. 1973). However, common sense dictates that arrests should not be made at unreasonable hours of the night or on the Sabbath, except in cases of pressing necessity.

Safety Considerations

In Washington v. Chrisman, 455 U.S. 1, 102 S.Ct. 812, 70 L.Ed.2d 778 (1982), the U.S. Supreme Court held:

> [I]t is not "unreasonable" under the Fourth Amendment for a police officer, as a matter of course, to monitor the movements of an arrested person, as his judgement dictates, following the arrest. The officer's need to ensure his own safety—as well as the integrity of the arrest—is compelling. Such surveillance is not an impermissible invasion of the privacy or personal liberty of an individual who has been arrested. 455 U.S. at 7, 102 S.Ct. at 817, 70 L.Ed.2d at 785.

In the *Chrisman* case, the officer arrested a college student for possession of alcoholic beverages by a person under twenty-one, and the student asked permission to go to his room to get his identification. The officer accompanied the student to his room, and while in the room, the officer observed marijuana in plain view. The Court held that the officer had a right to remain literally at the student's elbow at all times and that no showing of "exigent circumstances" was necessary to authorize the officer to accompany the student into the room. The Court said:

> Every arrest must be presumed to present a risk of danger to the arresting officer. . . . There is no way for an officer to predict reliably how a particular subject will react to arrest or the degree of potential danger. Moreover, the possibility that an arrested person will attempt to escape if not properly supervised is obvious. 455 U.S. at 7, 102 S.Ct. at 817, 70 L.Ed.2d at 785.

Executing an Arrest Warrant

Several additional considerations are involved in effecting an arrest when the arrest is carried out under authority of a warrant. First of all, when officers are directed to serve a warrant of arrest, their belief in the guilt of the defendant or their personal knowledge of facts pertaining to the offense is immaterial. There is no requirement that the offense be committed in their presence or that they have probable cause to believe that the defendant committed the offense. Officers are simply required to carry out the command as stated in the warrant, and the only questions of concern are (1) whether the person to be arrested is the person identified in the warrant, and (2) whether the warrant is valid on its face.

When the accused is identified in the warrant by name or description, a law enforcement officer is required to exercise reasonable diligence to make sure that the person designated in the warrant and no one else is arrested. If the person being arrested claims not to be the person identified in the warrant and there is a reasonably simple and direct means of checking that claim, the officer who arrests without checking may be liable for false arrest or false imprisonment. The officer must be very careful in determining whether the person arrested is the person identified in the warrant.

A warrant that is invalid on its face gives the law enforcement officer executing it no protection and no authority to arrest. The officer is bound to examine the warrant and acts at his or her peril in executing it if it is obviously invalid on its face. An arrest warrant is invalid on its face if one or more of the following are true.

1. The court issuing the warrant clearly has no jurisdiction.
2. The warrant fails to adequately indicate the crime charged.
3. The warrant fails to name or describe any identifiable person.
4. The warrant is not signed by the issuing magistrate.
5. The warrant is not directed to the officer who is about to execute it. (If the warrant is directed to all law enforcement officers in the state, any sworn officer may execute it. If, however, the warrant is directed only to the sheriff of a particular county, only that sheriff or a deputy sheriff may execute it.)

Once an officer determines that a warrant is valid on its face, the officer must carry out the warrant's commands and arrest the person identified in the warrant. The officer no longer has any personal discretion and is merely carrying out an order of the court:

> When the warrant purports to be for a matter within the jurisdiction of the justice (magistrate), the ministerial officer is obliged to execute it, and of course must be justified by it. He cannot inquire upon what evidence the judicial officer proceeded, or whether he committed an error or irregularity in his decision..., the constable has nothing to look to but the warrant as his guide.... Alexander v. Lindsey, 55 S.E.2d 470, 473-74 (N.C. 1949).

Most states allow arrest warrants for violations of state law to be executed at any place within the boundaries of the state. However, a law enforcement officer of one state may not go into another state to arrest under a warrant except in cases of fresh pursuit, which are discussed later.

Officers arresting with a warrant should give the same notice, discussed earlier, that they would ordinarily give in making any arrest. In addition, officers should have the warrant in their possession at the time of arrest and should show the warrant to the person arrested. In some states, however, officers may make a legal arrest pursuant to a warrant even though the warrant is not in their possession. They must, however, inform the defendant of the offense charged and of the existence of the warrant. If the defendant requests, officers must produce the warrant as soon as possible.

Like a warrantless felony arrest, an arrest made under a warrant (for a felony or misdemeanor) need not be made immediately. Officers have considerable discretion as to the time of making an arrest under a warrant. They may have lawful strategic reasons for delay or they may wish to select a time when the arrest can be accomplished with the least difficulty. "[T]he general rule is that, while execution should not be unreasonably delayed, law enforcement officers have a reasonable time in which to execute a warrant and need not arrest at the first opportunity." United States v. Drake, 655 F.2d 1025, 1027 (10th Cir. 1981).

An officer executing an arrest warrant must make a return of the warrant. The return is made by entering on the warrant the date of the arrest, signing the warrant, and filing the warrant with the court. Failure to return a warrant may invalidate that arrest and subject the officer to civil liability for false arrest or false imprisonment.

Service of a Summons

As discussed earlier, a magistrate may, under certain circumstances, issue a summons instead of an arrest warrant. A summons is served by personally delivering a copy to the defendant, or by leaving it at the defendant's dwelling house or usual place of abode with some person of suitable age and discretion who resides there. It may also be served by mailing it to the defendant's last known address. As with an arrest warrant, most states provide that a summons for a violation of state law may be served at any place within the state. In addition, a summons must be returned by the officer serving it to the proper magistrate before the return date appearing on the summons.

Assistance

Law enforcement officers may request private citizens to aid them in making an arrest. The laws of some states require that any person called upon by a law enforcement officer to assist the officer in the execution of his or her official duties, including the arrest of another person, is legally obligated to obey the officer. Refusal to aid an officer may be punishable under state law.

When private citizens act in aid of a known law enforcement officer, they have the same rights and privileges as the officer. While so acting, they have the status of a temporary law enforcement officer, including the right to use force and to enter property. If the person called upon acts in good faith, he or she is protected from liability even if the officer was acting illegally:

> It would be manifestly unfair to impose civil liability upon a private person for doing that which the law declares it a misdemeanor for him to refuse to do. Peterson v. Robison, 277 P.2d 19, 24 (Cal. 1954).

Discretion

Even though a law enforcement officer clearly has the ability and authority to arrest, good police practice may call for restraint of that power. It is beyond the scope of this chapter to give detailed guidelines in this area, but a brief discussion is necessary to set out general principles.

A law enforcement officer's primary job is to protect the public at large. Therefore, when an arrest may cause greater risk of harm to the public or will only cause embarrassment to a person who poses no real threat to the community, proper police practice may call for a decision not to arrest. For example, when a crowd is present, it is often unwise to arrest a person or persons who are creating a minor disturbance. An arrest may aggravate the disturbance and possibly precipitate a riot or civil disorder. Less drastic ways to handle the matter should be explored even though there may be legal grounds for an arrest. The same considerations apply to minor domestic disputes and disturbances by intoxicated persons who are creating no danger and may need no more than an assist in getting home. *An arrest is a significant restraint on a person's freedom and should always be justified by circumstances.*

Some law enforcement agencies have policies covering discretion to arrest. Where no policies exist, officers must use their common sense and good judgment. *Authority to arrest does not always mean duty to arrest.*

PLACE OF ARREST

In most states, law enforcement officers acting under authority of a warrant may make an arrest at any place within the state where the defendant may be found. Similarly, officers may serve a summons at any place within the state.

However, an officer generally has no official authority to arrest *without* a warrant outside the territorial or geographical limits of the county or district for which he or she has been elected or appointed. This area is usually referred to as the officer's *bailiwick*. Thus, sheriffs may not arrest without a warrant beyond the counties in which they have been elected, nor may municipal police officers arrest without a warrant beyond the limits of the cities in which they have been appointed. On the other hand, the authority of state law enforcement officers is statewide and their power to arrest without a warrant runs throughout the state. However, a law enforcement officer of one state has no authority to arrest in another state.

There are two exceptions to the rule that an officer may not arrest outside his or her bailiwick:

1. Arrests made as a private citizen
2. Arrests made in fresh pursuit

Citizen's Arrest Authority

As private citizens, law enforcement officers have the same authority as any other private citizens to make an arrest without a warrant. This authority comes from the common law, a body of unwritten law that was developed in England and based upon court decisions and that receives its binding force from traditional usage, custom, and universal acceptance. Under the common law rule in force in most states, private citizens have the authority to arrest any person who they have probable cause to believe has committed a felony. However, they can justify the arrest only by further showing that the felony was *actually committed*. The citizen's arrest authority, therefore, differs significantly from the arrest authority of law enforcement officers operating within their bailiwick. Private citizens act at their peril if no felony was actually committed, whereas law enforcement officers are protected if the arrest is based on probable cause.

Under the common law, private citizens may also arrest for felonies and "breach of the peace" misdemeanors *committed in their presence*. In the case of a felony, exercise of the authority to arrest is not only a privilege but a duty. A breach of the peace misdemeanor can be defined generally as a misdemeanor that causes or threatens direct physical harm to the public.

Therefore, in a state where the common law rule on citizen's arrest is followed, a law enforcement officer may arrest without a warrant in the previously described circumstances anywhere in the state. Furthermore, unless neighboring states have modified the common law rule by statute, a law enforcement officer may also arrest outside the borders of his or her state as a private citizen. However, the officer risks civil liability for a felony arrest made on probable cause as a private citizen if the officer cannot prove that a felony was actually committed.

Fresh Pursuit

Under the common law and most statutes, a law enforcement officer may make a lawful arrest without a warrant beyond the borders of his or her bailiwick in cases of fresh pursuit. Fresh pursuit means an officer's immediate pursuit of a criminal suspect into another jurisdiction after the officer has attempted to arrest the suspect in the officer's bailiwick.

The common law allowed a warrantless arrest in fresh pursuit only in felony cases, but today most state statutes allow warrantless arrests for both felonies and misdemeanors. For a warrantless arrest in fresh pursuit to be legal, all of the following conditions must be met.

1. The officer must have authority to arrest for the crime in the first place.

2. The pursuit must be of a fleeing criminal attempting to avoid immediate capture.

3. The pursuit must begin promptly and must be maintained continuously.

The main requirement is that the pursuit be fresh. The pursuit must flow out of the act of attempting to make an arrest and must be a part of the continuous process of apprehension. The pursuit need not be instantaneous but it must be made without unreasonable delay or interruption. There should be no side trips or diversions even for other police business. However, the continuity of pursuit is not legally broken by unavoidable interruptions connected with the act of apprehension, such as eating, sleeping, summoning assistance, or obtaining further information.

Fresh pursuit may lead a law enforcement officer outside the boundaries of his or her state. Ordinarily, an officer has no authority beyond that of a private citizen to make arrests in another state. However, many states have adopted the Uniform Act on Fresh Pursuit or similar legislation, which permits law enforcement officers from other states, entering in fresh pursuit, to make an arrest. The Uniform Fresh Pursuit Law of Iowa is typical:

> Any member of a duly organized state, county, or municipal law enforcing unit of another state of the United States who enters this state in fresh pursuit, and continues within this state in such fresh pursuit, of a person in order to arrest him on the ground that the person is believed to have committed a felony in such other state, shall have the same authority to arrest and hold such person in custody, as has any member of any duly organized state, county or municipal law enforcing unit of this state to arrest and hold in custody a person on the ground that the person is believed to have committed a felony in this state. Iowa Code Ann. § 806.1.

Since some states extend the privilege to make an arrest in fresh pursuit to out-of-state officers only on a reciprocity basis, a law enforcement officer must be familiar not only with his or her state's statute, but also with the fresh pursuit statutes of all neighboring states.

A law enforcement officer who makes an arrest in fresh pursuit under such a statute in a neighboring state must take the arrested person before an appropriate judicial officer without unreasonable delay. Some states allow an arresting officer from another state to take a person arrested in fresh pursuit back to the officer's home state after the arrested person is brought before an appropriate judicial officer. Other states allow this only upon extradition or waiver of extradition. Extradition is a procedure whereby authorities in one state (the demanding state) demand from another state (the asylum state) that a fugitive from justice in the demanding state, who is present in the asylum state, be delivered to the demanding state. Most states have adopted the Uniform Criminal Extradition Act, which provides uniform extradition procedures among the states.

USE OF FORCE

A law enforcement officer's right to use force to make an arrest depends upon the degree of force used and the context in which it is used. This section examines various aspects of arrest and discusses the degree of force appropriate in each situation.

Felony Arrests

Under the common law rule, a law enforcement officer could use any reasonably necessary *nondeadly* force to arrest for a felony. Most states retain this rule today, either by statute or by court decision: "[T]he use of any significant force...not reasonably necessary to effect an arrest—as where the suspect neither resists nor flees or where the force is used after a suspect's resistance has been overcome or his flight thwarted—would be constitutionally unreasonable." Kidd v. O'Neil, 774 F.2d 1252, 1256–57 (4th Cir. 1985).

The common law rule also allowed officers to use *deadly* force to arrest any fleeing felony suspect. Under the rule, an officer was not required to retreat from effecting an arrest to avoid extreme measures, but was required to press on and use all necessary force to bring the offender into custody. Use of deadly force was therefore permitted as a last resort if the only alternative was to abandon the attempt to arrest.

An examination of the history of the common law rule reveals that it originated in an era when all felonies were punishable by death, all felons were considered dangerous, defendants had meager rights, and few of those arrested and tried for felonies escaped conviction and death. Consequently, use of deadly force to apprehend fleeing felons was viewed merely as a more timely and less costly implementation of the eventual penalty for their offenses. In addition, police as such did not exist at that time; the responsibility for apprehending fleeing felons fell upon the unarmed and untrained citizens who responded to the hue and cry. Weapons were primitive and the use of force often meant hand-to-hand combat, which was seldom deadly, although it posed significant danger to the arresting person.

Today, most felonies are not punishable by death; fewer felons are convicted or executed; and police are organized, trained, equipped with sophisticated weapons, and capable of killing accurately at a distance and under circumstances posing little danger to officers or others, especially if the felon is unarmed. Operation of the common law rule under these changed circumstances would allow police to kill persons merely suspected of offenses that, upon conviction, would likely result in only brief imprisonment or even probation.

Although it is generally agreed that the police should be able to use as much force as necessary to protect the public against violent offenders and to protect themselves, the common law rule on deadly force has been much criticized as overly broad to fulfill these legitimate functions. As a result, the U.S. Supreme Court in 1985 declared unconstitutional Tennessee's statute that codified the common law rule. The Court reasoned that in authorizing police to use deadly force to apprehend *any* fleeing felony suspect, whether armed and dangerous or not, the statute violated the Fourth Amendment's guarantee against unreasonable seizures. Killing a suspect, the Court noted, is the ultimate seizure.

The use of deadly force to prevent the escape of all felony suspects, whatever the circumstances, is constitutionally unreasonable. It is not better that all felony suspects die than that they escape. Where the suspect poses no immediate threat to the officer and no threat to others, the harm resulting from failing to apprehend him does not justify the use of deadly force to do so. It is no doubt unfortunate when a suspect who is in sight escapes, but the fact that the police arrive a little late or are a little slower afoot does not always justify killing a suspect. A police officer may not seize an unarmed, nondangerous suspect by shooting him dead. . . . Where the officer has probable cause to believe that the suspect poses a threat of serious physical harm, either to the officer or to others, it is not constitutionally unreasonable to prevent escape by using deadly force. Thus, if the suspect threatens the officer with a weapon or there is probable cause to believe that he has committed a crime involving the infliction or threatened infliction of serious physical harm, deadly force may be used if necessary to prevent escape, and if, where feasible, some warning has been given. Tennessee v. Garner, 471 U.S. 1, 11–12, 105 S.Ct. 1694, 1701, 85 L.Ed.2d 1, 9–10 (1985).

Even before the U.S. Supreme Court decision in the *Garner* case, criticism of the common law rule on deadly force in felony cases resulted in abolition of the rule in many jurisdictions and in changes such as Section 3.07(2)(b) of the Model Penal Code, which reads as follows:

The use of deadly force is not justifiable under this Section unless:

   (i) the arrest is for a felony; and

  (ii) the person effecting the arrest is authorized to act as a peace officer or is assisting a person whom he believes to be authorized to act as a peace officer; and

 (iii) the actor believes that the force employed creates no substantial risk of injury to innocent persons; and

 (iv) the actor believes that:

   (1) the crime for which the arrest is made involved conduct including the use or threatened use of deadly force; or

   (2) there is substantial risk that the person to be arrested will cause death or serious bodily harm if his apprehension is delayed.

Some states have adopted this section of the Model Penal Code or variations of it. Other states have unclear positions on the use of deadly force.

An officer should make every effort to clearly ascertain the law on deadly force in his or her state and the policy in his or her department, but at a minimum, the officer must comply with the standards of the U.S. Supreme Court as set out in the *Garner* case. Very serious consequences can result from the unwarranted use of deadly force, such as death or injury to the officer or other persons, or liability of the officer both civilly and criminally.

Misdemeanor Arrests

As with felonies, most states retain the common law rule allowing law enforcement officers to use any reasonably necessary nondeadly force to arrest for a misdemeanor. However, an officer is *never* justified in using deadly force to arrest for a misdemeanor. State v. Wall, 286 S.E.2d 68 (N.C. 1982). *The rule is that it is better that a misdemeanant escape rather than a human life be taken.* The use of deadly force on a misdemeanant is excessive force constituting an assault. An officer who kills the suspect may be guilty of murder or manslaughter.

Self-Defense

Whether an offense is a felony or misdemeanor, a law enforcement officer making a lawful arrest may use whatever force is necessary under the circumstances, including deadly force, if the officer reasonably believes that the person to be arrested is about to commit an assault and that the officer is in danger of death or serious bodily injury. The law enforcement officer's duty is to be the aggressor and to press forward to bring the person under restraint. This cannot be accomplished by purely defensive action on an officer's part. Therefore, if an officer has lawful authority to arrest, the officer is not required to back down in the face of physical resistance to the arrest. State v. Williams, 148 A.2d 22 (N.J. 1959). An officer faced with the choice of abandoning an arrest or using deadly force in *self-defense* has the right to use deadly force if necessary for self-protection.

Resisting Arrest

Resisting arrest is a crime involving opposition by direct, forcible means against an officer's person in order to prevent the officer from taking the accused into custody. Under statutes defining the crime, indirect interference or hindrance of an officer will usually not support a conviction. Resistance requires active opposition such as shooting, striking, pushing, or otherwise struggling with the officer. Mere flight, concealment, or other avoidance or evasion of arrest will not constitute resistance.

> The fact that the accused sought to escape the officer by merely running away was not such an obstruction as the law contemplates. While it is the duty of every citizen to submit to a lawful arrest, yet flight is not such an offense as will make a person amenable to the charge of resisting or obstructing an officer who is attempting to make an arrest, as there is a broad distinction between avoidance and resistance or obstruction. Jones v. Commonwealth, 126 S.E. 74, 76–77 (Va. 1925).

Nor will verbal objections, protests, or threats unaccompanied by force constitute resisting arrest. However, a serious threat that is accompanied by the apparent ability and present intention to execute it, and which prevents an officer from acting because of reasonable fear of serious bodily injury, may constitute resistance to arrest.

Under the common law rule, the crime of resisting arrest requires that the arrest be lawful. If an arrest is unlawful, the person being arrested has the *right* to resist. A person being arrested also has a right to resist if the person making the arrest is not an officer of the law, or if the officer does not proceed in a lawful manner in making the arrest. Therefore, it is very important for law enforcement officers making an arrest to

1. establish their identity, if not already known or obvious; and

2. explain their purpose and authority.

Under the common law rule, a person threatened with an illegal arrest may not only resist the arrest, but may use any force reasonably necessary for self-defense and prevention of impending injury. State v. McGowan, 90 S.E.2d 703 (N.C. 1956). Since the impending injury resulting from an arrest is ordinarily only a brief unlawful detention, the degree of force a person may use is strictly limited. A person who uses more force than is reasonably necessary for the purpose may be guilty of an assault and battery on the officer. Deadly force is rarely justified to resist an unlawful arrest, except when a person has reasonable grounds to fear death or serious bodily injury at the hands of an officer.

The law on resisting arrest and other interferences with law enforcement officers differs from state to state. For example, some states prohibit a private citizen from using force to resist an arrest made by one who the citizen knows or has good reason to believe is an authorized police officer engaged in the performance of official duties, whether or not the arrest is illegal. If, however, the officer uses excessive and unnecessary force in effecting the arrest, the citizen may respond or counter with reasonable force for self-protection.

> Despite his duty to submit quietly without physical resistance to an arrest made by an officer acting in the course of his duty, even though the arrest is illegal, his right to freedom from unreasonable seizure and confinement can be protected, restored and vindicated through legal processes. However, the rule permitting reasonable resistance to excessive force of the officer, whether the arrest is lawful or unlawful, is designed to protect a person's bodily integrity and health and so permits resort to self-defense. Simply stated, the law recognizes that liberty can be restored through legal processes but life or limb cannot be repaired in a courtroom. And so it holds that the reason for outlawing resistance to an unlawful arrest and requiring disputes over its legality to be resolved in the courts has no controlling application on the right to resist an officer's excessive force. . . .
>
> Two qualifications on the citizen's right to defend against and to repel an officer's excessive force must be noticed. He cannot use greater force in protecting himself against the officer's unlawful force than reasonably appears to be necessary. If he employs such greater force, then he becomes the aggressor and forfeits the right to claim self-defense to a charge of assault and battery on the officer. . . . Furthermore, if he knows that if he desists from his physically defensive measures and submits to arrest the officer's unlawfully excessive force would cease, the arrestee must desist or lose his privilege of self-defense. State v. Mulvihill, 270 A.2d 277, 280 (N.J. 1970).

As illustrated by the *Mulvihill* case, the modern trend is away from the common law rule allowing resistance to any illegal arrest, because of the dangers inherent in the rule and because the consequences of an illegal arrest are at the most a brief period of detention during which arrested persons can resort to nonviolent legal remedies for regaining their liberty.

Entry of Dwellings

Under the common law, the right of a law enforcement officer to enter a dwelling to arrest depended upon whether the officer had legal authority to arrest. Legal authority to arrest, with or without a warrant, carried with it the authority to forcibly enter any dwelling house and search for the suspect who the officer had probable cause to believe was in that dwelling house.

> An agent must have probable cause to believe that the person he is attempting to arrest, with or without a warrant, is in a particular building at the time in question before that agent can legitimately enter the building by ruse or any other means. To hold otherwise is to grant the agent a license to go from house to house employing ruse entries in violation of the right of privacy of the respective occupants. United States v. Phillips, 497 F.2d 1131, 1136 (9th Cir. 1974).

This authority to enter a dwelling house to arrest applied even to misdemeanor arrests.

The common law rule is no longer valid. In recent years, the U.S. Supreme Court decided several cases dealing with the entry of dwellings to arrest. The general rule now is that a law enforcement officer may not enter a dwelling to arrest a person without a warrant, unless there is consent or exigent circumstances. Whether an arrest warrant or search warrant is required for entry depends on whether the dwelling to be entered is the suspect's home or someone else's home.

ENTRY OF A SUSPECT'S HOME. In Payton v. New York, 445 U.S. 573, 100 S.Ct. 1371, 63 L.Ed.2d 639 (1980), the U.S. Supreme Court held that, absent exigent circumstances or consent, a law enforcement officer may not make a warrantless entry into a suspect's home in order to make a routine felony arrest. The Court said that the physical entry of the home is the chief evil against which the wording of the Fourth Amendment is directed and that the warrant procedure minimizes the danger of needless intrusions of that sort. The Court went on to say that an arrest warrant requirement, although providing less protection than a search warrant requirement, was sufficient to interpose the magistrate's determination of probable cause between a zealous officer and a citizen. The Court concluded that "an arrest warrant founded on probable cause implicitly carries with it the limited authority to enter a dwelling in which the suspect lives when there is reason to believe the suspect is within." 445 U.S. at 603, 100 S.Ct. at 1388, 63 L.Ed.2d at 661. Therefore, absent consent or exigent circumstances, a law enforcement officer must have at least an arrest warrant to lawfully enter a suspect's home to arrest the suspect.

In United States v. Holland, 755 F.2d 253 (2d Cir. 1985), the court held that the *Payton* rule did not apply to vestibules and common areas of multitenant buildings because there can be no expectation of privacy in those areas and because police protection is needed in those areas. In that case, the court upheld a nonconsensual, nonemergency arrest of a defendant who answered the doorbell in the vestibule of his two-apartment building. The arresting officer had probable cause to believe that the defendant was involved in illegal drug sales.

In *Payton*, the Court did not specify the nature of the exigent circumstances that would justify a warrantless entry of a home to make an arrest. In Welsh v. Wisconsin, 466 U.S. 740, 753, 104 S.Ct. 2091, 2099, 80 L.Ed.2d 732, 745 (1984), however, the Court held that:

> [A]n important factor to be considered when determining whether any exigency exists is the gravity of the underlying offense for which the arrest is being made. Moreover, although no exigency is created simply because there is probable cause to believe that a serious crime has been committed . . . application of the exigent-circumstances exception in the context of a home entry should

rarely be sanctioned when there is probable cause to believe that only a minor offense . . . has been committed.

In the *Welsh* case, the warrantless arrest of the defendant in his home for a non-criminal traffic offense was held illegal.

ENTRY OF A THIRD PERSON'S HOME. In Steagald v. United States, 451 U.S. 204, 101 S.Ct. 1642, 68 L.Ed.2d 38 (1981), the U.S. Supreme Court held that an arrest warrant does not authorize law enforcement officers to enter the home of a third person to search for the person to be arrested, in the absence of consent or exigent circumstances. To protect the Fourth Amendment privacy interests of persons not named in an arrest warrant, a search warrant must be obtained to justify the entry into the home of any person other than the person to be arrested.

This requirement places a heavy practical burden on law enforcement officers, causing them to seek both an arrest warrant and a search warrant in many situations. An alternative, suggested by the U.S. Supreme Court, is that in most instances the police may avoid altogether the need to obtain a search warrant simply by waiting for a suspect to leave the third person's home before attempting to arrest the suspect. When the suspect leaves either the home of a third person or the suspect's own home and is in a public place, officers may arrest on probable cause alone. Neither an arrest warrant nor a search warrant is required to support an arrest made in a public place.

ENTRY OF DWELLINGS IN HOT PURSUIT. When the arrest of a suspect is set in motion in a public place, but the suspect retreats into his or her home, the right of officers to enter the home in hot pursuit is governed by the case of United States v. Santana, 427 U.S. 38, 96 S.Ct. 2406, 49 L.Ed.2d 300 (1976). In that case, police officers drove to the defendant's house after receiving information that the defendant had in her possession marked money used to make a heroin buy arranged by an undercover agent. The defendant was standing in the doorway of her house holding a paper bag as the police pulled up within fifteen feet of her. The officers got out of the car, shouting "Police," and the defendant retreated into the vestibule of her house where she was apprehended. When the defendant tried to pull away, envelopes containing heroin fell to the floor from the paper bag. Some of the marked money was found on her person.

The Court held that while standing in the doorway of her house, the defendant was in a "public place" for purposes of the Fourth Amendment. Since she was not in an area where she had any expectation of privacy and she was exposed to public view, speech, hearing, and touch, it was the same as if she had been standing completely outside her house. When police sought to arrest her, they merely intended to make a warrantless arrest in a public place upon probable cause. Under United States v. Watson, 423 U.S. 411, 96 S.Ct. 820, 46 L.Ed.2d 598 (1976), such an arrest would not violate the Fourth Amendment. By retreating into a private place, the defendant could not defeat an otherwise proper arrest that had been set in motion in a public place. Since the officers needed to act quickly to prevent the destruction of evidence, there was a true hot pursuit, even though there was only a very short chase. Thus the warrantless entry to make the arrest was justified, as was the search incident to that arrest.

FORCED ENTRY. Before officers may lawfully force their way into a dwelling to arrest someone inside, they must first knock on the door, announce their authority and purpose, and then demand admittance. If this demand is refused or met with silence, officers may enter forcibly after waiting a reasonable time under the circumstances.

> The requirement of prior notice of authority and purpose before forcing entry into a home is deeply rooted in our heritage, and should not be given grudging application. . . . Every householder, the good and the bad, the guilty and the innocent, is entitled to the protection designed to secure the common interest against unlawful invasion of the house. The petitioner could not be lawfully arrested in his home by officers breaking in without first giving him notice of their authority and purpose. Because the petitioner did not receive that notice before the officers broke the door to invade his home, the arrest was unlawful, and the evidence seized should have been suppressed. Miller v. United States, 357 U.S. 301, 313–14, 78 S.Ct. 1190, 1198, 2 L.Ed.2d 1332, 1340–41 (1958).

In this context, forcible entry of a dwelling does not necessarily mean only the violent breaking down of a door or the smashing of a window. The U.S. Supreme Court stated that "[a]n unannounced intrusion into a dwelling . . . is no less an unannounced intrusion whether officers break down a door, force open a chain lock on a partially open door, open a locked door by use of a passkey, or . . . open a closed but unlocked door." Sabbath v. United States, 391 U.S. 585, 590, 88 S.Ct. 1755, 1758, 20 L.Ed.2d 828, 834 (1968). Again, before making any entry of this type to arrest, officers must first knock, announce their authority and purpose, and demand admittance.

The failure to knock, announce, and demand admittance will be excused in the following situations:

1. When the officer's purpose is already known to the offender or other person upon whom demand for entry is made. As the U.S. Supreme Court stated in the *Miller* case:

> It may be that, without an express announcement of purpose, the facts known to officers would justify them in being virtually certain that the petitioner already knows their purpose so that an announcement would be a useless gesture. 375 U.S. at 310, 78 S.Ct. at 1196, 2 L.Ed.2d at 1338.

2. When the personal safety of the officer or other persons might be imperiled. United States v. Guyon, 717 F.2d 1536 (6th Cir. 1983).

3. When the delay to knock and announce might defeat the arrest by allowing the offender to escape. State v. Fair, 211 A.2d 359 (N.J. 1965).

4. When knocking and announcing might allow persons inside to destroy evidence, such as in drug cases, where evidence is often small and easily destroyed or disposed of. In Ker v. California, 374 U.S. 23, 83 S.Ct. 1623, 10 L.Ed.2d 726 (1963), the U.S. Supreme Court held that an unannounced entry into the defendant's apartment was proper when otherwise evidence of narcotics activity would have been destroyed. However, officers must be able to justify an unannounced entry by the particular facts of a case. In the *Ker* case, not

only did the officers reasonably believe that the defendant was in possession of narcotics, but the defendant's furtive conduct in eluding officers shortly before the arrest gave the officers grounds to believe that he might have been expecting the police. In Meyer v. United States, 386 F.2d 715 (9th Cir. 1967), the officers had nothing to justify their unannounced entry into a dwelling except the claim of a general propensity of narcotics violators to destroy evidence. The court held that the entry was unlawful:

> Under the Fourth Amendment, a specific showing must always be made to justify any kind of police action tending to disturb the security of the people in their homes. Unannounced forcible entry is in itself a serious disturbance of that security and cannot be justified on a blanket basis. Otherwise, the constitutional test of reasonableness would turn only on practical expediency, and the amendment's primary safe-guard—the requirement of particularity, would be lost. Just as the police must have sufficient particular reason to enter at all, so must they have some particular reason to enter in the manner chosen. 386 F.2d at 718.

DISPOSITION OF AN ARRESTED PERSON

Initial Appearance before the Magistrate

After arresting a person, with or without a warrant, a law enforcement officer must take the person before a magistrate, or deliver the person according to the mandate of the warrant. State statutes require that this be done promptly, using phrases such as "immediately," "without unnecessary delay," "forthwith," or other similar language. These state statutes confer a substantial right upon the defendant and create a corresponding duty upon law enforcement officers.

The reasons behind the rule requiring arrested persons to be brought before a magistrate without unnecessary delay are as follows:

1. To advise arrested persons of the charges against them, so that they may prepare their defense.

2. To advise arrested persons of their rights, such as the right to a preliminary hearing, right to counsel, and right to remain silent.

3. To protect arrested persons from being abandoned in jail and forgotten by or otherwise cut off from contact with people who can help them.

4. To prevent secret and extended interrogation of arrested persons by law enforcement officers.

5. To give arrested persons an early opportunity to secure their release on bail while awaiting the final outcome of the proceedings against them.

6. To give arrested persons an opportunity to speedily conclude proceedings on charges of minor offenses by pleading guilty to the charges, paying their fines, and going on their way.

7. To obtain a prompt, neutral "judicial determination of probable cause as a prerequisite to extended restraint of liberty following arrest." Gerstein v. Pugh, 420 U.S. 103, 114, 95 S.Ct. 854, 863, 43 L.Ed.2d 54, 65 (1975). Not all states provide for a judicial determination of probable cause at the initial appearance before a magistrate.

There is no single preferred pretrial procedure, and the nature of the probable cause determination usually will be shaped to accord with a State's pretrial procedure viewed as a whole....It may be found desirable, for example, to make the probable cause determination at the suspect's first appearance before a judicial officer, the determination may be incorporated into the procedure for setting bail or fixing other conditions of pretrial release. In some States, existing procedures may satisfy the requirement of the Fourth Amendment. Others may require only minor adjustment, such as acceleration of existing preliminary hearings. Current proposals for criminal procedure reform suggest other ways of testing probable cause for detention. Whatever procedure a State may adopt, it must provide a fair and reliable determination of probable cause as a condition for any significant pretrial restraint on liberty, and this determination must be made by a judicial officer either before or promptly after arrest. 420 U.S. at 123–25, 95 S.Ct. at 868–69, 43 L.Ed.2d at 71–72.

Courts are quite flexible in interpreting the meaning of "immediately," "without unnecessary delay," "forthwith," and like phrases in statutes requiring arrested persons to be brought before a magistrate. Courts realize that a certain amount of delay is necessary for an officer to perform required duties and other unavoidable activities connected with an arrest, such as booking the arrested person, routinely questioning and searching the person (if legally allowed), and checking facts.

> The duty enjoined upon arresting officers to arraign "without unnecessary delay" indicates that the command does not call for automatic obedience. Circumstances may justify a brief delay between arrest and arraignment, as for instance, where the story volunteered by the accused is susceptible of quick verification through third parties. Williams v. United States, 273 F.2d 781, 797–98 (9th Cir. 1959).

An officer may also delay bringing an arrested person before a magistrate because the arrested person is physically or mentally incapacitated or because a magistrate is not readily available, either because the courts are closed or because the distance to be traveled to reach a magistrate is great.

Therefore, "immediately," "without unnecessary delay," "forthwith," or other similar statutory language cannot be defined in terms of minutes and hours but must be interpreted in light of all the circumstances. If an officer takes an arrested person before a magistrate as soon as one is available, and does not unreasonably detain or otherwise deprive the arrested person of constitutional rights, the requirements of the rule should be satisfied.

Protection and Welfare of an Arrested Person

When delay in taking an arrested person before a magistrate is unavoidable, the officer must keep the arrested person safely in custody for the period of the delay. The officer may reasonably restrain the person to prevent escape and may even confine the person in a jail or other suitable place. Handcuffs may be used at the officer's discretion, depending on the person's reputation or record for violence, the time of day, the number of other persons in custody, and the duration of the detention.

The officer is responsible for the health and safety of the arrested person, including the provision of adequate medical assistance, if necessary. Any unnecessary use of force or negligent failure to prevent the use of force by others against the arrested person may subject the officer to civil liability.

Property of an Arrested Person

When a person is arrested and taken into custody, as part of the routine administrative procedure incident to booking and jailing the person, police may search the person and any container or article in his or her possession, in accordance with established inventory procedures. In Illinois v. Lafayette, 462 U.S. 640, 103 S.Ct. 2605, 77 L.Ed.2d 65 (1983), the U.S. Supreme Court held that stationhouse inventory searches were an incidental step following arrest and preceding incarceration. The justification for these searches does not rest on probable cause, and thus the absence of a warrant is immaterial to the reasonableness of the searches. The Court said that the governmental interests justifying a stationhouse inventory search are different from, and may in some circumstances be even greater than, those supporting a search incident to arrest (see Chapter 7). Among those interests are prevention of theft of the arrested person's property; deterrence of false claims regarding that property; prevention of injury from belts, drugs, or dangerous instruments such as razor blades, knives, or bombs; and determination or verification of the person's identity. Furthermore, it does not matter that there might be less intrusive means of satisfying those governmental interests. The Court said:

> It is evident that a stationhouse search of every item carried on or by a person who has lawfully been taken into custody by the police will amply serve the important and legitimate governmental interests involved.
> Even if less intrusive means existed of protecting some particular types of property, it would be unreasonable to expect police officers in the everyday course of business to make fine and subtle distinctions in deciding which containers or items may be searched and which must be sealed as a unit. 462 U.S. at 648, 103 S.Ct. at 2610, 77 L.Ed.2d at 72.

A stationhouse inventory search need not be conducted immediately upon the arrested person's arrival at the stationhouse. The U.S. Supreme Court held that a seizure of a prisoner's clothing in the morning, several hours after his arrest and incarceration the previous evening, was reasonable. No substitute clothing had been available at the time of arrest and, therefore, the normal processes incident to arrest and custody had not be completed.

> [O]nce the accused is lawfully arrested and is in custody, the effects in his possession at the place of detention that were subject to search at the time and place of his arrest may lawfully be searched and seized without a warrant even though a substantial period of time has elapsed between the arrest and subsequent administrative processing, on the one hand, and the taking of the property for use as evidence, on the other. United States v. Edwards, 415 U.S. 800, 807, 94 S.Ct. 1234, 1239, 39 L.Ed.2d 771, 778 (1974).

Sometimes, especially when a vehicle is involved, officers must take positive steps to protect the defendant's property or become liable in damages for failure to do so. To protect against liability of this nature, many law enforcement agencies have adopted standard procedures for impounding arrested persons' vehicles and making an inventory of their contents. (For a further discussion of impoundment and inventory of vehicles, see Chapter 10.)

Identification and Examination of Arrested Persons

Pre-trial procedures for identifying and examining arrested persons take many different forms. One form is confrontation of the arrested person with victims or witnesses of the crime, sometimes accomplished through the use of a police lineup or showup. The arrested person has no right to object to being viewed by witnesses for identification purposes and also has no right to demand to be placed in a lineup. (For a discussion of pre-trial identification techniques and the right to counsel, see Chapter 14.)

Law enforcement officers may take fingerprints, footprints, or photographs of the arrested person for purposes of identification or evidence. These may be taken by force if necessary. Schmerber v. California, 384 U.S. 757, 86 S.Ct. 1826, 16 L.Ed.2d 908 (1966). Officers may also obtain voice exemplars or have a dentist examine a defendant's mouth for a missing tooth for identification purposes.

> [T]he Fourth Amendment does not protect "what a person knowingly exposes to the public even in his home or office. . . . Like a man's facial characteristics, or handwriting, his voice is repeatedly produced for others to hear. No person can have a reasonable expectation that others will not know the sound of his voice, any more than he can reasonably expect that his face will be a mystery to the world." This doctrine is applicable as well to a missing tooth. United States v. Holland, 378 F.Supp. 144, 155 (E.D.Pa. 1974).

Law enforcement officers may physically examine arrested persons for measurements, scars, bruises, tattoos, and so on, and may require persons to disrobe against their will:

> Such procedures and practices and tests may result in freeing an innocent man accused of crime, or may be part of a chain of facts and circumstances which help identify a person accused of a crime or connect a suspect or an accused with the crime of which he has been suspected or has been accused. The law is well settled that such actions, practices, and procedures do not violate any constitutional right. Commonwealth v. Aljoe, 216 A.2d 50, 52–53 (Pa. 1966).

The U.S. Supreme Court has held that there is no denial of due process of law in taking a blood sample from a person who is unconscious and unable to give consent, and no unreasonable search and seizure or violation of the privilege against self-incrimination when such specimen is taken without consent from a person in lawful custody. Schmerber v. California, 384 U.S. 757, 86 S.Ct. 1826, 16 L.Ed.2d 908 (1966). In the *Schmerber* case, the blood sample was taken in a hospital by a physician following accepted medical procedures. There was a need for immediate action because the sample was needed to measure the blood's alcoholic content, which would quickly dissipate. The Court said:

> [W]e reach this judgment only on the facts in the present record. The integrity of an individual's person is a cherished value of our society. That we today hold that the Constitution does not forbid the State's minor intrusions into an individual's body under stringently limited conditions in no way indicates that it permits more substantial intrusions or intrusions under other conditions, 384 U.S. at 772, 86 S.Ct. at 1836, 16 L.Ed.2d at 920.

In a case involving a more substantial intrusion, the U.S. Supreme Court refused, on Fourth Amendment grounds, to allow the prosecution to compel an armed robbery suspect to undergo a surgical procedure under a general anesthetic for removal of a bullet lodged in his chest. Winston v. Lee, 470 U.S. 753, 105 S.Ct. 1611, 84 L.Ed.2d 662 (1985). The Court applied the same balancing test used in *Schmerber* and found that the potential threat to the suspect's health and safety combined with the extensive intrusion on the suspect's personal privacy and bodily integrity were not counterbalanced by a compelling need for evidence. Of particular importance was the Court's finding that the prosecution had substantial additional evidence that the suspect was the person who committed the robbery. The Court said:

> The Fourth Amendment is a vital safeguard of the right of the citizen to be free from unreasonable governmental intrusions into any area in which he has a reasonable expectation of privacy. Where the Court has found a lesser expectation of privacy . . . or where the search involves a minimal intrusion on privacy interests . . . the Court has held that the Fourth Amendment protections are correspondingly less stringent. Conversely, however, the Fourth Amendment's command that searches be "reasonable" requires that when the State seeks to intrude upon an area in which our society recognizes a significantly heightened privacy interest, a more substantial justification is required to make the search "reasonable." Applying these principles, we hold that the proposed search in this case would be "unreasonable" under the Fourth Amendment. 470 U.S. at 767, 105 S.Ct. at 1620, 84 L.Ed.2d at 673.

EFFECT OF ILLEGAL ARREST

Jurisdiction to try a person for a crime is not affected by an illegal arrest.

> [T]he power of a court to try a person for crime is not impaired by the fact that he had been brought within the court's jurisdiction by reason of a "forcible abduction." . . . [D]ue process of law is satisfied when one present in court is convicted of crime after having been fairly apprised of the charges against him and after a fair trial in accordance with constitutional procedural safeguards. There is nothing in the Constitution that requires a court to permit a guilty person rightfully convicted to escape justice because he was brought to trial against his will. Frisbie v. Collins, 342 U.S. 519, 522, 72 S.Ct. 509, 511–12, 96 L.Ed. 541, 545–46 (1952).

However, although an illegal arrest does not affect jurisdiction to try an offender, the exclusionary rule may affect the trial adversely. The exclusionary rule, as it relates to arrest, states that any evidence obtained by exploitation of an unlawful arrest will be inadmissible in court in a prosecution against the person arrested. Therefore, if the only evidence that the state has against an armed robbery suspect is a gun, a mask, and a roll of bills taken during a search incident to an unlawful arrest, the offender will very likely go free because these items will be inadmissible in court. (The exclusionary rule is discussed in detail in Chapter 3.)

A confession obtained by exploitation of an illegal arrest will also be inadmissible in court. Officers cannot avoid the effect of an illegal arrest by simply giving the arrested person the *Miranda* warnings. Other factors indicating that the confession was sufficiently an act of free will must be present.

The *Miranda* warnings are an important factor, to be sure, in determining whether the confession is obtained by exploitation of illegal arrest. But they are not the only factor to be considered. The temporal proximity of the arrest and the confession, the presence of intervening circumstances, . . . and, particularly, the purpose and flagrancy of the official misconduct are all relevant. Brown v. Illinois, 422 U.S. 590, 603–4, 95 S.Ct. 2254, 2261–62, 45 L.Ed.2d 416, 427 (1975).

The prosecution has a difficult burden in curing the effect of an illegal arrest on a subsequent confession. In Taylor v. Alabama, 457 U.S. 687, 102 S.Ct. 2664, 73 L.Ed.2d 314 (1982), police made an investigatory arrest without probable cause, based on an uncorroborated informant's tip, and transported the defendant against his will to the station for interrogation in the hope that something would turn up. The Court held that there was no meaningful intervening event to break the causal connection between the arrest and the confession, even though (1) six hours elapsed between the arrest and the confession; and (2) the confession may have been voluntary for purposes of the Fifth Amendment in the sense that *Miranda* warnings were given and understood, the defendant was permitted a short visit with his girlfriend, and the police did not physically abuse the defendant.

Many factors must be considered to determine whether a confession is obtained by exploitation of an illegal arrest; thus, it is difficult to predict how a particular court will rule. For example, despite only a two-hour lapse between an illegal arrest and a confession, in People v. Vance, 185 Cal.Rptr. 549 (Cal. App. 1982), the court held the defendant's confession admissible because of the following circumstances:

1. Proper *Miranda* warnings were given;

2. the defendant was confronted with information that tied him to the crimes;

3. the defendant was allowed to speak privately with his common law wife; and

4. there was no purposeful or flagrant police activity.

Since circumstances in control of the police are often the determinant of the admissibility of a confession following an illegal arrest, officers should do everything possible to ensure that a confession is a product of the suspect's free will.

In general, unless an exception to the exclusionary rule comes into play, any evidence obtained soon after and closely intertwined with an illegal arrest will be declared inadmissible.

Finally, a law enforcement officer may be subject to civil liability for false arrest or false imprisonment if an arrest is illegal or is made with excessive or unreasonable force. Civil liability may also be imposed if an officer's application for an arrest warrant is so lacking in indicia of probable cause as to render official belief in its existence unreasonable.

SUMMARY

A formal arrest can be defined as the apprehension or detention of a person so that the person may be held to answer for an alleged crime. The basic elements constituting a formal arrest are (1) an intention to arrest, under real or pretended authority; (2) an actual or constructive seizure of the person to be arrested; (3) a communication by the officer of the intention to arrest; and (4) an understanding of the officer's intention by the person to be arrested. Even though these basic elements are not all present, courts may find that an encounter between a law enforcement officer and a person entails such a significant intrusion on the person's freedom of action that it is in important respects indistinguishable from a formal arrest. Such an encounter, sometimes called a seizure tantamount to arrest, must be supported by probable cause or it is illegal. The test to determine whether a seizure is tantamount to arrest is whether, in view of all the circumstances surrounding the encounter, a reasonable person would have believed that he or she was not free to leave.

Although warrantless arrests on probable cause are permitted in certain circumstances, courts always prefer arrests made under authority of an arrest warrant. An arrest warrant is a written judicial order directing a law enforcement officer to arrest a particular person. The warrant is issued by a magistrate on the basis of a complaint stating the essential facts constituting the offense charged, if the magistrate is satisfied that the offense was committed and that the person to be arrested committed it. The magistrate may also issue a summons that merely directs the defendant to appear rather than ordering an arrest.

Law enforcement officers may make a warrantless public arrest for a felony if they have probable cause to believe that a felony has been or is being committed and that the person to be arrested has committed or is committing the felony. Officers may make a warrantless public arrest for a misdemeanor, however, only if the misdemeanor was committed in their presence. A warrantless misdemeanor arrest must be made immediately, but a warrantless felony arrest may be delayed for various reasons, so long as the defendant's rights are not prejudiced by the delay.

When law enforcement officers make an arrest, they should notify the person arrested that he or she is under arrest and notify that person of the officers' authority and of the cause of the arrest. If the arrest is made under authority of a warrant, officers should examine the warrant to make sure it is valid on its face before carrying out the commands of the warrant. When the arrest warrant is executed, officers should return the warrant as directed and explain what they have done in carrying out its commands.

Officers have no official authority to arrest without a warrant outside their bailiwick—the geographical area for which they were elected or appointed. Nevertheless, even though outside their bailiwick, they have the authority of any private citizen to arrest for breach of the peace misdemeanors committed in their presence and for felonies on probable cause. They may also arrest outside their bailiwick in fresh pursuit of a criminal who has fled their bailiwick, if the pursuit is begun promptly inside the bailiwick and maintained continuously.

Officers may use only the amount of force reasonably necessary under the circumstances to effect an arrest. Deadly force may be used only as a last resort and then only in specifically limited circumstances. Deadly force may never be used to accomplish an arrest for a misdemeanor. But officers may use deadly force in self-defense to protect themselves from death or serious bodily injury, and officers need not abandon an attempt to arrest in the face of physical resistance to the arrest.

Officers may not enter a dwelling to arrest a person without a warrant unless there is consent or exigent circumstances. An arrest warrant is required to enter a suspect's home to arrest the suspect. A search warrant is required to enter the home of a third person to arrest a suspect. But if an arrest is begun in a public place, officers may enter a dwelling without a warrant in hot pursuit, in order to complete the arrest. Before officers may lawfully enter a dwelling forcibly to arrest a person, they must be refused admittance after knocking, announcing their authority and purpose, and demanding admittance. Failure to knock and announce is excused if an officer's purpose is already known or if knocking and announcing would cause danger to the officer, cause the escape of the suspect, or result in the loss or destruction of evidence.

Duties of the officer after an arrest is effected include the following: bringing the arrested person before a magistrate without unnecessary delay; ensuring the health and safety of the prisoner while in the officer's custody; conducting a stationhouse inventory search of the prisoner, which may include searching and seizing any container or object in the prisoner's possession; and conducting identification procedures, including fingerprinting, photographing, physical examinations, and lineups.

Although an illegal arrest will not affect the jurisdiction of the court to try a person, any evidence obtained by exploitation of an illegal arrest will be inadmissible in a criminal proceeding against the defendant. In addition, the law enforcement officer may be liable both civilly and criminally for making an illegal arrest or for using excessive force.

REVIEW AND DISCUSSION QUESTIONS

1. Is it possible to formally arrest an insane or extremely mentally retarded person? Explain.

2. Name several ways in which a law enforcement officer or officers can prevent a routine encounter with a person on the street from being considered a seizure tantamount to arrest.

3. Give three practical reasons why a law enforcement officer should obtain an arrest warrant if possible.

4. How is a law enforcement officer's authority to arrest affected by time?

5. Is it valid to say that if an officer has strong probable cause to arrest someone, the officer may arrest the person anywhere in the country? Explain.

6. Under what circumstances may a law enforcement officer use deadly force, and what are the potential consequences of an illegal use of deadly force? Name several circumstances under which little or no force should be used to make an arrest.

7. Do law enforcement officers have a broader right to self-defense when they are assaulted while making an arrest than when they are assaulted while simply walking or cruising their beat?

8. Assume that a law enforcement officer has probable cause to arrest a defendant for armed assault and probable cause to believe that the person is hiding in a third person's garage, which is attached to the house. What warrants, if any, does the officer need to enter the garage to arrest the defendant? What if the officer is in hot pursuit of the defendant? What if the defendant is known to be injured and unarmed?

9. Give reasons to support an argument that a law enforcement officer should never have to knock and announce before entering a dwelling to arrest a dangerous felon or a drug offender.

10. If a law enforcement officer has probable cause to arrest, does the officer have to make an arrest? If not, what alternatives to arrest are available and under what circumstances should they be used?

CHAPTER 5
Search Warrants

Like the law of arrest, the law governing search warrants is based upon guarantees in the Fourth Amendment to the U.S. Constitution.

> The right of the people to be secure in their persons, houses, papers and effects, against unreasonable searches and seizures, shall not be violated, and no Warrants shall issue, but upon probable cause, supported by Oath or affirmation, and particularly describing the place to be searched and the persons or things to be seized. U.S.C.A.Const.Amend.IV.

Whereas the main concern of the previous chapter on arrest was the *seizure* of the *person*, this chapter's concern is with a broader array of matters including the search of persons *and* places and the seizure of a variety of things. The U.S. Supreme Court definitions of *search* and *seizure*, set out in Chapter 3, are repeated here for emphasis.

> A "search" occurs when an expectation of privacy that society is prepared to consider reasonable is infringed. A "seizure" of property occurs when there is some meaningful interference with an individual's possessory interests in that property. United States v. Jacobsen, 466 U.S. 109, 113, 104 S.Ct. 1652, 1656, 80 L.Ed.2d 85, 94 (1984).

Probable cause, which is a common aspect of both arrest and search and seizure law, is discussed in detail in Chapter 6.

HISTORY

The Fourth Amendment to the U.S. Constitution was adopted in response to abuses of governmental search and seizure authority originating in England in the seventeenth and eighteenth centuries. The early development of legally authorized searches and seizures under English common law is somewhat obscure. It appears that search warrants were first used in cases involving stolen property. Use of warrants to recapture stolen goods became widespread and increasingly violative of citizens' privacy. Eventually, use of warrants was extended to the enforcement of other laws. For example, in the eighteenth century the government issued general warrants to enforce strict libel laws. A general warrant is one that fails to specify the person or place to be searched or the person or item to be seized, and which leaves the time and manner of the search to the discretion of the searching officer. These general warrants were abused by law enforcement officers, and soon no person or property was free from unlimited search conducted at the whim of an officer on the mere suspicion that the person possessed literature critical of the king or of others in high places.

Despite their unpopularity with the citizenry, these abusive practices were transplanted to the American colonies. In mid-eighteenth century, Parliament enacted legislation authorizing general searches, called writs of assistance, to be conducted against the colonists to enforce the Trade Acts. Writs of assistance authorized royal customs officers to search houses and ships at will in order to discover and seize smuggled goods or goods on which the required duties had not been paid. The reaction of the colonists against the writs of assistance was strong and was one of the major causes of the American Revolution. As stated in the 1886 U.S. Supreme Court case of Boyd v. United States:

> The practice had obtained in the colonies of issuing writs of assistance to the revenue officers, empowering them, in their discretion, to search suspected places for smuggled goods, which James Otis pronounced "the worst instrument of arbitrary power, the most destructive of English liberty and the fundamental principles of law, that ever was found in an English law book;" since they placed "the liberty of every man in the hands of every petty officer." This was in February, 1761, in Boston, and the famous debate in which it occurred was perhaps the most prominent event which inaugurated the resistance of the colonies to the oppressions of the mother country. "Then and there," said John Adams, "then and there was the first scene of the first act of opposition to the arbitrary claims of Great Britain. Then and there the child of Independence was born." 116 U.S. 616, 625, 6 S.Ct. 524, 528–29, 29 L.Ed. 746, 749 (1886).

The experiences of the founding fathers with general warrants and writs of assistance caused them to insist upon including in the basic charters of the states and of the nation suitable guarantees against unreasonable searches and seizures. A prohibition against searches conducted at the whim of a law enforcement officer without any restrictions on the person or place to be searched or the person or item to be seized was first embodied in the Virginia Bill of Rights adopted in 1776. By the close of the revolutionary war, most of the states had adopted similar provisions. The present Fourth Amendment to the U.S. Constitution, with its emphasis on the protection of warrants issued upon probable cause, was included in the Bill of Rights in 1791. Today, the constitution of every state in the Union contains a similar provision.

The policy underlying the warrant requirement of the Fourth Amendment was stated by the U.S. Supreme Court:

> The point of the Fourth Amendment, which often is not grasped by zealous officers, is not that it denies law enforcement the support of the usual inferences which reasonable men draw from evidence. Its protection consists in requiring that those inferences be drawn by a neutral and detached magistrate instead of being judged by the officer engaged in the often competitive enterprise of ferreting out crime. Any assumption that evidence sufficient to support a magistrate's disinterested determination to issue a search warrant will justify

the officers in making a search without a warrant would reduce the Amendment to a nullity and leave the people's homes secure only in the discretion of police officers. . . . When the right of privacy must reasonably yield to the right of search is, as a rule, to be decided by a judicial officer, not by a policeman or Government enforcement agent. Johnson v. United States, 333 U.S. 10, 13–14, 68 S.Ct. 367, 369, 92 L.Ed. 436, 440 (1948).

DEFINITION

A search warrant is (1) an order in writing; (2) issued by a proper judicial authority; (3) in the name of the people; (4) directed to a law enforcement officer; (5) commanding the officer to search for certain personal property; and (6) commanding the officer to bring that property before the judicial authority named in the warrant. A search warrant is similar to an arrest warrant, which is an order to take a *person* into custody and bring the person before the proper judicial authority. In this chapter, the terms of the preceding definition are clarified and important relationships between search warrants and arrest warrants are highlighted.

OBTAINING A SEARCH WARRANT

Law enforcement officers must conform to established laws and procedures in applying for a search warrant. Failure to do so will result in no warrant being issued or in later invalidation of the warrant by a court. In either instance, valuable evidence will be unavailable to be used in the prosecution of a criminal case.

Search warrant procedures differ from state to state and are found in various statutes, rules, and court decisions. The procedures common to most states are summarized and discussed in this chapter.

Who May Issue Search Warrants

Only judicial officers who have been specifically authorized to do so may issue search warrants. Most states give this authority to judicial officers such as clerks of court, magistrates, complaint justices, justices of the peace, and judges. Law enforcement officers need to know which judicial officers are authorized to issue search warrants in their states. These judicial officers may be different from those authorized to issue arrest warrants. A search warrant issued by a person without authority is of no legal effect, and a search made under such a warrant is unlawful. For convenience, the term *magistrate* is used in this chapter to designate an official authorized to issue search warrants.

The main requirement of a magistrate is that he or she be impartial, or as is sometimes stated, "neutral and detached." The U.S. Supreme Court held that the following persons were not sufficiently impartial to issue warrants:

1. A state attorney general who was also the state's chief investigator and was later to be the chief prosecutor at trial. Coolidge v. New Hampshire, 403 U.S. 443, 91 S.Ct. 2022, 29 L.Ed.2d 564 (1971).

2. A magistrate who received a fee for issuing a search warrant but received nothing for denying a warrant. Connally v. Georgia, 429 U.S. 245, 97 S.Ct. 546, 50 L.Ed.2d 444 (1977).

3. A magistrate who participated in a search, helping officers in determining what to seize. Lo-Ji Sales, Inc. v. New York, 442 U.S. 319, 99 S.Ct. 2319, 60 L.Ed.2d 920 (1979).

Grounds for Issuance

Before issuing a search warrant, the magistrate must have probable cause to believe that items subject to seizure are in a particular place or on a particular person at the time of the issuance of the warrant. A law enforcement officer seeking a search warrant must supply the magistrate with the grounds for issuance of the warrant. This is done by means of an affidavit, which is merely a written declaration or statement of facts sworn to before the magistrate. An example of a typical affidavit for search warrant form appears on page 111.

If a law enforcement officer knowingly and intentionally, or with reckless disregard for the truth, makes false statements in an affidavit supporting a request for a search warrant, the warrant may not be issued or evidence seized under the warrant may be suppressed. In Franks v. Delaware, 438 U.S. 154, 98 S.Ct. 2674, 57 L.Ed.2d 667 (1978), the U.S. Supreme Court held that a defendant may challenge the veracity of an affidavit used by the police to obtain a search warrant. The Court said:

> [W]here the defendant makes a substantial preliminary showing that a false statement knowingly and intentionally, or with reckless disregard for the truth, was included by the affiant in the warrant affidavit, and if the allegedly false statement is necessary to the finding of probable cause, the Fourth Amendment requires that a hearing be held at the defendant's request. In the event that at the hearing the allegation of perjury or reckless disregard is established by the defendant by a preponderance of the evidence, and, with the affidavit's false material set to one side, the affidavit's remaining content is insufficient to establish probable cause, the search warrant must be voided and the fruits of the search excluded to the same extent as if probable cause was lacking on the face of the affidavit. 438 U.S. at 155–56, 98 S.Ct. at 2676–77, 57 L.Ed.2d at 672.

In addition, if a warrant application is so lacking in indicia of probable cause as to render official belief in its existence unreasonable, the officer making the application may be held liable for damages in a civil suit. Malley v. Briggs, 475 U.S. 335, 106 S.Ct. 1092, 89 L.Ed.2d 271 (1986).

The following discussion covers in detail the information that must be presented to the magistrate to establish grounds for the issuance of a search warrant.

PROBABLE CAUSE. Some states require that an affidavit contain *all* the information upon which a magistrate is to base a finding of probable cause to issue a search warrant. State v. Case, 363 So.2d 486 (La. 1978). Other states allow supplementation of a defective or incomplete affidavit by sworn oral testimony given before the magistrate. State v. Hendricks, 328 N.E.2d 822 (Ohio 1974). A small minority of states permit issuance of search warrants over the telephone.

AO 106 (Rev. 5/85) Affidavit for Search Warrant ⊕

United States District Court

_____ DISTRICT OF _____

In the Matter of the Search of
(Name, address or brief description of person or property to be searched)

**APPLICATION AND AFFIDAVIT
FOR SEARCH WARRANT**

CASE NUMBER:

I _____ being duly sworn depose and say:

I am a(n) _____ and have reason to believe
                                     Official Title

that ☐ on the person of or ☐ on the premises known as (name, description and/or location)

in the _____ District of _____
there is now concealed a certain person or property, namely (describe the person or property)

which is (give alleged grounds for search and seizure under Rule 41(b) of the Federal Rules of Criminal Procedure)

in violation of Title _____ United States Code, Section(s) _____
The facts to support the issuance of a Search Warrant are as follows:

Continued on the attached sheet and made a part hereof.   ☐ Yes   ☐ No

_____
Signature of Affiant

Sworn to before me, and subscribed in my presence

_____   at   _____
Date   City and State

_____   _____
Name and Title of Judicial Officer   Signature of Judicial Officer

---

These states require that the information telephoned by the affiant to the magistrate be taken under oath and be recorded.

Writing all the information upon which probable cause is based in the affidavit is preferred because it forces the law enforcement officer to think carefully about the case before applying for a warrant and it provides a complete record for a court to review the magistrate's decision, if the warrant is later challenged. This chapter proceeds on the assumption that a written affidavit is the exclusive vehicle for applying to a magistrate for a search warrant.

An affidavit should inform a magistrate (1) that a criminal offense has been or is being committed and (2) that seizable evidence relating to that offense is in a particular place at a particular time. The amount of proof required to persuade the magistrate to issue a search warrant is essentially the same as that required for the issuance of an arrest warrant or that required before an officer may arrest without a warrant for a felony. The constitutional term used to describe this amount of proof is *probable cause*. (Probable cause is discussed in Chapter 3 and in further detail in Chapter 6.) For purposes of applying for a search warrant, the essential requirement is that the underlying facts and circumstances upon which probable cause is based must be stated in the affidavit. An officer's mere conclusions, beliefs, or opinions will not suffice to establish probable cause.

Probable cause to search differs in two important respects from probable cause to arrest. First, probable cause to search and probable cause to arrest will usually arise out of different sets of facts. In order to find probable cause to arrest, a magistrate must find sufficient facts to show that an offense was committed and that a particular suspect committed it. Probable cause to search requires sufficient facts to show that particular items are connected with criminal activity and that they will be found in a particular place. Therefore, the same set of facts and circumstances might provide probable cause to arrest, but not probable cause to search, and vice versa.

Another difference between probable cause to arrest and probable cause to search is that time is a very important factor in determining probable cause to search. The items to be seized must be in the place or on the person to be searched at the time the application for a search warrant is made or, in the case of a warrantless search, at the time the search is executed. If there is too long a delay between the time when the information upon which probable cause is based is gathered and the time when the search is executed, there may no longer be good reason to believe that the property is still at the same location. Probable cause is said to be "stale" in this situation.

The length of time that an item of property is likely to remain at a given location depends upon the nature of the property, the nature of the criminal activity, the duration of the criminal activity, the criminal suspects, and many other factors. In crimes involving property that is likely to disappear or be moved, probable cause can go stale very quickly. For example, in State v. Willey, 363 A.2d 739 (Me. 1976), the court held that even though the informant had made three purchases of marijuana from the defendant in one week, this information was insufficient to justify the conclusion that thirty-one days after the last purchase, marijuana was still at the defendant's premises.

In contrast, an affidavit stating that hand grenades had been observed at the defendant's residence within the past thirty days was not insufficient because of stale probable cause. The court said that "[u]nlike many other items of contraband, hand grenades are not, to the best of our knowledge, in great demand even by the criminal element in our society; and they do not lend themselves to rapid disposition in the marketplace." United States v. Dauphinee, 538 F.2d 1 (1st Cir. 1976). Evidence of continuing crimes, especially white-collar crimes, is also not likely to disappear or be moved rapidly. The U.S. Supreme Court found that business records of an illegal real estate scheme would probably remain at their location for an extended period of time after the business transactions had taken place.

The business records sought were prepared in the ordinary course of petitioner's business in his law office or that of his real estate corporation. It is eminently reasonable to expect that such records would be maintained in those offices for a period of time and surely as long as the three months required for the investigation of a complex real estate scheme. Andresen v. Maryland, 427 U.S. 463, 479, n. 9, 96 S.Ct. 2737, 2747, n. 9, 49 L.Ed.2d 627, 641, n. 9 (1976).

ITEMS SUBJECT TO SEIZURE. State laws permit a warrant to be issued to search for and seize certain types of property. Although these laws differ, the following list is typical of the types of property allowed to be seized:

1. Property stolen or embezzled

2. Property designed or intended for use or which is or has been used as a means of committing a criminal offense (instrumentalities)

3. Property the possession of which is unlawful (contraband)

4. Property consisting of nontestimonial evidence that will aid in a particular apprehension or conviction

The first three listed types of property are self-explanatory. The fourth type of property is sometimes called mere evidence. Examples of mere evidence are clothing, blood, hair, or business records. Mere evidence was added to the list by many states in response to the U.S. Supreme Court decision in Warden v. Hayden, 387 U.S. 294, 87 S.Ct. 1642, 18 L.Ed.2d 782 (1967), which abolished the rule that search warrants could not be used as a means of gaining access to a person's house or office and papers solely for the purpose of searching for mere evidence to be used against the person in a criminal proceeding.

One limitation on the seizure of mere evidence is that the evidence must be nontestimonial. This requirement protects persons from being compelled to be witnesses against themselves in violation of their Fifth Amendment rights. It was originally assumed that private personal papers and business records could not be seized under this limitation because of their testimonial nature. The U.S. Supreme Court held, however, that a seizure of personal papers or business records from persons under a search warrant does not necessarily compel those persons to be witnesses against themselves. Andresen v. Maryland, 427 U.S. 463, 96 S.Ct. 2737, 49 L.Ed.2d 627 (1976). The Court quoted an earlier case stating that "'a party is privileged from producing the evidence, but not from its production.'" 427 U.S. at 473, 96 S.Ct. at 2745, 49 L.Ed.2d at 638. The Court held that the defendant in the *Andresen* case was not compelled to be a witness against himself because he was not required to say or to do anything during the search. If law enforcement authorities had attempted to subpoena the records, however, the defendant could have refused to give up the records by exercising his Fifth Amendment rights. The Court said:

> [A]lthough the Fifth Amendment may protect an individual from complying with a subpoena for the production of his personal records in his possession because the very act of production may constitute a compulsory authentication of incriminating information, . . . a seizure of the same materials by law enforcement officers differs in a crucial respect—the individual against whom the search is directed is not required to aid in the discovery, production, or authentication of incriminating evidence. 427 U.S. at 473–74, 96 S.Ct. at 2745, 49 L.Ed.2d at 638.

Bank records have even less protection. In United States v. Miller, 425 U.S. 435, 96 S.Ct. 1619, 48 L.Ed.2d 71 (1976), the U.S. Supreme Court held that a person's bank records are not private papers of the kind protected against compulsory production by the Fifth Amendment. By choosing to deal with a bank, people lose their expectation of Fourth Amendment protection against government investigation:

> The checks are not confidential communications but negotiable instruments to be used in commercial transactions. All of the documents obtained, including financial statements and deposit slips, contain only information voluntarily conveyed to the banks and exposed to their employees in the ordinary course of business. 425 U.S. at 442, 96 S.Ct. at 1624, 48 L.Ed.2d at 79.

The *Miller* case concerned a subpoena, but either a search warrant or subpoena could be used to obtain a person's bank records without violating the person's Fifth Amendment right against compulsory self-incrimination.

Both the *Andresen* and *Miller* cases serve to highlight a basic principle regarding the obtaining of papers as evidence in criminal cases: "There is no special sanctity in papers, as distinguished from other forms of property, to render them immune from search and seizure, if only they fall within the scope of the principles of the cases in which other property may be seized, and if they be adequately described in the affidavit and warrant." Gouled v. United States, 255 U.S. 298, 309, 41 S.Ct. 261, 265, 65 L.Ed. 647, 652 (1921). Nevertheless, officers seizing items such as business records or personal papers under a warrant should not require the defendant to assist them in any way. Otherwise the evidence may be suppressed because of a violation of the defendant's Fifth Amendment rights.

Another limitation on the seizure of mere evidence is that the evidence must aid in a particular apprehension or conviction. The reason for this requirement was stated by the U.S. Supreme Court:

> The requirements of the Fourth Amendment can secure the same protection of privacy whether the search is for "mere evidence" or for fruits, instrumentalities or contraband. There must of course be a nexus—automatically provided in the case of fruits, instrumentalities or contraband—between the item to be seized and criminal behavior. Thus in the case of "mere evidence," probable cause must be examined in terms of cause to believe that the evidence sought will aid in a particular apprehension or conviction. In doing so, consideration of police purposes will be served. Warden v. Hayden, 387 U.S. 294, 306–7, 87 S.Ct. 1642, 1650, 18 L.Ed.2d 782, 792 (1967).

An affidavit for a search warrant should indicate, for each item of property sought in the warrant, the type of seizable property under which the item is classified according to state law. This informs the magistrate that the items sought are connected with criminal activity. For the remainder of this chapter, items of property allowed to be seized under state law are referred to as items subject to seizure.

PARTICULAR DESCRIPTION OF PLACE OR PERSON.   The affidavit for a search warrant for a place must contain a description of the premises to be searched which points directly to a definitely ascertainable place to the exclusion of all others. The U.S. Supreme Court stated that "[i]t is enough if the description is such that the officer with a search warrant can with reasonable effort ascertain and identify the place intended." Steele v. United States, 267 U.S. 498, 503, 45 S.Ct. 414, 416, 69 L.Ed. 757, 760 (1925).

A street address is usually sufficient to identify premises in an urban area. For example, in State v. McClelland, 523 P.2d 357 (Kan. 1974), a search warrant was issued for "Premises of 1315 Monroe, Topeka, Shawnee County, Kansas." The court held:

> With that description any officer could have reasonably ascertained and identified the premises delineated in the warrant. We are of the opinion the term "premises" . . . included all property necessarily a part of and appearing so inseparable as to be considered a portion thereof. 523 P.2d at 359.

The location of rural property is more difficult to describe, but there is also less chance that an error will be made in locating a particular piece of rural property. Therefore, a description of a farm or other rural property by the name of the owner, the color and style of the dwelling, and general directions will usually suffice. Gatlin v. State, 559 S.W.2d 12 (Ark. 1977).

When the place to be searched is a multiple-occupancy dwelling such as an apartment house, hotel, or rooming house, the affidavit must go beyond merely stating the location of the premises. In Manley v. Commonwealth, 176 S.E.2d 309 (Va. 1970), the affidavit upon which the warrant was based read as follows:

> Place to be searched: 313 West 27th Street, a dwelling. The apartment of Melvin Lloyd Manley.

The defendant objected to the search on the ground that the apartment to be searched was not sufficiently described in the affidavit and warrant. The court held that the defendant's apartment was sufficiently described for the searching officers to locate it with very little effort:

> It has been generally held that a search warrant directed against a multiple-occupancy structure is invalid if it fails to describe the particular sub-unit to be searched with sufficient definiteness to preclude search of other units located in the larger structure and occupied by innocent persons. But there are exceptions to the general rule. Even though a search warrant against a multiple-occupancy structure fails to describe the particular sub-unit to be searched, it will ordinarily not be held invalid where it adequately specifies the name of the occupant of the sub-unit against which it is directed and provides the searching officers with sufficient information to identify, without confusion or excessive effort, such apartment unit. 176 S.E.2d at 314.

Whenever possible, however, information like room number, apartment number, and floor should be included in the affidavit. If necessary, a diagram showing the location should be attached to the affidavit.

In another case involving a multiple-occupancy dwelling, the description in the warrant of the place to be searched (a four-building apartment complex) gave a wrong street address but correctly stated the apartment number. Since there was only one apartment with that number in the entire complex, the court held that the description was sufficient:

> [T]he determining factor as to whether a search warrant describes the premises to be searched with sufficient particularity is not whether the description is technically accurate in every detail but rather whether the description is sufficient to enable the executing officer to locate and identify the premises with

reasonable effort, and whether there is any reasonable probability that another premises might be mistakenly searched which is not the one intended to be searched under the search warrant. United States v. Darensbourg, 520 F.2d 985, 987 (5th Cir. 1975).

To obtain sufficiently descriptive information, an officer may need to view the premises, examine floor plans, or make inquiries of landlords, tenants, or others to determine the correct limits of the place to be searched. The U.S. Supreme Court said that "[t]he validity of the warrant must be assessed on the basis of the information that the officers disclosed, or had a duty to discover and to disclose, to the issuing magistrate." Maryland v. Garrison, 480 U.S. 79, 85, 107 S.Ct. 1013, 1018, 94 L.Ed.2d 72, 81 (1987). Nevertheless, the sufficiency of the description will be judged in light of the information available to the officer at the time he or she prepared the affidavit. The later discovery of facts demonstrating that a warrant was unnecessarily broad does not retroactively invalidate the warrant. In short, if an officer is diligent in gathering the information upon which his or her description of the place to be searched is based, the warrant will be valid even though hindsight reveals that honest mistakes were made.

A warrant may be issued for the search of premises of an innocent third party who is not suspected of any crime. In a case involving the search of newspaper offices, the U.S. Supreme Court said that search warrants are not directed at persons, but at the seizure of things. "The critical element in a reasonable search is not that the owner of the property is suspected of crime but that there is reasonable cause to believe that the specific 'things' to be searched for and seized are located on the property to which entry is sought." Zurcher v. The Stanford Daily, 436 U.S. 547, 556, 98 S.Ct. 1970, 1977, 56 L.Ed.2d 525, 535 (1978).

A search warrant may also be issued to search a person for particular items of evidence, but the more common procedure is to arrest the person and conduct a search incident to arrest (see Chapter 7). Again the standard for determining the validity of a warrant to search a person is whether the warrant describes the person to be searched with sufficient particularity to enable identification with reasonable certainty. Even though a person's name is unknown or incorrectly stated, a warrant may still be valid if a description of the person is included. United States v. Ferrone, 438 F.2d 381 (3d Cir. 1971). A law enforcement officer applying for a warrant for the search of a person should not only state the person's name, if known, but also give a complete description including weight , height, age, race, clothing, address, and any aliases. State v. Tramantano, 260 A.2d 128 (Conn. Super. 1969). If the name in the affidavit is incorrect, the backup information will still enable the person to be identified.

Some courts hold that any search of a person that requires surgery is prohibited by the Fourth Amendment. Adams v. State, 299 N.E.2d 834 (Ind. 1973). Other courts require additional information in the affidavit to justify the issuance of a search warrant requiring surgery. Relevant additional information would be medical opinions on the risks of surgery; the seriousness of the crime; the relevance and importance of the evidence sought; the likelihood of surgery's producing the evidence; and alternatives or lack of alternatives to surgery. In addition, a defendant may be entitled to an adversary hearing and an opportunity to appeal an order directing surgery. United States v. Crowder, 543 F.2d 312 (D.C. Cir. 1976).

The U.S. Supreme Court has established exceptions to the warrant requirement allowing warrantless searches of motor vehicles under certain circumstances. However, the basic rule is that a warrant is required for the search of a motor vehicle. Since vehicles are considered *places* for search and seizure purposes, an affidavit is required to contain a description of the vehicle to be searched that is sufficiently particular that the vehicle can be located with reasonable certainty. Some courts have held that only the license plate number is necessary to sufficiently describe a motor vehicle for purposes of issuance of a warrant. Bowling v. State, 408 S.W.2d 660 (Tenn. 1966). Nevertheless, other descriptive information such as the make, body style, color, year, location, and owner or operator of the vehicle should be included, if known.

Mail may also be considered a *place* for search and seizure purposes. Courts have ruled that first-class domestic mail may not be lawfully opened without a warrant. (Domestic mail is any letter or package traveling wholly within the United States.) Therefore, law enforcement officers must follow the same procedures to obtain a warrant to search first-class domestic mail as to search places, persons, and vehicles.

A problem arises in describing the place to be searched when a search warrant is sought to install a tracking device such as a beeper, because the location of a place is precisely what is sought to be discovered. The U.S. Supreme Court responded to this issue as follows:

> [I]t will still be possible to describe the object into which the beeper is to be placed, the circumstances that led agents to wish to install the beeper, and the length of time for which beeper surveillance is requested. In our view, this information will suffice to permit issuance of a warrant authorizing beeper installation and surveillance. United States v. Karo, 468 U.S. 705, 718, 104 S.Ct. 3296, 3305, 82 L.Ed.2d 530, 543 (1984).

PARTICULAR DESCRIPTION OF THINGS. The affidavit for a search warrant must contain a particular description of the items to be seized. The U.S. Supreme Court explained the reason for this requirement:

> The requirement that warrants shall particularly describe the things to be seized makes general searches under them impossible and prevents the seizure of one thing under a warrant describing another. As to what is to be taken, nothing is left to the discretion of the officer executing the warrant. United States v. Marron, 275 U.S. 192, 196, 48 S.Ct. 74, 76, 72 L.Ed. 231, 237 (1927).

In general, the items to be seized must be described with sufficient particularity so that the officer executing the warrant (1) can identify the items with reasonable certainty, and (2) is left with no discretion as to which property is to be taken. The primary concern of courts evaluating descriptions of things to be seized in affidavits for search warrants is to ensure that a person will not be deprived of lawfully possessed property by a seizure made under an imprecise warrant.

A description of items merely as "stolen goods," "obscene materials," or "other articles of merchandise too numerous to mention," for instance, would be inadequate. Marcus v. Search Warrants, 367 U.S. 717, 81 S.Ct. 1708, 6

L.Ed.2d 1127 (1961). When an item can be described in detail, all available information about it should be included in the affidavit. For example, number, size, color, weight, condition, brand name, and other distinguishing features of items to be seized should be a part of the description where applicable. The affidavit should also indicate how the item is connected with criminal activity by stating the category of items subject to seizure within which the item falls.

A more general description may be allowed when specificity is impossible or difficult. For example, a court upheld the sufficiency of a warrant that authorized a search for:

> Certain items of property, to-wit:
>   "Various instruments and tools used in performing abortion, which were instrumentalities of such offense. . . ."

The court held that because of the unusual nature of the items to be seized, they were described with reasonable particularity in the warrant. A technical identification or description would have required the experience of a trained surgeon. State v. Brown, 470 P.2d 815, 819–20 (Kan. 1970).

A more general description may also be allowed when a large number of items to be seized are of a common nature and not unique. The general description should be accompanied by strong evidence that the items to be seized at a particular place are the actual items that offend against the law, and by evidence that the seizable items cannot be differentiated from similar innocent items. In United States v. Scharfman, 448 F.2d 1352 (2d Cir. 1971), a shipment containing hundreds of furs had been hijacked. The Federal Bureau of Investigation applied for a warrant to search the defendant's fur store for "fur coats, stoles, jackets and other finished fur products. . . ." 448 F.2d at 1353 n. 1. The court upheld the general description in the warrant because the affidavit stated that an informant experienced in the fur trade and an employee of the fur shipment's owner had informed the FBI that furs from the shipment were in the defendant's store. The court concluded from these facts that there was a reasonable likelihood that a large collection of similar stolen furs was in the defendant's store.

A general description will usually not be allowed if a more specific description is possible. In United States v. Townsend, 394 F.Supp. 736 (E.D. Mich. 1975), a search warrant commanded the seizure of "Stolen firearms, appr. ten (10), which are stored in the basement of the above location, and in bedrooms, and any and all other stolen items, contraband." The court held that the phrase "any and all other stolen items" was impermissibly vague. With respect to the description "10 firearms," the court said:

> Firearms may be easily characterized by color, length, type and other defining attributes. Therefore, further description in the instant case is far from a "virtual impossibility," and the generic description in combination with the other defects in particularity, constitutes a violation of defendant's Fourth Amendment guarantee. 394 F.Supp. at 747.

Courts generally allow greater leeway in descriptions of contraband material.

> If the purpose of the search is to find a specific item of property, it should be so particularly described in the warrant as to preclude the possibility of the officer

seizing the wrong property; whereas, on the other hand, if the purpose is to seize not a specific property, but any property of a specified character, which by reason of its character is illicit or contraband, a specific particular description of the property is unnecessary and it may be described generally as to its nature or character. People v. Schmidt, 473 P.2d 698, 700 (Colo. 1970).

In the *Schmidt* case, the court allowed a description specifying "marijuana, (Cannabis Sativa L.) Dangerous Drugs, Stimulant Drugs, and hallucinogenics . . . Together with such vessels, implements, and furniture in which drugs are found and the vessels, implements, and furniture used in connection with the manufacture, production, or dispensing of such drugs. . . ." General descriptions of gambling paraphernalia will also be allowed. In United States v. Appoloney, 761 F.2d 520 (9th Cir. 1985), the court allowed a description of "'wagering paraphernalia' such as betting slips, bottom sheets and owe sheets, and journals and schedules of sporting events."

General descriptions will not be allowed, however, if the items to be searched for or seized are books, films, recordings, or other materials that have not yet been adjudged obscene. Since these materials are presumed protected by the First Amendment, a very high degree of particularity is required in both the affidavit and the warrant. As the U.S. Supreme Court stated, "[T]he constitutional requirement that warrants must particularly describe the 'things to be seized' is to be accorded the most scrupulous exactitude when the 'things' are books, and the basis for their seizure is the ideas which they contain." Stanford v. Texas, 379 U.S. 476, 485, 85 S.Ct. 506, 511–12, 13 L.Ed.2d 431, 437 (1965). Therefore, in a case in which a magistrate viewed two films from the defendant's adult book store, concluded they were obscene, and issued a warrant authorizing the seizure of all other obscene materials, the U.S. Supreme Court held that the warrant was a prohibited general warrant:

> [T]he search left it entirely to the discretion of the officials conducting the search to decide what items were likely obscene and to accomplish their seizure. . . . Nor does the Fourth Amendment countenance open-ended warrants, to be completed while a seizure is being conducted and items seized or after the seizure has been carried out. Lo-Ji Sales, Inc. v. New York, 442 U.S. 319, 325, 99 S.Ct. 2319, 2324, 60 L.Ed.2d 920, 927–28 (1979).

MULTIPLE AFFIDAVITS. A law enforcement officer applying for a search warrant may submit more than one affidavit to the magistrate. The additional or supplemental affidavits may be prepared by the officer or by someone else.

> Since the object of the proceedings before the magistrate is to establish probable cause to justify issuance of a search warrant, law enforcement officers should not be hindered in their efforts to describe the basis for probable cause in supporting affidavits. So long as these affidavits are satisfactorily incorporated to all related documents necessary to the application for the warrant . . . the reviewing court will be assured of the simultaneous presence of these documents before the magistrate, and the search may be subjected to authoritative judicial review. State v. Gamage, 340 A.2d 1, 7 (Me. 1975).

The essential requirement is that all "affidavits are satisfactorily incorporated to all related documents necessary to the application for the warrant." The following procedure is suggested to ensure proper incorporation:

1. Entitle the first or primary affidavit Affidavit and Request for Search Warrant.

2. Entitle all additional affidavits Supplemental Affidavit 1, Supplemental Affidavit 2, and so forth.

3. Include the following statement in the first or primary affidavit: "This request is, also based upon the information in the sworn statements in Supplemental Affidavit 1, Supplemental Affidavit 2, . . . which are attached." (The law requires that clear reference be made to all supplemental affidavits).

4. Securely attach all supplemental affidavits to the primary affidavit. Use a stapler or other semipermanent method of binding. A paper clip would be unsatisfactory because of its tendency to slip off.

By following these simple steps, the officer ensures that the magistrate will be simultaneously presented with all the information upon which probable cause is to be based and that the appellate court will be able to effectively review the magistrate's decision.

Securing of Dwelling while Warrant Is Being Sought

When officers have probable cause to believe that evidence of criminal activity is in a dwelling, a temporary securing of the dwelling to prevent removal or destruction of evidence while a search warrant is being sought is not an unreasonable seizure of either the dwelling or its contents. The U.S. Supreme Court said:

> [T]he home is sacred in Fourth Amendment terms not primarily because of the occupant's *privacy* interests in the activities that take place within . . . [A] seizure affects only possessory interests, not privacy interests. Therefore, the heightened protection we accord privacy interests is simply not implicated where a *seizure* of premises, not a search, is at issue. Segura v. United States, 468 U.S. 796, 810, 104 S.Ct. 3380, 3389, 82 L.Ed.2d 599, 612 (1984).

Furthermore, the *Segura* case held that insofar as the *seizure* of the premises is concerned, it made no difference whether the premises were secured by stationing officers within the premises or by establishing a perimeter stakeout after a security check of the premises revealed that no one was inside. Under either method, officers control the premises pending arrival of the warrant. Both an internal securing and a perimeter stakeout interfere to the same extent with the possessory interests of the owners.

Anticipatory Search Warrants

An *anticipatory* search warrant, also called a *prospective* search warrant, is a warrant to search a particular place for a particular seizable item that has not yet arrived at the place where the search is to be executed. In recent years, law enforcement officers have applied for anticipatory search warrants in increasing numbers, especially in cases involving contraband in the mails and in cases involving informants or undercover officers. In People v. Glen, 331 N.Y.S.2d 656, 282 N.E.2d 614 (N.Y. 1972), law enforcement officers applied for a warrant to search a package allegedly containing narcotics. The affidavit stated that the package was consigned to the defendant, a known drug user, and that it was due to arrive at a Greyhound Bus Depot. The affidavit added that the defendant had called for the package earlier that morning, but the package had not yet arrived. The information in the affidavit was based on a tip from an informant whose reliability was adequately demonstrated. The warrant was issued, and shortly thereafter the officers were advised by a Greyhound clerk that the package had arrived. When the package went uncalled for that day, the officers removed it and examined it, finding marijuana. They returned the package to the depot the next morning. Later that day the defendant accepted delivery of the package and was arrested while leaving the depot.

The defendant contended on appeal that the warrant was invalid because no crime had been committed before its issuance and because there was no present and continuing possession of the contraband at the time of issuance. The court said:

> The ultimate answer to the problem is that as long as the evidence creates substantial probability that the seizable property will be on the premises when searched, the warrant should be sustained. To be sure, where there is no present possession the suppporting evidence for the prospective warrant must be strong that the particular possession of particular property will occur and that the elements to bring about that possession are in process and will result in the possession at the time and place specified. Otherwise, the hated general writs of assistance of pre-Revolutionary times would be revived, in effect, despite the constitutional limitations. Moreover, the issuing Judge should be satisfied that there is no likelihood that the warrant will be executed prematurely. 30 N.Y.2d at 259, 331 N.Y.S.2d at 661, 282 N.E.2d at 617.

Law enforcement officers applying for anticipatory search warrants must describe how the elements to bring about the possession or presence of particular property at a particular time and place are in process. A search warrant was held invalid in State v. Vitale, 530 P.2d 394 (Ariz. App. 1975), because of failure to satisfy that requirement. In that case, a warrant to search the defendant's pawn shop was issued on the basis that a reliable informant had agreed to sell a stolen television set to the defendant at the pawn shop. The police had the television in their possession at the time they applied for the warrant. After the sale, the warrant was executed and the television was seized.

The court held that there was no probable cause that a crime had been committed at the time the warrant was issued.

> The informant had not yet approached appellant regarding the television set at the time the . . . search warrant was issued; also there had not been any recent dealings between the informant and appellant. . . .
>
> In the instant case, no crime was in progress and it was a matter of speculation whether one would be committed in the future. The course of events strongly suggests that the duty to determine probable cause was improperly shifted from the magistrate to the police. 530 P.2d at 397–98.

If there had been some deal or arrangement between the informant and the defendant before the police applied for the warrant, the court might have found the warrant valid on the ground that a crime was in progress or at least was very likely to occur.

To ensure that a magistrate is provided with sufficient information to justify the issuance of an anticipatory search warrant, law enforcement officers should present strong evidence in an affidavit that the continuation of a process *already initiated* will result in seizable items arriving at a particular place at a particular time. To guard against premature execution of the warrant, the affidavit should carefully specify the time when the item to be seized will arrive at the place where the search is to occur and the time thereafter when the execution of the warrant is planned. This information will help satisfy the magistrate that the warrant will not be executed prematurely.

Redaction of Search Warrants

Search warrants may contain some clauses that are constitutionally sufficient and some that are not. Should courts suppress all evidence under these warrants or only the evidence seized under the constitutionally insufficient clauses? To avoid the severe remedy of total suppression of all evidence under these warrants, many courts have adopted the theory of *redaction,* also called *partial suppression* and *severability.* Redaction involves invalidating clauses in a warrant that are constitutionally insufficient for lack of probable cause or particularity while preserving clauses that satisfy the Fourth Amendment.

Not all courts have adopted the concept of redaction. Those that have point out that redaction is not inconsistent with the deterrent effect of the exclusionary rule. Illegally seized evidence is still suppressed, thereby discouraging law enforcement officials from attempting to evade Fourth Amendment requirements and preventing the government from benefiting from its own wrongdoing. Yet redaction mitigates the heavy social costs of unnecessarily excluding legally seized evidence. As a further constitutional safeguard, courts have been careful not to use redaction when "the warrant, when read with the affidavit, is essentially general in character but as to some tangential items meets the requirement of particularity." United States v. Cook, 657 F.2d 730, 735 n. 6 (5th Cir. 1981).

The Third Circuit Court of Appeals found that redaction is consistent with all five purposes of the warrant requirement:

> First, with respect to the search and seizure conducted pursuant to the valid portion of the redacted warrant, the intrusion into personal privacy has been justified by probable cause to believe that the search and seizure will serve society's need for law enforcement. Second, because it is a duly issued warrant that is being redacted, the objective of interposing a magistrate between law enforcement officials and the citizen has been attained. Third, even though it may not be coterminous with the underlying probable cause showing, the scope of a search pursuant to a particularized, overbroad warrant is nevertheless limited by the terms of its authorization. In the case of a warrant containing some invalid general clauses, redaction neither exacerbates nor ratifies the unwarranted intrusions conducted pursuant to the general clauses, but merely preserves the evidence seized pursuant to those clauses particularly describing items to be seized. Fourth, as to the valid portions of the warrant salvaged by redaction, the individual whose property is to be searched has received notification of the lawful authority of the executing officer, his need to search, and the limits of his power to search. Fifth, redaction does not affect the generation of a record susceptible to subsequent judicial review. United States v. Christine, 687 F.2d 749, 758 (3d Cir. 1982).

CONTENTS OF THE WARRANT

Although search warrants differ from state to state, most search warrants contain the following information.

1. The caption of the court or division of the court from which the warrant issues

2. A particular description of the place or person to be searched

3. A particular description of the property to be seized

4. The names of persons whose affidavits have been taken in support of the warrant

5. A statement of grounds for issuance of the warrant

6. The name of the officer or names of the officers to whom the warrant is directed together with a command to search the person or place named for the property specified

7. A specification of the time during the day when the search may be conducted

8. The name of the judicial officer to whom the warrant is to be returned

9. The date of issuance

10. The signature of the issuing magistrate together with a statement of the magistrate's official title

A typical search warrant form appears on page 125.

EXECUTION OF THE WARRANT

The execution of a search warrant is essentially the carrying out of the command or commands appearing on the face of the warrant itself. The U.S. Supreme Court stated that "the Fourth Amendment confines an officer executing a search warrant strictly within the bounds set by the warrant. . . ." Bivens v. Six Unknown Named Agents, 403 U.S. 388, 394 n. 7, 91 S.Ct. 1999, 2004 n. 7, 29 L.Ed.2d 619, 625 n. 7 (1971). Officers can determine many of their duties from simply reading the warrant; however, several aspects of the execution of search warrants need further explanation.

Who May Execute

A search warrant is directed to a particular officer or class of officers. Only the named officer or a member of the named class of officers may execute the warrant. If a warrant is directed to a particular officer such as a sheriff, a deputy may execute the warrant and the sheriff need not be present. Private persons may be enlisted to help in the execution of a warrant, but an officer to whom the warrant is directed must be personally present at the search scene.

Time Considerations

Three different aspects of time affect a law enforcement officer in the execution of a search warrant. First is the allowable delay between the warrant's issuance and its execution. In states with no time limit fixed by statute, court rule, or judicial decision, a warrant must be executed within a reasonable time after issuance. Reasonableness depends on the facts and circumstances of each case.

The chief concern of the courts is that probable cause does not become stale before execution of the warrant. Some states require that a search warrant be executed and returned within ten days after its date of issuance. Some of these states *also* require that the warrant be executed "forthwith." To resolve this apparent ambiguity, courts require that the warrant be executed within a reasonable time after issuance, so long as it is executed within the statutory period. United States v. Harper, 450 F.2d 1032 (5th Cir. 1971). *Therefore, even though an officer executed the warrant within the statutory ten (10) day period, the search could still be held unlawful if there were unnecessary delay resulting in legal prejudice to the defendant.*

Unnecessary delay is determined from the facts and circumstances of each case. In a case interpreting a statute with both a "ten day" provision and a "forthwith" provision, a warrant for the seizure of equipment used to manufacture LSD was executed six days after its issuance. The court held that the execution was timely, as the premises were under daily surveillance, and no activity was noted until after the first five days. The court said:

> While it is desirable that police be given reasonable latitude to determine when a warrant should be executed, it is also necessary that search warrants be executed with some promptness in order to lessen the possibility that the facts upon which probable cause was initially based do not become dissipated.
>
> We adopt the reasoning of the Second Circuit in *Dunnings* to the effect that "forthwith" means any time within 10 days after the warrant is issued, provided that the probable cause recited in the affidavit continues until the time of execution, giving consideration to the intervening knowledge of the officers and the passage of time. United States v. Nepstead, 424 F.2d 269, 271 (9th Cir. 1970).

There are many justifications for delaying the execution of a search warrant. For example, weather conditions, long travel distances, traffic problems, and similar obstacles may prevent the prompt execution of the warrant. Delays may be necessary to gather sufficient human resources for the search, to protect the safety of the searching officers, to prevent the destruction of evidence, and to prevent the flight of a suspect. When the warrant is for the search of both a person and premises, the search may be delayed until the person is present on the premises. People v. Stansberry, 268 N.E.2d 431 (Ill. 1971).

Another aspect of time affecting the execution of a search warrant is the time of day during which the warrant may be executed. In general, search warrants should be executed in the daytime. Courts have always frowned upon nighttime searches. The U.S. Supreme Court said that "it is difficult to imagine a more severe invasion of privacy than the nighttime intrusion into a private home. . . ." Jones v. United States, 357 U.S. 493, 498, 78 S.Ct. 1253, 1257, 2 L.Ed.2d 1514, 1519 (1958). Furthermore, nighttime searches are more likely to be met with armed resistance. State v. Brock, 633 P.2d 805 (Or. App. 1981). As a result, to obtain a warrant authorizing a nighttime search, some states require

---

AO 93
(Rev. 8/82)

SEARCH WARRANT ON WRITTEN AFFIDAVIT

𝔘𝔫𝔦𝔱𝔢𝔡 𝔖𝔱𝔞𝔱𝔢𝔰 𝔇𝔦𝔰𝔱𝔯𝔦𝔠𝔱 𝔠𝔬𝔲𝔯𝔱	DISTRICT	
UNITED STATES OF AMERICA v.	DOCKET NO.	MAGISTRATE'S CASE NO.
	TO:	

Affidavit(s) having been made before me by the below-named affiant that he/she has reason to believe that (on the person of) (on the premises known as) _____

_____

in the _____ District of _____ there is now being concealed certain property, namely

and as I am satisfied that there is probable cause to believe that the property so described is being concealed on the person or premises above-described and the grounds for application for issuance of the search warrant exist as stated in the supporting affidavit(s),

YOU ARE HEREBY COMMANDED to search on or before _____
(not to exceed 10 days) the person or place named above for the property specified, serving this warrant and making the search (in the daytime — 6:00 A.M. to 10:00 P.M.) (at any time in the day or night)* and if the property be found there to seize it, leaving a copy of this warrant and receipt for the property taken, and prepare a written inventory of the property seized and promptly return this warrant to _____
_____ as required by law.   *U.S. Judge or Magistrate*

NAME OF AFFIANT	SIGNATURE OF JUDGE ** OR US MAGISTRATE	DATE/TIME ISSUED

*If a search is to be authorized "at any time in the day or night" pursuant to Federal Rules of Criminal Procedure Rule 41(c), show reasonable cause therefor.
**United States Judge or Judge of a State Court of Record.

---

the affidavit to set forth specific facts showing a necessity for a nighttime search. Justification for a nighttime search has been found where a nighttime delivery of contraband was expected, where the property to be seized was likely to be removed promptly, and where part of a criminal transaction was to take place at night. United States v. Curry, 530 F.2d 636 (5th Cir. 1976).

Courts differ in their interpretations of when daytime and nighttime begin and end. A rule of thumb is that it is daytime when there is sufficient natural light to recognize a person's features. Otherwise, it is nighttime. Even if a night-time search is not authorized, the execution of a search warrant that was begun in the daytime may be continued into the nighttime if it is a reasonable continuation of the daytime search. An officer is not required to cut short the reasonable execution of a daytime search warrant just because it becomes dark outside. United States v. Joseph, 278 F.2d 504 (3d Cir. 1960).

The third aspect of time, as it relates to the execution of a search warrant, is the amount of time allowed for the law enforcement officer to perform the search *once it is initiated*. The general rule was stated by the New Hampshire Supreme Court: "The police, in executing a search warrant for a dwelling, may remain on the premises only so long as it is reasonably necessary to conduct the search." State v. Chaisson, 486 A.2d 297, 303 (N.H. 1984). Furthermore, as stated by the Tenth Circuit Court of Appeals, "once a search warrant has been fully executed and the fruits of the search secured, the authority under the warrant expires and further governmental intrusion must cease." United States v. Gagnon, 635 F.2d 766, 769 (10th Cir. 1980). Therefore, after all the objects described in a warrant have been found, the warrant provides no authorization to search further. If, however, the executing officers have found some but not necessarily all of the described items, the search may lawfully continue.

Gaining Entry

State statutes require law enforcement officers to knock and announce their authority and purpose before entering premises to execute a search warrant. Usually an announcement of identity as a law enforcement officer together with a statement that the officer has a search warrant is sufficient. A person may not refuse entry to an officer executing a warrant, but must submit voluntarily. State v. Valentine, 504 P.2d 84 (Or. 1972). If entry is refused, the officer may enter using force, including the breaking open of doors and windows. The occupant must be given a brief opportunity to respond before entry is forced. But failure to respond or other behavior inconsistent with voluntary compliance is equivalent to refusal. Unoccupied premises may be entered, forcefully if reasonably necessary, as if officers had been refused entry. The sound of footsteps, whispers, or flushing toilets, indicating possible escape or destruction of evidence, may create exigent circumstances justifying an immediate forcible entry. United States v. Mitchell, 783 F.2d 971 (10th Cir. 1986).

The purposes of the so-called knock and announce requirements are as follows:

1. To prevent violence to the police or other persons on the premises

2. To protect the privacy of the occupants of the premises from unexpected intrusions

3. To prevent property damage

4. To provide the occupant an opportunity to examine the warrant and point out a possible mistaken address or other errors

Several exceptions to the knock and announce requirement are recognized. First, officers need not knock and announce when they have reasonable grounds to believe that to do so would endanger themselves or others. In

United States v. Guyon, 717 F.2d 1536 (6th Cir. 1983), the court found exigent circumstances justifying an unannounced forcible entry where the defendant was known to be a fugitive from justice, knew the FBI was looking for him, and was armed and dangerous.

Officers may enter without knocking and announcing when they have reasonable grounds to believe that evidence will be destroyed or concealed or that an occupant will attempt to escape. Reasonable grounds must be based on specific facts and not mere speculation. Failure to comply with the knock and announce requirement will not be justified simply because a case involves narcotics or gambling. State v. Rauch, 586 P.2d 671 (Idaho 1978). In the *Rauch* case, which involved seizure of narcotics, the court found insufficient grounds for noncompliance, where the officer merely stated that he feared that people in the house were aware of the presence of officers outside. The officer gave no factual basis for his fear or any other reason to justify an unannounced entry.

> Under the Fourth Amendment, a specific showing must always be made to justify any kind of police action tending to disturb the security of the people in their homes. Unannounced forcible entry is in itself a serious disturbance of that security and cannot be justified on a blanket basis. Otherwise, the constitutional test of reasonableness would turn only on practical expediency, and the amendment's primary safeguard—the requirement of particularity—would be lost. Just as the police must have sufficiently particular reason to enter at all, so must they have some particular reason to enter in the manner chosen. People v. Gastelo, 67 Cal.2d 586, 588–89, 63 Cal.Rptr. 10, 12, 432 P.2d 706, 708 (Cal. 1967).

Finally, knocking and announcing "is excused when the officers are justifiably and virtually certain that the occupants already know their purpose." United States v. Eddy, 660 F.2d 381 (8th Cir. 1981). In United States ex rel. Dyton v. Ellingsworth, 306 F. Supp. 231 (D.Del. 1969), officers with a search warrant knocked on the defendant's apartment door and the door swung open partially so that the officer and occupants were clearly visible to each other. One of the officers was known to the occupants as a narcotics officer. The officers made no announcement of purpose, but waited about twenty seconds and then entered the apartment to conduct the search. The court held that the unannounced entry was reasonable because the defendant was reasonably certain of the police purpose before the officers entered his apartment. A formal announcement of authority and purpose would have been a useless gesture. However, since compliance with the knock and announce requirement is simple and effortless, it is seldom wise for an officer to assume a defendant's knowledge and risk the loss of evidence by noncompliance. A defendant may know the officer's authority and purpose, but may not know of the existence of a warrant.

A separate issue is whether law enforcement officers executing a search warrant may lawfully gain access to the area to be searched by entering areas not particularly described in the warrant. In general, courts have approved any means of gaining entry that was both reasonable and necessary. In Dalia v. United States, the U.S. Supreme Court approved a covert entry into a dwelling by officers attempting to install electronic surveillance equipment pursuant to a warrant. The Court said that it is generally left to the discretion of the executing officers to determine the details of conducting the search under the warrant. The Court added:

> Often in executing a warrant the police may find it necessary to interfere with privacy rights not explicitly considered by the judge who issued the warrant. For example, police executing an arrest warrant commonly find it necessary to enter the suspect's home in order to take him into custody, and they thereby impinge on both privacy and freedom of movement.... Similarly, officers executing search warrants on occasion must damage property in order to perform their duty. 441 U.S. 238, 257–58, 99 S.Ct. 1682, 1693–94, 60 L.Ed.2d 177, 193 (1979).

Therefore, officers executing a search warrant may use whatever method is necessary to gain access to premises to be searched, even to the extent of damaging property, if no reasonable alternative is available.

Search and Seizure of Third Persons and Their Property

When a search warrant is issued for the search of a named person or a named person *and* premises, officers executing the warrant clearly can detain and search the person named. However, may a person on the premises but not named in the warrant be detained or searched? *The general rule is that the search warrant for premises gives a law enforcement officer no authority to search a person not named in the warrant who merely happens to be on the premises.* In Ybarra v. Illinois, 444 U.S. 85, 100 S.Ct. 338, 62 L.Ed.2d 238 (1979), the defendant was a mere patron in a bar and the police had a warrant to search the bar and the bartender. The U.S. Supreme Court held that the search of the defendant was illegal because the police did not have probable cause particularized with respect to the defendant. The Court said that a warrant to search a place cannot normally be construed to authorize a search of each person in that place. Therefore, if an officer wishes to search a place and also wishes to search specific persons expected to be at that place, the officer should obtain a search warrant to search the place and each specific person. In order to obtain such a warrant, the officer must establish in the affidavit probable cause to search the place and each specific individual.

Detention of persons present on premises to be searched under a warrant may be allowed in certain circumstances, however. In Michigan v. Summers, 452 U.S. 692, 101 S.Ct. 2587, 69 L.Ed.2d 340 (1981), the U.S. Supreme Court held that officers executing a valid search warrant for contraband may detain the occupants of the premises while the search is being conducted. The Court said that "[i]f the evidence that a citizen's residence is harboring contraband is sufficient to persuade a judicial officer that an invasion of the citizen's privacy is justified, it is constitutionally reasonable to require that citizen to remain while officers of the law execute a valid warrant to search his home." 452 U.S. at 704–5, 101 S.Ct. at 2595, 69 L.Ed.2d at 351. In explaining the justification for the detention, the Court emphasized the limited additional intrusion represented by the detention once a search of the home had been authorized by a warrant. The Court also pointed out that when a search warrant for contraband is involved, law enforcement officers have a legitimate interest in preventing flight if incriminating evidence is found and in minimizing the risk of harm to themselves. The execution of a search warrant for contraband, especially narcotics, "is the kind of transaction that may give rise to sudden violence or frantic efforts to conceal or destroy evidence." 452 U.S. at 702, 101 S.Ct. at 2549, 69 L.Ed.2d at 349–50.

An officer also has authority to conduct a limited pat-down search or frisk for weapons of any person at the search scene who the officer reasonably believes is dangerous. The officer must be able to justify the frisk with specific facts and circumstances to support the belief that a particular person was dangerous. A mere suspicion or hunch that a person was dangerous will not justify a protective frisk. (See Chapter 12 for details on conducting protective searches.)

If an officer at a search scene obtains information constituting probable cause to make a felony arrest, or if a crime is being committed in the officer's presence, the officer may arrest the offender and search him or her incident to the arrest. (See Chapter 7 for details on search incident to arrest.)

Similar rules apply to the search and seizure of the *property* of third persons on the premises described in a warrant. For purposes of this discussion, a third person is a person who is not the target of the warrant and is not a resident of the target premises. In general, when a law enforcement officer executing a search warrant knows or reasonably should know that personal property located within the described premises belongs to a third person, the officer may not search or seize the property under authority of the warrant. In State v. Lambert, 710 P.2d 693 (Kan. 1985), a police officer executing a warrant for an apartment and its male occupant discovered three women in the kitchen of the apartment. The officers searched a purse lying on the kitchen table and found drugs. The court invalidated the search, finding that the officer had no reason to believe that the purse either belonged to the occupant of the premises or was part of the premises described in the search warrant. However, where officers neither know nor have reason to believe that property belongs to a third person, a search or seizure of the property will be upheld. In Carman v. State, 602 P.2d 1255 (Alaska 1979), the court upheld the search of a purse because the court found that the police did not know whether the purse belonged to a permanent resident of the apartment or a visitor.

Intensity of the Search

A search warrant authorizing the search of particularly described premises will justify a search of the described land, all of the buildings on the land, and other things attached to or annexed to the land. United States v. Meyer, 417 F.2d 1020 (8th Cir. 1969). Courts have generally also allowed a search of any vehicles owned or controlled by the owner of the premises and found on the premises. United States v. Percival, 756 F.2d 600 (7th Cir. 1985). Searches of areas neighboring or adjacent to the particularly described premises are usually not allowed. However, if neighboring or adjacent areas are only nominally separate and are actually used as a single living or commercial area, courts may allow the search of the entire area despite a limited warrant description. In United States v. Principe, 499 F.2d 1135 (1st Cir. 1974), a search of a cabinet in a hallway several feet away from the apartment described in the search warrant was justified where the owner testified that the cabinet "went with the apartment."

Officers executing a search warrant may look only where the items described in the warrant might be concealed. The U.S. Supreme Court stated the general rule: "A lawful search of fixed premises generally extends to the entire area in which the object of the search may be found and is not limited by the possibility that separate acts of entry or opening may be required to complete the search." United States v. Ross, 456 U.S. 798, 820–21, 102 S.Ct. 2157, 2170–71, 72 L.Ed.2d 572, 591 (1982). The court provided the following useful examples of the application of the rule:

> [A] warrant that authorizes an officer to search a home for illegal weapons also provides authority to open closets, chests, drawers, and containers in which the weapon might be found. A warrant to open a footlocker to search for marijuana would also authorize the opening of packages found inside. A warrant to search a vehicle would support a search of every part of the vehicle that might contain the object of the search. When a legitimate search is under way, and when its purpose and its limits have been precisely defined, nice distinctions between closets, drawers, and containers, in the case of a home, or between glove compartments, upholstered seats, trunks and wrapped packages, in the case of a vehicle, must give way to the interest in the prompt and efficient completion of the task at hand. 456 U.S. at 821.

An inaccurate description of the premises to be searched may cause officers to exceed the scope of a warrant, especially with respect to multiple-occupancy dwellings In Maryland v. Garrison, 480 U.S. 79, 107 S.Ct. 1013, 94 L.Ed.2d 72 (1987), officers obtained and executed a warrant to search the person of Lawrence McWebb and "the premises known as 2036 Park Avenue third floor apartment." The officers reasonably believed, on the basis of the information available, that there was only one apartment on the third floor. In fact, the third floor was divided into two apartments, one occupied by McWebb and one by the defendant. Before the officers discovered that they were in the wrong person's apartment, they had discovered contraband which led to the defendant's conviction.

The Court concluded that the officers had made a reasonable effort to ascertain and identify the place intended to be searched and that their failure to realize the overbreadth of the warrant was objectively understandable and reasonable. Nevertheless, the Court said:

> If the officers had known, or should have known, that the third floor contained two apartments before they entered the living quarters on the third floor, and thus had been aware of the error in the warrant, they would have been obligated to limit their search to McWebb's apartment. Moreover . . . they were required to discontinue the search of respondent's apartment as soon as they discovered that there were two separate units on the third floor and therefore were put on notice of the risk that they might be in a unit erroneously included within the terms of the warrant. 480 U.S. at 86–87, 107 S.Ct. at 1018, 94 L.Ed.2d at 82.

Therefore, although some latitude is allowed for honest mistakes in executing search warrants, officers may not rely blindly on the descriptions in a warrant, but must make a reasonable effort to determine that the described place to be searched is the place *intended* to be searched.

Officers executing a search warrant must use only reasonable force in conducting the search. An otherwise reasonable search may become unreasonable owing to the manner in which it is conducted. A search warrant gives officers authority to break into a house or other objects of search and to damage property in order to perform their duty. In a case involving a search of a vehicle for contraband, the U.S. Supreme Court said:

> An individual undoubtedly has a significant interest that the upholstery of his automobile will not be ripped or a hidden compartment within it opened. These interests must yield to the authority of a search, however.... United States v. Ross, 456 U.S. 798, 823, 102 S.Ct. 2157, 2172, 72 L.Ed.2d 572, 593 (1982).

Nevertheless, officers must exercise great care to avoid unnecessary damage to premises or objects. They must conduct a search in a manner designed to do the least damage possible, while still making a thorough examination of the premises. They should carefully replace objects that were necessarily moved or rearranged during the search. Generally, "[i]n executing a search warrant, to the extent possible, due respect should be given to the property of the occupants of the premises searched." State v. Sierra, 338 So.2d 609, 616 (La. 1976).

Finally, common decency mandates that officers executing a search warrant avoid any unnecessary injury to the feelings of persons present at the premises searched.

Seizure of Items Not Named in the Warrant

In Cady v. Dombrowksi, 413 U.S. 433, 93 S.Ct. 2523, 37 L.Ed.2d 706 (1973), police were investigating a possible homicide. The defendant informed them that he believed there was a body lying near his brother's farm. The police found the body and the defendant's car at the farm. Looking in through the window of the car, the police observed a pillowcase, backseat, and briefcase that were covered with blood, Police then obtained a warrant to search the car. While executing the warrant, police discovered, in "plain view" in the car, a blood-covered sock and floormat, which they seized. The defendant claimed that the sock and the floormat taken from his car were illegally seized since they were not specifically listed in the affidavit for the search warrant.

The Court held that the seizure of the items was constitutional. Since the warrant was validly issued, and the car was the item designated to be searched, the police were authorized to search the car. Although the sock and floormat were not listed in the warrant, the officers discovered these items in plain view in the car while executing the warrant and therefore could constitutionally seize them without a warrant.

The U.S. Supreme Court did not elaborate on this decision. However, decisions of many courts since the *Cady* decision have established the rule that *a law enforcement officer lawfully executing a valid search warrant may seize items not particularly described in the warrant that are found at the searched premises, if the seizure satisfies all the requirements of the plain view doctrine.* (See Chapter 9 for a complete discussion of the plain view doctrine.)

Duties After Search Is Completed

Proper execution of a search warrant entails several duties after the actual search is completed. Most states require that the officer conducting the search inventory all the property seized and leave a copy of the warrant and inventory with the occupants, or on the premises if no occupant is present. The warrant, together with a copy of the inventory, must be returned to the magistrate designated in the warrant. A typical form for the return and inventory (which is usually on the back of the search warrant) appears on page 133.

Courts unanimously hold that these postsearch duties are ministerial acts and that failure to perform them will not result in suppression unless the defendant demonstrates legal prejudice or shows that the failure was intentional or in bad faith. United States v. Marx, 635 F.2d 436 (5th Cir. 1981).

ADMINISTRATIVE SEARCH WARRANTS

An administrative search is a routine inspection of a home or business to determine compliance with various statutes and regulations. An administrative search seeks to enforce fire, health, and housing codes, licensing provisions, and the like. It differs from a criminal search in that a criminal search is directed toward gathering evidence in order to convict a person of a crime. An administrative search ordinarily does not result in a criminal prosecution.

Before 1967, courts consistently held that administrative searches were not subject to the restrictions of the the Fourth Amendment and that a search warrant was not needed to inspect residential or commercial premises for violations of regulatory and licensing provisions. In 1967, in Camara v. Municipal Court, 387 U.S. 523, 87 S.Ct. 1727, 18 L.Ed.2d 930, and See v. City of Seattle, 387 U.S. 541, 87 S.Ct. 1737, 18 L.Ed.2d 943, the U.S. Supreme Court reversed earlier decisions and held that administrative inspections were subject to the warrant requirement of the Fourth Amendment. The basis for both the *Camara* and *See* decisions was the Court's belief that a person's right of privacy should not be determined by the nature of the search. In *Camara*, the Court said, "It is surely anomalous to say that the individual and his private property are fully protected by the Fourth Amendment only when the individual is suspected of criminal behavior." 387 U.S. at 530, 87 S.Ct. at 1732, 18 L.Ed.2d at 936. Nevertheless, the Court held that, because administrative searches differ in nature and purpose from criminal searches, the probable cause standard for administrative searches differs in nature and is less stringent than the standard for criminal searches.

> The warrant procedure is designed to guarantee that a decision to search private property is justified by a reasonable governmental interest. But reasonableness is still the ultimate standard. If a valid public interest justifies the intrusion contemplated, then there is probable cause to issue a suitably restricted search warrant. 387 U.S. at 539, 87 S.Ct. at 1736, 18 L.Ed.2d at 941.

Despite the less stringent probable cause standard, the U.S. Supreme Court and other courts have carved out various exceptions to the warrant requirement for administrative searches. Exceptions based on emergency, consent, plain view, and open fields are similar to exceptions to the warrant require-

<table>
<tr><td colspan="3" align="center">**RETURN**</td></tr>
</table>

DATE WARRANT RECEIVED	DATE AND TIME WARRANT EXECUTED	COPY OF WARRANT AND RECEIPT FOR ITEMS LEFT WITH

INVENTORY MADE IN THE PRESENCE OF

INVENTORY OF PROPERTY TAKEN PURSUANT TO THE WARRANT

CERTIFICATION

I swear that this inventory is a true and detailed account of all the property taken by me on the warrant.

_____

Subscribed, sworn to, and returned before me this date.

_____   _____
                U.S. Judge or Magistrate   *Date*

ment for criminal searches discussed in Part Three of this book, but the standards are generally less stringent than those required for criminal searches. Another exception, allowing warrantless inspection of certain *licensed and closely regulated enterprises*, has been recognized by the U.S. Supreme Court. In United States v. Biswell, 406 U.S. 311, 92 S.Ct. 1593, 32 L.Ed.2d 87 (1972), the Court upheld a warrantless search of a storeroom of a gun dealer licensed under the Gun Control Act of 1968. The Court said:

> [I]f inspection is to be effective and serve as a credible deterrent, unan-
> nounced, even frequent, inspections are essential. In this context, the prereq-
> uisite of a warrant could easily frustrate inspections; and if the necessary flexi-
> bility as to time, scope and frequency is to be preserved, the protections
> afforded by a warrant would be negligible.
>
> It is also plain that inspections for compliance with the Gun Control Act pose
> only limited threats to the dealer's justifiable expectations of privacy. When a
> dealer chooses to engage in this pervasively regulated business and to accept a
> federal license, he does so with the knowledge that his business records, fire-
> arms, and ammunition will be subject to effective inspection. 406 U.S. at 316,
> 92 S.Ct. at 1596, 32 L.Ed.2d at 92–93.

The U.S. Supreme Court held that inspections of licensed and closely regulated enterprises are reasonable only if they satisfy three criteria:

1. A "substantial" government interest must support the regulatory scheme
under which the inspection is made;

2. the warrantless inspections must be necessary to further the regulatory
scheme; and

3. the regulatory statute must provide a constitutionally adequate substitute
for a warrant by advising the owner of commercial premises that the search is
being made pursuant to the law and has a properly defined scope and by limiting the discretion of the inspecting officers. New York v. Burger, 482 U.S. ____,
107 S.Ct. 2636, 96 L.Ed.2d 601 (1987).

In the *Burger* case, the Court found that a New York statute allowing warrantless inspection of automobile junkyards satisfied these criteria. The state had a
substantial interest in regulating the automobile junkyard industry because
motor vehicle theft had increased in the state and because the problem of theft
was associated with this industry. Warrantless inspections were necessary because frequent and unannounced inspections provide an element of surprise
crucial to regulating the market in stolen cars and parts. Finally, the statute
gave adequate notice to automobile junkyard operators and authorized inspections only during business hours and within a narrowly defined scope.

In another instance of weakened privacy interests and heightened governmental interests, the U.S. Supreme Court created an exception to the warrant
requirement for searches of students conducted by school officials and again
applied a standard of reasonableness stopping short of probable cause. In New
Jersey v. T.L.O., 469 U.S. 325, 105 S.Ct. 733, 83 L.Ed.2d 720 (1985), the Court
held that school officials carrying out searches and other functions pursuant to
disciplinary policies act as representatives of the state and not merely as surro-
gates for parents, and that they are therefore subject to the Fourth Amendment.
However, in attempting to balance the legitimate privacy rights of students
against the substantial interests of teachers and administrators in maintaining
discipline in the classroom and on school grounds, the Court held that school
officials need not obtain a warrant before searching students under their authority. The warrant requirement would unduly interfere with the maintenance of the swift and informal disciplinary procedures needed in the schools.
Furthermore, rather than require strict adherence to the requirement that a
search be based on probable cause to believe that the subject of the search has

violated or is violating the law, "the legality of a search of a student should depend simply on the reasonableness, under all the circumstances, of the search." 469 U.S. at 341, 105 S.Ct. at 742, 83 L.Ed.2d at 734.

Determining the reasonableness of any search involves an inquiry into (1) whether the action was justified at its inception, and (2) whether the search as actually conducted was reasonably related in scope to the circumstances that justified the interference in the first place. The Court said:

> Under ordinary circumstances, a search of a student by a teacher or other school official will be "justified at its inception" when there are reasonable grounds for suspecting that the search will turn up evidence that the student has violated or is violating either the law or the rules of the school. Such a search will be permissible in its scope when the measures adopted are reasonably related to the objectives of the search and not excessively intrusive in light of the age and sex of the student and the nature of the infraction. 469 U.S. at 341–42, 105 S.Ct. at 744, 83 L.Ed.2d at 734–35.

Administrative searches are not discussed in further detail because they are seldom conducted for purposes of the criminal law. However, the line between an administrative and a criminal search can sometimes become blurred. When an administrative search begins to take on the characteristics of a criminal search, the stricter standards applicable to criminal searches come into play. If these stricter standards are not satisfied, any evidence obtained will be inadmissible in a criminal prosecution.

The line between administrative and criminal searches often becomes blurred in fire investigation cases, because several different purposes may be served by a fire investigation and fire scenes present varying degrees of emergency. In addition, reasonable privacy expectations may remain in fire-damaged premises, thereby affecting the necessity to obtain a warrant.

> Privacy expectations will vary with the type of property, the amount of fire damage, the prior and continued use of the premises, and in some cases the owner's efforts to secure it against intruders. Some fires may be so devastating that no reasonable privacy interests remain in the ash and ruins, regardless of the owner's subjective expectations. The test essentially is an objective one: whether "the expectation [is] one that society is prepared to recognize as 'reasonable.'" . . . If reasonable privacy interests remain in the fire-damaged property, the warrant requirement applies, and any official entry must be made pursuant to a warrant in the absence of consent or exigent circumstances. Michigan v. Clifford, 464 U.S. 287, 292–93, 104 S.Ct. 641, 646, 78 L.Ed.2d 477, 483 (1984).

If a warrant is necessary, the purpose of the search determines the type of warrant required. If the primary purpose is to determine the cause and origin of a recent fire, only an administrative warrant is needed. To obtain an administrative warrant, fire officials need show only that "a fire of undetermined origin has occurred on the premises, that the scope of the proposed search is reasonable and will not intrude unnecessarily on the fire victim's privacy, and that the search will be executed at a reasonable and convenient time." Michigan v. Clifford, 464 U.S. 287, 294, 104 S.Ct. 641, 647, 78 L.Ed.2d 477, 484 (1984). If the primary purpose of the search is to gather evidence of criminal activity, a criminal search warrant may be obtained only on a showing of probable cause to believe that particularly described seizable property will be found in the place to be searched.

If evidence of criminal activity is discovered during the course of a valid administrative search, it may be seized under the plain view doctrine and used to establish probable cause to obtain a criminal search warrant. Fire officials may not, however, rely on this evidence to expand the scope of their administrative search without first satisfying an independent judicial officer that probable cause exists. The purpose of the search is important even if exigent circumstances exist.

> Circumstances that justify a warrantless search for the cause of a fire may not justify a search to gather evidence of criminal activity once that cause has been determined. If, for example, the administrative search is justified by the immediate need to ensure against rekindling, the scope of the search may be no broader than reasonably necessary to achieve its end. A search to gather evidence of criminal activity not in plain view must be made pursuant to a criminal warrant upon a traditional showing of probable cause. Michigan v. Clifford, 464 U.S. 287, 294–95, 104 S.Ct. 641, 647, 78 L.Ed.2d 477, 484–85 (1984).

An administrative search took on the characteristics of a criminal search in Michigan v. Tyler, 436 U.S. 499, 98 S.Ct. 1942, 56 L.Ed.2d 486 (1978), a case involving a late-night fire in a furniture store leased by the defendant. When the fire was reduced to smoldering embers, the fire chief, while investigating the cause of the fire, discovered two plastic containers of flammable liquid. The chief summoned a police detective to investigate possible arson. The detective took several pictures, but because visibility was hindered by darkness, steam, and smoke, the investigators departed the scene at 4:00 A.M. and returned shortly after daylight to continue the investigation. More evidence of arson was found and seized at that time. About a month later, a state police arson investigator made several visits to the fire scene and obtained evidence that was used at trial in convicting the defendant. At no time was any warrant or consent to search obtained.

The Court held that the investigative activity on the date of the fire was legal, but that the evidence-gathering activity a month after the fire was an illegal search and seizure.

> [W]e hold that an entry to fight a fire requires no warrant, and that once in the building, officials may remain there for a reasonable time to investigate the cause of the blaze. Thereafter, additional entries to investigate the cause of the fire must be made pursuant to the warrant procedures governing administrative searches. . . . Evidence of arson discovered in the course of such investigations is admissible at trial, but if the investigating officials find probable cause to believe that arson has occurred and require further access to gather evidence for a possible prosecution, they may obtain a warrant only upon a traditional showing of probable cause applicable to searches for evidence of crime. 436 U.S. at 511–12, 98 S.Ct. at 1951, 56 L.Ed.2d at 500.

Once a search is directed toward gathering evidence for a criminal prosecution, a criminal search warrant must be obtained. This requirement cannot be avoided by using other governmental officials to conduct searches under the guise of an administrative or regulatory inspection.

EFFECT OF ILLEGAL SEARCH AND SEIZURE

The most important effect of an illegal search or seizure is the exclusion of the evidence obtained from being used in court against the person whose rights were violated by the search. (The exclusionary rule is discussed in detail in Chapter 3.) Application of the exclusionary rule in a particular case will often result in a lost case for the prosecution and release of the person charged with crime.

Other possible effects of an illegal search and seizure are civil and criminal liability of the officer conducting the search and seizure. As with an illegal arrest, the consequences for the officer depend upon the circumstances of each case, including the officer's good faith, the degree of care used, the degree of force used, the seriousness of the violation, and the extent of injury or intrusion suffered by the defendant.

SUMMARY

The general rule is that all searches and seizures conducted without a warrant are unreasonable and in violation of the Fourth Amendment to the U.S. Constitution. Although there are many well-defined exceptions to this rule, searches made under the authority of a warrant are not only greatly preferred by the courts, but also give the law enforcement officer greater protection from liability.

A search warrant is a written order issued by a proper judicial authority (the magistrate) commanding a law enforcement officer to search for certain personal property and bring it before the judicial authority named in the warrant. An officer may obtain a search warrant by submitting to a magistrate a written application in the form of a sworn affidavit. The affidavit must state underlying facts and circumstances supporting probable cause to believe that particularly described items are located in a particularly described place or on a particularly described person. Only items connected with criminal activity, such as stolen property, contraband, and instrumentalities and evidence of crime, may be seized.

If a magistrate finds probable cause to search, he or she will issue a search warrant directing an officer or class of officers to execute the warrant. Officers must conduct the search within a reasonable time after the warrant's issuance and within any time period specified by state law or court rule. Before entering premises by force to execute the warrant, officers must knock and announce their authority and purpose, unless this notice will result in the loss or destruction of evidence, the escape of a suspect, or danger to an officer or others. Persons on the premises may not be searched, unless the search warrant authorizes the search of a particular person. Property of persons who are not the target of the warrant and not residents of the target premises may not be seized. If officers are executing a warrant to search for contraband, persons on the premises may be detained during the course of the search. Any person on the premises whom officers reasonably believe to be dangerous may be frisked for weapons.

A search under authority of a search warrant may extend to the entire premises described in the warrant, but only to those areas of the premises where the items to be seized might be concealed. The search must be conducted in a manner to avoid unnecessary damage to the premises or objects. Items not named in the warrant may be seized if all elements of the plain view doctrine are satisfied. After the search is completed, the officer must leave at the searched premises a copy of the warrant and a receipt for property taken. The officer must return the warrant along with a written inventory of property seized to the judicial officer designated in the warrant.

An administrative search is a routine inspection of a home or business to determine compliance with codes and licensing provisions dealing with fire safety, health, housing, and so on. Although administrative searches are not directed toward convicting a person of a crime, they are still subject to the warrant requirement of the Fourth Amendment. The probable cause standard for administrative searches is less stringent than the standard for criminal searches. If, however, an administrative search takes on the characteristics of a criminal search, the traditional probable cause standard applies.

An illegal search and seizure, whether caused by a failure to comply with warrant procedures or by a failure to satisfy one of the exceptions to the warrant requirement, will result in application of the exclusionary rule. The evidence seized during the search will be inadmissible in court, a situation often resulting in termination of the prosecution and release of the person charged. Furthermore, officers conducting an illegal search may be civilly or criminally liable for their actions.

REVIEW AND DISCUSSION QUESTIONS

1. Why is time a more important factor in determining probable cause to search than it is in determining probable cause to arrest?

2. Formulate a set of circumstances in which there is probable cause to search but not probable cause to arrest; in which there is probable cause to arrest but not probable cause to search; in which there is probable cause both to arrest and to search.

3. Name three kinds of property that are *unlikely* to remain in a particular place for longer than a week. Name three kinds of property that are *likely* to remain in a particular place for longer than a week.

4. Why should law enforcement officers executing a search warrant refrain from asking the person against whom the search is directed to assist them in any way?

5. Assume that you are a law enforcement officer attempting to obtain a search warrant for urban premises, rural premises, a multiple-unit dwelling, and a motor vehicle. Describe, as you would in the affidavit, one of each of these places that is familiar to you. (For example, describe for purposes of a search warrant application a friend's farm in the country.)

6. Discuss three ways in which a search warrant and an arrest warrant are affected by time differently.

7. Law enforcement officers have a search warrant to search a house for heroin and to search the person of the house owners' eighteen-year-old daughter. When the officers arrive to execute the warrant, the following persons are present at the house:
   a. The owners
   b. The eighteen-year-old daughter
   c. The daughter's fifteen-year-old brother, who appears extremely nervous
   d. The daughter's boyfriend, whom the officers recognize as a local gang member who is known to carry a knife
   e. An unidentified elderly couple
To what extent may the officers search or detain each person present?

8. A law enforcement officer has a search warrant to search the defendant's house for cameras stolen from a particular department store. May the officer:
   a. Look in desk drawers?
   b. Search the defendant's body?
   c. Seize a brown paper bag containing a white powder resembling heroin, found in a desk drawer?
   d. Search the defendant's garage?
   e. Look in the defendant's wife's jewelry box?
   f. Break open a locked wall safe?
   g. Seize a portable radio found on a table with a tag from the department store attached to it?

9. Is each of the following descriptions in a search warrant of items to be seized sufficiently particular?
   a. An unkown-make .38 caliber blue steel with wood grips, revolver. See United States v. Wolfenbarger, 696 F.2d 750 (10th Cir. 1982).
   b. Videotape and equipment used in a copyright infringement. See United States v. Smith, 686 F.2d 234 (5th Cir. 1982).
   c. All doctor's files concerning an accident patient. See United States v. Hershenow, 680 F.2d 847 (1st Cir. 1982).
   d. Plaques, mirrors, and other items. See United States v. Apker, 705 F.2d 293 (8th Cir. 1983).
   e. Items related to the smuggling, packing, distribution, and use of controlled substances. See United States v. Ladd, 704 F.2d 134 (4th Cir. 1983).
   f. Business papers that are evidence and instrumentalities of a violation of a general tax fraud statute. See United States v. Cardwell, 680 F.2d 75 (9th Cir. 1982).

10. Does a warrant to search a house authorize a search of a tent set up on the premises near the house? Does a warrant authorizing the seizure of stolen typewriters authorize the seizure of nonstolen typewriters commingled with them? Is the seizure of an entire book of accounts permissible when only two or three pages of the book are relevant to the specifications of the search warrant?

CHAPTER 6
Probable Cause

Probable cause is discussed to a limited extent in Chapter 3, as one of the basic underlying concepts of criminal procedure. This chapter attempts to impart a practical working knowledge of all aspects of probable cause as it concerns both arrest and search and seizure. This chapter is therefore designed to be read in conjunction with the preceding chapters.

DEFINITION

Two different but similar definitions of probable cause are quoted here, one for search and one for arrest, because different types of information are required to establish probable cause in each instance. An often quoted definition of probable cause to *search* is that found in Carroll v. United States, 267 U.S. 132, 45 S.Ct. 280, 69 L.Ed. 543 (1925), in which the Court said that probable cause exists when:

> [T]he facts and circumstances within their [the officers,] knowledge and of which they had reasonably trustworthy information [are] sufficient in themselves to warrant a man of reasonable caution in the belief that [seizable property would be found in a particular place or on a particular person]. (bracketed material supplied) 267 U.S. at 162, 45 S.Ct. at 288, 69 L.Ed. at 555.

Paraphrasing the *Carroll* case, the Court defined probable cause to *arrest* in Brinegar v. United States, 338 U.S. 160, 175–76, 69 S.Ct. 1302, 1310–11, 93 L.Ed. 1879, 1890 (1949):

> Probable cause exists where "the facts and circumstances within their [the officers'] knowledge and of which they had reasonably trustworthy information [are] sufficient in themselves to warrant a man of reasonable caution in the belief that" an offense has been or is being committed [by the person to be arrested]. (final bracketed material added)

These definitions differ only in that the facts and circumstances that would justify an arrest may be different from those that would justify a search. This chapter is primarily concerned with the part of the definition of probable cause that is common to both arrests and searches, namely, the nature, quality, and amount of information necessary to establish probable cause. In this regard, another U.S. Supreme Court definition of probable cause may be helpful.

> "The term 'probable cause,' according to its usual acceptation, means less than evidence which would justify condemnation. . . ." Finely tuned standards such as proof beyond a reasonable doubt or by a preponderance of the evidence, useful in formal trials, have no place in the magistrate's decision. While an effort to fix some general, numerically precise degree of certainty corresponding to "probable cause" may not be helpful, it is clear that "only the probability, and not a prima facie showing, of criminal activity is the standard of probable cause. . . ." Illinois v. Gates, 462 U.S. 213, 235, 103 S.Ct. 2317, 2330, 76 L.Ed.2d 527, 546 (1983).

This chapter is designed to clarify the meaning of terms in this definition while concentrating on specific examples of information that law enforcement officers must have before they may arrest or search, with or without a warrant.

Sources of Information

Information upon which probable cause may be based can come to the attention of a law enforcement officer in two possible ways: (1) the officer may perceive the information, or (2) someone else may perceive the information and relay it to the officer. These information sources are treated differently by the courts and are discussed separately here.

INFORMATION OBTAINED THROUGH THE OFFICER'S OWN SENSES

Law enforcement officers applying for an arrest or search warrant must state *in writing* in the complaint or affidavit the underlying facts upon which probable cause for the issuance of the warrant is based (see Chapters 4 and 5). Most warrantless arrests and searches must also be based on probable cause. No written document is required, but officers must be prepared to justify a warrantless arrest or search with underlying facts if its validity is later challenged. Therefore, whether or not a warrant is sought, officers must have sufficient information supporting probable cause in their minds *before* conducting an arrest or search.

One type of information used to support probable cause is information from the officer's own senses. This includes what an officer perceives through the senses of sight, hearing, smell, touch, and taste. Furthermore, an officer's perceptions may be given additional credence because of personal experience or expertise in a particular area.

> Among the pertinent circumstances to be considered is the qualification and function of the person making the arrest. An officer of a narcotics detail may find probable cause in activities of a suspect and in the appearance of paraphernalia or physical characteristics which to the eye of a layman could be without significance. His action should not, therefore, be measured by what might not

be probable cause to an untrained civilian passerby, but by a standard appropriate for a reasonable, cautious, and prudent narcotics officer under the circumstances of the moment. State v. Poe, 445 P.2d 196, 199 (Wash. 1968).

Indications of Criminal Activity That Support Probable Cause

A law enforcement officer's perceptions of a crime being committed in his or her presence clearly provide probable cause to arrest the person committing the crime. Crimes are seldom committed in an officer's presence, however, and usually an officer must develop probable cause over time from perceptions of a variety of facts and circumstances. The following discussion focuses on specific facts and circumstances indicative of criminal activity, together with court cases explaining their relative importance in the probable cause equation.

FLIGHT. The flight of a suspect when approached by a law enforcement officer may be considered in determining probable cause. In United States v. Brock, 408 F.2d 322 (5th Cir. 1969), officers in a patrol car were radioed a description of a car and its occupants, who were suspected of illegal activities involving non-tax-paid whiskey. When the officers spotted the car, they pulled up to it and called out the nickname of the defendant, whom they recognized. The defendant threw his car into reverse and sped away. The officers overtook him after a short chase. As they approached his car, they smelled the odor of moonshine whiskey and observed tin cans and plastic jugs in the backseat of the vehicle. They arrested the defendant.

The court held that the arrest was valid and supported by probable cause. The court specifically held that the flight of the defendant was one factor *among others* to be considered in determining probable cause.

Flight by itself, however, will not support a finding of probable cause. In Wong Sun v. United States, 371 U.S. 471, 83 S.Ct. 407, 9 L.Ed.2d 441 (1963), federal officers arrested a man named Hom Way at two o'clock in the morning and found narcotics in his possession. Hom Way told the officers that he had purchased an ounce of heroin from a person named Blackie Toy. At six o'clock that same morning, the officers went to a laundry operated by James Wah Toy. When Toy answered the door, one officer identified himself, whereupon Toy slammed the door and ran to his living quarters at the rear of the building. The officers broke in and followed Toy to his bedroom where they arrested him.

The U.S. Supreme Court held that the arrest was made without probable cause. First, the officers had no basis in experience for confidence in the reliability of Hom Way's information. (More is said about reliability of informants later.) Second, the mere fact of Toy's flight did not provide a justification for a warrantless arrest without further information.

> Toy's refusal to admit the officers and his flight down the hallway thus signified a guilty knowledge no more clearly than it did a natural desire to repel an apparently unauthorized intrusion. . . .
>
> A contrary holding here would mean that a vague suspicion could be transformed into probable cause for arrest by reason of ambiguous conduct which the arresting officers themselves have provoked. 371 U.S. at 483–84, 83 S.Ct. at 415, 9 L.Ed.2d at 452–53.

REAL OR PHYSICAL EVIDENCE. Officers may establish probable cause by the observation and evaluation of real or physical evidence. In State v. Heald, 314 A.2d 820 (Me. 1973), officers were summoned at 2:00 A.M. to a store that had recently been burglarized. The officers discovered two sets of footprints in fresh-fallen snow leading from the store to the tire tracks of an automobile. Since the automobile tire tracks were identifiable by a distinctive tread, the officers followed them. After a short distance, the officers met another officer who had found a checkbook belonging to the store owner in the road. Farther down the road the officers found a bag containing electrical parts. Then the officers came upon a car parked in the middle of the road with its lights off—the only other vehicle the officers had seen since leaving the scene of the crime, except a vehicle driven by a person known to the officers. As the patrol car approached the parked car, the parked car's lights came on and the car was driven away. The officers stopped the car and arrested its two occupants for breaking and entering.

The court found that the items of real evidence found and the reasonable inferences drawn from the evidence, together with the highly suspicious circumstances, provided probable cause to arrest the defendants. The court added:

> Although the possibility of mistake existed, as it invariably does in a probable cause situation, they would have been remiss in their duty if they had not arrested the defendants promptly. 314 A.2d at 825.

FURTIVE CONDUCT. Law enforcement officers frequently observe persons engaged in secretive or furtive conduct, arousing suspicion of impending criminal activity or concealment of evidence of criminal activity. Usually, this conduct will at least justify an officer's further investigation to determine whether a crime is being or is about to be committed. (See Chapter 12 on stop and frisk.) Furtive conduct by itself, however, will usually be insufficient to establish probable cause to arrest because the observed person may be making a totally innocent gesture, exhibiting a physical or mental problem, or reacting in fear to an officer's presence. A person's nervousness in the presence of a law enforcement officer will not alone amount to probable cause. The Supreme Court of Colorado stated that "[i]t is normal for law-abiding persons, as well as persons guilty of criminal activity, to be nervous when stopped by a policeman for a traffic offense." People v. Goessl, 526 P.2d 664, 665 (Colo. 1974). A person should not be subject to arrest or search on the basis of a mistaken interpretation of an innocent action.

In Gallik v. Superior Court, 97 Cal.Rptr. 693, 489 P.2d 573 (Cal. 1971), a police officer spotted a car parked illegally with the defendant sitting in it. The officer pulled up next to the vehicle in order to advise the defendant that the car was illegally parked. As the officer approached, he noticed the defendant lean forward in the driver's seat. The officer directed the defendant to get out of the car, patted him down, and searched under the seat of the car, finding marijuana.

The court held the search and seizure illegal. To constitute probable cause for search, something more than a motorist bending over in the front seat is required. The gesture must have some guilty significance arising either from specific information known to the officer or from additional suspicious circumstances observed by the officer. In this case, there was no guilty significance and the search was invalidated.

When accompanied by additional circumstances, however, furtive conduct may be considered in determining probable cause. In People v. Rodriquez, 79 Cal.Rptr. 240 (Cal.App. 1969), officers entered the home of Bracamonte to execute a search warrant. As they entered, they observed the defendant standing in the living room. The officers recognized the defendant because they had been told by informants that he was a narcotics dealer, and they had observed him in the company of narcotics suppliers on several occasions. The officers noticed that the defendant's right hand was clenched in a fist behind his right leg, and they asked him what he was concealing. He made a further gesture to conceal his hand from view and then raised it in an upward motion toward his mouth. One officer grabbed his hand and opened his fist, finding a balloon that contained what was later determined to be heroin. The defendant was arrested.

The court held that the officers had probable cause to arrest the defendant. The defendant's presence in a place suspected of narcotics activity and his past dealings in narcotics, combined with his furtive movements, supplied the necessary probable cause. With respect to furtive movements, the court said:

> [T]o add to the highly suspicious circumstances, appellant not only attempted to hide something behind his leg in a clenched fist, but when the officer inquired as to what he was hiding, appellant moved his clenched fist rapidly toward his mouth. Swallowing narcotics is a popular method of avoiding detection, and movements of the hand toward the mouth have consistently been held to be the type of furtive movement that may be assessed in the probable cause equation. 79 Cal.Rptr. 243–44.

Furtive conduct must be evaluated in light of all the facts and circumstances, including time of day, setting, weather conditions, persons present, and nature of the crime.

ADMISSIONS. A person's admission of criminal conduct to a law enforcement officer may provide probable cause to arrest. In People v. Hubbard, 88 Cal.Rptr. 411 (Cal.App. 1970), officers observed a vehicle driven by the defendant fail to stop for a traffic light and they followed it into a gas station. The officers intended only to issue a traffic citation. When the vehicle stopped, the defendant and two passengers stepped from the vehicle and advanced toward the officers. The officers conducted pat-down searches to protect themselves, and one officer felt capsules in the defendant's pocket. The officer asked the defendant if he had any pills in his pocket, and the defendant responded, "They're reds. They belong to my mother." The officer then asked the defendant to take out the pills, and the officer seized them. Later chemical analysis indicated they were seconal.

The court found that the usage of the term "reds" to describe seconal was so common that they could take judicial notice of it. The admission by the defendant was held to be sufficient in itself to provide probable cause to arrest.

The court also held that *Miranda* warnings were not required before the questioning because the defendant was subjected to only a "transitory" restraint and was not in custody for *Miranda* purposes. Nevertheless, whenever an admission or confession is obtained from a defendant, *Miranda* and voluntariness requirements must be satisfied, if they apply. (These requirements are discussed in Chapter 13.)

FALSE OR IMPLAUSIBLE ANSWERS. False or implausible answers to routine questions may be considered in determining probable cause, but will usually not provide probable cause standing alone. In United States v. Gomori, 437 F.2d 312 (4th Cir. 1971), state police were notified that rental trucks were being used to transport stolen goods in a certain area of the state. An officer patrolling in this area stopped a rental truck for a routine check for registration, driver's license, and rental papers. Noticing that the truck was heavily loaded, the officer asked the defendant what he was carrying. The defendant claimed that his truck was empty. A subsequent search revealed a cargo of stolen cigarettes.

The court held that probable cause to search was provided by the officer's knowledge that rental trucks were being used in the area to transport stolen goods combined with the defendant's obvious lie. A search warrant was not needed in this situation because the truck was a moveable vehicle stopped on the highway and could be searched under the *Carroll* doctrine once there was probable cause to search. (Search and seizure of vehicles without a warrant is discussed in Chapter 10.)

PRESENCE IN A HIGH CRIME AREA OR AT A CRIME SCENE. Suspicious activity in a high-crime area may contribute to probable cause. In People v. Nieto, 72 Cal.Rptr. 764 (Cal.App. 1968), at 3:30 A.M. officers observed a parked car with its headlights on in an area in which drug offenses were frequently committed. They noticed a man in a second car across the street receiving something from a white paper sack held by the driver of the first car. The officers approached the second car and observed a broken left window vent and the defendant in the backseat stuffing something behind the seat cushion. They ordered all four occupants out of the car. As the occupants emerged, a sack fell to the ground and broke, revealing numerous pills and capsules resembling dangerous drugs. The occupants of the car were arrested.

The court held that the combinations of circumstances—the high-crime neighborhood, the hour, the apparent transfer of something, the suspicious conduct of some of the men, the broken window vent, and finally the broken bag full of pills and capsules—was sufficient to give the officers probable cause to arrest the occupants of the car. Mere presence in a high-crime area, without other indications of criminal activity, would not have provided probable cause to arrest.

Presence at the scene of a recent crime provides an even stronger indication of probable cause. In State v. Mimmovich, 284 A.2d 282 (Me. 1971), an officer received a radio report that a break was in progress at a certain building. When the officer arrived at the building, he discovered that the rear window had been broken and metal bars over the window spread wide enough to permit the entrance of a person. He observed no suspects at the scene but heard voices coming from the second-floor porch of an adjoining building. The officer entered this building and went up to the roof, where he found the defendants, lightly clad on a cold night, attempting to conceal themselves. He arrested them, frisked them for weapons, and found coins that were later admitted into evidence.

The court found that the radio warning that a break was in progress, the observations of the officer at the scene, the presence of the defendants near the scene of the crime, lightly clad on a cold winter night, and the defendants' attempt to conceal themselves were sufficient to give the officer probable cause to arrest the defendants.

ASSOCIATION WITH OTHER KNOWN FELONS. Association of a suspect with other known felons may be considered in determining probable cause but will not alone be sufficient to provide probable cause. In United States v. Whitney, 425 F.2d 169 (8th Cir. 1970), police had arrested two associates of the defendant and her companion in connection with a bank robbery and had found part of the stolen money on those associates. The police knew that the defendant, her companion, and the alleged robbers had been staying at the same motel when the alleged robbers were arrested only two days after the robbery. The police also knew that they had recovered only a portion of the money from the bank. The defendant and her companion had moved from the motel where they were staying immediately after their associates were arrested and had registered under assumed names at another motel. The court held that this combination of circumstances provided probable cause to arrest the defendant.

PAST CRIMINAL CONDUCT. The mere fact that a suspect has a known criminal record will not alone provide probable cause to arrest.

> We do not hold that the officer's knowledge of the petitioner's physical appearance and previous record was either inadmissible or entirely irrelevant upon the issue of probable cause. . . . But to hold that knowledge of either or both of these facts constituted probable cause would be to hold that anyone with a previous criminal record could be arrested at will. Beck v. Ohio, 379 U.S. 89, 97, 85 S.Ct. 223, 228, 13 L.Ed.2d 142, 148 (1964).

As the Court stated, however, prior criminal activity of a suspect is relevant to the determination of probable cause. In State v. Temple, 488 P.2d 1380 (Or. App. 1971), an officer observed in plain view in the back of a truck coils of copper wire. The coils were of a type and amount not readily available to the ordinary citizen, nor would the ordinary citizen ever have use for that type and amount. The officer knew this because he had considerable experience investigating copper wire thefts. Furthermore, the officer knew the defendant to be a copper wire thief and had arrested him on several felony charges before.

The court found probable cause to seize the wire in the truck. The court emphasized that the officer could not have seized the wire unless he had a reasonable foundation for the belief that it was stolen. The large amount and unusual nature of the copper wire provided this reasonable foundation. The observations of an experienced officer plus the officer's knowledge of the defendant's prior criminal activity provided probable cause to seize the wire.

FACTS ARISING DURING INVESTIGATION OR TEMPORARY DETENTION. Probable cause to arrest or search may arise during routine investigation or questioning of a person. An officer may initially only be seeking information or investigating suspicious circumstances. Yet during the course of investigation other facts may come to the officer's attention, either from the words or actions of a temporarily detained person or from other sources. For example the detained person may give evasive answers, attempt to flee, or act in a furtive manner, or the officer may perceive any of the other indications of possible criminal activity discussed earlier. If the combination of facts and circumstances is sufficient to establish probable cause to arrest or search, the officer may act accordingly.

The most important case on this subject is the U.S. Supreme Court case of Terry v. Ohio, 392 U.S. 1, 88 S.Ct. 1868, 20 L.Ed.2d 889 (1968), the leading case on stop and frisk. (In Chapter 12, the *Terry* case and other stop and frisk cases illustrate how probable cause to arrest or search may arise from routine investigation and questioning.)

INFORMATION OBTAINED BY THE OFFICER THROUGH INFORMANTS

Most crimes are committed out of the presence of law enforcement officers, and thus usually officers must rely on information from sources other than their own perceptions to establish probable cause to arrest or search. This information must come from ordinary citizen informants or criminal informants who have themselves personally perceived observations of criminal activity. (The term *informant* is used in this chapter to refer to any person from whom a law enforcement officer obtains information on criminal activity.) The problem with using information from informants is ensuring that the information is trustworthy enough to be acted upon. Over the years, courts have developed elaborate rules and procedures for establishing probable cause when the information comes from informants.

The method of establishing probable cause through the use of an informant's information is sometimes referred to as the hearsay method, as opposed to the direct observation method discussed previously. The hearsay method was the subject of a landmark decision by the U.S. Supreme Court in 1983. That decision, Illinois v. Gates, 462 U.S. 213, 103 S.Ct. 2317, 76 L.Ed.2d 527, abandoned an approach to determining probable cause through the use of informants that had been established by two previous U.S. Supreme Court decisions, Aguilar v. Texas, 378 U.S. 108, 84 S.Ct. 1509, 12 L.Ed.2d 723 (1964), and Spinelli v. United States, 393 U.S. 410, 89 S.Ct. 584, 21 L.Ed.2d 637 (1969). The *Aguilar* and *Spinelli* decisions had established specific requirements for law enforcement officers to follow in preparing complaints or affidavits when using information received from informants. The *Gates* decision abandoned rigid adherence to these specific requirements in favor of a "totality of the circumstances" approach to determining probable cause.

Despite the changes brought about by the *Gates* decision, there are good reasons for discussing the *Aguilar* and *Spinelli* decisions in detail. First, the underlying rationales of these decisions and other cases interpreting them retain their vitality and help in analyzing the totality of circumstances under *Gates*. Second, several states have rejected the *Gates* decision based on their state constitutions or statutes. These states still require complaints and affidavits to be prepared according the *Aguilar* and *Spinelli* requirements.

Therefore, this discussion of the hearsay method of determining probable cause begins with a detailed analysis of the *Aguilar-Spinelli* line of cases. It then evaluates the effect of the *Gates* totality of the circumstances approach to the hearsay method of determining probable cause. The discussion concentrates on the situation in which a law enforcement officer is applying for a search warrant based upon information from informants. This approach is used to help focus the discussion and to emphasize again that the officer should *write down*, in the complaint or affidavit, all the information upon which probable cause is based. The same probable cause considerations are involved in arrest warrants and in warrantless arrests and searches, except that the information need not be written down in the warrantless situation.

Aguilar v. Texas

Before the *Gates* decision, the leading case on establishing probable cause under the hearsay method was the U.S. Supreme Court case of Aguilar v. Texas, 378 U.S. 108, 84 S.Ct. 1509, 12 L.Ed.2d 723 (1964). The *Aguilar* case set out a *two-pronged test* for determining probable cause when the information in an affidavit was either entirely or partially obtained from an informant:

1. The affidavit must describe underlying circumstances from which a neutral and detached magistrate may determine that the informant had a sufficient basis for his or her knowledge and that the information was not the result of mere rumor or suspicion.

2. The affidavit must describe underlying circumstances from which the magistrate may determine that the informant was credible or that the informant's information was reliable.

Both prongs of the *Aguilar* test had to be satisfied in order to establish probable cause. Each prong of the *Aguilar* test is discussed separately here, emphasizing the duties of the law enforcement officer in each case.

PRONG 1: INFORMANT'S BASIS OF KNOWLEDGE. A law enforcement officer must demonstrate to the magistrate in the affidavit underlying circumstances enabling the magistrate to independently evaluate the accuracy of an informant's conclusion. This is usually done by showing how the informant knows the supplied information. To satisfy this requirement, the affidavit must show either:

1. that the informant personally perceived the information given to the officer; or

2. that the informant's information came from another source, but there is good reason to believe it.

Informant's Information Is Firsthand. If the informant came upon the information by personal perception, the law enforcement officer should have few problems in satisfying the first prong of the *Aguilar* test. The officer merely has to state, in the affidavit, *how, when,* and *where* the informant obtained the information furnished to the officer. In State v. Daniels, 200 N.W.2d 403 (Minn. 1972), the officer stated in the affidavit:

> For approximately the past two months I have received information from an informant whose information has recently resulted in narcotic arrests and con-

> victions that a Gregory Daniels who resides at 929 Logan N, (down) has been selling marijuana, hashish and heroin. My informant further states that he has seen Daniels sell drugs, namely: heroin and further that he has seen Daniels with heroin on his person. The informant has seen heroin on the premises of 929 Logan N, (down) within the past 48 hours. 200 N.W.2d at 404.

The court said:

> There seems to be no dispute that such personal observation satisfies that part of the *Aguilar* test which requires that the affidavit contain facts to enable the magistrate to judge whether the informant obtained his knowledge in a reliable manner. 200 N.W.2d at 406.

Stating in the affidavit the *time* when the informant obtained the information is very important, especially in applications for search warrants, because probable cause to search can become stale with time. In Windsor v. State, 265 So.2d 916 (Ala. Crim. App. 1972), a law enforcement officer stated in his affidavit for a search warrant that his informant had told him that he had sold certain (stolen) property to the defendant. But the officer did not state when the sale took place. The court said that the affidavit was deficient because it failed to show that the information received from the informant was fresh.

Despite painstaking care by a law enforcement officer in establishing the basis of an informant's knowledge, courts will not find probable cause when errors in the informant's information result in serious injustice. In United States v. Mackey, 387 F.Supp. 1121 (D. Nev. 1975), officers detained the defendant for hitchhiking and sent his name through the computer at the National Crime Information Center (NCIC), a national clearinghouse for law enforcement agencies administered by the FBI. The computer reported that the defendant was wanted in another city for a parole violation. The officers arrested the defendant and subsequently found a gun in his possession. The NCIC report was later found to be false; the defendant had satisfied the parole violation five months earlier. The court ordered the suppression of all evidence resulting from the defendant's arrest.

> [A] computer inaccuracy of this nature and duration, even if unintended, amounted to a capricious disregard for the rights of the defendant as a citizen of the United States. The evidence compels a finding that the government's action was equivalent to an arbitrary arrest, and that an arrest on this basis deprived defendant of his liberty without due process of law. 387 F.Supp. at 1125.

Therefore, although the officers acted properly in all respects, evidence was ruled inadmissible through no fault of their own. (Note that "information received from the NCIC computer bank has been routinely accepted in establishing probable cause for a valid arrest." United States v. Hines, 564 F.2d 925 [10th Cir. 1977]. Officers should ordinarily feel free to act on such information.)

Informant's Information Is Hearsay. If the informant's information comes from a third person, that person and his or her information must satisfy both prongs of the *Aguilar* test. The officer preparing the affidavit must show how the third person knows the information furnished to the informant. For example, if the third person saw criminal activity taking place at a particular time, a statement in the affidavit to that effect would be sufficient to satisfy the first prong of the *Aguilar* test. The officer must, however, also satisfy prong 2 of the *Aguilar* test with respect to *both* the informant *and* and the third person. (Prong 2 of *Aguilar* is discussed later in this chapter.)

Detailing Informant's Information. Courts recognize one other method of satisfying the first prong of the *Aguilar* test besides stating how, when, and where the informant came by the information provided. In the U.S. Supreme Court case of Spinelli v. United States, 393 U.S. 410, 89 S.Ct. 584, 21 L.Ed.2d 637 (1969), the Court said:

> In the absence of a statement detailing the manner in which the information was gathered, it is especially important that the tip describe the accused's criminal activity in sufficient detail that the magistrate may know that he is relying on something more substantial than a casual rumor circulating in the underworld or an accusation based merely on an individual's general reputation. 393 U.S. at 416, 89 S.Ct. at 589, 21 L.Ed.2d at 644.

The *Spinelli* case cited another U.S. Supreme Court case, Draper v. United States, 358 U.S. 307, 79 S.Ct. 329, 3 L.Ed.2d 327 (1959), as an example of sufficient use of detail to satisfy the first prong of the *Aguilar* test. In the *Draper* case, the informant did not state the manner in which he had obtained his information. The informant did, however, report that the defendant had gone to Chicago the day before by train and that he would return to Denver by train with three ounces of heroin on one of two specified mornings. The informant went on to describe, with minute particularity, the clothes that the defendant would be wearing and the bag he would be carrying upon arrival at the Denver station. The Supreme Court said:

> A magistrate, when confronted with such detail, could reasonably infer that the informant had gained his information in a reliable way. 393 U.S. at 417, 89 S.Ct. at 589, 21 L.Ed.2d at 644.

In Soles v. State, 299 A.2d 502 (Md. Spec. App. 1973), probable cause to conduct a warrantless search of an automobile was found even though the officer was unable to tell how, when, or where the informant obtained his information. The court held that the information given by the informant was sufficiently detailed to indicate that he had gained his information in a reliable way. Relevant parts of the officer's testimony at the motion to suppress hearing are quoted as follows, because the testimony indicates the type of detail that courts require to show that an informant spoke from personal knowledge.

The informant described the appellant in the following detail:

> "A. The source described Mr. Soles. He gave—told me that the name of the subject was Soles. He didn't know any other name. Just Soles. He described Mr. Soles as being approximately five foot eight inches in height, approximately 160 pounds, as being a Negro male, approximately in his early 30's. I believe one age was 35 years of age. He said he had a receding hairline slightly, a small bush cut. He said his hair wasn't a big bush. He said it was short. He said he had a goatee and he was light skinned."

The informant described the appellant's automobile in the following detail:

> "A. It was a late model blue convertible with a white top bearing New York tags, I believe WQ 9579, something like that; WX 9579. My recollection isn't real good on that."

The informant described the operation generally and the cocaine specifically in the following detail:

> "THE WITNESS: The source called me at home and related to me that he had information about a male subject from New York who was a major distributor of cocaine to several known narcotics dealers in Washington. He related to me that this source was named Soles. He also indicated to me that he had given the tag number of Soles' car to my partner, Officer Robert Polzin, earlier that week, and in the conversation with this source he related to me that Soles had in excess of an eighth of a kilo of cocaine in his trunk of his car inside a briefcase. He said this cocaine would be inside a glass jar. He stated that Soles had several thousand dollars in cash on him, which were the assets from the sale of part of the cocaine he brought down from New York. He stated he was armed with a pistol, and stated that he would be leaving Washington for New York before three o'clock that evening."

> The trial judge, "when confronted with such detail, could reasonably infer that the informant had gained his information in a reliable way," . . . that is, via first-hand observation. Upon our independent review, we draw such an inference. 16 Md.App. at 663–66, 299 A.2d at 507–8.

In summary, if a law enforcement officer does not know how, when, or where an informant obtained information, the officer can still satisfy the first prong of the *Aguilar* test by obtaining as much detail as possible from the informant and stating *all* of it in the affidavit.

PRONG 2: INFORMANT'S VERACITY. The second prong of *Aguilar* requires the officer to demonstrate to the magistrate in the affidavit underlying circumstances to convince the magistrate of the informant's veracity (i.e., that the informant is credible or that the informant's information is reliable). In one of the few cases dealing with the reliability of an informant's information, the court found that information supplied by an unnamed street drug seller to one of his clients about a future drug "drop" was "reliable." The court said:

> Though from the criminal milieu, to be sure, he was not, wittingly at least, working with the police. He was not in the position of the "common informant . . . hidden behind a cloak of immunity from prosecution for his own misdeeds." . . . This street seller was, so far as he knew, engaged in a purely commercial venture for his own profit. He was dealing with a regular and presumably valued customer. Being unable initially to satisfy his customer's demand, it was to his every advantage to assure the prompt return of that customer as soon as fresh merchandise was available for sale. He simply had no purpose in misleading his own clientele. The circumstances in which the seller passed on the information to a customer and confidant are replete, we think, with reasonable assurances of trustworthiness. Upon our constitutionally-mandated independent review, we believe the information furnished by this secondary informant to have been reliable, notwithstanding his utter lack of demonstrated credibility. Thompson v. State, 298 A.2d 458, 462 (Md. 1973).

Most cases have dealt with the "credibility" aspect of the informant's veracity rather than with the reliability of the informant's information. The amount and type of information required to establish credibility depends upon whether the informant is an ordinary citizen informant or a criminal informant.

Ordinary Citizen Informant. An ordinary citizen informant is usually presumed credible and no further evidence of credibility need be stated in the affidavit beyond the informant's name and address and his or her status as a victim of or witness to crime.

> One cannot approach the problem of informants whose information may or may not be sufficient to create "probable cause" as if there was only two classes: reliable informants whose information has previously been tested by the police and "all others." A multitude of cases . . . attest to the fact that information from a citizen who purports to be the victim of or to have witnessed a crime may, under certain circumstances, provide a sufficient basis for an arrest. People v. Griffin, 58 Cal.Rptr. 707, 711 (Cal.App. 1967).

The reason behind this rule was stated by the Supreme Court of Wisconsin:

> [A]n ordinary citizen who reports a crime which has been committed in his presence, or that a crime is being or will be committed, stands on much different ground than a police informer. He is a witness to criminal activity who acts with an intent to aid the police in law enforcement because of his concern for society or for his own safety. He does not expect any gain or concession for his information. An informer of this type usually would not have more than one opportunity to supply information to the police, thereby precluding proof of his reliability by pointing to previous accurate information which he has supplied. State v. Paszek, 184 N.W.2d 836, 843 (Wis. 1971).

Another reason for accepting the credibility of an ordinary citizen is the average person's fear of potential criminal or civil action for deliberately or negligently providing false information. People v. Hicks, 378 N.Y.S.2d 660, 341 N.E.2d 227 (N.Y. 1975).

Nevertheless, some courts have required more information to establish credibility of an ordinary citizen informant. The Arkansas Supreme Court held that there was no probable cause to arrest when the only information officers had was an anonymous telephone tip that a certain car was occupied by two armed men. The court said:

> [I]f this arrest must be upheld on the basis of sufficient probable cause, any officer may arrest anyone at any time and justify his action by attributing it to an anonymous telephone call. The protection of the Bill of Rights is not to be so readily circumvented. Conor v. State, 538 S.W.2d 304, 305 (Ark. 1976).

The court indicated that the officers should have either obtained more information about the informant or more facts pointing to the commission of an offense before the court would find probable cause to arrest.

The Supreme Court of Virginia found an ordinary citizen informant credible where the affidavit stated that, although the informant had not previously furnished information to the police concerning violations of the narcotics laws, he was steadily employed, was a registered voter, enjoyed a good reputation in his neighborhood, and had expressed concern for young people involved with narcotics. Brown v. Commonwealth, 187 S.E.2d 160 (Va. 1972). In another Virginia case, an officer's affidavit for a search warrant stated that the officer had known the ordinary citizen informant and his family for many years and that the informant was known to be credible. The court said:

> Although more extensive background information would be highly desirable, "a common sense and realistic" interpretation of the affidavit . . . leads us to the

conclusion that it contains information reported by a first time citizen informer whose name was withheld by the affiant.

Public-spirited citizens should be encouraged to furnish to the police information of crimes. Accordingly, we will not apply to citizen informers the same
standard of reliability as is applicable when police act on tips from professional
informers or those who seek immunity for themselves, whether such citizens
are named . . . or, as here, unnamed. Guzewicz v. Commonwealth, 187 S.E.2d
144, 148 (Va. 1972).

These cases indicate that the more information provided in the affidavit about
an ordinary citizen informant, the more likely the informant will be found to be
credible.

Criminal Informant. Unlike the ordinary citizen's credibility, which may sometimes be presumed, the criminal informant's credibility must always be established by a statement of underlying facts and circumstances. Criminal informants may be professional police informants, persons with a criminal record,
accomplices in a crime, or persons seeking immunity for themselves. Usually,
criminal informants will not want their identities disclosed in an affidavit. The
U.S. Supreme Court held that an informant's identity need not be disclosed if
his or her credibility is otherwise satisfactorily established. In McCray v. Illinois, 386 U.S. 300, 306–7, 87 S.Ct. 1056, 1060, 18 L.Ed.2d 62, 68 (1967), the
Court quoted the New Jersey Supreme Court with approval:

"If a defendant may insist upon disclosure of the informant in order to test the
truth of the officer's statement that there is an informant or as to what the informant related or as to the informant's reliability, we can be sure that every defendant will demand disclosure. He has nothing to lose and the prize may be
the suppression of damaging evidence if the State cannot afford to reveal its
source, as is so often the case. And since there is no way to test the good faith
of a defendant who presses the demand, we must assume the routine demand
would have to be routinely granted. The result would be that the State could
use the informant's information only as a lead and could search only if it could
gather adequate evidence of probable cause apart from the informant's data.
Perhaps that approach would sharpen investigatorial techniques, but we doubt
that there would be enough talent and time to cope with crime upon that basis.
Rather we accept the premise that the informer is a vital part of society's defensive arsenal. The basic rule protecting his identity rests upon that belief."

Whether or not the informant's identity is disclosed in the affidavit, a statement
of underlying facts and circumstances supporting credibility must be included.
The following facts and circumstances are relevant.

1. Informant has given accurate information in the past. The usual method of
establishing the credibility of a criminal informant is by showing that the informant has in the past given accurate information that has led to arrests, convictions, recovery of stolen property, or some like accomplishment. This is sometimes referred to as establishing the informant's track record.

Magistrates will not evaluate affidavits that attempt to establish the credibility of informants with undue technicality. United States v. Ventresca, 380 U.S.
102, 85 S.Ct. 741, 13 L.Ed.2d 684 (1965). Nevertheless, a law enforcement officer may not merely state the conclusion that the informant is credible because
of proven credibility. The officer must state facts demonstrating that the informant has given accurate information in the past.

The main concern of the magistrate is the *accuracy* of the information supplied by the informant in the past. In People v. Lawrence, 273 N.E.2d 637 (Ill.App. 1971), the court found the informant credible even though none of his prior tips had resulted in convictions.

> Convictions, while corroborative of an informer's reliability, are not essential in establishing his reliability. Arrests, standing alone, do not establish reliability, but information that has been proved accurate does. Arrestees may not be prosecuted; if prosecuted they may not be indicted; if indicted they may not be tried; if tried, they may not be convicted. If a case is tried, the informer may never testify; his credibility may never be passed upon in court. The true test of his reliability is the accuracy of his information. 273 N.E.2d at 639.

In United States v. Dunnings, 425 F.2d 836, 839 (2d Cir. 1969), the court found sufficient a statement that the informant had "furnished reliable and accurate information on approximately 20 occasions over the past four years." 425 F.2d at 839. In State v. Daniels, 200 N.W.2d 403 (Minn. 1972), the court held that the credibility of the informant was sufficiently shown where the affidavit stated that the informant's information "has recently resulted in narcotic arrests and convictions." 200 N.W.2d at 406–7. In United States v. Smith, 462 F.2d 456 (8th Cir. 1972), the informant's credibility was established by an affidavit that specified:

> The informant has previously provided reliable information to agents of the Bureau of Narcotics and Dangerous Drugs. On one occassion [*sic*] within the last two weeks a search warrant was issued pursuant to the informants [*sic*] information and narcotics were seized. On another occassion [*sic*] within the last month the informant introduced me to an individual who he said was a dealer. I purchased heroin from the individual.

Generally, the more information provided about an informant's track record, the more likely the magistrate will find the informant credible. Types of information considered relevant are as follows:

1. The time when previous information was furnished by the informant

2. Specific examples of verification of the accuracy of the informant's information

3. Description of how the informant's information helped in bringing about an arrest, conviction, or other result

4. Documentation of the informant's consistency in providing accurate information

5. Details of the informant's "general background, employment, personal attributes that enable him to observe and relate accurately, position in the community, reputation with others, personal connection with the suspect, any circumstances which suggest the probable absence of any motivation to falsify, the apparent motivation for supplying the information, the presence or absence of a criminal record or association with known criminals, and the like." United States v. Harris, 403 U.S. 573, 600, 91 S.Ct. 2075, 2090, 29 L.Ed.2d 723, 743 (1971) (dissenting opinion).

If an officer has no *personal* knowledge of circumstances demonstrating that an informant is credible, the officer may state in the affidavit information about the informant's credibility received from other law enforcement officers. State

v. Lambert, 363 A.2d 707 (Me. 1976). The officer should state the names of other law enforcement officers and should state in detail how those officers acquired personal knowledge of the informant's credibility.

A dog trained to react to controlled substances may also be considered an informant. The dog's credibility can also be established by presenting the track record of the dog and its handler. In United States v. Race, 529 F.2d 12 (1st Cir. 1976), a dog reacted positively to two wooden crates in an airline warehouse containing some 300 crates. The dog's reaction provided the basis for probable cause to arrest the defendant. The Court said:

> We do not, of course, suggest that any dog's excited behavior could, by itself, be adequate proof that a controlled substance was present, but here the government laid a strong foundation of canine reliability and handler expertise. Murphy [the dog's handler] testified that the dog had undergone intensive training in detecting drugs in 1971, that he had at least four hours a week of follow-up training since then, as well as work experience, and that the strong reaction he had to the crates was one that in the past had invariably indicated the presence of marijuana, hashish, heroin or cocaine. 529 F.2d at 14.

2. Informant made admissions or turned over evidence against the informant's own penal interest.   In United States v. Harris, 403 U.S. 573, 91 S.Ct. 2075, 29 L.Ed.2d 723 (1971), the U.S. Supreme Court held that an admission made by an informant against the informant's own penal interest is sufficient to establish the credibility of the informant.

> People do not lightly admit a crime and place critical evidence in the hands of the police in the form of their own admissions. Admissions of crime, like admissions against proprietary interests, carry their own indicia of credibility—sufficient at least to support a finding of probable cause to search. That the informant may be paid or promised a "break" does not eliminate the residual risk and opprobrium of having admitted criminal conduct. 403 U.S. at 583–84, 91 S.Ct. at 2082, 29 L.Ed.2d at 734.

In State v. Appleton, 297 A.2d 363 (Me. 1972), the court held that an informant's turning over criminal evidence against the informant's penal interest was also strongly convincing evidence of credibility. The informant purchased certain drugs at the defendant's apartment and the same day brought those drugs to the police to be tested. A law enforcement officer applied for a warrant to search the defendant's apartment, stating both that the informant had purchased the drugs and that he had delivered them to the police. The court held that the informant's actions justified a belief in the credibility of his story. "An informant is not likely to turn over to the police such criminal evidence unless he is certain in his own mind that his story implicating the persons occupying the premises where the sale took place will withstand police scrutiny." 297 A.2d at 369.

CORROBORATION

An officer with insufficient information to satisfy either or both prongs of the *Aguilar* test may be able to bolster that information by corroboration. Corroboration means strengthening or confirming the information supplied by the informant by stating in the affidavit supporting information obtained by law enforcement officers. For example, an officer may receive a tip from an informant about criminal activity. In addition, through surveillance or independent investigation, the officer or fellow officers may personally perceive further indications of criminal activity. By writing this corroborating information in the affidavit in addition to the information directed toward satisfying the *Aguilar* test, the officer enables a magistrate to consider all facts that may bear upon probable cause, no matter what the source of the information.

The corroborative information provided by the law enforcement officer in the affidavit may work in three possible ways:

1. The information obtained by the officer may *in itself* provide probable cause independent of the informant's information (See earlier under "Indications of Criminal Activity That Support Probable Cause.") Corroborating information of this degree will provide probable cause to search even if neither prong of the *Aguilar* test is met.

2. The officer's information may confirm or verify the information provided by the informant. For example, if an officer cannot satisfy prong 2 of the *Aguilar* test, the corroborating information may provide the necessary verification of the informant's report. In other words, if some significant details of the informant's information are shown to be true by independent observation of a law enforcement officer, the magistrate is more likely to be convinced of the informant's veracity.

3. The officer's information may be added to an informant's information that meets *Aguilar* standards. Although neither standing alone is sufficient to establish probable cause, a combination of all the information may be sufficient.

Therefore, to ensure that a magistrate is presented with sufficient information on which to base a determination of probable cause, the affidavit should include the following:

1. All information directed toward satisfying the *Aguilar* two-prong test

2. All information perceived by law enforcement officers that corroborates the informant's information

3. All additional corroborating information perceived by law enforcement officers relating to the criminal activity for which the search warrant is being sought

To illustrate how courts deal with corroboration, two cases with similar fact situations but different results are discussed in detail.

Spinelli v. United States

The U.S. Supreme Court case of Spinelli v. United States, 393 U.S. 410, 89 S.Ct. 584, 21 L.Ed.2d 637 (1969), is the leading case on corroboration. In that case, the defendant was convicted of traveling to St. Louis, Missouri from a nearby Illinois suburb with the intention of conducting gambling activities prohibited by Missouri law. On appeal, the defendant challenged the validity of a search warrant that was used to obtain incriminating evidence against him. The affidavit in support of the search warrant contained the following allegations:

1. The FBI had kept track of the defendant's movements during five days in August 1965. On four of the five days, the defendant was seen crossing a bridge from Illinois to St. Louis between 11 A.M. and 12:15 P.M. and was seen parking his car in a lot used by residents of a certain apartment house between 3:30 P.M. and 4:45 P.M. On one day, the defendant was followed further and was seen to enter a particular apartment in the building.

2. An FBI check with the telephone company revealed that this apartment contained two telephones listed under the name of Grace Hagen and carried two different numbers.

3. The defendant was known to the officer preparing the affidavit (the affiant) and to federal law enforcement agents and local law enforcement agents as a "bookmaker, an associate of bookmakers, a gambler, and an associate of gamblers." 393 U.S. at 414, 89 S.Ct. at 588, 21 L.Ed.2d at 642.

4. The FBI had been informed by a confidential reliable informant that the defendant was operating a handbook and accepting wagers and disseminating wagering information by means of telephones assigned the same numbers as the phones in the previously mentioned apartment.

The court first discussed in detail allegation number 4, the information obtained from the informant. The Court said:

> The informer's report must first be measured against *Aguilar's* standards so that its probative value can be assessed. If the tip is found inadequate under *Aguilar*, the other allegations which corroborate the information contained in the hearsay report should then be considered. 393 U.S. at 415, 89 S.Ct. at 588, 21 L.Ed.2d at 643.

The court found that prong 2 of *Aguilar* was not satisfied because the affiant merely stated that he had been informed by a "confidential reliable informant." This was a mere conclusion or opinion of the affiant because no *underlying circumstances* were stated to show the magistrate that the informant was credible.

Nor was prong 1 satisfied. The affidavit failed to state sufficient *underlying circumstances* from which the informant concluded that the defendant was running a bookmaking operation. There was no statement as to how, when, or where the informant received his information—whether he personally observed the defendant at work or whether he ever placed a bet with him. If the informant obtained his information from third persons, there was no explanation why these sources were credible or how they obtained their information.

Finally, the affidavit did not describe the defendant's alleged criminal activity in sufficient detail to convince a magistrate that the information was more than mere rumor or suspicion. The only facts supplied were that the defendant was using two specified telephones to conduct gambling operations. As the court said, this meager report could easily have been obtained from an offhand remark at a neighborhood bar.

The Court then considered allegations 1 and 2 of the affidavit to see if they provided sufficient corroboration of the informant's information or provided probable cause in themselves. The Court found that these two items contained no suggestion of criminal conduct. The defendant's travels to and from the apartment building and his entry into a particular apartment could not be taken as indicative of gambling activity. And there was certainly nothing unusual about an apartment containing two separate telephones. The Court, therefore, concluded:

> At most, these allegations indicated that Spinelli could have used the telephones specified by the informant for some purpose. This cannot by itself be said to support both the inference that the informer was generally trustworthy and that he had made his charge against Spinelli on the basis of information obtained in a reliable way. 393 U.S. at 417, 89 S.Ct. at 589, 21 L.Ed.2d at 644.

Finally, the Court considered allegation 3—that the defendant was "known" to the FBI and others as a gambler. The Court called this a bald and unilluminating assertion of police suspicion and said that it may not be used to give additional weight to allegations that would otherwise be insufficient.

Since the *Spinelli* decision, the U.S. Supreme Court has decided that the alleged criminal reputation of a suspect *may* be considered by a magistrate in evaluating an affidavit for a search warrant. United States v. Harris, 403 U.S. 573, 91 S.Ct. 2075, 29 L.Ed.2d 723 (1971). The Court said that criminal reputation couldn't be used in *Spinelli* because *Spinelli* contained no factual indication of the defendant's past criminal activities to back up the assertion. The affiant in the *Harris* case stated in the affidavit that the defendant had a reputation for four years as a trafficker of non-tax-paid distilled spirits, that the officer had received information from all types of persons as to the defendant's activities, and that during this period a sizable stash of illicit whiskey had been found in an abandoned house under the defendant's control. The Court held that when criminal reputation is supported by factual statements indicating prior criminal conduct, reputation can be considered along with other allegations.

The *Spinelli* case is instructive because it traces through all the *Aguilar* requirements for establishing probable cause using an informant's information and gives reasons why each test was not met by the affidavit. It then considers other information in the affidavit as corroboration of the informant's information and gives specific reasons why the corroborative information is inadequate.

Dawson v. State, 276 A.2d 680 (Md.Spec.App. 1971) is a case similar to the *Spinelli* case, except that the search warrant in *Dawson* was found to be valid. The discussion of the *Dawson* case centers on the differences between the two cases that caused the court in the *Dawson* case to reach a different conclusion.

Dawson v. State

In the *Dawson* case, the defendant was convicted of unlawfully maintaining premises for the purpose of selling lottery tickets and of unlawfully betting, wagering, or gambling on the results of horse races. He appealed, claiming among other things that the search warrant of his home was illegal because probable cause was lacking. The affidavit for the warrant contained nine paragraphs. The first paragraph listed the investigative experience of the affiant and ended with his conclusion that gambling activities were at that time being conducted at the defendant's premises. The third through ninth paragraphs contained the direct observations of the affiant officer. (These paragraphs are considered later.) The second paragraph dealt with an informant's information and is quoted here:

> That on Thursday April 17, 1969 your affiant interviewed a confidential source of information who has given reliable information in the past relating to illegal gambling activities which has resulted in the arrest and conviction of persons arrested for illegal gambling activities and that the source is personally known to your affiant. That this source related that there was illegal gambling activities taking place at 8103 Legation Road, Hyattsville Prince George's County, Maryland by a one Donald Lee Dawson. That the source further related that the source would call telephone #577–5197 and place horse and number bets with Donald Lee Dawson. 276 A.2d at 685.

The court analyzed the second paragraph in terms of the two-pronged *Aguilar* test. Considering the informant's basis of knowledge first, the court found that *Aguilar* was satisfied. The affidavit stated that the informant had personally called the phone number 577–5197 and had placed horse and number bets with the defendant. In contrast, in the *Spinelli* case, nothing was said about how the informant obtained his information.

The *Dawson* court found the information supplied about the credibility of the informant to be barely sufficient. The affidavit stated that both arrests and convictions had resulted from the informant's information in the past, which was more than a mere conclusion or opinion of the affiant. The affidavit also went further to establish the informant's credibility than did the affidavit in *Spinelli*, where the informant was merely described as a "confidential reliable informant." The court implied that more specific information on the informant's credibility would have been desirable but said:

> It may well be that the facts here recited are enough to establish the credibility of the informant. In view of the strong independent verification hereinafter to be discussed, however, it is unnecessary for the State to rely exclusively on such recitation. 276 A.2d at 686.

The court assumed for purposes of discussion that the credibility of the informant had *not* been adequately established and proceeded to discuss *corroboration*, making a concerted effort to compare the affidavit in this case with that in *Spinelli*.

Paragraphs three through nine of the *Dawson* affidavit stated that a surveillance of the defendant's activities had been conducted during a six-day period in April 1969 and that the following information was obtained:

— The defendant was observed to be engaged in no apparent legitimate employment during the period.

— The defendant had two telephones in his residence with two separate lines, both of which had silent listings.

— One of the defendant's silent listings had been picked up in the course of a raid on a lottery operation three years earlier in another town.

— On each day of observation, the defendant was observed to purchase an Armstrong Scratch Sheet, which gives information about horses running at various tracks that day.

— On each morning of observation, the defendant was observed to leave his house between 9:02 and 10:20 A.M., to return to his house between 11:20 A.M. and 12:06 P.M., and to remain in his house until after 6:00 P.M., The affiant, who was experienced and expert in gambling investigations, stated that during the hours between noon and 6:00 P.M., horse and number bets can be placed and the results of betting become available.

— On each day of observation, the defendant was observed during his morning rounds to stop at a number of places, including liquor stores and restaurants, for very short periods of time. He never purchased anything from any of the stores nor did he eat or drink at the restaurants. The affiant stated that such brief regular stops are classic characteristics of the pickup-man phase of a gambling operation:

> He picks up the "action" (money and/or list of bets) from the previous day or evening from prearranged locations—"drops." At the same time, he delivers cash to the appropriate locations for the payoff of yesterday's successful players. 11 Md.App. at 711, 276 A.2d at 689.

— On one of the days, the defendant was observed in close association all day with another person who was known to have been arrested for alleged gambling violations three years before.

— Finally, the defendant had been arrested and convicted of gambling violations about three years before.

The court considered each allegation in detail. Although each allegation, taken separately, could admittedly have been consistent with innocent conduct on the defendant's part, the court refused to consider each allegation separately. Instead, the court said:

> [P]robable cause emerges not from any single constituent activity but, rather, from the overall pattern of activities. Each fragment of conduct may communicate nothing of significance, but the broad mosaic portrays a great deal. The whole may, indeed, be greater than the sum of its parts. 276 A.2d at 687.

Furthermore, the court relied heavily on the investigating officer's experience in investigating gambling activities and the interpretations he was able to place on the defendant's conduct.

The court, therefore, concluded:

> In reviewing the observations, the ultimate question for the magistrate must be What is revealed by the whole pattern of activity? In the case at bar, the various strands of observation, insubstantial unto themselves, together weave a strong web of probable guilt. 276 A.2d at 689.

The court compared this case with the *Spinelli* case and explained why the affidavit here was sufficient to provide probable cause while the one in *Spinelli* was not.

— In *Spinelli*, there were no observations of the pickup-man type of activity.

— In *Spinelli*, there was no observed association with a previously arrested gambler.

— In *Spinelli*, there was no daily purchase of an Armstrong Scratch Sheet to evidence some daily interest in horse races.

— In *Spinelli*, neither Spinelli's nor Grace Hagen's phone number had been previously picked up in a raided gambling headquarters.

— In *Spinelli*, Spinelli was not a convicted gambler.

— Finally, and perhaps most importantly, the confidential informant's information in *Spinelli* was so inadequate under *Aguilar* as to lend *no* additional light or interpretation to the direct observations. In contrast, the confidential informant's information in the *Dawson* case was very substantial and significantly enhanced the direct observations.

> The hearsay information may, of course, reinforce the direct observation just as the direct observation may reinforce the hearsay information. There is no one-way street from direct observation to hearsay information. Rather, each may simultaneously cross-fertilize and enrich the other. 276 A.2d at 690.

The court's emphasis on analyzing the overall pattern of activities and the totality of facts and circumstances in the *Dawson* case was an early harbinger of the approach to probable cause taken in the landmark decision of the U.S. Supreme Court in *Illinois v. Gates*.

TOTALITY OF THE CIRCUMSTANCES TEST

In the 1983 case of *Illinois v. Gates*, the U.S. Supreme Court abandoned the *Aguilar-Spinelli* two-pronged test for determining probable cause through the use of informants for a totality of the circumstances test. More correctly, the court abandoned a rigid adherence to the *Aguilar-Spinelli* test, since the elements of the *Aguilar-Spinelli* test remain important considerations under the new *Gates* test. This discussion of the *Gates* test begins with the facts of the case.

On May 3, 1978, the Bloomingdale, Illinois, Police Department received an anonymous letter that included statements that the defendants, a husband and wife, made their living selling drugs; that the wife would drive their car to Florida on May 3 and leave it to be loaded up with drugs; that the husband would fly down in a few days to drive the car back loaded with over $100,000 worth of drugs; and that the defendants had over $100,000 worth of drugs in the basement of their home. Acting on the tip, a police officer obtained the defendants' address and learned that the husband had made a reservation for a May 5 flight to Florida. The officer then made arrangements with a Drug Enforcement Administration (DEA) agent for surveillance of the May 5 flight. The surveillance revealed that the husband took the flight, stayed overnight in a motel room registered to his wife, and the next morning headed north with an unidentified woman toward Bloomingdale in a car bearing Illinois license plates issued to the husband. A search warrant for the defendants' residence and automobile was obtained, based on these facts and the anonymous letter. When the defendants arrived home, the police searched the car and the residence and found marijuana.

The Illinois Supreme Court found that the *Aguilar-Spinelli* two-pronged test had not been satisfied. First, the "veracity" prong was not satisfied because there was no basis for concluding that the anonymous person who wrote the letter to the police department was credible. Second, the "basis of knowledge" prong was not satisfied because the letter gave no information on how its writer knew of the defendants' activities. The court therefore concluded that no showing of probable cause had been made.

The U.S. Supreme Court said:

> We agree with the Illinois Supreme Court that an informant's "veracity," "reliability" and "basis of knowledge" are all highly relevant in determining the value of his report. We do not agree, however, that these elements should be understood as entirely separate and independent requirements to be rigidly exacted in every case, which the opinion of the Supreme Court of Illinois would imply. Rather . . . they should be understood simply as closely intertwined issues that may usefully illuminate the commonsense, practical question whether there is "probable cause" to believe that contraband or evidence is located in a particular place. 462 U.S. at 230, 103 S.Ct. at 2327–28, 76 L.Ed.2d at 543.

In effect, the Court said that the elements of the *Aguilar-Spinelli* two-pronged test are important considerations in determining the existence of probable cause, but should be evaluated only as part of the ultimate commonsense determination and not as rigid rules to be applied mechanically. The Court believed that this totality of the circumstance approach was more in keeping with the nature of probable cause as a fluid concept, which depends on probabilities arising from varying fact situations, and does not lend itself to a neat set of legal rules. The Court reiterated the following quotation from Brinegar v. United States, 338 U.S. 160, 175, 69 S.Ct. 1302, 1310, 93 L.Ed. 1879, 1890 (1949):

> In dealing with probable cause . . . as the very name implies, we deal with probabilities. These are not technical; they are the factual and practical considerations of everyday life on which reasonable and prudent men, not legal technicians, act.

The Court suggested that originally the two prongs of the *Aguilar-Spinelli* test were intended simply as guides to a magistrate's determination of probable cause, not as inflexible, independent requirements applicable in every case. The two prongs should be understood as "relevant considerations in the totality of circumstances that traditionally has guided probable cause determinations: a deficiency in one may be compensated for, in determining the overall reliability of a tip by a strong showing as to the other, or by some other indicia of reliability." 462 U.S. at 233, 103 S.Ct. at 2329, 76 L.Ed.2d at 545. The entire process of determining probable cause could, therefore, be simplified as follows:

> The task of the issuing magistrate is simply to make a practical, common-sense decision whether, given all the circumstances set forth in the affidavit before him, including the "veracity" and "basis of knowledge" of persons supplying hearsay information, there is a fair probability that contraband or evidence of a crime will be found in a particular place. And the duty of a reviewing court is simply to ensure that the magistrate had a "substantial basis for . . . conclud[ing]" that probable cause existed. 462 U.S. at 238–39, 103 S.Ct. at 2332, 76 L.Ed.2d at 548.

The *Gates* totality of the circumstances test should cause little change in procedure for law enforcement officers applying for search warrants. If officers follow the advice in this chapter for preparing affidavits under the *Aguilar-Spinelli* test, the affidavits will have as good a chance or a better chance of satisfying the *Gates* test. The *Gates* emphasis on the value of corroborating information should, however, make it less difficult to obtain a search warrant based partially on information from an anonymous informant. As the *Gates* opinion indicated, overly rigid application of the two-pronged test tended to reject anonymous tips, because ordinary citizens generally do not provide extensive recitations of the basis of their everyday observations and the veracity of anonymous informants is largely unknown and unknowable. The Court said:

> [A]nonymous tips seldom could survive a rigorous application of either of the . . . prongs. Yet, such tips, particularly when supplemented by independent police investigation, frequently contribute to the solution of otherwise "perfect crimes." While a conscientious assessment of the basis for crediting such tips is required by the Fourth Amendment, a standard that leaves virtually no place for anonymous citizen informants is not. 462 U.S. at 237–38, 103 S.Ct. at 2332, 76 L.Ed.2d at 548.

With respect to the anonymous letter in the *Gates* case, the Court said that the corroboration of predictions that the defendants' car would be in Florida, that the husband would fly to Florida in a few days, and that the husband would drive the car back to Illinois indicated that the informant's other assertions were also true. The letter's accurate predictions of the defendants' future actions, especially, made it more likely that the informant also had access to reliable information of the defendants' alleged illegal activities. Although the tip was corroborated only as to the defendants' seemingly innocent behavior, and although it by no means indicated with certainty that illegal drugs would be found, the Court believed that it sufficed "for the practical, common-sense judgment called for in making a probable cause determination. It is enough, for purposes of assessing probable cause, that 'corroboration through other sources of information reduced the chances of a reckless or prevaricating tale,' thus providing 'a substantial basis for crediting the hearsay.'" 462 U.S. at 244, 103 S.Ct. at 2335, 76 L.Ed.2d at 552.

SUMMARY

Probable cause exists when the facts and circumstances within a law enforcement officer's knowledge and of which the officer has reasonably trustworthy information are sufficient in themselves to warrant a person of reasonable caution in the belief either that:

1. a particular person has committed or is committing a crime; or
2. seizable items are located at a particular place or on a particular person.

Probable cause does not require certainty or proof beyond a reasonable doubt, but it does require something beyond mere suspicion. It is a practical, nontechnical, commonsense concept dealing with probabilities arising out of the varying facts and circumstances of everyday life.

Information upon which probable cause is to be based may come to a law enforcement officer's attention in two possible ways:

1. Through the officer's own perceptions

2. Through the perceptions of an informant who relays the information to the officer

Some indications of criminal activity that may contribute to probable cause are as follows:

1. Flight

2. Real or physical evidence such as fingerprints or weapons

3. Furtive conduct

4. Incriminating admissions

5. False or implausible answers

6. Presence at a crime scene or in a high-crime area

7. Association with other known criminals

8. Past criminal conduct

9. Facts arising during investigation or temporary detention

Standing alone, none of these indications of criminal activity may be sufficient to establish probable cause. However, when combined with other indications, each is a relevant factor in determining whether an arrest or a search is justified. Before law enforcement officers act, either to apply for a warrant or to conduct a warrantless arrest or search (in the proper circumstances), they should make sure that they have sufficient information upon which to base their actions and that they can justify their actions before a magistrate or judge.

When information about criminal activity comes from an informant, an officer must satisfy the totality of circumstances test set out in the case of *Illinois v. Gates*. That test simply requires the officer to provide underlying facts and circumstances indicating a substantial basis for a magistrate to determine that probable cause to arrest or search exists. Highly relevant to this determination are the elements of the *Aguilar-Spinelli* two-pronged test. To satisfy this test, the officer must provide underlying circumstances indicating the basis of the informant's knowledge about the criminal activity and underlying circumstances from which the officer concluded that the informant was credible or that the information was reliable. These requirements need not be applied in a rigid, technical manner, but mere conclusions or opinions of the officer will not suffice to establish probable cause. The magistrate must be satisfied that the informant's information is not mere rumor, suspicion, or reckless or malicious fabrication. Corroboration of the details of an informant's tip by independent police work is a valuable means of satisfying the totality of the circumstances test for determining probable cause.

Law enforcement officers applying for a warrant should write down in the affidavit, in an orderly manner, the following:

1. All information directed toward satisfying the *Aguilar* two-prong test

2. All information perceived by law enforcement officers to corroborate the informant's information

3. All additional corroborating information perceived by law enforcement officers relating to the criminal activity for which the search warrant is being sought

REVIEW AND DISCUSSION QUESTIONS

1. Why is it important for a law enforcement officer to write down in a complaint or affidavit the facts and circumstances upon which probable cause is based?

2. Give an example of a strong indication of probable cause to *arrest* that is arrived at through each of the five senses—sight, hearing, smell, taste, and touch.

3. Give an example of a strong indication of probable cause to *search* that is arrived at through each of the five senses—sight, hearing, smell, taste, and touch.

4. List three possible strong indications of probable cause to *arrest* for each of the following crimes:
   a. Theft
   b. Assault
   c. Arson
   d. Breaking and entering
   e. Rape
   f. Driving to endanger

5. Discuss the significance in the probable cause context of the phrase "conduct innocent in the eyes of the untrained may carry entirely different 'messages' to the experienced or trained . . . observer." Davis v. United States, 409 F.2d 458, 460 (D.C.Cir. 1969). Discuss specifically in terms of drug offenses and gambling offenses.

6. Must law enforcement officers know exactly the elements and name of the specific crime for which they are arresting or searching in order to have probable cause? See People v. Georgev, 230 N.E.2d 851 (1967).

7. What does *corroboration* mean and why is it important to a law enforcement officer in establishing probable cause through the use of informants?

8. How did the U.S. Supreme Court case of *Illinois v. Gates* change the requirements for establishing probable cause through the use of informants? Does the *Gates* decision make the law enforcement officer's task easier or harder?

9. Mr. A walks into a police station, drops three wristwatches on a table, and tells an officer that Mr. B robbed a local jewelry store two weeks ago. Mr. A will not say anything else in response to police questioning. A quick investigation reveals that the three watches were among a number of items stolen in the jewelry store robbery. Do the police have probable cause to do each of the following?
   a. Arrest Mr. A
   b. Arrest Mr. B
   c. Search Mr. A's home
   d. Search Mr. B's home

10. If you answered no to any of the items in question 9, explain why in detail. If you answered yes to any of them, draft the complaint or affidavit for a warrant or explain why a warrant is not needed.

PART THREE
Exceptions to the Search Warrant Requirement

CHAPTER 7
Search Incident to Arrest

The early chapters of this book emphasize the law's preference for warrants based upon probable cause as the chief means of balancing the need for efficient and effective law enforcement against the need to protect the rights of individual citizens to be secure against unreasonable searches and seizures. In Aguilar v. Texas, 378 U.S. 108, 84 S.Ct. 1509, 12 L.Ed.2d 723 (1964), the U.S. Supreme Court stated that the preference for warrants is so strong that less persuasive evidence will justify the issuance of a warrant than would justify a warrantless search or warrantless arrest.

> [W]hen a search is based upon a magistrate's, rather than a police officer's determination of probable cause, the reviewing courts will accept evidence of a less "judicially competent or persuasive character than would have justified an officer in acting on his own without a warrant," . . . and will sustain the judicial determination so long as "there was a substantial basis for [the magistrate] to conclude that [seizable evidence was] probably present. . . ." 378 U.S. at 111, 84 S.Ct. at 1512, 12 L.Ed.2d at 726.

The warrant procedure is preferred because it places responsibility for deciding the delicate question of probable cause with a neutral and detached judicial officer. Law enforcement is served, because law enforcement officers may search certain persons or places and seize certain persons or things when the officers can show reasonable grounds that a person, place, or thing is significantly connected with criminal activity. The Fourth Amendment rights of citizens are also served, because the decision to allow a search and seizure is removed from the hurried judgment of overzealous law enforcement officers engaged in the competitive enterprise of investigating crime.

Nevertheless, in practice, situations often arise in which the time and effort needed to obtain a warrant would unjustifiably frustrate enforcement of the laws. To ensure that the delicate balance between individual rights and law enforcement is maintained, courts have carved out various exceptions to the warrant requirement and have allowed warrantless searches in certain situations.

One important exception is a search incident to arrest. Coverage of the exceptions to the search warrant requirement begins, therefore, with a discussion of Chimel v. California, 395 U.S. 752, 89 S.Ct. 2034, 23 L.Ed.2d 685 (1969), the leading case on search incident to arrest.

CHIMEL v. CALIFORNIA

Since 1969, the law of search incident to arrest has been controlled by the U.S. Supreme Court case of Chimel v. California. In that case, law enforcement officers arrived at the defendant's home with a warrant for his arrest for the burglary of a coin shop. The defendant was not at home, but his wife let the officers in to wait for him. When the defendant arrived, the officers handed him the warrant and asked if they could look around. He objected, but the officers searched the entire house anyway on the basis of the lawful arrest. The officers found coins and other items that were later used in court to obtain a conviction against the defendant.

The U.S. Supreme Court found the search of the entire house unreasonable.

> When an arrest is made, it is reasonable for the arresting officer to search the person arrested in order to remove any weapons that the latter might seek to use in order to resist arrest or effect his escape. Otherwise, the officer's safety might well be endangered, and the arrest itself frustrated. In addition, it is entirely reasonable for the arresting officer to search for and seize any evidence on the arrestee's person in order to prevent its concealment or destruction. And the area into which an arrestee might reach in order to grab a weapon or evidentiary items must, of course, be governed by a like rule. A gun on a table or in a drawer in front of one who is arrested can be as dangerous to the arresting officer as one concealed in the clothing of the person arrested. There is ample justification, therefore, for a search of the arrestee's person and the area "within his immediate control"—construing that phrase to mean the area from within which he might gain possession of a weapon or destructible evidence. 395 U.S. 752, 762–63, 89 S.Ct. 2034, 2040, 23 L.Ed.2d 685, 694.

The *Chimel* decision drastically changed the area allowed to be searched incident to arrest from that allowed under previous law. Under pre-*Chimel* law, an officer was allowed to search incident to arrest the area considered to be in the "possession" or under the "control" of the arrested person. These vague standards were interpreted by the courts to include areas that were not necessarily under the defendant's "physical control" but were within his or her "constructive possession." Under this interpretation, law enforcement officers could search an entire residence incident to an arrest made in the residence and had almost free reign in deciding what would be searched. Furthermore, because neither a written application for a warrant nor a demonstration of probable cause before a magistrate was required, the search incident to arrest was administratively more convenient and was heavily used by law enforcement officers.

Although a warrant or probable cause is still not needed to conduct a search incident to arrest, *Chimel* has made it much more difficult for officers to obtain admissible evidence as a result of such a search. This chapter discusses various ramifications of the limitations *Chimel* places on a law enforcement officer's power to search incident to arrest.

SCOPE

The allowable scope of a search incident to arrest depends largely on the allowable purposes of a search incident to arrest. *Chimel* allows a law enforcement officer to search a person incident to arrest for only two purposes:

1. To search for and remove weapons that the arrestee might use to resist arrest or effect an escape

2. To search for and seize evidence in order to prevent its concealment or destruction

Seizable Property

In a search incident to arrest, as in any search and seizure, a law enforcement officer may search for and seize the following types of property.

1. *Weapons* that the arrested person may use to injure the officer or others or to effect an escape,

2. *Fruits of the crime* for which the arrest is made,

3. *Instrumentalities* used to commit the crime,

4. *Contraband,*

5. *Evidence* of the crime or evidence that the person arrested committed the crime. People v. Lewis, 311 N.Y.S.2d 905, 909, 260 N.E.2d 538, 541 (N.Y. 1970).

In addition, an officer may seize evidence of crimes other than the crime for which the arrest was made. In United States v. Simpson, 453 F.2d 1028 (10th Cir. 1972), the defendant was arrested under a warrant for possessing and transporting explosives. During a search incident to the arrest, the arresting officer found a third person's Selective Service Certificate and Classification Card, the possession of which was illegal. The court held that the certificate and card were admissible in court, even though they did not relate to the offense of possessing explosives.

> The general rule is that incident to a lawful arrest, a search without a warrant may be made of portable personal effects in the immediate possession of the person arrested. The discovery during a search of a totally unrelated object which provides grounds for prosecution of a crime different than that which the accused was arrested for does not render the search invalid. 453 F.2d at 1031.

Search of Arrestee's Body

The *Chimel* case gives few guidelines as to the allowable extent of the search of an arrestee's body. However, the later cases of United States v. Robinson, 414 U.S. 218, 94 S.Ct. 467, 38 L.Ed.2d 427 (1973), and Gustafson v. Florida, 414 U.S. 260, 94 S.Ct. 488, 38 L.Ed.2d 456 (1973), held that a law enforcement officer may conduct a *full* search of a person's body incident to the arrest of the person. In each case, the Court upheld an inspection of the contents of a cigarette package seized incident to the arrest of the defendant for a traffic violation. Illegal drugs were found in both cases. In the *Robinson* case, the Court said:

> It is the fact of the lawful arrest which establishes the authority to search, and we hold that in the case of lawful custodial arrest a full search of the person is not only an exception to the warrant requirement of the Fourth Amendment, but is also a "reasonable" search under that Amendment. 414 U.S. at 235, 94 S.Ct. at 477, 38 L.Ed.2d at 441.

This language was quoted with approval in the *Gustafson* decision, 414 U.S. at 263–64, 94 S.Ct. at 491, 38 L.Ed.2d at 460. Therefore, under the *Robinson-Gustafson* rule, whenever officers make a lawful custodial arrest, they may make a full search of the arrestee's body incident to the arrest.

FULL SEARCH OF ARRESTEE'S BODY. The *Robinson-Gustafson* rule raises the question as to what constitutes a full search of the arrestee's body. The following principles can be derived from court decisions dealing with this question.

1. A full search of the arrestee's body allows the seizure of evidence on or in the body. Such evidence might include hair samples and fingernail clippings on the body and blood or drugs in the body. Officers must use reasonable and painless procedures in obtaining such evidence. In Commonwealth v. Tarver, 345 N.E.2d 671 (Mass. 1975), the court upheld a seizure of hair samples from the head, chest, and pubic area of a person incident to the arrest of that person for murder and sexual abuse of a child.

2. A full search of the arrestee's body allows the *seizure* of items of evidence or weapons immediately associated with the arrestee's body, such as clothing, billfolds, jewelry, wristwatches, and weapons strapped or carried on the person. In this context, immediately associated means attached in a permanent or semipermanent way to the arrestee's body or clothing. In State v. Smith, 203 N.W.2d 348 (Minn. 1972), the court held that the seizure of the defendant's boots at the time of booking was a valid search and seizure incident to arrest.

3. A full search of the arrestee's body allows a *search* of property seized under item 2 here. Such a search might include going through the pockets of clothing; examining clothing for bloodstains, hair, or dirt; and examining weapons for bloodstains, fingerprints, or serial numbers. In Parker v. State, 544 S.W.2d 149 (Tex. Crim. App. 1976), officers on surveillance stopped the defendant and another man as they emerged from an apartment that was suspected of containing illegal drugs. While the officers were attempting to obtain information about the apartment, they discovered a weapon on the defendant and a bag containing a white powder nearby. They arrested the defendant, searched him, and seized his billfold. In the billfold were found packets of a white powder that was later determined to be cocaine. The court held that the officers had probable cause to arrest the defendant. The full search of the defendant and the seizure and search of his billfold incident to the lawful custodial arrest were held reasonable under the Fourth Amendment.

4. A full search of the arrestee's body allows the *seizure* of other personal property and containers that are *not* immediately associated with the arrestee's body, but which the arrestee is carrying or otherwise has under his immediate control. Property that might be seized includes luggage, attache cases, bundles, or packages. Before 1977, this type of property not only could have been *seized*, but also could have been *searched*. In 1977, however, in United States v. Chadwick, 433 U.S. 1, 97 S.Ct. 2476, 53 L.Ed.2d 538, the U.S. Supreme Court severely limited the *search* of luggage and other personal property after it has been seized incident to arrest.

In the *Chadwick* case, the defendants arrived in Boston from San Diego by train and loaded a large double-locked footlocker, which they had transported with them, into the trunk of their waiting car. Federal narcotics agents, who had probable cause to arrest and to search the footlocker, but no warrants, arrested the defendants. The agents took exclusive control over the footlocker and took it and the defendants to the federal building in Boston. An hour and a half later, the agents, without the defendants' consent and without a search warrant, opened the footlocker and found large amounts of marijuana.

The U.S. Supreme Court held that the search of the footlocker was illegal.

> The potential dangers lurking in all custodial arrests make warrantless searches of items within the "immediate control" area reasonable without requiring the arresting officer to calculate the probability that weapons or destructible evidence may be involved. [citing United States v. Robinson and Terry v. Ohio] However, warrantless searches of luggage or other property seized at the time of an arrest cannot be justified as incident to that arrest either if the "search is remote in time and place from the arrest," . . . or no exigency exists. Once law enforcement officers have reduced luggage or other personal property not immediately associated with the person of the arrestee to their exclusive control, and there is no longer any danger that the arrestee might gain access to the property to seize a weapon or destroy evidence, a search of that property is no longer an incident of the arrest.
>
> Here the search was conducted more than an hour after federal agents had gained exclusive control of the footlocker and long after respondents were securely in custody; the search therefore cannot be viewed as incidental to the arrest or as justified by any other exigency. Even though on this record the issuance of a warrant by a judicial officer was reasonably predictable, a line must be drawn. In our view, when no exigency is shown to support the need for an immediate search, the Warrant Clause places the line at the point where the property to be searched comes under the exclusive dominion of police authority. Respondents were therefore entitled to the protection of the Warrant Clause with the evaluation of a neutral magistrate, before their privacy interests in the contents of the footlocker were invaded. 433 U.S. at 15–16, 97 S.Ct. at 2485–86, 53 L.Ed.2d at 550–51.

Footnotes to the *Chadwick* opinion indicate that the Court's decision was based in large part on its belief that the defendants' legitimate privacy interests were violated. In footnote 10 the Court said:

> Unlike searches of the person, United States v. Robinson, 414 U.S. 218 (1973); United States v. Edwards, 415 U.S. 800 (1974), searches of possessions within an arrestee's immediate control cannot be justified by any reduced expectations of privacy caused by the arrest. Respondents' privacy interest in the

contents of the footlocker was not eliminated simply because they were under arrest. 433 U.S. at 16 n. 10, 97 S.Ct. at 2486 n. 10, 53 L.Ed.2d at 551 n. 10.

In footnote 8 the Court said:

> Respondents' principal privacy interest in the footlocker was of course not in the container itself, which was exposed to public view, but in its contents. A search of the interior was therefore a far greater intrusion into Fourth Amendment values than the impoundment of the footlocker. Though surely a substantial infringement with respondents' use and possession, the seizure did not diminish respondents' legitimate expectation that the footlocker's contents would remain private. 433 U.S. at 13–14 n. 8, 97 S.Ct. at 2485 n. 8, 53 L.Ed.2d at 550 n. 8.

To summarize, law enforcement officers may *seize* incident to arrest luggage and other personal property not immediately associated with the arrestee's body if that property is within the arrestee's immediate control. Once officers have the property under their exclusive control and there is no further danger that the arrestee might gain access to the property to seize a weapon or destroy evidence, officers may *not search* the property without a warrant or consent. However, if officers reasonably believe that the property contains some immediately dangerous instrumentality, such as explosives, or that some other genuine emergency exists, they may search the property immediately and disarm the weapon or otherwise end the danger.

STATE DEPARTURES FROM ROBINSON-GUSTAFSON RULE. Based on interpretations of their state constitutions, some state courts have refused to follow the *Robinson-Gustafson* rule allowing a full body search incident to a lawful custodial arrest. Several states, including Alaska, Colorado, Hawaii, and Oregon, have placed various limitations on the *Robinson-Gustafson* rule. The Supreme Court of Hawaii limited the warrantless search of an arrestee's person incident to a lawful custodial arrest (1) to disarming the arrested person when there is reason to believe from the facts and circumstances that the person may be armed; and (2) to discovering evidence related to the crime *for which the person was arrested.* State v. Kaluna, 520 P.2d 51, 60 (Hawaii 1974). Under this more restrictive rule, officers may not search for *evidence* incident to offenses that would not produce evidence (such as loitering and minor traffic offenses), and officers may not search for weapons unless they can point to specific facts and circumstances indicating the likelihood that the arrested person was armed and dangerous.

The California Supreme Court also refused to go along with the U.S. Supreme Court's decisions in the *Robinson* and *Gustafson* cases. In California, an officer may not conduct a full body search of an arrested person when the arrest will be disposed of by a mere citation or the arrested person will be transported in a law enforcement vehicle to a police facility where the opportunity to post bond is available. Officers may, however, conduct a pat-down frisk for weapons before placing an arrested person in a law enforcement vehicle for transportation to the stationhouse. The court recognized the increased danger to law enforcement officers in this situation. People v. Longwill, 123 Cal.Rptr. 297, 538 P.2d 753 (Cal. 1975).

SEARCH OF AREA WITHIN ARRESTEE'S IMMEDIATE CONTROL

> And the area into which an arrestee might reach in order to grab a weapon or evidentiary items must, of course, be governed by a like rule. A gun on a table or in a drawer in front of one who is arrested can be as dangerous to the arresting officer as one concealed in the clothing of the person arrested. There is ample justification, therefore, for a search of the arrestee's person and the area "within his immediate control"—construing that phrase to mean the area from within which he might gain possession of a weapon or destructible evidence. 395 U.S. at 763, 89 S.Ct. at 2040, 23 L.Ed.2d at 694.

This quotation from the *Chimel* case gives definite guidelines as to the extent of the area around an arrestee that is "within his immediate control" and is therefore subject to search by an officer. This determination of the permissible area of search depends on several factors such as the size and shape of the room, the size and agility of the arrestee, whether the arrestee was handcuffed or otherwise subdued, the size and type of evidence being sought, the number of people arrested, and the number of officers present.

Several other cases have further refined the *Chimel* guidelines. In People v. Spencer, 99 Cal.Rptr 681 (Cal. App. 1972), officers went to the defendant's trailer home to arrest him for participating in an armed robbery. They found him lying in bed. One officer immediately searched under the blankets for a gun as other officers attempted to subdue the defendant, who was resisting. Two revolvers were found in a box at the foot of the bed. The court held that this box was within the area of the defendant's reach and that the revolvers were admissible in evidence.

If a person is arrested out of doors, a search of that person's home or apartment cannot be justified as incident to the arrest. In Frazier v. State, 488 P.2d 613 (Okla. Crim. App. 1971), the defendant was arrested in his backyard and the arresting officers then went up to his apartment and searched it. The court held that the search was unreasonable because it extended beyond the arrestee's reach.

If it is necessary for an arrested person to go into a different area of the premises from that in which he or she was arrested, the officer may, for protective purposes, accompany the person and search if necessary. In Giacalone v. Lucas, 445 F.2d 1238, 1247 (6th Cir. 1971), an arrest under warrant for conspiracy to commit extortion took place early in the morning when the arrested person was in his bedclothes. An officer suggested that the defendant change into street clothes before leaving for the station. The defendant agreed and went to his bedroom followed by the officers. As the defendant went to a chest of drawers to obtain clothing, one officer searched the drawer and found a blackjack and several other weapons. The defendant was convicted of illegal possession of a blackjack.

The court held the search was lawful:

> Certainly, if immediately after a lawful arrest, the arrestee reads the arrest warrant and without coercion consents to go to his bedroom to change into more appropriate clothing, the arresting officers—incident to that arrest—may search the areas upon which the arrestee focuses his attention and are within his reach to gain access to a weapon or to destroy evidence. 445 F.2d at 1247.

Search of Motor Vehicles

In New York v. Belton, 453 U.S. 454, 460–61, 101 S.Ct. 2860, 2864, 69 L.Ed.2d 768, 775 (1981), the U.S. Supreme Court held:

> [W]hen a policeman has made a lawful custodial arrest of the occupant of an automobile, he may, as a contemporaneous incident of that arrest, search the passenger compartment of that automobile.
>
> It follows from this conclusion that the police may also examine the contents of any containers found within the passenger compartment, for if the passenger compartment is within the reach of the arrestee, so also will containers in it be within reach. . . . Such a container may, of course, be searched whether it is open or closed, since the justification for the search is not that the arrestee has no privacy interest in the container, but that the lawful custodial arrest justifies the infringement of any privacy interest the arrestee may have.

In a footnote, the Court defined a container as any object capable of holding another object. A container thus includes "closed or open glove compartments, consoles or other receptacles located anywhere within the passenger compartment, as well as luggage, boxes, bags, clothing, and the like." 453 U.S. at 460–61 n. 4, 101 S.Ct. at 2684 n. 4, 69 L.Ed.2d at 775 n. 4. The court also pointed out that only the interior of the passenger compartment of an automobile, and not the trunk, may be searched incident to arrest.

The *Belton* case deals only with the search incident to arrest exception to the warrant requirement and has nothing to do with the so-called automobile exception under the *Carroll* doctrine. (See Chapter 10.) The Court specifically referred to the *Chimel* case, stating that articles inside the relatively narrow compass of the passenger compartment of an automobile are in fact generally, even if not inevitably, within "the area into which an arrestee might reach in order to grab a weapon or evidentiary item." 395 U.S. at 763, 89 S.Ct. at 2040, 23 L.Ed.2d at 694. Therefore, the holding in the *Belton* case does not apply unless there has been a custodial arrest of the occupant of an automobile. And it is the custodial arrest that provides the justification for examining the contents of containers seized from the passenger compartment of the automobile. Moreover, as the previously quoted passage from the *Belton* case indicates, the searching of any containers found in the automobile must be substantially contemporaneous with the arrest of the automobile's occupant. If a container is seized and searched some time later, after it is in the exclusive control of the police, the *Chadwick* case requires that a warrant be obtained.

Search of Persons Other Than the Arrestee

When an arrest is made, other persons besides the arrested person are often in the vicinity. Courts generally allow a limited search of an arrestee's companion or companions in the immediate area of the arrest, when the arresting officer reasonably believes that these persons may present a danger or may destroy evidence. The allowed search is limited to a pat-down search of the companion's body and a search of the area within his or her immediate control for weapons or destructible evidence.

> Where . . . an arresting officer by his own calculation which must survive objective review, determines that a dangerous situation may exist under the circumstances due to the presence of a third party, we do not propose, out of regard

for the safety of the officers, to limit the search to a "pat down" when the actual danger is seen reasonably to exist in easy access to items within the companion's immediate control. United States v. Simmons, 567 F.2d 314, 319 (7th Cir. 1977).

Some courts apply a totality of the circumstances test in determining whether a search of an arrestee's companions is justified. In United States v. Flett, 806 F.2d 823 (8th Cir. 1986), the court upheld a pat-down search of an arrestee's companion, even though the companion made no threatening moves toward the officer and the officer noticed no bulge in the companion's clothing. The court said that the focus of the judicial inquiry was not whether the officer had an indication that the person was armed and dangerous, but rather, "whether the officer reasonably perceived the subject of the frisk as potentially dangerous." 806 F.2d at 828. The court found that the pat-down search was justified by the following circumstances:

1. The arrestee was the subject of an arrest warrant for narcotics violations.

2. The arrestee was a known member of a national motorcycle gang with violent propensities.

3. The arrestee was the "enforcer" of the local chapter of the motorcyle gang and had been previously charged with a firearms violation.

4. The companion was in the arrestee's house, was dressed in attire similar to that of gang members, and physically resembled known gang members.

5. The officer had 15 years' experience in law enforcement.

SEARCH OF OTHER AREAS OF THE PREMISES

Under the rule of the *Chimel* case, officers may not search any other areas of the premises other than the limited area within the arrestee's immediate control. Officers may, however, be justified in going into other areas for other reasons. For example, for their own protection, officers may look into other rooms to see if other persons are present. This is sometimes referred to as a protective walkthrough. Officers also may have to go through other rooms in entering or leaving the premises. These movements into other areas of the premises are not considered searches because the officers are not looking for weapons or incriminating evidence. Nevertheless, an officer who observes a weapon or other seizable item lying open to view may seize it, and that item will be admissible in court if the requirements of the plain view doctrine are satisfied (see Chapter 9).

In a bank robbery case, the defendant was arrested in his girl friend's apartment. At the time of his arrest, the apartment was dark and the defendant was nude. An officer went to get clothing for the defendant and found two jackets of the type that had been described as having been worn by the bank robbers. On the way out of the apartment, an officer turned on the kitchen light so he could see his way. Money taken during the robbery was observed on the kitchen floor.

The court held that both the jackets and the money were admissible in evidence. Finding no violation of the *Chimel* rule, the court said:

> Since they were bound to find some clothing for Titus rather than take him nude to FBI headquarters on a December night, the fatigue jackets were properly seized under the "plain view" doctrine. Welch was entitled to turn on the kitchen lights, both to assist his own exit and to see whether the other robber might be about; when he saw the stolen money, he was permitted to seize it. Everything the agents took was in their "plain view" while they were where they had a right to be; there was no general rummaging of the apartment. . . . United States v. Titus, 445 F.2d 577, 579 (2d Cir. 1971).

In United States v. Miller, 449 F.2d 974 (D.C.Cir. 1971), officers arrested the defendant in a dentist's office for robbery of a liquor store. They went into other rooms of the dentist's suite to look for possibly dangerous persons and found a stolen bottle of whiskey in plain view in the dentist's laboratory.

The court held that the bottle of whiskey was admissible in evidence. The officers had no way of knowing who else might be on the premises. They were justified in conducting a search of the suite to assure themselves that no hostile and possibly dangerous persons were hiding in other rooms. The bottle of whiskey was in plain view in the dentist's laboratory, and there was no evidence that the officers engaged in any general search of the premises beyond that necessary to find other persons who might have been present. If, however, the facts indicate that a protective walkthrough was a mere pretext or excuse for a search for evidence, any evidence seized will be inadmissible.

OTHER REQUIREMENTS FOR A VALID SEARCH INCIDENT TO ARREST

Several other requirements for a valid search incident to arrest may have been touched on in the previous discussion. This section treats each of these requirements in further detail under a separate heading for each requirement.

Lawful Custodial Arrest.

To justify a full search incident to arrest, an arrest must be a lawful custodial arrest. The word *custodial* is important here because in some states the term *arrest* is applied to situations in which an officer stops a person and issues a ticket, citation, or notice to appear in court, instead of taking the person into custody. A full search would not be authorized in situations in which the officer merely issued a ticket, citation, or notice to appear. In other words, the officer must take the arrested person into custody to justify a full search.

When conducting a search incident to arrest, an officer need not have a specific object or class of objects in mind. Even if the arrest is for an offense that could produce no evidence, the officer is still allowed to conduct a full search of the arrestee's body. The lawful custodial arrest, in itself, justifies the search.

Finally, officers need not satisfy any standard of probability that weapons or evidence will be found as a result of a search. Whether or not there is any such probability, the lawful custodial arrest alone provides sufficient justification for the search. Officers need not provide any underlying facts and circumstances justifying the need to search.

Contemporaneousness

In general, a search incident to arrest is not reasonable unless it is contemporaneous with the arrest. To be contemporaneous, a search must be conducted as close in time to the arrest as practically possible. In a U.S. Supreme Court case on this point, the defendant, a suspected possessor of narcotics, was lawfully arrested on a downtown street corner. The officers then took him to his home some distance away and conducted an intensive search that yielded narcotics.

The Court held the search unreasonable:

> In the circumstances of this case, however, the subsequent search of the petitioner's home cannot be regarded as incident to his arrest on a street corner more than two blocks away. A search "can be incident to an arrest only if it is substantially contemporaneous with the arrest and is confined to the immediate vicinity of the arrest." James v. Louisiana, 382 U.S. 36, 37, 86 S.Ct. 151, 151, 15 L.Ed.2d 30, 31 (1965).

The reason for this rule is that officers may search incident to arrest only (1) to protect themselves and (2) to prevent the destruction or concealment of evidence. A delayed search indicates that the officers were not concerned about either of these possibilities and that the search was conducted for another, impermissible, purpose.

Sometimes circumstances prevent an officer from conducting an immediate search incident to arrest. For example, body cavity searches and searches of persons of the opposite sex usually must be delayed. In these situations, the officer should remove the arrested person from the scene and conduct the search as soon as favorable circumstances prevail. In United States v. Miles, 413 F.2d 34 (3d Cir. 1969), an arrest for an armed bank robbery took place in a crowded hotel lobby, which was lit only by candles because of a power failure. The court held that under these circumstances it was proper for officers to make a cursory search for weapons at the hotel and to make a more thorough search later at the station.

Even though it is feasible to search an arrested person at the time of arrest, under certain circumstances courts will allow a delay between the arrest and search for a good reason. The U.S. Supreme Court made such an exception to the general rule in the case of United States v. Edwards, 415 U.S. 800, 94 S.Ct. 1234, 39 L.Ed.2d 771 (1974). In that case, the defendant was arrested shortly after 11:00 P.M. for attempting to break into a building. The defendant was taken to jail. Law enforcement officials had probable cause to believe that the defendant's clothing contained paint chips from the crime scene. Since the police had no substitute clothing for the defendant, they waited until the next morning to seize his clothing without a warrant. Paint chips matching those at the break scene were found on the clothing.

The Court held that, despite the delay, the clothing was lawfully seized incident to the defendant's arrest. The administrative process and the mechanics of arrest had not yet come to a halt the next morning. The police had custody of the defendant and the clothing and could have seized the clothing at the time of arrest. It was reasonable to delay the seizure until substitute clothing was available.

> [O]nce the accused is lawfully arrested and is in custody, the effects in his possession at the place of detention that were subject to search at the time and place of his arrest may lawfully be searched and seized without a warrant even though a substantial period of time has elapsed between the arrest and subsequent administrative processing, on the one hand, and the taking of the property for use as evidence on the other. 415 U.S. at 807, 94 S.Ct. at 1239, 39 L.Ed.2d at 778.

The *Edwards* case does *not* allow law enforcement officers to delay a search incident to arrest for as long as they wish. Nor does the case sanction *all* delays in searching and seizing evidence incident to arrest. Officers must be able to provide good reasons for delaying a search incident to arrest, and the duration of a delay must be reasonable under the circumstances. Otherwise the search and seizure may be declared illegal.

The contemporaneousness requirement does not necessarily mean that the arrest must precede the search. Although this is usually the case, the search may precede the arrest and still be a valid search incident to arrest, if

1. probable cause to arrest exists at the time of the search and does not depend on the fruits of the search; and

2. the arrest follows quickly on the heels of the search. Rawlings v. Kentucky, 448 U.S. 98, 100 S.Ct. 2556, 65 L.Ed.2d 633 (1980).

Who May Conduct the Search

If possible, the law enforcement officer making the arrest should conduct the search incident to the arrest. If an officer makes an arrest and does not search the arrested person right away, but later allows another officer to search the person, the later search may be held unlawful. It would not meet the requirement of contemporaneousness nor would it indicate a concern for the protection of the officer or the prevention of the destruction or concealment of evidence.

Nevertheless, if the arresting officer transfers an arrested person to the custody of another officer, the second officer may again search the arrested person. This second search is allowed because the second officer is entitled to take personal safety measures and need not rely on the assumption that the arrestee has been thoroughly searched for weapons by the arresting officer. United States v. Dyson, 277 A.2d 658 (D.C. App. 1971).

Use of Force

Law enforcement officers searching a person incident to arrest may use the degree of force necessary to protect themselves, prevent escape, and prevent the destruction or concealment of evidence. Courts will review the use of force strictly, and officers should use as little force as is necessary to accomplish their legitimate purpose.

In Salas v. State, 246 So.2d 621 (Fla. Dist. Ct. App. 1971), a seizure of drugs incident to arrest was upheld even though the arresting officer put a choke hold on the arrestee and forced him to spit out drugs he was attempting to swallow. However, before more intrusive measures are taken, such as pumping the stomach or probing body cavities, the following conditions must be satisfied:

1. The officer must have good reason to believe that the person's body contains evidence that should be removed. For example, in People v. Jones, 97 Cal.Rptr. 492 (Cal. App. 1971), officers observed the defendant thrust drug capsules into his mouth and quickly swallow them.

2. If possible, the procedure should be performed by a doctor working under sanitary conditions and in a medically approved manner.

3. Only the amount of force reasonably necessary to make the person submit to the examination may be used. Blackford v. United States, 247 F.2d 745 (9th Cir. 1957).

Arrest Must Not Be a Pretext to Justify Search

A law enforcement officer may not use an arrest as a pretext to search for evidence incident to the arrest. Even though an arrest is technically valid, if the officer's primary purpose is to use the arrest as a convenient excuse for an otherwise illegal search, the search will still be illegal.

> Whether or not an arrest is a mere pretext to search is a question of the motivation or primary purpose of the arresting officer. Improper motivation has been found where the arrest for a minor offense which serves as a mere "sham" or "front" for a search for evidence of another unrelated offense for which there is no probable cause to arrest or search . . . It has also been found where the arresting officer deliberately delays making the arrest in order to allow the arrestee to enter the premises which the officer desires to search. Williams v. United States, 418 F.2d 159, 161 (9th Cir. 1969).

SEARCH INCIDENT TO DETENTION

In Cupp v. Murphy, 412 U.S. 291, 93 S.Ct. 2000, 36 L.Ed.2d 900 (1973), the U.S. Supreme Court decided that a law enforcement officer may conduct a limited warrantless search of a person merely *detained* for investigation. In that case, the defendant was notified of his wife's strangulation, and then voluntarily came to the police headquarters and met his attorney there. Police noticed a dark spot on the defendant's finger and asked if they could take a scraping from his fingernails. The defendant refused. Under protest and without a warrant, police proceeded to take the samples, which turned out to include particles of skin and blood of the defendant's wife and fabric from her clothing. The evidence was admitted at trial and the defendant was convicted of second-degree murder.

The Court held that the momentary seizing of the defendant to get the fingernail scrapings constituted a seizure governed by the Fourth Amendment. The Court, citing the *Chimel* case, also recognized that under prescribed conditions warrantless searches incident to an arrest are constitutionally valid. In this case, however, without an arrest or search warrant, a full *Chimel* search of the defendant's body and the area within his immediate control would not have been permissible.

Nevertheless, the Court validated the search under a limited application of the *Chimel* rule based on the unique facts of the case:

1. The defendant was not arrested but was detained only long enough to take the fingernail scrapings.

2. The search was very limited in extent, involving only the scraping of fingernails. (The Court was careful to point out that a full *Chimel* search would not have been justified without an arrest. The officers therefore could not have searched the defendant's body and the area within his immediate control.)

3. The evidence—blood and skin on the fingernails—was readily destructible.

4. The defendant made attempts to destroy the evidence, creating exigent circumstances.

5. There was probable cause to arrest the defendant, even though he was not actually arrested.

All five of these conditions were essential to the Court's decision and must be satisfied to make a search incident to detention legal. Otherwise a warrant must be obtained before a search is conducted.

SUMMARY

Search incident to arrest is a recognized exception to the warrant requirement of the Fourth Amendment. The U.S. Supreme Court case of *Chimel v. California* permits the search of a lawfully arrested person for the limited purposes of removing weapons and preventing the concealment or destruction of evidence. If the arrest is a custodial arrest, a full search for weapons and seizable evidence is permitted, whether or not there is any likelihood of danger or any reason to believe evidence will be found.

A search incident to arrest must be substantially contemporaneous with the arrest and may extend to the arrestee's body and to the area within his or her immediate control—the area from which the arrestee might gain possession of a weapon or destructible evidence. Any weapon or seizable evidence found within this area may be seized. If, however, the item seized is luggage or other personal property not immediately associated with the person of the arrestee, a delayed search of the property, after it has come within the exclusive control of the police, may not be conducted without a warrant. A search incident to the arrest of an occupant of a motor vehicle may extend to the passenger area of the vehicle and may include a search of containers found in the vehicle, if the search is contemporaneous with the arrest.

Searches of persons in the vicinity of the arrested person and the areas within their immediate control may be conducted incident to the arrest, if reasonably necessary to remove weapons and prevent the concealment or destruction of evidence. Searches of areas of the premises beyond the immediate control of the arrestee or companions may not be conducted. Nevertheless, if officers are in a place or position in which they have a right to be, they may seize evidence lying open to view under the plain view doctrine. Searches incident to arrest may be delayed in a variety of circumstances, but there must be good reason for a delay and the duration of the delay must be reasonable under the circumstances.

The U.S. Supreme Court has approved a limited warrantless search of a person merely detained for investigation. Such a search may be conducted, however, only if there is probable cause to arrest the suspect and if there is an imminent danger that crucial evidence will be destroyed if the search is not made immediately.

REVIEW AND DISCUSSION QUESTIONS

1. Assume that while riding in the first-class section of an airplane, a person is legally arrested for transporting illegal drugs. Can the arresting officers immediately conduct searches of the following items and places incident to the arrest?
   a. The person's clothing
   b. The person's suitcase
   c. The entire first-class section of the airplane
   d. The person's body cavities

If you approved any of the preceding searches, consider whether each search *should* be made and what are the possible alternatives.

2. If a defendant is arrested in an automobile for stealing the automobile, may the arresting officer search other passengers in the automobile incident to the defendant's arrest?

3. In a typical search incident to arrest situation, the arrest is followed by a search and then by a seizure. Is a search followed by a seizure and then by an arrest valid? Is a seizure followed by an arrest and then by an additional search valid?

4. What search incident to an arrest problems are presented when the person arrested is a person of the opposite sex?

5. Does the nature of the offense arrested for have any effect on the scope of a search incident to arrest?

6. Assume that a defendant is arrested in the kitchen of his home for the armed robbery of a bank earlier that day. The arresting officers have an arrest warrant but no search warrant. The defendant is one of three persons wanted in the robbery. The defendant's automobile, the suspected getaway car, is parked in his driveway. Indicate the full extent of the arresting officers' authority to search the defendant, his premises, and his automobile.

7. Assume the same facts as in question 6 except that the defendant is arrested while running from his house to his automobile. Indicate the full extent of the arresting officers' authority to search the defendant, his premises, and his automobile. What if the officers have only a search warrant for the defendant's house, and no arrest warrant? What if it is raining heavily?

8. Is the scope of a search incident to arrest affected by any of the following circumstances?
   a. The defendant is handcuffed and chained to a pole.
   b. The defendant is unconscious.
   c. The defendant is surrounded by a group of friends.
   d. The defendant is arrested on a dark street.

9. Since the search of containers in the passenger compartment of an automobile is now allowed incident to a custodial arrest under the ruling in *New York v. Belton*, should law enforcement officers wait until a defendant is in an automobile before making an arrest, when possible? Should officers make custodial arrests for offenses for which they would ordinarily not make custodial arrests?

10. Discuss the meaning of the statement, "It is not at all clear that the 'grabbing distance' authorized in the *Chimel* case is conditioned upon the arrested person's continued capacity 'to grab.'" People v. Fitzpatrick, 346 N.Y.S.2d 793, 797, 300 N.E.2d 139, 143 (N.Y. 1973).

CHAPTER 8
Consent Searches

Another well-established exception to the search warrant requirement is the *consent search*. A consent search occurs when a person voluntarily allows a law enforcement officer to search his or her body, premises, or belongings. The consenting individual relinquishes any right to object to the search on constitutional grounds, and any evidence seized as a result of the search is admissible in court even though there was no warrant and no probable cause to search. A consent search may also provide a benefit to a consenting party who is innocent of any wrongdoing.

> If the search is conducted and proves fruitless, that in itself may convince the police that an arrest with its possible stigma and embarrassment is unnecessary, or that a far more extensive search pursuant to a warrant is not justified. In short, a search pursuant to consent may result in considerably less inconvenience for the subject of the search, and, properly conducted, is a constitutionally permissible and wholly legitimate aspect of effective police activity. Schneckloth v. Bustamonte, 412 U.S. 218, 228, 93 S.Ct. 2041, 2048, 36 L.Ed.2d 854, 863 (1973).

The consent search is frequently used by law enforcement officers, because it is faster than warrant procedures and does not require the often difficult determination of whether there is probable cause, either to search or to arrest. There are, however, many opportunities for abuse of a person's Fourth Amendment rights by law enforcement officers. To protect those rights, courts closely examine the circumstances surrounding every consent search to determine if the consent was truly voluntary. The U.S. Supreme Court said:

> [T]he Fourth and Fourteenth Amendments require that consent not be coerced, by explicit or implicit means, by implied threat or covert force. For, no matter how subtly the coercion were applied, the resulting "consent" would be no more than a pretext for the unjustified police intrusion against which the Fourth Amendment is directed. . . .
>
>   The problem of reconciling the recognized legitimacy of consent searches with the requirement that they be free from any aspect of official coercion cannot be resolved by any infallible touchstone. To approve such searches without

the most careful scrutiny would sanction the possibility of official coercion; to place artificial restrictions upon such searches would jeopardize their basic validity. Just as was true with confessions the requirement of "voluntary" consent reflects a fair accommodation of the constitutional requirements involved. In examining all the surrounding circumstances to determine if in fact the consent to search was coerced, account must be taken of subtly coercive police questions, as well as the possibly vulnerable subjective state of the person who consents. Those searches that are the product of police coercion can thus be filtered out without undermining the continuing validity of consent searches. In sum, there is no reason for us to depart in the area of consent searches, from the traditional definition of "voluntariness." Schneckloth v. Bustamonte, 412 U.S. 218, 229, 93 S.Ct. 2041, 2048–49, 36 L.Ed.2d 854, 864 (1973).

When the prosecuting attorney attempts to introduce into court evidence obtained as a result of a consent search, the court requires proof by "clear and convincing evidence" that the consent was voluntary and was not the result of duress or coercion, express or implied. The prosecutor's proof will consist almost entirely of the law enforcement officer's testimony about the circumstances surrounding the obtaining of the consent and the conducting of the search. The remainder of this chapter is devoted to explaining in detail the meaning of the voluntariness requirement and providing guidelines for the law enforcement officer in conducting consent searches.

VOLUNTARINESS REQUIREMENT

There are no set rules for determining whether or not a consent to search is voluntary. Courts will examine all the circumstances surrounding the giving of the consent in making this decision. The following examples illustrate the circumstances courts consider important in deciding the question of voluntariness of consent.

Force or Threat of Force

Courts always find consent involuntary if law enforcement officers used force or threats of force in obtaining the consent. In a case in which the defendant was confronted by police officers with drawn guns and was told the officers would get a warrant if necessary, the court held that the defendant did not give free and voluntary consent to search when he gave the officers the keys to his car in an atmosphere of "dramatic excitement." Weed v. United States, 340 F.2d 827 (10th Cir. 1965). Lack of valid consent was also found where officers told the defendant that if he didn't consent, the officers could and would get a search warrant which would allow them to tear the paneling off his walls and ransack his house. United States v. Kampbell, 574 F.2d 962 (8th Cir. 1978).

A mere threat by police to obtain a warrant if consent is withheld is usually not considered coercion, however, especially if the officer indicates that he or she must apply for the warrant from a neutral and detached judicial authority and if the threat that a warrant can be obtained is well-founded. United States v. Faruolo, 506 F.2d 490 (2d Cir. 1974).

Sometimes the initial encounter between a law enforcement officer and a suspect requires the officer to use force or threat of force for personal or public safety. Despite the coercive nature of the initial confrontation, an officer may still obtain a valid consent to search if the consent itself is obtained without coercion. In United States v. Alfonso, 759 F.2d 728 (9th Cir. 1985), police with guns drawn arrested the defendant in his motel room. After determining that no weapons or other persons were in the room, the officers holstered their guns. The officers informed the defendant of the purpose of their investigation, and the defendant, who was not handcuffed, responded that he had "nothing to hide." The court held that the defendant's consent to a search of his luggage was voluntary, despite the initial armed confrontation.

Submission to Fraudulent or Mistaken Claim of Authority

A subtler form of coercion is a law enforcement officer's assertion of a right to search, when the officer has no such right. A person's submission to this assertion of authority and consent to the search does not constitute a voluntary consent. Rather than an act of free will, it is merely a mistaken demonstration of respect for the law. It matters not whether the officer's assertion of authority was mistaken or was deliberately designed to deceive the person. In Bumper v. North Carolina, 391 U.S. 543, 88 S.Ct. 1788, 20 L.Ed.2d 797 (1968), officers went to the home of a rape suspect to look for evidence. The home was owned and occupied by the defendant's grandmother. The officers told the grandmother that they had a search warrant and she let them in. During the course of their search, a rifle was found. At the hearing on the motion to suppress the rifle as evidence, the prosecutor relied on the grandmother's consent rather than the warrant to support the legality of the search. (In fact, no warrant was ever returned nor was there any information about the conditions under which it was issued.)

The U.S. Supreme Court held that a search cannot be justified on the basis of consent when that consent has been given only after an announcement by the officers conducting the search that they have a search warrant:

> When a prosecutor seeks to rely upon consent to justify the lawfulness of a search, he has the burden of proving that the consent was, in fact, *freely and voluntarily given.* This burden cannot be discharged by showing no more than acquiescence to a claim of lawful authority. A search conducted in reliance upon a warrant cannot later be justified on the basis of consent if it turns out that the warrant was invalid. The results can be no different when it turns out that the State does not even attempt to rely upon the validity of the warrant, or fails to show that there was, in fact, any warrant at all.
>
> When a law enforcement officer claims authority to search a home under a warrant, he announces in effect that the occupant has no right to resist the search. The situation is instinct with coercion—albeit colorably lawful coercion. Where there is coercion there cannot be consent. 391 U.S. at 548–50, 88 S.Ct. at 1792, 20 L.Ed.2d at 802–3.

Misrepresentation or Deception

Coercion may also take the form of misrepresentation or deception on matters other than the officer's authority. A person's consent to search based on false impressions created by a law enforcement officer is not voluntary. In Commonwealth v. Wright, 190 A.2d 709 (Pa. 1963), officers arrested the defendant for robbery and murder and questioned him at police headquarters, but obtained no incriminating statements. The next day, officers, without a search warrant, went to the defendant's apartment to conduct a search. They falsely told the defendant's wife that the defendant had admitted the crime and had sent the police for the "stuff." The frightened and upset wife admitted the officers to the apartment and led them to money taken in the robbery. The Court held that the consent given by the wife was not voluntary: "[I]t is well established that the consent may not be gained through stealth, deceit, or misrepresentation, and that if such exists this is tantamount to implied coercion." 190 A.2d at 709, 711.

If, however, the deceit is carried out by an undercover officer and concerns only the officer's identity as a governmental agent, a person's misplaced confidence in the agent will not make the person's consent involuntary.

> Entry of an undercover agent is not illegal if he enters a home for the "very purposes contemplated by the occupant." . . . If the occupant reveals private information to the visitor under such circumstances, he or she assumes the risk the visitor will reveal it. United States v. Goldstein, 611 F.Supp. 624, 626 (N.D. Ill. 1985).

In the *Goldstein* case, the undercover officer gained entrance to the defendant's home for the purpose understood by the defendant's wife: to discuss the possible purchase of a stolen emerald. The court held that the wife's voluntarily showing the officer the emerald was the result of her misplaced trust in the officer and did not implicate any Fourth Amendment privacy interest.

Custody or Arrest

In United States v. Watson, 423 U.S. 411, 96 S.Ct. 820, 46 L.Ed.2d 598 (1976), the U.S. Supreme Court held that a consent to search is not involuntary solely because the person giving the consent is under arrest or is otherwise in custody. Nevertheless, courts tend to examine very carefully any consent given under these circumstances. A person who has been taken into custody or arrested is believed to be "more susceptible to duress or coercion from the custodial officers." United States v. Richardson, 388 F.2d 842, 845 (6th Cir. 1968). The Indiana Supreme Court held that because of the inherently coercive nature of in-custody interrogation, a person in custody of the police is entitled to the presence and advice of counsel before deciding whether to give consent to search. Pirtle v. State, 323 N.E.2d 634 (Ind. 1975).

In general, it will be harder to prove a consent was voluntary when the person giving the consent was in custody than if the person was not. However, if the person in custody is subjected to additional coercive action by a law enforcement officer, such as handcuffing, display of weapons, or incarceration, or if the officer interrogates the person without giving *Miranda* warnings, a subsequent consent to search is likely to be considered involuntary. Evasive or uncooperative conduct on the part of the person in custody is also considered to be an indication that the consent is not voluntary.

If the arrest or detention itself is illegal, courts will generally hold that any consent obtained as a result of the illegal conduct is "fruit of the poisonous tree" and necessarily involuntary unless there are attenuating circumstances.

In Florida v. Royer, 460 U.S. 491, 103 S.Ct. 1319, 75 L.Ed.2d 229 (1983), the U.S. Supreme Court, after finding that the defendant was being illegally detained when he consented to the search of his luggage, held that the consent was tainted by the illegality and was ineffective to justify the search. In United States v. Wellins, 654 F.2d 550 (9th Cir. 1981), however, despite an illegal arrest of the defendant, the court held that a consent to search obtained one and one-quarter hours after the illegal arrest was valid. Attenuating circumstances were found where the defendant was given *Miranda* warnings and was allowed to consult with his attorney and codefendant before signing a consent form. Another court held that the passage of a significant amount of time and the lack of flagrant misconduct by police helped to purge the taint of an illegal arrest. United States v. Cherry, 794 F.2d 201 (5th Cir. 1986).

Knowledge of Right to Refuse Consent

Before the U.S. Supreme Court decision in *Schneckloth v. Bustamonte* (discussed earlier), some courts held that in order to prove voluntary consent to search, the prosecution had to show that the person giving consent knew of the right to refuse consent. Other courts ruled that knowledge of the right to refuse consent was only one factor to be considered in determining voluntariness. *Schneckloth v. Bustamonte* adopted the latter view:

> Voluntariness is a question of fact to be determined from all the circumstances, and while the subject's knowledge of a right to refuse is a factor to be taken into consideration, the prosecution is not required to demonstrate such knowledge as a prerequisite to establishing a voluntary consent.... 412 U.S. at 248–49, 93 S.Ct. at 2059, 36 L.Ed.2d at 875.

A law enforcement officer seeking to obtain a valid consent to search from a person not in custody need not give any warnings or otherwise ensure that the person is aware of the right to refuse consent.

Nevertheless, even though formal warnings are not required for non-custodial consent searches, the courts still consider a person's knowledge of the right to refuse consent as very persuasive evidence of voluntariness. "[T]he . . . salutary practice of informing individuals that they are free to refuse consent to a search and to contact a lawyer . . . does not absolutely prove uncoerced consent, [but] it does in many instances assuage the fear of a court that an individual was intimidated into consent to a search." United States v. Berry, 670 F.2d 583, 597–98 (5th Cir. 1982). For example, in In re Joe. R., 165 Cal.Rptr. 837, 612 P.2d 927 (Cal. 1980), the court found voluntary consent to search despite the presence of several officers with drawn guns, where officers had explained the right to refuse consent. Therefore, an officer *may* give a person formal warning of this right to increase the chances that the consent will be voluntary. Furthermore, since the courts have not yet decided whether knowledge of the right to refuse consent is necessary for a valid consent when the consenting person is *in custody*, officers should so inform persons under arrest or otherwise in custody. The following warning should adequately inform a person of the right to refuse consent:

> I am a law enforcement officer. I would like to request permission from you to search your premises (person, belongings).

You have an absolute right to refuse to grant permission for me to search unless I have a search warrant.

If you do grant permission to search, anything found can be used against you in a court of law. If you refuse, I will not make a search at this time.

A consent to search given by a person after receiving such a warning is likely to be considered voluntary by a court, assuming there has been no coercion by the officer.

If an officer has clear indications that the consenting person already knows of the right to insist on a search warrant, there is no need for the officer to give any warnings. In United States v. Curiale, 414 F.2d 744 (2d Cir. 1969), when an officer asked the defendant to sign a Consent to Search form, the defendant said, "If I don't sign this, you are going to get a search warrant." The court found that this statement demonstrated the defendant's awareness of his right to resist the officer's search in the absence of a warrant. His subsequent signature on the form was therefore a relinquishment of a *known* right.

Some state courts have refused to follow the *Schneckloth v. Bustamonte* totality of the circumstances test and have required that consenting persons be aware of their right to refuse consent in addition to requiring that the consent be voluntary. The New Jersey Supreme Court held that the state constitution demands that "the validity of a consent to search, even in a noncustodial situation, must be measured in terms of waiver; i.e., where the state seeks to justify a search on the basis of consent it has the burden of showing that the consent was voluntary, an essential element of which is knowledge of the right to refuse consent." State v. Johnson, 346 A.2d 66, 68 (N.J. 1975). Likewise, Case v. State, 519 P.2d 523 (Okla. Crim. App. 1974), held that officers must give *Miranda* warnings before obtaining consent.

Clearness and Explicitness of Consent

Another issue in determining the voluntariness of consent is whether the expression of consent is clear, explicit, and unequivocal. Hesitation or ambiguity in the giving of consent could be an indication that the consent is not voluntary.

Both written and oral consent to search are equally effective in waiving a person's right to later object to the search on constitutional grounds. A signed and witnessed writing, however, provides the best proof of a clear, voluntary, waiver of a known right. A suggested form for obtaining a written consent to search appears on page 191.

Consent need not be expressed in words but may be implied from a person's acts or conduct. For example, in United States v. Miller, 589 F.2d 1117 (1st Cir. 1978), the defendant never expressly consented to a search of luggage. Nevertheless, valid consent was found where the defendant unlocked his vehicle, unlocked the luggage inside the vehicle, and disclaimed any knowledge or interest in the luggage.

Notification of Counsel

If a defendant has retained counsel in connection with a criminal charge, officers should notify the defendant's counsel before obtaining a consent to

---

CONSENT TO SEARCH

I, _____ , have been requested to consent to a search of my _____ , located at _____ _____ . I have also been advised of my constitutional rights to refuse consent and to require that a search warrant be obtained prior to any search. I have further been advised that if I do consent to a search, any evidence found as a result of the search can be seized and used against me in any court of law, and that I may withdraw my consent to search at any time prior to the conclusion of the search.

After having been advised of my constitutional rights as stated above, I hereby voluntarily waive those rights and consent to a search and authorize _____ and _____ to conduct a complete search of the above-described _____ .

_____

Signature

_____

Location and Date

WITNESSES:

_____

Signature, Title and Date

_____

Signature, Title and Date

---

search. In Tidwell v. Superior Court, 95 Cal.Rptr.213 (Cal. App. 1971), a law enforcement officer obtained from the defendant, who was being held in the county jail, consent to search the defendant's automobile. At the time, the defendant was represented by appointed counsel on a separate charge, but the officer did not notify counsel before obtaining consent. The court suppressed the evidence, holding that once counsel is appointed the police may not obtain consent to search without notifying counsel.

Physical, Mental, and Emotional Factors

Voluntariness of consent may be affected by the physical, mental, or emotional condition of the person giving consent. If a person is sick, injured, mentally ill, under the influence of alcohol or drugs, or otherwise impaired, that person's vulnerability to subtle forms of coercion may affect the voluntariness of consent. Likewise, if a person is immature, inexperienced, mentally retarded, illiterate, or emotionally upset, the impairment of perception and understanding may render any consent to search a mere submission to authority. United States v. Gallego-Zapata, 630 F.Supp. 655 (D. Mass. 1986).

The existence of any one of these conditions or states of mind standing alone will usually not invalidate an otherwise uncoerced consent. "[T]he mere fact that one has taken drugs, or is intoxicated, or mentally agitated, does not render consent involuntary." United States v. Rambo, 789 F.2d 1289, 1297 (8th Cir. 1986). In United States v. Gay, 774 F.2d 368, 377 (10th Cir. 1985), the court said:

> The issue squarely put is whether Gay was so intoxicated that his consent to search was not the product of a rational intellect and a free will. . . . The question is one of mental awareness so that the act of consent was that of one who knew what he was doing. It is elementary that one must know he is giving consent for the consent to be efficacious.

In the *Gay* case, the court found voluntary consent to search the defendant's automobile glove compartment despite the defendant's intoxication, based on evidence that the defendant:

— Was able to answer questions addressed to him;
— Produced his driver's license on request;
— Responded when asked if he had been drinking;
— Emptied his pockets upon request; and
— Denied access to the automobile's trunk, which was found to contain cocaine in a later search.

SCOPE

In general, the scope of a consent search is determined by the extent of search allowed by the person giving consent. A preliminary issue, however, is whether there has been a consent to search at all. Although a person may give a valid consent to an officer's requests, it may not be a consent to *search*. The best example of this is a person's consent to allow an officer to *enter* his or her home in compliance with the officer's request for an interview. This does *not* automatically give the officer a right to search. There is a vital distinction between the granting of admission to one's home for the purposes of conversation and the granting of permission to thoroughly search the home.

In Duncan v. State, 176 So.2d 840 (Ala. 1965), officers investigating a murder knocked on the defendant's hotel room door and were invited in by the defendant. The defendant was not advised that they were police officers nor did the officers make any request to search the defendant's room. Nevertheless, a search was conducted and incriminating evidence was found.

The court held that the invitation to enter his room, extended by the defendant to the person who knocked on the door, did not constitute a consent to search his room. Quoting from another case, the court said:

> "To justify the introduction of evidence seized by a police officer within a private residence on the ground that the officer's entry was made by invitation, permission, or consent, there must be evidence of a statement or some overt act by the occupant of such residence sufficient to indicate his intent to waive his rights to the security and privacy of his home and freedom from unwarranted intrusions therein. An open door is not a waiver of such rights. . . ." 176 So.2d at 853.

Plain View Doctrine

Although an invitation to enter premises is not the equivalent of a consent to search the premises, an officer need not ignore contraband or other criminal evidence lying in plain view. Under the *plain view doctrine*, if officers are in a place or position in which they have a legal right to be as the result of a prior valid intrusion into a constitutionally protected area, they may seize any criminal evidence that is lying open to view. In Robbins v. Mackenzie, 364 F.2d 45 (1st Cir. 1966), officers were investigating a robbery, and preliminary information led them to suspect a man named Albert. The officers went to Albert's apartment, knocked on the door, identified themselves, and were invited into the apartment by Albert, who opened the door and walked back into the room. The defendant was present in the apartment as a guest of Albert. While talking to the two men, the officers noticed various objects fitting the description of items stolen in the robbery lying in plain view. They arrested the two men and seized the evidence observed.

The court held that the evidence seized was admissible against the defendant (Albert's guest). Because the officers were rightfully in the room by Albert's invitation, they were also rightfully there with respect to the defendant. Seeing what was patently and obviously open to view was therefore not a search, and seizing the evidence was not a violation of the defendant's rights. (The plain view doctrine is discussed in detail in Chapter 9.)

Area of Search

Assuming that an officer obtains a valid consent not only to *enter* premises, but also to *search* the premises, the extent of the area allowed to be searched depends on the words or actions exchanged between the person giving the consent and the officer. In People v. Cruz, 40 Cal.Rptr. 841, 395 P.2d 889 (Cal. 1964), an officer obtained permission to "look around" an apartment. The court held that this did not authorize the officer to open and search boxes and suitcases that he had been informed were the property of persons other than the person giving consent. In other words, an officer can search only the parts of premises over which the person giving consent has some possessory right or control, and not personal property that the officer knows belongs to some other person. In State v. Johnson, 427 P.2d 705 (Wash. 1967), valid consent was given to officers to search the trunk of a car. The court held that this consent did not extend to search of the passenger area of the car and that evidence found in the passenger area was inadmissible in court.

The limitation on the area of search allowed by consent applies equally to searches of the person as to searches of premises. For example, in a case in which an individual consented to search of his person for *weapons*, the court held that "the scope of the search consented to must be limited to the scope of the right of search asserted, unless it should clearly appear that free and voluntary consent was given to a general and exploratory search." People v. Rice, 66 Cal.Rptr. 246, 249 (Cal. App. 1968). In *Rice*, the seizure of marijuana in a plastic bottle in the defendant's pocket was held illegal as beyond the scope of the consent granted. In another case, a Consent to Search form that authorized officers to search the defendant's car and remove "whatever documents or items of property whatsoever, which they deem pertinent to the investigation" was held to grant authority for a general and exploratory search. Therefore, officers did not exceed the scope of the consent by opening an unlocked suitcase found in the car's trunk. United States v. Kapperman, 764 F.2d 786 (11th Cir. 1985).

In a case involving both a nonverbal consent and a limitation on the area of the person allowed to be searched by consent, a police officer, while questioning the defendant with regard to narcotics, asked the defendant whether he was still using or carrying narcotics. When the defendant replied that he was not, the officer asked him if he minded if he checked him for needle marks. The defendant said nothing but put his arms out sideways. The officer did not check the defendant's arms but instead patted down his coat and found marijuana cigarettes.

The court held that the search went beyond the area to which the defendant had consented to allow a search:

> Bowen's putting out his arms sideways in response to a query whether he minded allowing the officer to check "if he had any marks on him" could hardly be said to be naturally indicative or persuasive of the giving of an intended consent to have the officer switch instead to a general search of his pockets—in which he had two marijuana cigarettes. Oliver v. Bowens, 386 F.2d 688, 691 (9th Cir. 1967).

As a general rule, if an officer asks for and obtains consent to search a specific area, whether in a place or on a person, the officer is limited to that specific area. If the search goes beyond that area, any evidence seized is likely to be held inadmissible in court.

Time

A person giving consent to search may also place a time limitation on the search. In State v. Brochu, 237 A.2d 418 (Me. 1967), officers investigating the death of the defendant's wife obtained a valid consent from the defendant to search his home. The officers conducted a search and found nothing, At this point in time, the defendant had not been accused of anything. However, later in the day, police received information giving them probable cause to arrest the defendant for his wife's murder and to obtain a search warrant for his premises. The defendant was arrested that evening and the search warrant was executed the next day. The validity of the warrant was challenged, and the prosecution attempted to justify the second search on the basis that the defendant's earlier consent continued in effect after his arrest to the next day. The court rejected this contention.

> The officers entered the defendant's home on the 5th under the protection of his consent. By nightfall, however, the defendant had ceased to be the husband assisting in the solution of his wife's death and had become the man accused of his wife's murder by poison (and) held under arrest for hearing.
>
> When the defendant became the accused, the protective cloak of the Constitution became more closely wrapped around him. . . .
>
> The consent of December 5 in our view should be measured on the morning of the 6th by the status of the defendant as the accused. There is no evidence whatsoever that the consent of the 5th was ever discussed with the defendant at or after his arrest, or that he was informed of the State's intent to enter and

search his home on the 6th on the strength of a continuing consent. We conclude, therefore, that consent of the defendant had ended by December 6, and accordingly the officers were not protected thereby on the successful search of the 6th. 237 A.2d at 421.

Once a consent search is terminated for a significant length of time, a new consent should be obtained before continuing to search, especially if intervening events suggest that a second consent might not be given so readily as the original consent. Otherwise, a search warrant should be obtained.

Object of Search

The scope of a consent search may be limited by the object for which the consenting person allows the officer to search. In People v. Superior Court (Arketa), 89 Cal.Rptr. 316 (Cal. App. 1970), a person gave officers consent to search his premises for a suspect of a crime. The officers conducted a thorough search of the house and its closets for a crowbar without advising the person that they wanted to look for a crowbar. The court invalidated the search because it went beyond the scope of the consent granted. Law enforcement officers should not look in areas where the object for which they have consent to search could not be located because of its size, shape, or character. If no limitation is placed on the objects to be searched for or seized, a search may be as broad as the officer's previously acquired knowledge about the crimes likely to have been committed and the items of evidence likely to be discovered. United States v. Sealey, 630 F.Supp. 801 (E.D. Cal. 1986).

Revocation of Consent

Consent may be revoked or withdrawn at any time after the search has been partially completed. In United States v. Bily, 406 F.Supp. 726 (E.D. Pa. 1975), the defendant consented to a search of his house for pornographic films. After an investigation of approximately two hours, during which certain films were discovered, the defendant stated, "That's enough, I want you to stop." The court held that this was a revocation of consent that took immediate effect. Only the seizures of film that took place before the revocation were held valid.

WHO MAY GIVE CONSENT

In general, the only person able to give a valid consent to a search is the person whose constitutional protection against unreasonable searches and seizures would be invaded by the search if it were conducted without consent. This means, for example, that when the search of a person's body or clothing is contemplated, only that person can consent to the search. The same rule applies to searches of property, except that when several people have varying degrees of interest in the same property, more than one person may be qualified to give consent to search.

In certain situations, the law recognizes authority in a third person to consent to a search of property even though he or she is not the person against whose interest the search is being conducted. In United States v. Matlock, 415 U.S. 164, 94 S.Ct. 988, 39 L.Ed.2d 242 (1974), the U.S. Supreme Court stated the test for determining whether a third person could consent to a search of premises or effects:

> [W]hen the prosecution seeks to justify a warrantless search by proof of voluntary consent, it is not limited to proof that consent was given by the defendant, but may show that permission to search was obtained from a third party who possessed *common authority over or other sufficient relationship to the premises or effects sought to be inspected.* 415 U.S. at 171, 94 S.Ct. at 993, 39 L.Ed.2d at 249–50 (emphasis supplied).

The Court then defined "common authority":

> Common authority is, of course, not to be implied from the mere interest a third party has in the property. The authority which justifies the third-party consent does not rest upon the law of property, with its attendant historical and legal refinements, . . . but rests rather on mutual use of the property by persons generally having joint access or control for most purposes, so that it is reasonable to recognize that any of the co-inhabitants has the right to permit the inspection in his own right and that the others have assumed the risk that one of their number might permit the common area to be searched. 415 U.S. at 171 n. 7, 94 S.Ct. at 993 n. 7, 39 L.Ed.2d at 250 n. 7.

Questions of who may give valid consent are often confusing and complicated, and courts tend to carefully scrutinize any waiver of a person's constitutional rights. The remainder of this chapter examines examples of consent search situations in which the person giving consent is not the person against whose interests the search is being conducted.

Persons Having Equal Rights or Interests in Property

It is well settled that when two or more persons have substantially equal rights of ownership, occupancy, or other possessory interest in property to be searched or seized, any one of the persons may legally authorize a search and any evidence found may be used against any of the other persons. In Wright v. United States, 389 F.2d 996 (8th Cir. 1968), police obtained a valid consent to search a defendant's apartment from a codefendant in a case involving a break into a bank. The codefendant was living with the defendant at the time, and evidence showed that the codefendant had a right to use and occupy the premises. The police found evidence incriminating the defendant in the apartment. The court held that the codefendant, being a joint tenant or resident of the apartment, could consent to the entry and search of the apartment: "This court and other courts have held that where there are multiple lawful residents of a premises, any one of such persons may give permission to enter and that if incriminating evidence is found, it may be used against all." 389 F.2d at 998.

In determining whether a person is a joint occupant of premises, courts will consider whether the person paid rent, how long the person stayed, whether the person left belongings on the premises, whether the person possessed a key, and whether there was any written or oral agreement among other parties as to the person's right to use and occupy the premises.

Consent to search given by a person with common authority over premises is not invalidated because that person gave consent with the expectation of receiving a reward. In Bertolotti v. State, 476 So.2d 130 (Fla. 1985), a women who knew of the possibility of a reward through a crime watch program consented to a search of an apartment she shared with the defendant, The Court said:

> A community-wide, regularly advertised program which rewards any citizen who provides information useful to the police in their criminal investigations is not tantamount to recruiting police agents; the state should not be penalized in the use of information so obtained. Mrs. Griest's consent to the search was not vitiated by the possibility of financial reward. 476 So.2d at 132.

In a case involving equal rights to personal property, the defendant, at his murder trial, objected to the introduction into evidence of clothing seized from his duffel bag. At the time of the seizure, the duffel bag was being used jointly by the defendant and his cousin, and had been left in the cousin's home. When police arrested the cousin, they asked him if they could have his clothing. The cousin directed them to the duffel bag, and both the cousin and his mother consented to its search. During the search, the officers came upon the defendant's clothing in the bag and it was seized as well.

The Court upheld the legality of the search over the defendant's objections:

> Since Rawls [the cousin] was a joint owner of the bag, he clearly had authority to consent to its search. The officers therefore found evidence against the petitioner while in the course of an otherwise lawful search. *[plain view doctrine]*
> . . . Petitioner argues that Rawls only had actual permission to use one compartment of the bag and that he had no authority to consent to a search of the other compartments. We will not, however, engage in such metaphysical subtleties in judging the efficacy of Rawls' consent. Petitioner, in allowing Rawls to use the bag and in leaving it in his house, must be taken to have assumed the risk that Rawls would allow someone else to look inside. We find no valid search and seizure claim in this case. Frazier v. Cupp, 394 U.S. 731, 740, 89 S.Ct. 1420, 1425, 22 L.Ed.2d 684, 693–94 (1969).

A third party who has common authority to use premises may give consent to a search of the premises even if not *actually* using the premises at the time of the search. In United States v. Cook, 530 F.2d 145 (7th Cir. 1976), the defendant's landlady consented to a search of a poultry house on her property. The poultry house consisted of a large room in which the landlady had segregated an area with wire fence for her exclusive use. She gave the defendant permission to use the remaining space, but she retained the right to use the space if necessary. The defendant claimed that since neither the landlady nor her family *actually* used the defendant's area, there was no common authority. The court upheld the search, however, ruling that the defendant had assumed the risk that the landlady would permit others to inspect the premises.

A third party cannot consent to a search of more than that over which he or she has common authority. In United States v. Gilley, 608 F.Supp. 1065 (S.D. Ga. 1985), the court held that a consent to search a home given by the home's occupant did not authorize a search of a guest's travel bag found in the living room. The guest had done nothing that diminished his natural expectation of privacy in the contents of the bag. The host lacked common authority over the bag, as she had not been authorized to open or use the bag, and she had not in fact opened the bag.

Landlord—Tenant

A landlord has *no* implied authority to consent to a search of a tenant's premises or a seizure of the tenant's property during the period of the tenancy, even though the landlord has the authority to enter the tenant's premises for the limited purposes of inspection, performance of repairs, or housekeeping services. Chapman v. United States, 365 U.S. 610, 81 S.Ct. 776, 5 L.Ed.2d 828 (1961). Once the tenancy has terminated, however, and the landlord has the primary right to occupation and control of the premises, the landlord may consent to a search of the premises, even though the former tenant has left personal belongings on the premises. People v. Urfer, 79 Cal.Rptr. 60 (Cal. App. 1969). Furthermore, since a landlord clearly has joint authority over and access to common areas of an apartment building, a landlord may give valid consent to search those areas. United States v. Kelly, 551 F.2d 760 (8th Cir. 1977).

Hotel Manager—Hotel Guest

The U.S. Supreme Court held that the principles governing a landlord's consent to a search of a tenant's premises apply to consent searches of hotel rooms allowed by hotel managers. In Stoner v. California, 376 U.S. 483, 84 S.Ct. 889, 11 L.Ed.2d 856 (1964), police investigating a robbery went to the defendant's hotel. The defendant was not in his room, and police obtained permission from the hotel clerk to search the defendant's room. Items of evidence incriminating the defendant in the robbery were found in the room.

The Court held that the search was illegal and that the items seized could not be used against the defendant in court. The defendant's constitutional right was at stake here—not the clerk's or the hotel's. Therefore, only the defendant, either directly or through an agent, could waive that right. There was no evidence that the police had any basis whatsoever to believe that the night clerk had been authorized by the defendant to permit the police to search his room:

> It is true . . . that when a person engages a hotel room he undoubtedly gives "implied or express permission" to "such persons as maids, janitors or repairmen" to enter his room "in the performance of their duties." . . . But the conduct of the night clerk and the police in the present case was of an entirely different order. . . .
>
> No less than a tenant of a house . . . a guest in a hotel room is entitled to constitutional protection against unreasonable searches and seizures. . . . That protection would disappear if it were left to depend upon the unfettered discretion of an employee of the hotel. 376 U.S. at 489–90, 84 S.Ct. at 893, 11 L.Ed.2d at 361.

When the term of a hotel guest's occupancy of a room expires, however, the guest loses his or her exclusive right to privacy in the room, whether or not the guest remains in the room. The hotel manager then has the right to enter the room and may consent to a search of the room and a seizure of items found in the room. United States v. Larson, 760 F.2d 852 (8th Cir. 1985).

Host—Guest

In general, the owner or primary occupant of premises (the host) may validly consent to a search of the premises and any evidence found will be admissible against a guest on the premises. In Woodard v. United States, 254 F.2d 312 (D.C. Cir. 1958), a homeowner had "taken in," without payment of rent, her grand-nephew and another young man. While she was tidying up her home, she found a loaded pistol and other items. She called the police and gave them permission to search the premises. The incriminating evidence found by the police as a result of this consent search was held admissible in court over the objections of the guests.

If, however, the person against whom a search for evidence is directed is a long-term guest and has an area of the premises set aside for exclusive personal use, the host may not consent to a search of that area of the premises. Reeves v. Warden, 346 F.2d 915 (4th Cir. 1965). The host's authority to consent to a search of the guest's area of the premises depends on the length of time of the guest's stay, the exclusiveness of the guest's control of a particular area of the premises, and the guest's reasonable expectation of privacy in that area of the premises.

Employer—Employee

In general, an employer may consent to a search of any part of the employer's premises over which the employer has authority and control. In State v. Robinson, 206 A.2d 779 (N.J. Super. 1965), the court held that an employer could validly consent to the search of an employee's locker in the employer's plant. The employer not only owned the premises, but under the terms of a contract between the employer and the employee's union, the employer retained a master key to all employee's lockers. In United States v. Carter, 569 F.2d 801 (4th Cir. 1977), an employer's consent to search a company vehicle in the custody of an employee was held valid. The employer not only owned the vehicle, but could tell the employee what and what not to do with it, and could designate any other use of it.

However, an employer may not effectively consent to a search of an area set aside for use by an employee and within the employee's exclusive control. In United States v. Blok, 188 F.2d 1019 (D.C. Cir. 1951), the court held that an employee's boss could not validly consent to a search of a desk assigned for the employee's exclusive use.

> In the absence of a valid regulation to the contrary, appellee was entitled to, and did keep private property of a personal sort in her desk. Her superiors could not reasonably search the desk for her purse, her personal letters, or anything else that did not belong to the government and had no connection with the work of the office. Their consent did not make such a search by the police reasonable. 188 F.2d at 1021.

An employee's ability to validly consent to a search of the employer's premises depends upon the scope of the employee's authority. The average employee, such as a clerk, janitor, maintenance person, driver, or other person temporarily in charge, may not give such consent. United States v. Block, 202 F.Supp. 705 (S.D.N.Y. 1962). If, however, the employee is a manager or other person of considerable authority who is left in complete charge for a substantial period of time, the employee probably would be able to effectively consent to a search of the employer's premises. United States v. Antonelli Fireworks Co., 155 F.2d 631 (2d Cir. 1946). In People v. Litwin, 355 N.Y.S.2d 646 (N.Y. App. Div. 1974), the court held that a babysitter has insufficient authority over the premises of his or her employer to give a valid consent to search the premises.

School Official—Student

The search by police of a high school student's locker, when consented to by a school official, is valid because of the relationship between school authorities and the students. The school authorities have an obligation to maintain discipline over students, and usually they retain partial access to the students' lockers so that neither has an exclusive right to use and possession of the lockers. Thus, in a case in which the locker of a student suspected of burglary was opened by police with the consent of school authorities and incriminating evidence was found, the court said:

> Although a student may have control of his school locker as against fellow students, his possession is not exclusive against the school and its officials. A school does not supply its students with lockers for illicit use in harboring pilfered property or harmful substances. We deem it a proper function of school authorities to inspect the lockers under their control and to prevent their use in illicit ways or for illegal purposes. We believe this right of inspection is inherent in the authority vested in school administrators and that the same must be retained and exercised in the management of our schools if their educational functions are to be maintained and the welfare of the student bodies preserved. State v. Stein, 456 P.2d 1, 3 (Kan. 1969).

Consent searches of college dormitory rooms are treated similarly to searches of hotel rooms. In Commonwealth v. McCloskey, 272 A.2d 271 (Pa. Super. 1970), police, aided by the dean of men, searched the defendant's room at a university and found marijuana. The evidence was held to be inadmissible in court. Even though the university had the right to check the room for damages, wear, and unauthorized appliances, this did *not* mean that the defendant "was not entitled to have a 'reasonable expectation of freedom from governmental intrusion', or that he gave consent to the police search, or gave the University authority to consent to such a search." 272 A.2d at 273.

Principal—Agent

A person clearly may give someone else authority to consent to a search of the person's property. For example, an attorney may consent to a search of a client's premises if the attorney has been specifically authorized to do so by the client. In Brown v. State, 404 P.2d 428 (Nev. 1965), a search of the defendant's premises and a seizure of his farm animals were upheld because consent to search had been given by the defendant's attorney after consultation with the defendant. Without a specific authorization to give consent to search, however, the mere existence of an attorney-client relationship gives an attorney no authority to waive a client's personal rights.

In another example, State v. Kellam, 269 S.E.2d 197 (N.C. App. 1980), home-owners gave their next-door neighbor the key to their house with instructions to "look after their house" while the owners were away. The court held that the neighbor's consent to search the house was valid.

Husband—Wife

In general, one spouse may consent to a search of family premises on the rationale that husband and wife are joint occupants with equal rights in the premises. In Roberts v. United States, 332 F.2d 892 (8th Cir. 1964), officers questioned the defendant's wife as part of a murder investigation. The wife volunteered information that the defendant had fired a pistol into the ceiling of their home some time ago. She later validly consented to a search and seizure of the bullet in the ceiling.

The court sustained the search on the basis that the consent was voluntary, the place of the search was the home of the defendant's wife, and the premises were under the immediate and complete control of the wife at the time of the search. Furthermore, the bullet could not be considered a personal effect of the husband, over which the wife would have no power to consent to search.

> It is not a question of agency, for a wife should not be held to have authority to waive her husband's constitutional rights. This is a question of the wife's own rights to authorize entry into premises where she lives and of which she had control. Roberts v. United States, 332 F.2d 892, 896–97 (8th Cir. 1964).

Many courts have even allowed estranged spouses to consent to the search of marital premises they have vacated. In United States v. Long, 524 F.2d 660 (9th Cir. 1975), the court held that an estranged wife, as a joint owner of a house she had vacated, could give consent to search the house even though her husband (the temporarily absent current occupant) had changed the locks on the doors.

Parent—Child

A parent's consent to search premises owned by the parent will usually be effective against a child who lives on those premises.

> Hardy's father gave his permission to the officers to enter and search the house and the premises *which he owned* and in which his son lived with him. Under the circumstances presented here the voluntary consent of Hardy's father to search *his own* premises is binding on Hardy and precludes his claim of violation of constitutional rights. Commonwealth v. Hardy, 223 A.2d 719, 723 (Pa. 1966).

A parent may not consent to a search of an area of the parent's home occupied by the child, however, if the child uses the room exclusively, has sectioned it off, has furnished it with his or her own furniture, pays rent, or otherwise establishes an expectation of privacy. State v. Peterson, 525 S.W.2d 599 (Mo.App. 1975). Furthermore, parents may not consent to a search of a child's room in their home if the child has already refused to grant such consent. "Constitutional rights may not be defeated by the expedient of soliciting several persons successively until the sought-after consent is obtained." People v. Mortimer, 46 A.D.2d 275, 277, 361 N.Y.S.2d 955, 958 (N.Y.App.Div. 1974).

In general, a child living in his or her parents' home does not have sufficient authority to consent to a search of the home in the absence of the parents. May v. State, 199 So.2d 635 (Miss. 1967).

Bailor—Bailee

A bailee of personal property may consent to a search of the property if the bailee has full possession and control. (A bailee is a person in rightful possession of personal property by permission of the owner or bailor). In United States v. Eldridge, 302 F.2d 463 (4th Cir. 1962), the defendant loaned his car to a friend for the friend's personal use. Police investigating a theft asked the friend for permission to search the trunk of the car. The friend opened the trunk and the police found incriminating evidence against the defendant.

The court held that the search was legal and that the evidence found was admissible against the defendant. The friend had been given rightful possession and control over the automobile and could do with it whatever was reasonable under the circumstances. The defendant had reserved no exclusive right to the trunk when he gave his friend the key. The friend's opening of the trunk for the police was a reasonable exercise of his control over the car for the period during which he was permitted to use it.

If the bailee giving consent has only limited control over the property, such as for shipment or storage purposes, evidence found by law enforcement officers would not be admissible in court against the owner of the property. Thus, an airline could not consent to the search of a package that the defendant had wrapped and tied and delivered to the airline solely for transportation purposes. Corngold v. United States, 367 F.2d 1 (9th Cir. 1966). Nor could the owner of a boat who had agreed to store certain of the defendant's items on his boat give a valid consent to police to search and seize the items. Commonwealth v. Storck, 275 A.2d 362 (Pa. 1971).

Voluntary Production of Evidence

If a person voluntarily produces incriminating evidence, without any attempt by police to obtain consent and without coercion, deception, or other illegal police conduct, there is no search and seizure and the evidence will be admissible in court. In the U.S. Supreme Court case of Coolidge v. New Hampshire, 403 U.S. 443, 91 S.Ct. 2022, 29 L.Ed.2d 564 (1971), two officers went to the defendant's home, while the defendant was at the police station under investigation for murder, in order the check out the defendant's story with his wife. The officers asked the wife if the defendant owned any guns, and she replied, "Yes, I will get them in the bedroom." She then took four guns out of a closet and gave them to the officers. The officers then asked her what her husband had been wearing on the night in question, and she produced several pairs of trousers and a hunting jacket. The police seized all this evidence, and it was used against the defendant in court.

The Court found no objection to the introduction of the previously described evidence in court. In fact, the Court found that the actions of the police did not even amount to a search and seizure. Because the Court discussed in detail the significance of the actions of the police, and because of the importance of the issue, the Court's opinion is quoted here at length:

[I]t cannot be said that the police should have obtained a warrant for the guns and clothing before they set out to visit Mrs. Coolidge, since they had no intention of rummaging around among Coolidge's effects or of dispossessing him of any of his property. Nor can it be said that they should have obtained Coolidge's permission for a seizure they did not intend to make. There was nothing to compel them to announce to the suspect that they intended to question his wife about his movements on the night of the disappearance or about the theft from his employer. Once Mrs. Coolidge had admitted them, the policemen were surely acting normally and properly when they asked her, as they asked those questioned earlier in the investigation, including Coolidge himself, about any guns there might be in the house. The question concerning the clothes Coolidge had been wearing on the night of the disappearance was logical and in no way coercive. Indeed, one might doubt the competence of the officers involved had they not asked exactly the questions they did ask. And surely when Mrs. Coolidge of her own accord produced the guns and clothes for inspection, rather than simply describing them, it was not incumbent on the police to stop her or avert their eyes. . . .

In assessing the claim that this course of conduct amounted to a search and seizure, it is well to keep in mind that Mrs. Coolidge described her own motive as that of clearing her husband, and that she believed that she had nothing to hide. She had seen her husband himself produce his guns for two other policemen earlier in the week, and there is nothing to indicate that she realized that he had offered only three of them for inspection on that occasion. The two officers who questioned her behaved, as her own testimony shows, with perfect courtesy. There is not the slightest implication of an attempt to coerce or dominate her, or for that matter, to direct her actions by the more subtle techniques of suggestion that are available to officials in circumstances like these. To hold that the conduct of the police here was a search and seizure would be to hold, in effect, that a criminal suspect has constitutional protection against the adverse consequences of a spontaneous, good-faith effort by his wife to clear him of suspicion. 403 U.S. at 488–90, 91 S.Ct. at 2049–50, 29 L.Ed.2d at 596.

Reasonable Expectation of Privacy

Since the U.S. Supreme Court decision in Katz v. United States, 389 U.S. 347, 88 S.Ct. 507, 19 L.Ed.2d 576 (1967), courts have considered a person's reasonable expectation of privacy as a major factor in determining whether consent to search that person's property could be given by a third person. In United States v. Novello, 519 F.2d 1078 (5th Cir. 1975), the defendant rented an enclosed storage area which was accessible only to the rental agent and to those working with the agent. The defendant stored his truck containing marijuana in the area. Law enforcement officers, acting on an informant's tip, obtained consent to enter the enclosed area from one of the persons having access and discovered marijuana in the truck. The court held that the defendant had no reasonable expectation of privacy in the storage area and upheld the search. The court said, "One who knows that others have of right general and untrammeled access to an area, a right as extensive as his own, can scarcely have much expectation of secrecy in it or confidence about whom they may let inspect it." 519 F.2d at 1080.

The Oregon Court of Appeals relied upon a defendant's reasonable expectation of privacy to invalidate the search of a bedroom in a private residence that the defendant occupied under a rental agreement. A father and his two daughters leased and occupied the residence along with the defendant. The defendant was the only occupant of a private room under an agreement with the father. One of the daughters gave consent to search the defendant's room, where incriminating evidence was found. The court held that the daughter could not consent to a search of the defendant's room. The defendant had a reasonable expectation of privacy in the room because he rented it, was its sole occupant, and had never given anyone permission to enter it. State v. Fitzgerald, 530 P.2d 553 (Or. App. 1974).

SUMMARY

A consent search occurs when a person allows a law enforcement officer to search his or her body, premises, or belongings. Consent searches are convenient for law enforcement officers, requiring no justification such as probable cause or a warrant, but consent searches present many opportunities for abuse. For this reason, courts exercise a strong presumption against consents to search and place a heavy burden on prosecutors to prove that a consent to search was voluntary. Voluntariness depends on the totality of circumstances surrounding the giving of consent. Among the circumstances considered are the following.

1. Force or threat of force by police
2. Fraudulent or mistaken claim of police authority
3. Misrepresentation or deception by police
4. Arrest or detention of consenting person
5. Consenting person's awareness of the right to refuse consent to search
6. Clearness and explicitness of consent
7. Physical, mental and emotional condition of consenting person

   The scope of a consent search may be limited in area, in time, and by the object for which the search is allowed. These limitations are usually determined by the intent of the consenting person as indicated by the exchange of words and actions between the person and the police. Consent to search may be revoked by the person giving it at any time.

   The constitutional right to refuse to consent to a search is a personal right of the individual against whom the search is directed. A person other than the person against whose interests the search is being conducted cannot effectively consent to a search of property unless (1) the person has been specifically authorized to do so, or (2) the person possesses common authority over or has other sufficient relationship to the premises or effects sought to be inspected. If a person establishes a reasonable expectation of privacy in property, another person may not consent to a search of the property.

REVIEW AND DISCUSSION QUESTIONS

   1. If a person is deprived of freedom of action in a significant way by law enforcement officers, should the person be given warnings of the right to refuse consent before being asked for consent to search?

2. If a law enforcement officer asks a person for consent to search his or her home for stolen jewelry when the officer's real purpose is to look for marked money, is the consent voluntary?

3. Assume that law enforcement officers have obtained a valid consent to search an arrested defendant's automobile for drugs, and an initial search proves fruitless. Can the officers search the automobile again two hours later without obtaining a new consent to search? What about two days later? What about two weeks later? What changes in the defendant's status might render the initial consent no longer valid?

4. If, after giving consent to search, a person becomes nervous and revokes or limits the scope of the search, can this reaction be used by the officers as an indication of probable cause to obtain a search warrant?

5. Are third-party consents to search the defendant's premises valid in the following circumstances?
    a. A husband, out of anger at his wife, the defendant, invites the police into the house and points out evidence incriminating the wife.
    b. The defendant's girlfriend, who lives with him part-time, consents to a search of the defendant's apartment.
    c. A wife disobeys the instructions of her husband, the defendant, not to allow a search of their home. Does it matter if the police know of the instructions or not?

6. Is it proper for a law enforcement officer to deliberately avoid attempting to obtain consent to search from the defendant and instead attempt to obtain consent from someone with equal authority over the defendant's premises? Does it matter whether the law enforcement officer had an opportunity to attempt to obtain consent from the defendant and deliberately failed to take it? What if the defendant was deliberately avoiding the police?

7. Is a consent to search voluntary if it is obtained after a law enforcement officer tells a person that a search warrant will be obtained if consent is refused? What if the officer only says that an attempt will be made to obtain a search warrant? What if the officer explains that it might not be possible to obtain a search warrant?

8. Should a person be able to limit the number of officers conducting a consent search? Should a person be able to choose which officer or officers will conduct the consent search? Should a person be allowed to follow around the officer conducting the search?

9. Can the following persons give a valid consent to search?
    a. A highly intoxicated person
    b. A five-year old; a seven-year old; a ten-year old
    c. A mentally retarded or senile person
    d. An emotionally upset person
    e. An uneducated person

10. Can the driver of a motor vehicle consent to a search of the vehicle even though a passenger objects? Can the owner of a store consent to a search of the store even though an employee objects? Can a parent consent to a search of his or her home even though a child objects?

CHAPTER 9
Plain View Doctrine

The plain view doctrine was simply stated in the U.S. Supreme Court decision in Harris v. United States: "It has long been settled that objects falling in the plain view of an officer who has a right to be in a position to have that view may be introduced in evidence. . . ." 390 U.S. 234, 236, 88 S.Ct. 992, 993, 19 L.Ed.2d 1067, 1069 (1968).

The plain view doctrine permits law enforcement officers to observe and seize evidence without a warrant, probable cause, or other justification. It is therefore usually considered an exception the the warrant requirement of the Fourth Amendment, even though a plain view observation technically does not constitute a *search*. A search occurs only if there is an infringement of a person's reasonable expectation of privacy; a law enforcement officer's mere observation of an item of evidence from a position in which the officer has a right to be is ordinarily not an infringement of a person's privacy rights. If there is no search, there can be no Fourth Amendment violation, and the observed item may be seized and introduced in evidence.

REQUIREMENTS OF THE PLAIN VIEW DOCTRINE

Despite the apparent simplicity and obviousness of its basic concept, the plain view doctrine does not give law enforcement officers a license to look around anywhere, any time, and under any circumstances and to seize anything they wish. The doctrine has carefully prescribed requirements developed through court decisions over the years. These requirements can be summarized as follows:

1. The officer, as the result of a prior valid intrusion into a constitutionally protected area, must be in a position in which he or she has legal right to be.

2. The officer must not unreasonably intrude on any person's reasonable expectation of privacy.

3. The officer must actually observe the item of evidence.

4. The item of evidence must by lying in the open.

5. The officer must have probable cause to believe that the item observed is subject to seizure.

6. The discovery of the item of evidence by the officer must be inadvertent.

Before the seizure of an item of evidence can be justified under the plain view doctrine, the law enforcement officer seizing the item must satisfy all six of these requirements. The remainder of this chapter is devoted to a discussion of these requirements.

The Officer, as the Result of a Prior Valid Intrusion into a Constitutionally Protected Area, Must Be in a Position in Which He or She Has a Legal Right to Be

The situations in which a law enforcement officer is in a position in which he or she has a legal right to be are too numerous to present an exhaustive listing. The U.S. Supreme Court gave several examples in Coolidge v. New Hampshire:

> What the "plain view" cases have in common is that the police officer in each of them had a prior justification for an intrusion in the course of which he came inadvertently across a piece of evidence incriminating the accused. The doctrine serves to supplement the prior justification—whether it be a warrant for another object, hot pursuit, search incident to lawful arrest, or some other legitimate reason for being present unconnected with a search directed against the accused—and permits the warrantless seizure. . . . 403 U.S. at 466, 91 S.Ct. at 2038, 29 L.Ed.2d at 583.

This section discusses several examples in which this requirement of the plain view doctrine has been applied.

EFFECTING AN ARREST OR SEARCH INCIDENT TO ARREST. A law enforcement officer may lawfully seize an object that comes into view during a lawfully executed arrest or a search incident to arrest. The law of search incident to arrest and the plain view doctrine must be clearly distinguished. Under the rule of *Chimel v. California* (see Chapter 7), a law enforcement officer may search a person incident to arrest only for weapons or to prevent the destruction or concealment of evidence. The extent of the search is limited to the arrestee's body and the area within the arrestee's immediate control, "construing that phrase to mean the area from within which he might gain possession of a weapon or destructible evidence." 395 U.S. at 763, 89 S.Ct. at 2040, 23 L.Ed.2d at 694.

The plain view doctrine does *not* extend the permissible area of search incident to arrest. In the *Chimel* case, the Court specifically said:

> There is no comparable justification, however, for routinely searching any room other than that in which an arrest occurs—or for that matter, for searching through all the desk drawers or other closed or concealed areas in that room itself. Such searches in the absence of well-recognized exceptions, may be made only under the authority of a search warrant. 395 U.S. at 763, 89 S.Ct. at 2040, 23 L.Ed.2d at 694.

Nevertheless, the law of search incident to arrest does not require a law enforcement officer to ignore or avert his or her eyes from objects readily visible in the room where the arrest occurs. If the arresting officer inadvertently observes an item of evidence open to view, but outside the area under the immediate control of the arrestee, the officer may seize it, so long as the observation was made in the course of a lawful arrest or an appropriately limited search incident to arrest. The item of evidence will be admissible in court if all requirements of the plain view doctrine are satisfied.

CONDUCTING A STOP AND FRISK. A seizable item observed by an officer during the course of a lawful stop and frisk may also be seized without a warrant. (See Chapter 12 for a discussion of stop and frisk.) Again, the plain view doctrine does not extend the area of search permissible under stop and frisk law, but it does give the officer authority to seize readily visible objects. This authority extends to the passenger compartment of an automobile. "If while conducting a legitimate *Terry* search of the interior of the automobile, the officer should . . . discover contraband other than weapons, he clearly cannot be required to ignore the contraband, and the Fourth Amendment does not require its suppression in such circumstances." Michigan v. Long, 463 U.S. 1032, 1050, 103 S.Ct. 3469, 3481, 77 L.Ed.2d 1201, 1220 (1983).

EXECUTING A SEARCH WARRANT. In the case of Cady v. Dombrowski, 413 U.S. 433, 93 S.Ct. 2523, 37 L.Ed.2d 706 (1973), the U.S. Supreme Court held that an officer executing a valid search warrant could legally seize items of evidence lying in plain view even though they were not particularly described in the warrant. For purposes of this discussion, law enforcement officers executing a valid search warrant are in a position in which they have a legal right to be.

An officer without a warrant may not enter premises to secure the premises while a search warrant is being obtained, unless there are exigent circumstances. Evidence observed open to view after such an illegal entry will not be admissible under the plain view doctrine, because the officer was not in a position in which he or she had a legal right to be. United States v. Griffin, 502 F.2d 959 (6th Cir. 1974).

MAKING CONTROLLED DELIVERIES. The U.S. government has the right to inspect all incoming goods from foreign countries at the port of entry. In addition, common carriers have a common law right to inspect packages they accept for shipment, based on their duty to refrain from carrying contraband. Although the sheer volume of goods in transit prevents systematic inspection of all or even a large percentage of these goods, common carriers and customs officials inevitably discover contraband in transit in a variety of circumstances. When such a discovery is made, it is routine procedure to notify the appropriate authorities, so that the authorities may identify and prosecute the person or persons responsible for the movement of the contraband. The arrival of law enforcement authorities on the scene to confirm the presence of contraband and to determine what to do with it does not convert the otherwise legal search by the common carrier or customs official into a government search subject to the Fourth Amendment. United States v. Edwards, 602 F.2d 458 (1st Cir. 1979).

Law enforcement authorities, rather than simply seizing the contraband and destroying it, will often make a so-called controlled delivery of the container, monitoring the container on its journey to the intended destination. The person dealing in the contraband can then be identified upon taking possession of and asserting control over the container. The typical pattern of a controlled delivery has been described as follows:

> They most ordinarily occur when a carrier, usually an airline, unexpectedly discovers what seems to be contraband while inspecting luggage to learn the identity of its owner, or when the contraband falls out of a broken or damaged piece of luggage, or when the carrier exercises its inspection privilege because some suspicious circumstance has caused it concern that it may unwittingly be transporting contraband. Frequently, after such a discovery, law enforcement agents restore the contraband to its container, then close or reseal the container, and authorize the carrier to deliver the container to its owner. When the owner appears to take delivery he is arrested and the container with the contraband is seized and then searched a second time for the contraband known to be there. United States v. Bulgier, 618 F.2d 472, 476 (7th Cir. 1980).

The U.S. Supreme Court, relying on the plain view doctrine, held that no protected privacy interest remains in contraband in a container once government officers lawfully have opened that container and identified its contents as illegal. Furthermore, the simple act of resealing the container to enable the police to make a controlled delivery does not operate to revive or restore the lawfully invaded privacy rights. The Court said:

> The plain view doctrine is grounded on the proposition that once police are lawfully in a position to observe an item first-hand, its owner's privacy interest in that item is lost; the owner may retain the incidents of title and possession but not privacy . . . [O]nce a container has been found to a certainty to contain illicit drugs, the contraband becomes like objects physically within the plain view of the police, and the claim to privacy is lost. Consequently, the subsequent reopening of the container is not a "search" within the intendment of the Fourth Amendment. Illinois v. Andreas, 463 U.S. 765, 771–72, 103 S.Ct. 3319, 3324, 77 L.Ed.2d 1003, 1010 (1983).

In the *Andreas* case, the Court acknowledged that there are often unavoidable interruptions of control or surveillance of a container and that at some point after such an interruption, courts should recognize that the container may have been put to other uses, thereby reinstating the individual's legitimate expectation of privacy in the container. The Court decided that a workable, objective standard that limits the risk of intrusion on legitimate privacy interests when there is such an interruption is whether there is a substantial likelihood that the contents of the container have been changed during the gap in surveillance. If there is no such likelihood, the officer may legally open the container without a warrant.

PURSUING A FLEEING SUSPECT. Law enforcement officers who are lawfully on premises in hot pursuit of a dangerous person may seize items of evidence observed open to their view. In Warden v. Hayden, 387 U.S. 294, 87 S.Ct. 1642, 18 L.Ed.2d 782 (1967), the police were informed that an armed robbery had taken place and that a suspect wearing a light cap and dark jacket had entered a certain house less than five minutes before the officers arrived. Several officers entered the house and began to search for the described suspect and for weapons that he had used in the robbery and that he might use against them. One officer, while searching the cellar, found in a washing machine clothing of the type that the fleeing man was said to have worn. The Court held that the seizure of the clothing was lawful:

> [T]he seizures occurred prior to or immediately contemporaneous with Hayden's arrest, as part of an effort to find a suspected felon, armed, within the house into which he had run only minutes before the police arrived. The permissible scope of search must, therefore, at the least, be as broad as may reasonably be necessary to prevent the dangers that the suspect at large in the house may resist or escape. 387 U.S. at 299, 87 S.Ct. at 1646, 18 L.Ed.2d at 787.

If, however, the suspect had already been taken into custody when the officer looked into the washing machine, the seizure of the clothing would have been unlawful. There no longer would have been any danger of the fleeing suspect's using a weapon against the officers and, therefore, no reason to look for weapons in the washing machine.

To summarize, officers who enter a constitutionally protected area in hot pursuit of a fleeing suspect are in a position in which they have a legal right to be and may seize items of evidence observed lying open to view during the conduct of the hot pursuit and the protective search for weapons. Note that hot pursuit does not necessarily involve a violent crime or a dangerous person. The U.S. Supreme Court held that there was a hot pursuit when officers chased the defendant, who the officers had probable cause to believe had just purchased illegal drugs, from her doorway into her house. United States v. Santana, 427 U.S. 38, 96 S.Ct. 2406, 49 L.Ed.2d 300 (1976).

RESPONDING TO AN EMERGENCY. Related to the hot pursuit situation is the situation in which an officer responds to an emergency and observes items of evidence open to view. In People v. Clark, 68 Cal.Rptr. 713 (Cal.App. 1968), two police officers responded to a citizen's report that a woman was screaming for help in a certain house. A man answered the door, said "Wait a minute," and then closed the door again. One officer heard shuffling inside the apartment and the other officer observed a man attempting to escape out a back window. After identifying himself and demanding admittance (which was not granted), the officer at the entrance to the house kicked in the door. While investigating the situation inside, he observed marijuana open to view on a table.

The court found that the combination of circumstances presented to the officer justified his forced entry:

> The probability that a woman within the apartment was the unwilling victim of some criminal act was increased rather than lessened by the conduct of those within the apartment after the police presented themselves at the door; that conduct can only have had the effect of heightening the sense of emergency. . . .
>
> Having entered reasonably in an emergency "they did not have to blind themselves to what was in plain sight simply because it was disconnected with the purpose for which they entered." 68 Cal.Rptr. at 717.

In State v. Moulton, 481 A.2d 155 (Me. 1984), police had probable cause to believe that a dangerous criminal suspect was on the premises of an auto repair complex. The officers believed that the suspect not only had stolen motor vehicles and parts, but had driven one vehicle into a lake and had set another on fire. The auto repair complex was large, with many exits, making it difficult to secure. The likely presence of tools, vehicles, and flammable liquids added to the danger, and the hour was late, adding to the difficulty of obtaining a warrant. Under these exigent circumstances the court found that the officers were justified in entering the building without a search warrant for the suspect. Once inside the building, officers observed criminal evidence lying in plain view and seized it. These warrantless seizures were held reasonable under the Fourth Amendment, and a subsequent search warrant obtained in part on the basis of the items found in plain view was valid.

Police may thus enter premises and search without a warrant for a criminal suspect (especially a dangerous one) if

1. the police have probable cause to believe that the criminal suspect is on the premises; and

2. there are exigent circumstances precluding police from securing the premises long enough to obtain a search warrant.

Once police have made a valid intrusion into the premises, they may seize items of evidence lying in plain view.

Law enforcement officers may be tempted to justify otherwise illegal searches by resorting to this combination of the plain view doctrine and response to an emergency. Courts will carefully examine these situations and will invalidate a search if a genuine emergency does not exist or if a search goes beyond what is necessary to respond to the emergency. The U.S. Supreme Court stated that "a warrantless search must be 'strictly circumscribed by the exigencies which justify its initiation,'. . ." Mincey v. Arizona, 437 U.S. 385, 393, 98 S.Ct. 2408, 2414, 57 L.Ed.2d 290, 300 (1978). In the *Mincey* case, the prosecution attempted to justify an extensive four-day warrantless search of a murder victim's apartment on the basis of a "murder scene exception" to the warrant requirement. The search occurred when there was no emergency threatening life or limb and after all persons in the apartment had been located.

The court said that police may make warrantless entries on premises where they reasonably believe that a person within is in need of immediate aid. Police may also make a prompt warrantless protective search of the area to see if other potentially dangerous persons are still on the premises. Any evidence observed in plain view during the course of these legitimate emergency activities may be seized. However, the Court held that absent an emergency, "the 'murder scene exception'. . . is inconsistent with the Fourth and Fourteenth Amendments—that the warrantless search of Mincey's apartment was not constitutionally permissible simply because a homicide had recently occurred there." 437 U.S. at 395, 98 S.Ct. at 2414, 57 L.Ed.2d at 302. In Thompson v. Louisiana, 469 U.S. 17, 105 S.Ct. 409, 83 L.Ed.2d 246 (1984), the Court reiterated that even a limited two-hour general nonemergency search of a murder scene remains a significant intrusion on a person's privacy and may not be conducted without a warrant.

The Officer Must Not Unreasonably Intrude on Any Person's Reasonable Expectation of Privacy

Not all observations made by law enforcement officers who are in a position in which they have a legal right to be will satisfy Fourth Amendment requirements. If an observation intrudes on a person's reasonable expectation of privacy, the observation will be considered an illegal search unless it is supported by a warrant or falls within a recognized exception to the warrant requirement.

In a case illustrating this principle, a law enforcement officer observed the defendant and another man enter the men's room of a city park and not exit for about five minutes. The officer then entered the plumbing access area of the rest room and observed the men performing illegal sexual acts. The officer had observed no other suspicious acts by the defendant before the defendant entered the men's room. The court held that this was not plain view observation by the officer but an illegal search.

> The People here urge us to hold that clandestine observation of doorless stalls in public rest rooms is not a "search" and hence is not subject to the Fourth Amendment's prohibition of unreasonable searches. This would permit the police to make it a routine practice to observe from hidden vantage points the rest room conduct of the public whenever such activities do not occur within fully enclosed toilet stalls and would permit spying on the "innocent and guilty alike." Most persons using public rest rooms have no reason to suspect that a hidden agent of the state will observe them. The expectation of privacy a person has when he enters a rest room is reasonable and is not diminished or destroyed because the toilet stall being used lacks a door.
>
> Reference to expectations of privacy as a Fourth Amendment touchstone received the endorsement of the United States Supreme Court in Katz v. United States, 389 U.S. 347, 88 S.Ct. 507, 19 L.Ed.2d 576 (1968). Viewed in the light of Katz, the standard for determining what is an illegal search is whether defendant's "reasonable expectation of privacy was violated by unreasonable governmental intrusion." People v. Triggs, 106 Cal.Rptr. 408, 412–13, 506 P.2d 232, 236–37 (Cal. 1973).

If, however, a person has no reasonable expectation of privacy in a place or an object, plain view observations by law enforcement officers violate no Fourth Amendment rights. In New York v. Class, 475 U.S. 106, 106 S.Ct. 960, 89 L.Ed.2d 81 (1986), a law enforcement officer stopped an automobile for a traffic infraction. After the driver voluntarily got out of the vehicle, the officer entered the vehicle and removed some papers from the dashboard in order to ascertain the vehicle identification number (VIN). (Federal law requires the VIN to be placed in the plain view of someone outside the automobile to facilitate the VIN's usefulness for various governmental purposes such as research, insurance, safety, theft prevention, and vehicle recall.)

The Court held that there was no reasonable expectation of privacy in the VIN because of the important role played by the VIN in the pervasive governmental regulation of the automobile and because of the efforts of the federal government to ensure that the VIN is placed in plain view. Furthermore, the placement of papers on top of the VIN was insufficient to create a privacy interest in the VIN, since efforts to restrict access to an area do not generate a reasonable expectation of privacy where none would otherwise exist. The mere viewing of the formerly obscured VIN was not, therefore, a violation of the Fourth Amendment.

The Officer Must Actually Observe the Item of Evidence

The law enforcement officer must actually *see* the item of evidence lying in the open in order to lawfully seize it under the plain view doctrine. Information gathered through senses other than sight cannot be used to support seizures of evidence under the plain view doctrine. In People v. Marshall, 69 Cal.Rptr. 585, 442 P.2d 665 (Cal. 1968), officers legally entered an apartment to arrest some suspects. They did not find any of the suspects in the apartment, but they distinctly smelled fresh marijuana and they traced the smell to a closed bag inside a carton in a closet. The officers opened the bag, seized the marijuana, and arrested the defendant several hours later when he returned to the apartment.

The court held the seizure of the marijuana illegal. The court said that if the evidence had been in plain *sight*, the officers could have seized it, because the officers were rightfully on the premises looking for persons believed to be in hiding. In this case, however, the marijuana was *not* in plain sight. It was in cellophane bags inside a closed brown paper bag that was in an open box in an open closet. In smelling the marijuana and tracing it to the bag, the officers had *probable cause* to believe that marijuana was in the bag. They could, therefore, have obtained a *search warrant* for the marijuana based on probable cause. They could not however, legally go into the bag and seize the marijuana, because the marijuana itself was not in plain view. There were also no exigent circumstances to justify an immediate seizure of the marijuana

> However strongly convinced officers may be that a search will reveal contraband, their belief, whether based on the sense of smell or other sources, does not justify a search without a warrant. The point of the Fourth Amendment, which often is not grasped by zealous officers, is not that it denies law enforcement the support of the usual inferences which reasonable men draw from evidence. Its protection consists in requiring that those inferences be drawn by a neutral and detached magistrate instead of being judged by the officer engaged in the often competitive enterprise of ferreting out crime. Any assumption that evidence sufficient to support a magistrate's disinterested determination to issue a search warrant will justify the officers in making a search without a warrant would reduce the Amendment to a nullity and leave the people's homes secure only in the discretion of police officers. 69 Cal.Rptr. at 588–89, 442 P.2d at 668–69.

To summarize, a law enforcement officer who has made a valid intrusion into a constitutionally protected area and has probable cause to believe that an item of evidence is in a certain place, but does not *see* the item lying in plain view, must obtain a search warrant before the item can be legally seized unless there are exigent circumstances.

The Item of Evidence Must Be Lying in the Open

This requirement of the plain view doctrine simply means that the item of evidence must be readily visible to the law enforcement officer. Among the phrases used by courts in describing this requirement are "in plain view," "in plain sight," "in open view," and "open to view." These phrases mean essentially the same thing and are clear in the context of an object lying on a table, on a floor, or on the seat of an automobile. Questions have arisen, however, on the issues of mechanical or electrical observation aids and closer examination of items, giving rise to several court decisions interpreting this requirement of the plain view doctrine.

MECHANICAL OR ELECTRICAL AIDS. It is well settled that law enforcement officers may use mechanical or electrical aids to assist in observing items of evidence, so long as the officers are in a position in which they have a legal right to be and are not intruding upon someone's reasonable expectation of privacy. In Marshall v. United States, 422 F.2d 185 (5th Cir. 1970), when a law enforcement officer arrived at a drive-in restaurant, he was told that a car had been parked in the parking lot for an hour with its lights on and with a person lying in the backseat. The officer went over to the car to see if anything was wrong. He shined a flashlight into the car and observed the defendant lying in the back with a sawed-off shotgun resting on the floorboard between his feet. He arrested the defendant and seized the shotgun.

The court held that the observation of the shotgun by the officer was not a search. The officer was in a position in which he had a legal right to be and his use of the flashlight did not, in itself, make his observations unlawful:

> When the circumstances of a particular case are such that the police officer's observation would not have constituted a search had it occurred in daylight, then the fact that the officer used a flashlight to pierce the nighttime darkness does not transform his observation into a search. Regardless of the time of day or night, the plain view rule must be upheld where the viewer is rightfully positioned, seeing through eyes that are neither accusatory nor criminally investigatory. The plain view rule does not go into hibernation at sunset. 422 F.2d at 189.

In United States v. Grimes, 426 F.2d 706 (5th Cir. 1970), an officer stationed himself in a field about fifty yards from the defendant's house and with the aid of binoculars watched the activities of the defendant, a known liquor violator. The officer observed the defendant place two large cardboard boxes (each of which contained six gallons of untaxed whiskey) into a 1961 Buick. The liquor was later found in the car while the car was being operated on a public street by another person. The court held that the officer's use of binoculars to observe the defendant's activities did not constitute an illegal search. A defendant's reasonable expectation of privacy was violated, however, in a case in which police looked into an eighth-floor window from a vantage point two hundred to three hundred yards away using high-powered binoculars.

> We ... view the test of validity of the surveillance as turning upon whether that which is perceived or heard is that which is conducted with a reasonable expectation of privacy and not upon the means used to view it or hear it. So long as that which is viewed or heard is perceptible to the naked eye or unaided ear, the person seen or heard has no reasonable expectation of privacy in what occurs. Because he has no reasonable expectation of privacy, governmental authority may use technological aids to visual or aural enhancement of whatever type available. However, the reasonable expectation of privacy extends to that which cannot be seen by the naked eye or heard by the unaided ear. While

governmental authority may use a technological device to avoid detection of its own law enforcement activity, it may not use the same device to invade the protected right. People v. Arno, 153 Cal.Rptr. 624, 627 (Cal.App. 1979).

CLOSER EXAMINATION OF ITEMS. A difficult issue is how far an officer may go in examining an item more closely before the examination constitutes a search rather than a mere plain view observation. The U.S. Supreme Court gave some guidelines in a case in which police, investigating a shooting, entered the defendant's apartment to search for the shooter, for other victims, and for weapons. One officer noticed stereo components and, suspecting they were stolen, read and recorded their serial numbers, moving some of the equipment in the process. After checking with headquarters and learning that the components were stolen, the officer seized some of the components and obtained warrants for others. The Court analyzed the officer's actions in terms of search and seizure law.

> [T]he mere recording of the serial numbers did not constitute a seizure. . . . [I]t did not "meaningfully interfere" with respondent's possessory interest in either the serial numbers or the equipment, and therefore did not amount to a seizure. . . . Officer Nelson's moving of the equipment, however, did constitute a "search" separate and apart from the search for the shooter, victims, and weapons that was the lawful objective of his entry into the apartment. Merely inspecting those parts of the turntable that came into view during the latter search would not have constituted an independent search because it would have produced no additional invasion of respondent's privacy interest. . . . But taking action, unrelated to the objectives of the authorized intrusion, which exposed to view concealed portions of the apartment or its contents, did produce a new invasion of respondent's privacy unjustified by the exigent circumstance that validated the entry. Arizona v. Hicks, 480 U.S. 321, 324–25, 107 S.Ct. 1149, 1152, 94 L.Ed.2d 347, 353–54 (1987).

The lesson of the *Hicks* case is that an officer's examination of an item of property will be a *search* rather than a *plain view observation* if

1. the officer produces a new invasion of the person's property by taking action that exposes to view concealed portions of the premises or its contents; and

2. the officer's action is unrelated to and unjustified by the objectives of his or her authorized intrusion.

In People v. Eddington, 198 N.W.2d 297 (Mich. 1972), police were lawfully in the defendant's apartment for the purpose of arresting him. While they were looking for the defendant, one officer observed a pair of shoes believed to have been worn by the defendant at the time of the murder. The officer picked up the shoes and examined the heels. After obtaining a search warrant, he returned and seized the shoes. The shoes were introduced in evidence against the defendant.

The court held that the examination of the heels of the shoes was not an illegal search:

> Detective Shelby was lawfully in defendant's apartment. He reasonably believed defendant to be hiding in the apartment and had every right, supported by probable cause, to search for the suspected killer. Shelby's discovery of the

shoes was not the result of a general search for evidence. Rather, the pair of shoes was seen during the course of the search for Eddington. In our view, Shelby's subsequent action in lifting the shoes and examining their heels involved no more than "legitimate and restrained investigative conduct undertaken on the basis of ample factual justification". . . . 198 N.W.2d at 302.

Note that in the *Eddington* case, the examination of the shoes was closely related to and justified by the objectives of the officer's authorized intrusion, namely, to search for the defendant.

Ordinarily, the opening and examination of a closed container will be considered a search because of the serious invasion of privacy these actions usually entail. Nevertheless, the U.S. Supreme Court allowed an examination of a partially closed container by government agents after the container had been opened and its contents examined by a private party. In United States v. Jacobsen, 466 U.S. 109, 104 S.Ct. 1652, 80 L.Ed.2d 85 (1984), employees of a freight carrier examined a damaged cardboard box wrapped in brown paper and found a white powdery substance in the innermost of four plastic bags that had been concealed in a tube inside the package. The employees notified the Drug Enforcement Administration (DEA), replaced the plastic bags in the tube, and placed the tube back in the box. A DEA agent arrived and removed the tube from the box and the plastic bags from the tube. When he saw the white powder, he opened the bags and removed a small amount of the white powder. He then subjected the powder to a field chemical test. The test indicated that the powder was cocaine.

The U.S. Supreme Court found that the initial invasion of the package by the freight carrier employees did not violate the Fourth Amendment because it was a private rather than a governmental action. The Court then analyzed the additional invasions of privacy by the DEA agent in terms of the degree to which they exceeded the scope of the private search. The Court found that even if the white powder was not itself in plain view because it was enclosed in so many containers and covered with papers, the DEA agent could be virtually certain that nothing else of significance was in the package and that a manual inspection of the tube and its contents would not tell him anything more than he already had been told by the freight carrier employees. The agent's reexamination of the contents of the package merely avoided the risk of a flaw in the employees' recollection, rather than further infringing on someone's privacy. The Court said:

> Respondents could have no privacy interest in the contents of the package, since it remained unsealed and since the Federal Express employees had just examined the package and had, of their own accord, invited the federal agent to their offices for the express purpose of viewing its contents. The agent's viewing of what a private party had freely made available for his inspection did not violate the Fourth Amendment. . . . Similarly, the removal of the plastic bags from the tube and the agent's visual inspection of their contents enabled the agent to learn nothing that had not previously been learned during the private search. It infringed no legitimate expectation of privacy and hence was not a "search" within the meaning of the Fourth Amendment. 466 U.S. at 199–20, 104 S.Ct. at 1659–60, 80 L.Ed.2d at 98.

The Court further held that the agent's assertion of dominion and control over the package and its contents was a seizure, but that the seizure was reasonable, since it was apparent that the tube and plastic bags contained contraband and little else. The Court said that "it is well-settled law that it is constitutionally reasonable for law enforcement officials to seize 'effects' that cannot support a justifiable expectation of privacy without a warrant, based on probable cause to believe they contain contraband." 466 U.S. at 121–22, 104 S.Ct. at 1661, 80 L.Ed.2d at 99.

The Court then addressed the question of whether the additional intrusion occasioned by the field test, which had not been conducted by the freight carrier employees and therefore exceeded the scope of the private search, was an unlawful search or seizure within the meaning of the Fourth Amendment. The Court held that a chemical test that merely discloses whether or not a particular substance is cocaine, and no other arguably "private" fact, compromises no legitimate privacy interest. Furthermore, even though the test destroyed a quantity of the powder and thereby permanently deprived its owner of a protected possessory interest, the infringement was constitutionally reasonable. The Court reasoned that the law enforcement interests justifying the procedure were substantial and, because only a trace amount of material was involved, the seizure could have, at most, only a minimal effect on any protected property interest.

To summarize, a law enforcement officer may examine, without a warrant, a container whose contents are not open to view, if any privacy interest in the contents of the container has already been compromised by a private party and information about the contents has been made available to the officer by the private party. In addition, it is constitutionally permissible for the officer to seize the contents of the container, if the officer has probable cause to believe the contents are contraband, and to conduct a chemical field test so long as only a trace amount of the substance is destroyed by the test.

The Officer Must Have Probable Cause to Believe that the Item Observed Is Subject to Seizure.

In Arizona v. Hicks, 480 U.S. 321, 107 S.Ct. 1149, 94 L.Ed.2d 347 (1987), the U.S. Supreme Court held that probable cause is required to invoke the plain view doctrine. This simply means that before a law enforcement officer may seize an item of property that is observed open to view, the officer must have probable cause to believe that the property comes within one of the categories of property subject to seizure under state or federal law. These categories of property, as listed and discussed in Chapter 5, are as follows:

1. Property stolen or embezzled

2. Property designed or intended for use or which is or has been used as a means of committing a criminal offense (instrumentalities)

3. Property, the possession of which is unlawful (contraband)

4. Property consisting of nontestimonial evidence that will aid in a particular apprehension or conviction (mere evidence)

In Coolidge v. New Hampshire, 403 U.S. 443, 466, 91 S.Ct. 2022, 2038, 29 L.Ed.2d 564, 583 (1971), the Court said that a seizure of an item in plain view is justified "only where it is *immediately apparent* to the police that they have evidence before them." (emphasis supplied). The phrase "immediately apparent" has been broadly interpreted to give officers a reasonable time within which to make the probable cause determination. For example, in United States v. Johnston, 784 F.2d 416 (1st Cir. 1986), the court held that an item's incriminating nature need not be determined by the first officer who observes the item, but may be based on the collective knowledge of all officers lawfully on the premises after all have observed the item. In the *Johnston* case, an officer came across torn pages from a notebook while executing a search warrant for narcotics. Probable cause to seize the pages as incriminating evidence did not develop, however, until the team of searching officers completed a search of the rest of the premises and discovered related evidence of narcotics violations. So long as the officers had probable cause to believe the items were incriminating by the time of completion of the execution of the search warrant, the *immediately apparent* requirement was held to be satisfied.

In State v. Mosher, 270 A.2d 451 (Me. 1970), a Massachusetts police officer arrested the defendant and two companions for trespassing with their automobile on private property. While waiting for assistance, the officer observed articles of clothing wrapped in cellophane lying inside the car. Later, after the car had been removed to the police station, the officer learned through police channels that similar clothing had recently been stolen in Maine. He obtained a search warrant and seized the clothing.

The Court found the search warrant defective but upheld the seizure because the items of clothing were in the officer's plain view. The court said:

> Even where . . . no search is necessary, the accompanying seizure must be accompanied by probable cause or reasonable grounds to believe that the property falls within a category which warrants the seizure. 270 A.2d at 453.

When the officer seized the items, he had probable cause to believe that the articles of clothing were *stolen* based on the report that similar articles had been stolen in Maine. If the officer had seized the articles of clothing when he first observed them, the seizure would have been illegal. At that time, he had no reason to believe that they were stolen or that they came under any other category of seizable property. It was only after he received the report that similar clothing had been stolen in Maine that he had probable cause to believe the property was seizable.

Officers may use their background and experience to evaluate the facts and circumstances in arriving at a probable cause determination. In Texas v. Brown, 460 U.S. 730, 103 S.Ct. 1535, 75 L.Ed.2d 502 (1983), an officer stopped the defendant's automobile at night at a routine driver's license checkpoint, asked the defendant for his license, and shined a flashlight into the car. The officer observed an opaque, green party balloon, knotted about one-half inch from the tip. After shifting his position, the officer also observed several small vials, quantities of loose white powder, and an open bag of party balloons in the open glove compartment. The U.S. Supreme Court held that the officer had probable cause to believe that the balloon contained an illicit substance:

> [The officer] testified that he was aware, both from his participation in previous narcotics arrests and from discussions with other officers, that balloons tied in the manner of the one possessed by [the defendant] were frequently used to carry narcotics. This testimony was corroborated by that of a police depart-

ment chemist who noted that it was "common" for balloons to be used in packaging narcotics. In addition, [the officer] was able to observe the contents of the glove compartment of [the defendant's] car, which revealed further suggestions that [the defendant] was engaged in activities that might involve possession of illicit substances. The fact that [the officer] could not see through the opaque fabric of the balloon is all but irrelevant: the distinctive character of the balloon itself spoke volumes as to its contents—particularly to the trained eye of the officer. 460 U.S. at 742–43, 103 S.Ct. at 1543, 75 L.Ed.2d at 514.

In Shipman v. State, 282 So.2d 700 (Ala. 1973), however, the object containing drugs was found to be insufficiently distinctive in character to justify its seizure. In that case, law enforcement officers detained several persons on a store owner's complaint that they were acting in an unruly manner. An officer observed one the persons move an object to the top of his boot. The object, though clearly not a weapon, was seized and was later determined to contain heroin. The court held that even though the object was in plain view its seizure was illegal because the officer did not have probable cause to believe it was contraband.

> The reason for this rule is apparent. If the rule were otherwise, an officer acting on mere groundless suspicion, could seize anything and everything belonging to an individual which happened to be in plain view on the prospect that on further investigation some of it might prove to have been stolen or to be contraband. It would open the door to unreasonable confiscation of a person's property while a minute examination of it is made in an effort to find something criminal. Such practice would amount to the "general exploratory search from one object to another until something incriminating at last emerges" which was condemned in Coolidge v. New Hampshire. . . . Ex post facto justification of a seizure made on mere groundless suspicion, is totally contrary to the basic tenets of the Fourth Amendment. . . .
>
> For an item in plain view to be validly seized, the officer must possess some judgment at the time that the object to be seized is contraband and that judgment must be grounded upon probable cause. 282 So.2d at 704.

In certain instances, an officer may have occasion to *search* rather than *seize* items found in plain view. Recall that in Arizona v. Hicks, 480 U.S. 321, 107 S.Ct. 1149, 94 L.Ed.2d 347 (1987) (discussed earlier), an officer conducting an emergency search of an apartment after a shooting incident observed stereo equipment which he suspected was stolen. He searched the equipment, moving it for closer examination, and obtained the serial numbers. The equipment was determined to be stolen, and some was seized immediately and some was seized later under a warrant. The Court held that the same probable cause standard applies to plain view searches as applies to plain view seizures. Since the officer had only a suspicion that the stereo equipment was stolen, his search was not based on probable cause and was therefore unreasonable under the Fourth Amendment.

The Discovery of the Item of Evidence by the Officer Must Be Inadvertent

The *inadvertency* requirement of the plain view doctrine is best illustrated by the U.S. Supreme Court case of Coolidge v. New Hampshire, 403 U.S. 443, 91

S.Ct. 2022, 29 L.Ed.2d 564 (1971). In that case, police went to the defendant's house to arrest him for murder. They also had a warrant to search his Pontiac car for evidence of the murder. They seized the car, which was parked and plainly visible in the driveway, and brought it back to the station where it was searched. Vacuum sweepings from the car were used as evidence at the defendant's trial, and the defendant was convicted.

When the search warrant was later found to be invalid, the prosecution attempted to justify the seizure of the automobile on the theory that, since the car was an "instrumentality of the crime," and was seized while lying in plain view, no warrant was needed. The Court said that the plain view doctrine could not be used to justify the seizure in this case because the discovery of the evidence was not inadvertent:

> [T]he discovery of evidence in plain view must be inadvertent. The rationale of the exception to the warrant requirement, as just stated, is that a plain-view seizure will not turn an initially valid (and therefore limited) search into a "general" one, while the inconvenience of procuring a warrant to cover an inadvertent discovery is great. *But where the discovery is anticipated, where the police know in advance the location of the evidence and intend to seize it, the situation is altogether different. The requirement of a warrant to seize imposes no inconvenience whatever, or at least none which is constitutionally cognizable in a legal system that regards warrantless searches as "per se unreasonable" in the absence of "exigent circumstances."* (emphasis supplied) 403 U.S. at 470–71, 91 S.Ct. at 2040, 29 L.Ed.2d at 585–86.

Courts have generally interpreted the inadvertency requirement to not require that the discovery of evidence be *totally* unanticipated. Rather, the requirement is satisfied if the police may have had some expectation they would discover seizable items, but that expectation did not rise to the level of probable cause to obtain a warrant for those items.

> [F]or the inadvertent discovery rule to apply . . . it must appear that prior to the issuance of the warrant the police could reasonably and in good faith either have failed to recognize the existence of probable cause or believed that there was insufficient evidence of probable cause to search. . . . [T]he "inadvertent" limitation on "plain view" must be read neither to allow a premeditated seizure, nor to prevent effective police work. United States v. $10,000 in U.S. Currency, 780 F.2d 213, 218 (2d Cir. 1986).

The significance of the inadvertency requirement is that it reemphasizes the importance of obtaining a search warrant in situations in which, before arriving at the place to be searched, an officer has probable cause to believe a particular item of evidence is located in a particular place and the officer intends to seize the item. Unless there are exigent circumstances, a warrantless seizure in these situations will *not* be justified under the plain view doctrine.

In United States v. Lisznyai, 470 F.2d 707 (2d Cir. 1972), the court found sufficient exigent circumstances to justify the use of the plain view doctrine to support the warrantless seizure of items whose location law enforcement officers already knew. Law enforcement agents on several occasions observed the defendant purchase laboratory equipment and chemicals used in the manufacture of amphetamine and carry them into his home. On one occasion, the agents entered the apartment with the defendant's consent on the pretense of making an emergency phone call. They observed the laboratory equipment on a kitchen counter. The agents, stationed at a nearby apartment, also observed someone working in the laboratory, and they detected a smell of ether, which is employed in manufacturing amphetamine. Late one night, the agents observed the defendant dismantling the laboratory equipment. Believing that the defendant was attempting to flee, they called their superiors, who said they would attempt to obtain a search warrant. In the meantime, the agents at the scene went to "secure" the defendant's apartment while waiting for the delivery of the warrant. When they arrived at the apartment, they immediately arrested the defendant and seized the laboratory equipment, which was in plain view.

The defendant claimed that the seized equipment should not have been admitted into evidence because, although it was in plain view, the agents knew beforehand that the equipment was in the apartment. Citing *Coolidge v. New Hampshire*, the defendant claimed that the plain view doctrine applies only when the discovery of the evidence is inadvertent, not when the discovery is anticipated—when the police know in advance the location of the evidence, and intend to seize it.

The court held that the warrantless seizure was valid. The agents made efforts to obtain a search warrant; a warrantless seizure was not planned. When the agents saw the equipment being dismantled, however, they reasonably concluded that the defendant's flight was imminent and that incriminating evidence was about to be carried away. Immediate action by the agents was required:

> *Coolidge* does not require suppression of evidence seized in plain view during an arrest where the circumstances have become exigent merely because prior knowledge of the evidence was acquired shortly before the seizure. 470 F.2d at 710.

This case illustrates the strong preference of courts for warrants. The court likely would have held the search illegal had not the agents already begun the process of obtaining the search warrant when the emergency plain view search was made. The attempt to obtain a warrant clearly showed that a warrantless seizure of the evidence in plain view was *not* planned, but was in response to an emergency.

In Ludlow v. State, 314 N.E.2d 750 (Ind. 1974), law enforcement officers received information that narcotics were in a home occupied by five persons. When the officers discovered that they had arrest warrants for two of the five persons, they went to the home. The officers entered the home, discovered the narcotics lying open to view, and seized them. The court held that the discovery of the narcotics was not inadvertent because the entry to execute the arrest warrants was merely a pretext to search for the narcotics. Because the seizure of the narcotics was anticipated, the plain view doctrine did not apply and the seizure was unlawful.

SUMMARY

Under the plain view doctrine, an observation of items lying open to view by a law enforcement officer who has a right to be in a position to have that view is not a search, and the officer may seize the evidence without a warrant. The doctrine has six requirements, all of which must be satisfied before seizure of an item of evidence can be legally justified.

First, the officer, as a result of a prior valid intrusion into a constitutionally protected area, must be in a position in which he or she has a legal right to be. Some examples of situations in which an officer's intrusion is justified are effecting an arrest or search incident to arrest, conducting a stop and frisk, executing a search warrant, making controlled deliveries, pursuing a fleeing suspect, and responding to an emergency.

Second, the officer must not unreasonably intrude on any person's reasonable expectation of privacy. To satisfy this requirement, the officer must use common sense to keep the investigation of crime within reasonable bounds.

Third, the officer must observe the item of evidence. This requirement means that the officer must actually see the item of evidence. If the officer merely has probable cause to believe that the item of evidence is in a particular place, a search warrant must be obtained before the item may be seized.

Fourth, the item of evidence must be lying in the open. The officer may use mechanical or electrical aids, such as a flashlight or binoculars, to assist in observing the item, so long as this does not unreasonably intrude on someone's reasonable expectation of privacy. The officer may also examine items more closely, unless:

1. the officer produces a new invasion of the person's property by taking action that exposes to view concealed portions of the premises or its contents; and

2. the officer's action is unrelated to and unjustified by the objectives of his or her authorized intrusion.

Furthermore, the opening of a container to determine if incriminating evidence is inside is prohibited unless any privacy interest in the contents of the container has already been compromised by a private party and information about the contents has been made available to the officer by the private party.

Fifth, the officer must have probable cause to believe that the item observed is subject to seizure. This simply means that the officer must have probable cause to believe that the item comes within one of the categories of property that are allowed to be seized under state law. An officer may use his or her experience and background to assist in determining whether a particular item is seizable.

Sixth, the discovery of the item of evidence by the officer must be inadvertent. The plain view doctrine does not apply when, before arriving at the place to be searched, the officer has probable cause to believe a particular item of evidence is located in a particular place and the officer intends to seize the item. Nevertheless, if there are exigent circumstances, even a planned seizure of evidence in plain view may be justified, especially if efforts toward obtaining a search warrant have been made.

REVIEW AND DISCUSSION QUESTIONS

1. Should the requirement that the discovery of an item of evidence be inadvertent apply if the officer had insufficient time to obtain a search warrant after learning the location of the item?

2. If law enforcement officers are in a place in which they have a right to be and they observe bottles that appear to contain illegal drugs, may they open the bottles and examine the contents further? May law enforcement officers use their sense of smell, taste, or touch to determine if items are subject to seizure when they are not sure?

3. Assume that law enforcement officers have a warrant to arrest the defendant for stealing guns four months ago. The officers suspect that the guns are at the defendant's home, but that suspicion is based on stale information insufficient to obtain a search warrant. May the officers seize guns found in plain view when they arrest the defendant? Would it make any difference if the officers could have easily found out if the guns were still at the defendant's home by contacting a reliable informant?

4. May law enforcement officers take an item off the shelf in an antique store and examine it to determine if it is stolen? May officers do the same thing in a private home into which they have been invited by a person who does not know they are law enforcement officers?

5. Discuss the meaning of the following statement of the U.S. Supreme Court: "'Plain view' is perhaps better understood . . . not as an independent 'exception' to the warrant clause, but simply as an extension of whatever the prior justification for an officer's 'access to an object' may be." Texas v. Brown, 460 U.S. 730, 738–39, 103 S.Ct. 1535, 1540–1541, 75 L.Ed.2d 502, 511 (1983).

6. What problems are presented by an officer executing a search warrant for specified obscene materials, who seizes some magazines that are in plain view and were not specified in the warrant?

7. What are the limits on protective searches? May officers routinely look throughout a house for other suspects whenever they make an arrest or search? May officers go into other buildings on the premises? May officers go into neighboring homes? If an arrest is made in the hallway of a motel, may officers conduct a protective search of any or all of the rooms of the motel?

8. Does the plain view doctrine authorize a warrantless entry into a dwelling to seize contraband visible from outside the dwelling? Why or why not? What if an officer observes contraband from the hallway of a motel through the open door to one of the rooms? What if an officer observes contraband lying on the desk in someone's office?

9. Would it be proper for officers executing a search warrant for stolen property to bring along victims of the theft to aid the officers in seizing other stolen items not named in the warrant that might be in plain view? Why or why not?

10. If police officers are legitimately on premises, may they record the serial numbers of any objects that they suspect are stolen property? May they take photographs of these objects?

CHAPTER 10
Search and Seizure of Vehicles and Containers

The same basic legal principles apply to the search of motor vehicles as apply to the search of fixed premises. For instance, it is well settled that an automobile is a personal effect, a place, or a thing within the meaning of the Fourth Amendment and is protected against unreasonable searches and seizures. Therefore, law enforcement officers should obtain a warrant whenever they want to search a motor vehicle unless the situation falls within one of the exceptions to the warrant requirement discussed in this chapter or in other chapters of this book. (Guidelines for obtaining a warrant can be found in Chapters 5 and 6.)

Courts have created exceptions to the warrant requirement for motor vehicles because of the unique nature of motor vehicles. Some of their unique characteristics are their mobility, their use as transportation to and from crime scenes, and their employment in transporting dangerous weapons, stolen goods, contraband, and instrumentalities of crime. In addition, a person has a lesser expectation of privacy in a motor vehicle because it travels public thoroughfares where its occupants and contents are open to view; it seldom serves as a residence or permanent place for personal effects; it is required to be registered and its occupant is required to be licensed; it is extensively regulated with respect to the condition and manner in which it is operated on public streets and highways; it periodically undergoes an official inspection; and it is often taken into police custody in the interests of public safety.

This chapter discusses the exceptions to the warrant requirement for searches and seizures of motor vehicles and also examines the search and seizure of movable containers, because similar considerations apply to both areas of the law.

THE CARROLL DOCTRINE

The *Carroll* doctrine holds that a warrantless search of a motor vehicle stopped on the public ways by a law enforcement officer who has probable cause to believe that the vehicle contains items subject to seizure is not unreasonable under the Fourth Amendment. The *Carroll* doctrine is sometimes referred to as the *automobile exception* to the search warrant requirement. The doctrine originated in the case of Carroll v. United States, 267 U.S. 132, 45 S.Ct. 280, 69 L.Ed. 543 (1925), in which federal prohibition agents obtained information that the defendant and another person were bootleggers who frequently traveled a certain road in a certain automobile. The officers later unexpectedly encountered the two men driving on that road in that automobile. The officers pursued and stopped the automobile on the highway. The automobile was thoroughly searched and the officers found several bottles of illegal liquor concealed in the automobile's upholstery. No warrant had been obtained for the search.

The U.S. Supreme Court held:

> On reason and authority the true rule is that if the search and seizure without a warrant are made upon probable cause, that is, upon a belief, reasonably arising out of circumstances known to the seizing officer, that an automobile or other vehicle contains that which by law is subject to seizure and destruction, the search and seizure are valid. The Fourth Amendment is to be construed in the light of what was deemed an unreasonable search and seizure when it was adopted, and in a manner which will conserve public interests as well as the interests and rights of individual citizens. 267 U.S. at 149, 45 S.Ct. at 283, 69 L.Ed. at 549.

Probable Cause

The controlling consideration in the search of a vehicle without a warrant is probable cause to believe that the vehicle contains items that are connected with criminal activity and thus are subject to seizure. This was emphasized in the *Carroll* decision:

> Having thus established that contraband goods concealed and illegally transported in an automobile or other vehicle may be searched for without a warrant, we come now to consider under what circumstances such search may be made. It would be intolerable and unreasonable if a prohibition agent were authorized to stop every automobile on the chance of finding liquor and thus subject all persons lawfully using the highways to the inconvenience and indignity of such a search. Travellers may be so stopped in crossing an international boundary because of national self protection reasonably requiring one entering the country to identify himself as entitled to come in, and his belongings as effects which may be lawfully brought in. But those lawfully within the Country, entitled to use the public highways, have a right to free passage without interruption or search unless there is known to a competent official authorized to search, probable cause for believing that their vehicles are carrying contraband or illegal merchandise. 267 U.S. at 153–54, 45 S.Ct. at 285, 69 L.Ed. at 551–52.

Probable cause is discussed in detail in Chapters 3 and 6. In vehicle search and seizure cases, probable cause depends on the particular circumstances of each situation. The law enforcement officer's determination of probable cause must be based on objective facts that could justify the issuance of a warrant by a magistrate and not merely on the subjective good faith of the officer. Evidence seized from a vehicle that is not seized on the basis of probable cause will be inadmissible in court.

Impounding the Vehicle

Chambers v. Maroney, 399 U.S. 42, 90 S.Ct. 1975, 26 L.Ed.2d 419 (1970), expanded the *Carroll* doctrine's grant of authority to law enforcement officers to search vehicles to include vehicles impounded and removed after being stopped on the public ways. In that case, the police had information that armed robbers carrying the fruits of the crime had fled the robbery scene in a light blue compact station wagon. Four men were said to be in the vehicle, one wearing a green sweater and another wearing a trench coat. The police stopped a vehicle fitting the description, arrested the four occupants, and drove the vehicle to the police station. The vehicle was thoroughly searched at the station and evidence was seized leading to the defendant's conviction.

The U.S. Supreme Court upheld the search:

> In enforcing the Fourth Amendment's prohibition against unreasonable searches and seizures, the Court has insisted upon probable cause as a minimum requirement for a reasonable search permitted by the Constitution. As a general rule, it has also required the judgment of a magistrate on the probable cause issue and the issuance of a warrant before a search is made. Only in exigent circumstances will the judgment of the police as to probable cause serve as a sufficient authorization for a search. Carroll . . . holds a search warrant unnecessary where there is probable cause to search an automobile stopped on the highway; the car is movable, the occupants are alerted, and the car's contents may never be found again if a warrant must be obtained. Hence an immediate search is constitutionally permissible.
>
> Arguably, because of the preference for a magistrate's judgment, only the immobilization of the car should be permitted until a search warrant is obtained; arguably, only the "lesser" intrusion is permissible until the magistrate authorizes the "greater." But which is the "greater" and which the "lesser" intrusion is itself a debatable question and the answer may depend on a variety of circumstances. For constitutional purposes, we see no difference between on the one hand seizing and holding a car before presenting the probable cause issue to a magistrate and on the other hand carrying out an immediate search without a warrant. Given probable cause to search either course is reasonable under the Fourth Amendment.
>
> On the facts before us, the blue station wagon could have been searched on the spot when it was stopped since there was probable cause to search and it was a fleeting target for a search. The probable cause factor still obtained at the station house and so did the mobility of the car unless the Fourth Amendment permits a warrantless seizure of the car and the denial of its use to anyone until a warrant is secured. In that event there is little to choose in terms of practical consequences between an immediate search without a warrant and the car's

immobilization until a warrant is obtained. 399 U.S. at 51–52, 90 S.Ct. at 1981, 26 L.Ed.2d at 428–29.

Exigent Circumstances

In the passage just quoted the Supreme Court said that "[o]nly in exigent circumstances will the judgment of the police as to probable cause serve as a sufficient authorization for a search." Some lower courts have taken this to mean that the police must be able to demonstrate specific facts establishing exigent circumstances, in addition to probable cause, before searching a vehicle stopped on the road. The U.S. Supreme Court, however, has made it clear that this is not necessary. In Michigan v. Thomas, 458 U.S. 259, 261, 102 S.Ct. 3079, 3081, 73 L.Ed.2d 750, 753 (1982), the Court said:

> In *Chambers v. Maroney*. . . we held that when police officers have probable cause to believe there is contraband inside an automobile that has been stopped on the road, the officers may conduct a warrantless search of the vehicle, even after it has been impounded and is in police custody. We firmly reiterated this holding in *Texas v. White*, 423 U.S. 67, 96 S.Ct. 304, 46 L.Ed.2d 209 (1975). . . . It is thus clear that the justification to conduct such a warrantless search does not vanish once the car has been immobilized; nor does it depend upon a reviewing court's assessment of the likelihood in each particular case that the car would have been driven away, or that its contents would have been tampered with, during the period required for the police to obtain a warrant.

In short, the requirement that there must be exigent circumstances before the police's judgment as to probable cause will justify a warrantless search is automatically satisfied in the case of a motor vehicle stopped on the road. Some state courts, however, may interpret their own constitutions to require stricter standards than those of the U.S. Supreme Court.

When a motor vehicle has not been stopped on the public ways, the requirement of exigent circumstances in addition to the requirement of probable cause must be established by the law enforcement officer before conducting a search or seizure. Usually, exigent circumstances are established by demonstrating specific facts showing either that the vehicle may be moved to an unknown location or out of the jurisdiction, making a search under authority of a warrant impossible, or that items subject to seizure may be removed from the vehicle and concealed or destroyed.

For example, in California v. Carney, 471 U.S. 386, 105 S.Ct. 2066, 85 L.Ed.2d 406 (1985), Drug Enforcement Agency agents had probable cause to search a mobile motor home parked in a lot in the downtown area of a large city. The Court applied the standard that a search of a vehicle is justified under the *Carroll* doctrine if the vehicle "is being used on the highways, or if it is readily capable of such use and is found stationary in a place not regularly used for residential purposes—temporary or otherwise." 471 U.S. at 392, 105 S.Ct. at 2070, 85 L.Ed.2d at 414. The warrantless search of this mobile home was upheld because the vehicle was readily mobile by a turn of the ignition key and was so situated that an objective observer would conclude that it was being used not as a residence, but as a vehicle. In United States v. Levesque, 625 F.Supp. 428 (D.N.H 1985), however, the court disallowed a warrantless search of a motor home that was not readily mobile:

The trailer at issue . . . was situated in a trailer park and on a lot, objectively indicating that it was being used as a residence. Although the truck which tows the trailer was only a few feet from the trailer, the trailer was not readily mobile in light of the fact that one end of the trailer was elevated on blocks and that the trailer was connected to utilities at the campground, and also because of the three quarters of an hour lead time to connect the trailer and truck. The mobile home exception to the warrant requirement thus would appear to have no application herein. 625 F.Supp. 450–51.

In Cardwell v. Lewis, 417 U.S. 583, 94 S.Ct. 2464, 41 L.Ed.2d 325 (1974), the U.S. Supreme Court found exigent circumstances justifying the warrantless seizure of the defendant's automobile from a commercial parking lot in which the defendant had left it before his appearance at the police station, where he was arrested. The defendant had been fully aware that he was under investigation for several months, and he had told his attorney to see that his wife and family got the car. The Court based its finding of exigent circumstances on the possibility that the attorney or a family member might remove evidence from the car if the police delayed seizing it. In a case where there were no indications of the potential mobility of an automobile, however, the court disallowed a warrantless search of a parked, unoccupied automobile:

[A]ny search of an automobile that was parked, immobile and unoccupied at the time the police first encountered it in connection with the investigation of a crime must be authorized by a warrant issued by a magistrate or, alternatively, the prosecution must demonstrate that exigent circumstances other than the potential mobility of the automobile exist. Here, the prosecution failed to demonstrate any individualized exigent circumstances. State v. Kock, 725 P.2d 1285, 1287 (Or. 1986).

If a vehicle or its contents present a potential danger to the public safety if not searched immediately, the *exigent circumstances* requirement of the *Carroll* doctrine may be satisfied, even though the car is not movable. In United States v. Cepulonis, 530 F.2d 238 (1st Cir. 1976), a law enforcement officer observed, through the window of an automobile, a sawed-off shotgun protruding from beneath the front seat. The court upheld the immediate warrantless seizure of the shotgun, finding probable cause and also finding that someone other than the car's owner (who was in custody) could have moved the car. The court went on to say:

Moreover, a legitimate concern for public safety counselled against leaving the car, with a loaded shotgun visible through the window, unguarded in the Motel parking lot and "vulnerable to intrusion by vandals." . . . Under the circumstances the agents were faced with a choice whether to seize and hold the car while securing a warrant or to carry out an immediate warrantless search. 530 F.2d at 243.

In Coolidge v. New Hampshire, 403 U.S. 443, 91 S.Ct. 2022, 29 L.Ed.2d 564 (1971), the U.S. Supreme Court indicated that the exigent circumstances requirement would not be satisfied if there were no real possibility that someone would remove the car and conceal or destroy evidence within it. In the *Coolidge* case, the police had known for some time of the probable role of the defendant's automobile in a crime. The police went to the defendant's home, arrested him inside his house, and escorted his wife and children to another town to spend the night. There were no other adult occupants of the house. The vehicle was unoccupied and in the defendant's driveway. Police towed the vehicle to the stationhouse and searched it there without a warrant.

The Court held that the search of the automobile could not be justified under the *Carroll* doctrine because the car was not movable, nor were there any other exigent circumstances to justify the search:

> [S]urely there is nothing in this case to invoke the meaning and purpose of the rule of Carroll v. U.S.—no alerted criminal bent on flight, no fleeting opportunity on an open highway after a hazardous chase, no contraband or stolen goods or weapons, no confederates waiting to move the evidence, not even the inconvenience of a special police detail to guard the immobilized automobile. In short, by no possible stretch of the legal imagination can this be made into a case where "it is not practicable to secure a warrant," . . . and the "automobile exception," despite its label, is simply irrelevant. 403 U.S. at 462, 91 S.Ct. at 2035–36, 29 L.Ed.2d at 580.

Entry upon Private Premises

When law enforcement officers, acting on probable cause and following closely behind a vehicle, would have been authorized to stop and search the vehicle while on a public way, they may properly follow the vehicle onto private property and conduct the search there. In Scher v. United States, 305 U.S. 251, 59 S.Ct. 174, 83 L.Ed 151 (1938), an informant's tip and careful surveillance gave police officers probable cause to believe that a certain automobile contained contraband. The officers followed the auto until the defendant parked it in his garage. The subsequent warrantless search of the car in the garage was held valid by the Court:

> [I]t seems plain enough that just before he entered the garage the following officers properly could have stopped petitioner's car, [and] made search. . . .
> Passage of the car into the open garage closely followed by the observing officer did not destroy this right. 305 U.S. at 255, 59 S.Ct. at 176, 83 L.Ed. at 154.

Scope of Search

The permissible scope of a warrantless search of a motor vehicle under the *Carroll* doctrine has been defined in United States v. Ross, 456 U.S. 798, 102 S.Ct. 2157, 72 L.Ed.2d 572 (1982), a case involving the legitimate stopping of an automobile by police officers who had probable cause to believe that the automobile contained narcotics. During the search of the car, the searching officers found and opened a closed brown paper bag and a zippered leather pouch, discovering heroin in the bag and a large amount of money in the pouch. In holding the search legal, the U.S. Supreme Court said:

> [T]he scope of the warrantless search authorized by [the *Carroll*] exception is no broader and no narrower than a magistrate could legitimately authorize by warrant. If probable cause justifies the search of a lawfully stopped vehicle, it justifies the search of every part of the vehicle and its contents that may conceal the object of the search. 456 U.S. at 425, 102 S.Ct. at 2172, 72 L.Ed.2d at 572.

Emphasizing that the scope of a search under the *Carroll* doctrine depends entirely on the object of the search, the Court stated:

The scope of a warrantless search of an automobile thus is not defined by the nature of the container in which the contraband is secreted. Rather, it is defined by the object of the search and the places in which there is probable cause to believe that it may be found. Just as probable cause to believe that a stolen lawnmower may be found in a garage will not support a warrant to search an upstairs bedroom, probable cause to believe that undocumented aliens are being transported in a van will not justify a warrantless search of a suitcase. Probable cause to believe that a container placed in the trunk of a taxi contains contraband or evidence does not justify a search of the entire cab. 456 U.S. at 824, 102 S.Ct. at 2172, 72 L.Ed.2d at 593.

Furthermore, in United States v. Johns, 469 U.S. 478, 105 S.Ct. 881, 83 L.Ed.2d 890 (1985), the U.S. Supreme Court held that where officers have probable cause to search a vehicle for a specific object, the search of a container in the vehicle which could contain that object need not be conducted at the same time as the seizure or search of the vehicle. Customs agents in the *Johns* case had seized and impounded a vehicle under the *Carroll* doctrine on the basis of probable cause to believe it contained marijuana. The Court approved a warrantless search of plastic bags found in the vehicle conducted three days later.

To summarize, under the *Carroll* doctrine, if officers have probable cause to search an entire vehicle for a specific seizable item, they may search to the same extent as if they had a warrant to search for that item. But, if officers have only probable cause to search a particular movable container, which merely happens to be inside a motor vehicle, and not probable cause to search the entire vehicle, different rules apply. These rules are discussed in the following section.

MOVABLE CONTAINERS

The rationale justifying a warrantless search of an automobile believed to be transporting items subject to seizure arguably applies with equal force to any movable container believed to be carrying such an item. However, the U.S. Supreme Court has squarely rejected that argument. In United States v. Chadwick, 433 U.S. 1, 97 S.Ct. 2476, 53 L.Ed.2d 538 (1977), federal railroad officials became suspicious when they noticed that a large footlocker loaded onto a train was unusually heavy and was leaking talcum powder, a substance often used to mask the odor of marijuana. Narcotics agents met the train at its destination and a trained police dog signaled the presence of a controlled substance inside the footlocker. The agents did not seize the footlocker at that time. Instead, they waited until the defendant arrived and the footlocker was placed in the trunk of his automobile. Before the automobile's engine was started, the officers arrested the defendant and his two companions. The agents then removed the footlocker to a secure place, opened it without a warrant, and discovered a large quantity of marijuana.

The prosecution argued on appeal that the warrantless search was "reasonable" because a footlocker has some of the mobile characteristics that support warrantless searches of automobiles. The Supreme Court rejected the argument:

The factors which diminish the privacy aspects of an automobile do not apply to respondents' footlocker. Luggage contents are not open to public view, except as a condition to border entry or common carrier travel; nor is luggage subject to regular inspections and official scrutiny on a continuing basis. Unlike an automobile, whose primary function is transportation, luggage is intended as a repository of personal effects. In sum, a person's expectations of privacy in personal luggage are substantially greater than in an automobile. 433 U.S. at 13, 97 S.Ct. at 2484, 53 L.Ed.2d at 549.

The Court noted that the practical problems associated with the temporary detention of a piece of luggage during the period of time necessary to obtain a warrant are significantly less than those associated with the detention of an automobile. In holding the warrantless search of the footlocker unjustified, the Court reaffirmed the general principle that closed packages and containers may not be searched without a warrant. Thus, the court declined to extend the rationale of the automobile exception to permit a warrantless search of any movable container found in a public place.

In Arkansas v. Sanders, 442 U.S. 753, 99 S.Ct. 2586, 61 L.Ed.2d 235 (1979), a case similar to *Chadwick*, a police officer received information from a reliable informant that the defendant would arrive at the local airport on a specified flight that afternoon carrying a green suitcase containing marijuana. The officer went to the airport and observed the defendant arrive on schedule and retrieve a green suitcase from the airline baggage service. The defendant gave the suitcase to a waiting companion who placed it in the trunk of a taxi. The defendant and his companion drove off in the cab. Police officers followed and stopped the cab several blocks from the airport. The officers opened the trunk, seized the suitcase, and searched the suitcase on the scene without a warrant. The suitcase contained marijuana.

The U.S. Supreme Court ruled that the warrantless search of the suitcase was impermissible under the Fourth Amendment. As in *Chadwick*, the mere fact that the suitcase had been placed in the trunk of the vehicle did not render the automobile exception of *Carroll* applicable. The police had probable case to seize the suitcase before it was placed in the trunk of the cab and did not have probable cause to search the cab itself. Since the suitcase had been placed in the trunk, no danger existed that its contents could have been hidden elsewhere in the vehicle. Furthermore, none of the practical difficulties associated with the detention of a vehicle on a public highway that made the immediate search in *Carroll* reasonable could justify the immediate search of the suitcase, since the officers had no interest in detaining the taxi or its driver. The common thread in the *Chadwick* and *Sanders* cases is that in neither case did the police have probable cause to search the vehicle or anything in it except the footlocker in the *Chadwick* case and the green suitcase in the *Sanders* case. Without probable case to search the vehicles, the *Carroll* doctrine did not apply, and the searches should not have been conducted without a warrant.

IMPOUNDMENT AND INVENTORY OF VEHICLE

Impoundment

Some police department policies require officers to impound a motor vehicle when the driver or owner is taken into custody or is incapacitated by intoxication, illness, or some other condition. The usual procedure involves the police taking possession of the vehicle and moving it to a garage or police lot for safe-keeping. The main justification for such an impoundment policy is that the vehicle would otherwise be left unattended on a public street or highway, and would be an easy target for theft or vandalism, leaving the police open to potential liability.

Nevertheless, the right to impound a vehicle does not automatically follow upon the taking into custody or incapacitation of the driver or owner. Some courts have held that an impoundment of a vehicle must be necessary in order to be legal. In a case in which both occupants of an automobile were intoxicated, and there was no one else to drive or take care of the automobile, the court favored impoundment over leaving the car unattended on the street. People v. Havenstein, 84 Cal.Rptr. 528 (Cal.App. 1970).

If less intrusive alternate means of caring for the vehicle are available, however, they should be used. In a case involving a defendant arrested for driving under the influence, the defendant made arrangements to have his brother and mother take care of his car. The arresting officer, however, refused to relinquish the car and impounded it. The contents were later inventoried and LSD tablets were found. The court held that the impoundment of the car, and therefore the inventory search of it, was illegal. The court said, "We hold that where police assumed custody of defendant's automobile for no legitimate state purpose other than safekeeping, and where defendant had arranged for alternate means, not shown to be unreasonable, for the safeguarding of his property, impoundment of defendant's automobile was unreasonable and, therefore, the concomitant inventory was an unreasonable search under the Fourth Amendment." State v. Goodrich, 256 N.W.2d 506, 507 (Minn. 1977).

Law enforcement officers are not, however, constitutionally required to offer a defendant the opportunity to make other arrangements for the safekeeping of his or her vehicle nor must they always choose methods of dealing with a defendant's vehicle that are less intrusive than impoundment. As stated by the U.S. Supreme Court, "[t]he reasonableness of any particular governmental activity does not necessarily or invariably turn on the existence of alternative 'less intrusive' means." Illinois v. Lafayette, 462 U.S. at 647, 103 S.Ct. at 2610, 77 L.Ed.2d at 72 (1983). Therefore, nothing prohibits the exercise of police discretion to impound a vehicle rather than to park and lock it in a safe place, for instance, so long as that discretion is exercised according to standard criteria and on the basis of something other than suspicion of evidence of criminal activity. Colorado v. Bertine, 479 U.S. 367, 375, 107 S.Ct. 738, 743, 93 L.Ed.2d 739, 748 (1986).

The removal of an unoccupied parked vehicle is clearly justified when the vehicle constitutes a traffic hazard or otherwise violates local parking ordinances. The U.S. Supreme Court specifically authorized impoundment of vehicles under such circumstances:

> In the interests of public safety and as part of what the Court has called "community caretaking functions," . . . automobiles are frequently taken into police custody. Vehicle accidents present one such occasion. To permit the uninterrupted flow of traffic and in some circumstances to preserve evidence, disabled or damaged vehicles will often be removed from the highways or streets at the behest of police engaged solely in caretaking and traffic control activities. Police will also frequently remove and impound automobiles which violate parking ordinances which thereby jeopardize both the public safety and the efficient movement of vehicular traffic. The authority of police to seize and

remove from the streets vehicles impeding traffic or threatening public safety and convenience is beyond challenge. South Dakota v. Opperman, 428 U.S. 364, 368–69, 96 S.Ct. 3092, 3096, 49 L.Ed.2d 1000, 1005 (1976).

Inventory

Assuming that a vehicle has been lawfully impounded, may the vehicle then be searched for incriminating evidence without a warrant? Unless the situation satisfies the requirements of the *Carroll* doctrine, police have no authority to conduct a warrantless investigatory search of a lawfully impounded motor vehicle. In other words, police must obtain a search warrant to search an impounded vehicle unless they have probable cause to search the vehicle and the vehicle was originally stopped on the public ways or exigent circumstances make an immediate warrantless search of the vehicle necessary.

Nevertheless, in South Dakota v. Opperman, 428 U.S. 364, 96 S.Ct. 3092, 49 L.Ed.2d 1000 (1976), the U.S. Supreme Court approved a more limited search of impounded motor vehicles: the routine practice of local police departments of securing and inventorying the vehicle's contents. This limited search is allowed to protect the following:

1. The owner's property while it remains in police custody
2. The police against claims or disputes over lost or stolen property
3. The police from potential danger

This inventory procedure is not considered to be a search for purposes of the Fourth Amendment because its object is not to find incriminating evidence as part of a criminal investigation. Rather, it is considered to be a routine administrative-custodial procedure, and it may not be used as a pretext to conduct an exploratory search for incriminating evidence in order to circumvent the warrant requirement. Harris v. United States, 370 F.2d 477 (D.C.Cir. 1966).

The allowable scope of the inventory is restricted to accessible areas of the vehicle in which the owner's or occupant's personal belongings might be vulnerable to theft or damage. Areas covered by the inventory would usually include an unlocked glove compartment, an unlocked trunk, the sun visors, the front and rear seat areas, and other places in which property is ordinarily kept. People v. Andrews, 85 Cal.Rptr. 908 (Cal.App. 1970). The U.S. Supreme Court decision in Colorado v. Bertine, 479 U.S. 367, 107 S.Ct. 738, 93 L.Ed.2d 739 (1986), expanded the allowable scope of an inventory search to include closed containers and their contents found within the impounded vehicle. As a part of the inventory, a notation should be made of the vehicle identification number, the motor number, and the make, model, and license plate number of the car in order that the car may be easily identified later. Cotton v. United States, 371 F.2d 385 (9th Cir. 1967).

Officers should not open locked glove compartments or locked trunks to make inventories of their contents because the protection of the property, the officers, and others would not ordinarily require it and because inventorying locked areas may violate the owner's or occupant's reasonable expectation of privacy. State v. Boster, 539 P.2d 294 (Kan. 1975). But when officers reasonably believe that the contents of an automobile or the contents of a locked compartment in an automobile present a danger to themselves or others, they may make as extensive a search as necessary to end the danger.

The intensity of the inventory must also be limited by its purpose. Thus, if officers dismantle the vehicle, look behind the upholstery, or in any other manner indicate that their purpose is other than to protect and secure the vehicle's contents, the courts will consider the inventory a pretext for a search designed to uncover evidentiary materials. The inventory will then be considered an illegal warrantless search and the fruits of the search will be inadmissible in court.

Likewise, if police delay making an inventory of the contents of an impounded vehicle for an unreasonable period of time, the inventory may be ruled an illegal search. An unreasonably delayed inventory indicates that police were not really concerned about safeguarding the owner's property or protecting themselves against claims or from danger, but were primarily interested in looking for evidence. A vehicle inventory should be conducted as soon as possible after the impoundment, taking into consideration the police agency's human resources, facilities, work load, and other circumstances. If the inventory is delayed for more than a day or two without good reason, it is likely to be declared illegal.

Each law enforcement agency should have standard procedures for inventorying impounded vehicles, or the inventories may be declared illegal. In upholding the validity of an inventory of an impounded car in *South Dakota v. Opperman*, the U.S. Supreme Court emphasized that the police were using a standard inventory form pursuant to standard police procedures. The Court said, "The decisions of this Court point unmistakably to the conclusion reached by both federal and state courts that inventories pursuant to standard police procedures are reasonable." 428 U.S. at 372, 96 S.Ct. at 3098, 49 L.Ed.2d at 1007. The Ninth Circuit Court of Appeals invalidated an inventory of a legally impounded automobile because the local police department did not have a standard procedure regarding the inventorying of an impounded vehicle's contents.

> [E]ven if an investigatory motive was not shown, our decision would be the same because the inventorying of impounded cars was not shown to be a routine practice and policy of *this* police department, as was the case in *Opperman....* It is the inventorying practice and not the impounding practice that, if routinely followed and supported by proper noninvestigatory purposes, could render the inventory a reasonable search under *Opperman*. The fact that other police departments routinely follow such a practice may give support to the proposition that such a practice, if locally followed, is reasonable. It does not, however, render reasonable a search where the inventorying practice is not locally followed and the search, thus, is a departure from local practice. United States v. Hellman, 556 F.2d 442, 444 (9th Cir. 1977).

Plan View Doctrine

Although a law enforcement officer may not look for evidence of crime while conducting a bona fide inventory, if contraband or other items subject to seizure are inadvertently discovered, those items may lawfully be seized and are admissible in evidence. When the officer is lawfully conducting an inventory in the vehicle and there has been no search in the Fourth Amendment sense, the situation is governed by the plain view doctrine discussed in Chapter 9.

In a case illustrating the application of the plain view doctrine to the inventory situation, officers stopped a vehicle that was being operated without license plates. Neither of the occupants claimed to be the owner of the automobile nor did they know to whom it belonged. Furthermore, the driver's statement that he had borrowed the vehicle from a used car dealer was not consistent with information disclosed on the registration sticker. On the basis of these facts, the officers arrested the two men on a charge of auto theft. After the arrest, as a normal procedure before impounding the vehicle, the officers began an inventory of all personal property found in it. One officer picked up a jacket on the front seat where the defendant had been sitting and noticed in plain sight a burned cigarette. Since the cigarette appeared to him to be marijuana, the officer searched the jacket and found another similar cigarette in the left-hand pocket. The defendant later admitted that he had purchased the cigarettes approximately one week earlier.

The court held that the marijuana cigarette was legally seized by the officer:

> In the course of making the inventory of the contents of the car, the officer merely removed the jacket from the front seat revealing in plain sight the narcotic. How it got there could not be determined but it is clear that when the officer picked up the jacket the cigarette was there for all to see. Actually, the officer's observation of the cigarette was not the result of a search, for it appeared in plain sight in the normal course of the reasonable and valid activity of the officer in making the inventory incidental to impounding the car. People v. Nebbitt, 7 Cal.Rptr. 8, 13 (Cal.App. 1960).

IMPOUNDMENT OF VEHICLE UNDER FORFEITURE STATUTES

Another ground for allowing a warrantless search of a vehicle by law enforcement officers is the seizure and impoundment of the vehicle under authority of a state forfeiture statute. In the case of Cooper v. California, 386 U.S. 58, 87 S.Ct. 788, 17 L.Ed.2d 730 (1967), the defendant was arrested for selling heroin wrapped in brown paper to a police informer. At the time of the arrest, the defendant's car was seized and impounded pursuant to a state forfeiture statute. The statute required that any officer making an arrest for a narcotics offense involving the use of a vehicle must seize and hold the vehicle as evidence pending a judicial declaration of forfeiture or release. Evidence showed that the defendant used his vehicle in connection with his possession and transportation of narcotics. One week after the seizure, police searched the car and discovered a piece of brown paper in the glove compartment. The brown paper was later introduced at trial. The state had not acquired title to the car at the time of the search.

This search could not be justified under the *Carroll* doctrine because there were no exigent circumstances. The car had been in police custody for a week, during which time the police could easily have obtained a warrant. Nevertheless, the Court held the search legal, finding that the car was lawfully held by the police in connection with criminal activity under the state forfeiture statute. Since the car was to be held for a considerable period of time, and since the police could deny possession of the car to its owner, the police had possessory rights of their own for the limited purpose of searching the vehicle.

The *Cooper* case allows law enforcement officers to conduct a warrantless search of a vehicle, in the absence of exigent circumstances, when all the following conditions are met:

1. A state statute requires law enforcement officers to seize vehicles involved in certain offenses and hold them pending forfeiture proceedings.

2. A vehicle is seized by the officer in connection with an offense named in the state forfeiture statute and is impounded.

3. The search of the car is closely related to the reason the defendant was arrested, the reason the vehicle was impounded, and the reason the vehicle is being retained.

4. The officer expects that the car will be in police custody for a considerable time.

5. The officers can legally deny possession of the car to the owner.

The *Cooper* decision does not require that officers have probable cause to search a vehicle impounded under the forfeiture statute. Nevertheless, because of the general preference for warrants, if officers do have probable cause to search, they should obtain a search warrant.

EXPECTATION OF PRIVACY

In recent years, courts have begun to analyze warrantless searches and seizures of vehicles in terms of whether they intrude upon a person's reasonable expectation of privacy. In Cardwell v. Lewis, 417 U.S. 583, 94 S.Ct. 2464, 41 L.Ed.2d 325 (1974), the U.S. Supreme Court held that where probable cause exists, a warrantless examination of the exterior of a car is not unreasonable under the Fourth and Fourteenth Amendments.

> One has a lesser expectation of privacy in a motor vehicle because its function is transportation and it seldom serves as one's residence or as the repository of personal effects. A car has little capacity for escaping public scrutiny. It travels public thoroughfares where both its occupants and its contents are in plain view.... This is not to say that no part of the interior of an automobile has Fourth Amendment protection; the exercise of a desire to be mobile does not, of course, waive one's right to be free of unreasonable governmental intrusion. But insofar as Fourth Amendment protection extends to a motor vehicle, it is the right to privacy that is the touchstone of our inquiry. 417 U.S. at 590–91, 94 S.Ct. at 2469–70, 41 L.Ed.2d at 335.

In South Dakota v. Opperman, 428 U.S. 364, 96 S.Ct. 3092, 49 L.Ed.2d 1000 (1976), the U.S. Supreme Court approved the warrantless inventory of an automobile impounded for parking violations.

> Besides the elements of mobility, less rigorous warrant requirements govern because the expectation of privacy with respect to one's automobile is significantly less than that relating to one's home or office. In discharging their varied

> responsibilities for ensuring the public safety, law enforcement officials are necessarily brought into frequent contact with automobiles. Most of this contact is distinctly noncriminal in nature.... Automobiles, unlike homes, are subjected to pervasive and continuing governmental regulation and controls, including periodic inspection and licensing requirements. As an everyday occurrence, police stop and examine vehicles when license plates or inspection stickers have expired, or if other violations, such as exhaust fumes or excessive noise, are noted, or if headlights or other safety equipment are not in proper working order. 428 U.S. at 367–68, 96 S.Ct. at 3096, 49 L.Ed.2d at 1004.

Furthermore, a person does not have a greater expectation of privacy in a vehicle merely because the vehicle is capable of functioning as a home.

> In our increasingly mobile society, many vehicles used for transportation can be and are being used not only for transportation, but for shelter, i.e., as a "home" or "residence." To distinguish between respondent's motor home and an ordinary sedan for purposes of the vehicle exception would require that we apply the exception depending upon the size of the vehicle and the quality of its appointments. Moreover, to fail to apply the exception to vehicles such as a motor home ignores the fact that a motor home lends itself easily to use as an instrument of illicit drug traffic and other illegal activity.... We decline ... to distinguish between "worthy" and "unworthy" vehicles which are either on the public roads and highways, or situated such that it is reasonable to conclude that the vehicle is not being used as a residence. California v. Carney, 471 U.S. 386, 393–94, 105 S.Ct. 2066, 2070, 85 L.Ed.2d 406, 414–415 (1985).

The quoted passages indicate that the courts are imposing fewer restrictions on law enforcement officers with regard to warrantless searches of vehicles. Nevertheless, even though the reasonable expectation of privacy in a vehicle is less than that in a home or office, law enforcement officers must not violate that expectation when conducting searches or inventories of vehicles. For example, the U.S. Supreme Court stated that "a search, even of an automobile, is a substantial invasion of privacy. To protect that privacy from official arbitrariness, the Court always has regarded probable cause as the minimum requirement for a lawful search." United States v. Ortiz, 422 U.S. 891, 896, 95 S.Ct. 2585, 2588, 45 L.Ed.2d 623, 629 (1975).

Electronic Beepers

A *beeper* is a radio transmitter, usually battery operated, that emits periodic signals that can be picked up by a radio receiver. A beeper neither records nor transmits any sounds other than its signal, but the signal can be monitored by directional finders, enabling law enforcement officers to determine the beeper's location.

For the first time, the U.S. Supreme Court dealt with the Fourth Amendment implications of the use of beepers in the case of United States v. Knotts, 460 U.S. 276, 103 S.Ct. 1081, 75 L.Ed.2d 55 (1983). With the consent of a chemical company, officers installed a beeper in a five-gallon container of chloroform, a substance used to manufacture illicit drugs. One of the defendants purchased the container of chloroform and transported it by automobile to a codefendant's secluded cabin in another state. Law enforcement officers monitored the progress of the automobile carrying the chloroform all the way to its destination.

After three days of visual surveillance of the cabin, officers obtained a search warrant, searched the cabin, and found evidence of the illegal manufacture of drugs.

The Court held that the warrantless monitoring of the beeper by law enforcement officers to trace the location of the chloroform container did not violate the defendant's legitimate expectation of privacy:

> The governmental surveillance conducted by means of the beeper in this case amounted principally to the following of an automobile on public streets and highways.... A person travelling in an automobile on public thoroughfares has no reasonable expectation of privacy in his movements from one place to another. When [the defendant] travelled over the public streets he voluntarily conveyed to anyone who wanted to look the fact that he was travelling over particular roads in a particular direction, the fact of whatever stops he made, and the fact of his final destination when he exited from public roads onto private property. 460 U.S. at 281, 103 S.Ct. at 1085, 75 L.Ed.2d at 62.

Although the owner of the cabin and surrounding premises undoubtedly had a justifiable expectation of privacy within the cabin, the expectation did not extend to the visual observation of his codefendant's automobile arriving on his premises after leaving a public highway, nor to movements of objects such as the container of chloroform outside the cabin. That the officers relied not only on visual surveillance but on the use of the beeper to locate the automobile did not alter the situation. "Nothing in the Fourth Amendment prohibited the police from augmenting the sensory faculties bestowed upon them at birth with such enhancement as science and technology afforded them in this case." 460 U.S. at 282, 103 S.Ct. at 1086, 75 L.Ed.2d at 63.

The Court emphasized the limited use the officers made of the signals from the beeper. There was no indication that the beeper signal was received or relied upon after it had indicated that the chloroform container had ended its automotive journey at the defendant's camp. Moreover, there was no indication that the beeper was used in any way to reveal information as to the movement of the drum within the cabin, or in any way that would not have been visible to the naked eye from outside the cabin.

The U.S. Supreme Court case of United States v. Karo, 468 U.S. 705, 104 S.Ct. 3296, 82 L.Ed.2d 530 (1984), addressed the question of whether the monitoring of a beeper in a private residence, a location not open to visual surveillance, violates the Fourth Amendment rights of those who have a justifiable interest in the privacy of the residence. The Court found that the government's warrantless surreptitious use of an electronic device to obtain information it could not have obtained by observation from outside the curtilage of a house was the same, for purposes of the Fourth Amendment, as a law enforcement officer's warrantless surreptitious entry of the house to verify that the beeper was in the house. Even though the monitoring of a beeper inside a private residence is less intrusive than a full-scale search, it is illegal unless conducted under authority of a warrant. The Court said:

> Requiring a warrant will have the salutary effect of ensuring that the use of beepers is not abused, by imposing upon agents the requirement that they demonstrate in advance their justification for the desired search. This is not to say

that there are no exceptions to the warrant rule, because if truly exigent circumstances exist no warrant is required under general Fourth Amendment principles.

Therefore, the warrantless monitoring of a beeper is permissible only if the beeper, or the container containing the beeper, could have been observed from outside the curtilage of a house, or if there is an emergency. Otherwise, the monitoring of a beeper located in a place not open to visual surveillance is illegal without a warrant.

Searches by Dogs

In United States v. Solis, 536 F.2d 880 (9th Cir. 1976), the court held that the use of specially trained dogs to detect the smell of marijuana in a vehicle did not violate the reasonable expectation of privacy of the vehicle's owner. In that case, a drug agent suspected that marijuana was hidden in the floor of a certain semitrailer parked at the rear of a gas station. The agent went to the gas station and found the semitrailer with what appeared to be white talcum powder on its doors. The officer knew from his training and experience that marijuana was often smuggled in semitrailer floors and that talcum powder was often used to conceal marijuana's odor. The agent notified the customs office, which sent two customs officers with specially trained marijuana-sniffing dogs. The dogs, who were determined to be extremely reliable, reacted positively to marijuana in the semitrailer. A search warrant was obtained and the marijuana was seized.

The court held that the use of the dogs to help the officers establish probable cause to search was reasonable and did not violate the defendant's reasonable expectation of privacy. The court said:

> The dogs' intrusion such as it was into the air space open to the public in the vicinity of the trailer appears to us reasonably tolerable in our society. There was no invasion of the "curtilage"—the trailer. No sophisticated mechanical or electronic devices were used. The investigation was not indiscriminate, but solely directed to the particular contraband. There was an expectation that the odor would emanate from the trailer. Efforts made to mask it were visible. The method used by the officers was inoffensive. There was no embarrassment to or search of the person. The target was a physical fact indicative of possible crime, not protected communications. We hold that the use of the dogs was not unreasonable under the circumstances and therefore was not a prohibited search under the fourth amendment. 536 F.2d at 882–83.

Courts are in disagreement over the search and seizure implications of the use of drug-detecting dogs. The safest procedure for law enforcement officers is to make sure drug-detecting dogs are reliable and to obtain a warrant before conducting a search based on a dog's reactions.

SUMMARY

Although the search and seizure of motor vehicles are generally governed by the warrant requirement of the Fourth Amendment, courts have created certain exceptions to the warrant requirement for motor vehicles, based on the differences between a motor vehicle and fixed premises. A motor vehicle is mobile and is used to transport criminals, weapons, and fruits and instrumentalities of crime. It seldom serves as a residence or a permanent repository of personal effects. Furthermore, a person has a reduced expectation of privacy in a motor vehicle because the vehicle travels public thoroughfares where its occupants and contents are open to view, and because the vehicle is subject to extensive governmental regulation, including periodic inspection and licensing.

The most important exception to the warrant requirement is the so-called automobile exception as embodied in the *Carroll* doctrine. Under the *Carroll* doctrine, law enforcement officers may conduct a warrantless search of a motor vehicle if they have probable cause to believe that the vehicle contains items subject to seizure and if there are exigent circumstances that make obtaining a warrant impracticable. If the vehicle is stopped on the public ways, the exigent circumstances requirement is automatically satisfied and the police need not provide supporting facts and circumstances to establish the existence of exigent circumstances. In addition, police may conduct a warrantless search of a vehicle stopped on the public ways even after the vehicle has been impounded and is in police custody. The scope of the search is defined by the object of the search and the places in which there is probable cause to believe the object may be found. If police have probable cause to believe that a particular seizable item is located somewhere in a vehicle that has been lawfully stopped on the public ways, they may search the vehicle as if they had a search warrant for the item. This means they have the right to open and search closed, opaque containers, located inside the vehicle, in which the seizable item might be contained. If, however, police do not have probable cause to search the entire vehicle, but only probable cause to search a particular container inside the vehicle, they may not open and search the container without a warrant. Nevertheless, if police have probable cause to believe that the container holds an immediately dangerous instrumentality, such as explosives, they may open the container and disarm the instrumentality or otherwise end the danger. If a closed, opaque container is seized incident to the arrest of an occupant of a motor vehicle, the search and seizure of the contents of the container are governed by the case of *New York v. Belton* (discussed in Chapter 7).

The inventory of a lawfully impounded motor vehicle may also be conducted without a warrant. This procedure is not considered to be a search for Fourth Amendment purposes, but merely an administrative procedure. The officer making the inventory may not look for incriminating evidence but may be concerned only with protecting the owner's property, protecting the police against claims or disputes over lost or stolen property, and protecting the police from potential danger. The inventory of a vehicle must be limited in scope and intensity by the purposes for which it is allowed. Nevertheless, evidence of crime found in plain view during the inventory may be seized and will be admissible in court. Seizure and impoundment of a vehicle under a state forfeiture statute may also provide legal justification for a warrantless search of the vehicle.

Although courts are in disagreement, they generally approve the tracing of the location of a motor vehicle on public thoroughfares by means of an electronic beeper, and the detection of drugs in a motor vehicle by means of sniffing by specially trained dogs. Both these limited types of intrusion are allowed, based upon the reduced expectation of privacy in motor vehicles.

REVIEW AND DISCUSSION QUESTIONS

1. Are there any situations in which a warrant is required to search a motor vehicle? Is the warrant requirement essentially the exception rather than the rule in automobile cases?

2. Do the legal principles in this chapter apply to vehicles such as bicycles, rowboats, motor homes, trains, or airplanes?

3. If a law enforcement officer has probable cause to believe a vehicle contains small concealable items such as drugs, jewels, or rare coins, to what extent can the vehicle be searched without a warrant under the *Carroll* doctrine? Can the upholstery be ripped open? Can the vehicle be dismantled? Can the tires be taken off to look inside them? Can pillows, radios, clothing, and other potential containers be dismantled or ripped apart?

4. Under the *Carroll* doctrine, an officer with probable cause to search a motor vehicle has the choice to either conduct the search immediately or impound the vehicle and search it later at the stationhouse. What factors should be considered in making this choice?

5. Describe three situations in which there are exigent circumstances and probable cause to search a vehicle that has *not* been stopped on the highway.

6. If the postal service turns over to the police plastic bags believed to contain illegal drugs, may the police conduct chemical tests on the contents of the bags without a warrant?

7. Assume that a person is arrested for drunken driving late at night while driving alone on a city street. He tells the police that he doesn't want his car impounded and that a friend will pick up the car some time the next day. He says he will sign a statement absolving the police from any liability for any loss of or damage to the car or its contents. Should the police impound the car and inventory its contents?

8. Under the *Carroll* doctrine, do the police have to have probable cause to search the vehicle at the time it is stopped on the highway in order to search it later at the station? Suppose a person is arrested on the highway for a traffic violation and is told to accompany officers to the station to post bond. A routine check at the station reveals that the vehicle is stolen. May the officers search it without a warrant?

9. If officers have probable cause to search a vehicle stopped on the highway, but no probable cause to arrest the passengers of the vehicle, can the officers search the passengers also? Are the passengers "containers" under the ruling of the *Ross* case? Does the answer depend on the nature of the evidence the officers are looking for?

10. Is a warrantless installation of a beeper proper in each of the following circumstances?
   a. Attaching a beeper to the outside of an automobile
   b. Placing a beeper somewhere inside an automobile
   c. Opening a closed package or luggage to install a beeper
   d. Attaching a beeper to the outside of a package or luggage
   e. Placing a beeper with money taken in a bank robbery

CHAPTER 11
Open Fields and Abandoned Property

The Fourth Amendment to the U.S. Constitution guarantees "the right of the people to be secure in their persons, *houses*, papers, and effects, against unreasonable *searches* and seizures....(emphasis supplied) U.S.C.A. Const.Amend.IV. The word *houses* and the word *searches* are italicized because the meaning of open fields depends upon court interpretation of the word *houses*, and the meaning of abandoned property depends upon court interpretations of the word *searches*. The legal meanings of these terms and their interrelationships are introduced with a summary of Hester v. United States, 265 U.S. 57, 44 S.Ct. 445, 68 L.Ed. 898 (1924), which established the concepts of open fields and abandonment in the law of search and seizure.

HESTER v. UNITED STATES

In *Hester v. United States*, revenue officers, investigating suspected bootlegging, went to the house of Hester's father. As they approached, they saw Henderson drive up to the house. The officers concealed themselves and observed Hester come out of the house and hand Henderson a quart bottle. An alarm was given. Hester went to a nearby car and removed a gallon jug, and he and Henderson fled across an open field. One of the officers pursued, firing his pistol. Henderson threw away his bottle, and Hester dropped his jug, which broke, keeping about one quart of its contents. A broken jar, still containing some of its contents, was found outside the house. The officers examined the jug, the jar, and the bottle and determined that they contained illicitly distilled whiskey. The officers had neither a search warrant nor an arrest warrant.

The defendant was convicted of concealing distilled spirits, and contended on appeal that the testimony of the two officers was inadmissible because their actions constituted an illegal search and seizure. The Court said:

243

It is obvious that even if there had been a trespass, the above testimony was not obtained by an illegal search or seizure. The defendant's own acts, and those of his associates, disclosed the jug, the jar and the bottle—and there was no seizure in the sense of the law when the officers examined the contents of each after it had been *abandoned*. . . . The only shadow of a ground for bringing up the case is drawn from the hypothesis that the examination of the vessels took place upon Hester's father's land. As to that, it is enough to say that, apart from the justification, the special protection accorded by the Fourth Amendment to the people in their "persons, houses, papers and effects," is not extended to the *open fields*. The distinction between the latter and the house is as old as the common law. (emphasis supplied) 265 U.S. at 58–59, 44 S.Ct. at 446, 68 L.Ed. at 900.

The remainder of this chapter is devoted to a discussion of the law of search and seizure applied to open fields and abandoned property, as the law has developed since the *Hester* case.

OPEN FIELDS

The basic open fields doctrine was stated by the U.S. Supreme Court in the *Hester* case: "[T]he special protection accorded by the Fourth Amendment to the people in their 'persons, houses, papers and effects' is not extended to the open fields." 265 U.S. at 59, 44 S.Ct. at 446, 68 L.Ed. at 900.

The open fields doctrine allows law enforcement officers to search for and seize evidence in the open fields without a warrant, probable cause, or any other legal justification. Even if officers trespass on the land of another while searching the open fields, the evidence they seize will not be inadmissible by reason of trespass. Oliver v. United States, 466 U.S. 170, 104 S.Ct. 1735, 80 L.Ed.2d 214 (1984). Furthermore, the officers themselves will not be held liable for trespass in a civil suit if the trespass was required in the performance of their duties. Giacona v. United States, 257 F.2d 450 (5th Cir. 1958).

The key issue is determining where the area protected by the Fourth Amendment ends and the open fields begin. The answer is found in court decisions interpreting the word *houses* in the Fourth Amendment. The word *houses* has been given a very broad meaning by the courts. The Fourth Amendment has been held to protect people in their homes, whether owned, rented, or leased. The term *houses* has also been held to include any quarters in which a person is staying or living, whether permanently or temporarily. Examples of protected living quarters are hotel and motel rooms, apartments, rooming and boarding house rooms, and even hospital rooms.

Furthermore, the protection of the Fourth Amendment extends to places of business. United States v. Botsch, 364 F.2d 542, 547 (2d Cir. 1966). The protection extended to places of business is limited, however, to areas or sections that are not open to the public: "[A] private business whose doors are open to the general public is also to be considered open to entry by the police for any proper purpose not violative of the owner's constitutional rights—e.g., patronizing the place or surveying it to promote law and order or to suppress a breach of the peace." State v. La Duca, 214 A.2d 423, 426 (N.J. Super. 1965). For purposes of convenience, the word *house* is used in the remainder of this chapter to refer to either residential or commercial premises covered by the Fourth Amendment.

Courts have extended the meaning of *houses* under the Fourth Amendment to include the "ground and buildings immediately surrounding a dwelling." Rosencranz v. United States, 356 F.2d 310, 313 (1st Cir. 1966). This area is commonly known as the *curtilage*. The concept of curtilage is vital to the open fields doctrine because the open fields are considered to be all the space that is not contained within the curtilage. The following discussion focuses on the facts and circumstances that courts rely on in determining the extent of the curtilage.

Determination of Curtilage

To determine whether property to be searched falls within the curtilage of a house, the law enforcement officer must consider "the factors that determine whether an individual reasonably may expect that an area immediately adjacent to the home will remain private." Oliver v. United States, 466 U.S. 170, 180, 104 S.Ct. 1735, 1742, 80 L.Ed.2d 214 (1984). The Court described those factors in another case: "[W]e believe that curtilage questions should be resolved with particular reference to four factors: the proximity of the area claimed to be curtilage to the home, whether the area is included within an enclosure surrounding the home, the nature of the uses to which the area is put, and the steps taken by the resident to protect the area from observation by people passing by." United States v. Dunn, 480 U.S. 294, 301, 107 S.Ct. 1134, 1139, 94 L.Ed.2d 326, 334–35 (1987). These factors are not intended to produce a finely tuned formula, but rather are useful analytical tools to help determine whether the area in question should be placed under the same Fourth Amendment protection as the home. The Court emphasized that "the primary focus is whether the area in question harbors those intimate activities associated with domestic life and the privacies of the home." 480 U.S. at 301, n. 4, 107 S.Ct. at 1139, n. 4, 94 L.Ed. 2d at 335, n. 4.

The four factors are discussed here under various headings through an analysis of court decisions on the open fields doctrine.

RESIDENTIAL YARD. Courts differ as to whether the residential yard is within the curtilage. In State v. Buchanan, 432 S.W.2d 342 (Mo. 1968), law enforcement officers investigating a robbery obtained a search warrant to search the defendant's premises. The officers searched the residence and an outbuilding and finally found a shotgun in the front yard, eight to ten feet from the street. The warrant was later held to be invalid. The court held that the front yard was within the curtilage of the defendant's house and was subject to the same constitutional protection as the house itself. Since the officers' only justification for being on the premises was an invalid search warrant, the search was illegal.

In another case, however, the court held that entry into a residential yard, even if a trespass, and the observation of that which is open to view is not prohibited by the Fourth Amendment. An officer had received information that the defendant was growing marijuana under a fig tree outside his residence. The officer went to the defendant's residence to investigate. The premises were described by the court as a house that faced the street with a driveway that ran along the east of the house and terminated in a garage at the rear and east of the house. The defendant's residence was attached to the rear of the garage. The fig tree was about twenty feet from the defendant's door. The officer observed marijuana plants growing in a keg near the base of the tree, partially covered by the leaves and limbs of the tree.

In finding the seizure of the plants legal, the court said:

> [T]hey were located a scant 20 feet from defendant's door to which presumably delivery men and others came, and the front house, as well as defendant's house, apparently had access to the yard. Under the circumstances it does not appear that defendant exhibited a subjective expectation of privacy as to the plants. Furthermore, any such expectation would have been unreasonable. People v. Bradley, 81 Cal.Rptr. 457, 459, 460 P.2d 129, 131 (Cal. 1969).

The main difference between these two cases appears to be that the defendant's yard in the *Bradley* case was semipublic in nature because residents of the front house, people making deliveries, and others had access to it. Apparently, the defendant's yard in the *Buchanan* case did not allow such access. Judging by the different approaches taken by the courts in these two cases, it is impossible to definitely say whether the residential yard is or is not to be considered part of the curtilage. Law enforcement officers should treat the residential yard of a house as part of the curtilage unless there are clear indications that the person residing in the house had no reasonable expectation of privacy in the yard. Since there is considerable doubt as to whether the residential yard falls within the curtilage, an officer should obtain a warrant for searches of this area when possible.

FENCES. If the area immediately surrounding a house is enclosed by a fence, the area within the fence is usually defined as the curtilage. In Patler v. Commonwealth, 177 S.E.2d 618 (Va. 1970), law enforcement officers investigating a murder learned that the defendant had been seen target shooting in a field outside his farm before the murder. The officers obtained a search warrant (which was later held invalid), went to the farm, and found spent bullets and shell casings outside a fence and about 250 feet from the dwelling house.

The court held that the search and seizure without a valid warrant were legal because they were conducted in the open fields, outside the curtilage.

> The evidence discloses that the area around the dwelling and outbuildings habitually used and necessary and convenient for family purposes was enclosed by a substantial fence. When such fence is erected it ordinarily defines the curtilage, particularly in a rural area. 177 S.E.2d at 620.

Nevertheless, if a piece of land is already outside the curtilage, erecting fences around it or taking other steps to protect privacy in the land will not establish that the expectation of privacy in the land is legitimate and bring the land within the curtilage. In Oliver v. United States, to conceal their criminal activities, the defendants planted marijuana upon secluded land and erected fences and No Trespassing signs around the property. The U.S. Supreme Court said:

> [I]t may be that because of such precautions, few members of the public stumbled upon the marijuana crops seized by the police. Neither of these suppositions demonstrates, however, that the expectation of privacy was *legitimate* in

the sense required by the Fourth Amendment. The test of legitimacy is not whether the individual chooses to conceal asserted 'private' activity. Rather, the correct inquiry is whether the government's intrusion infringes upon the personal and societal values protected by the Fourth Amendment.... [W]e find no basis for concluding that a police inspection of open fields accomplishes such an infringement. 466 U.S. at 182–83, 104 S.Ct. at 1743, 80 L.Ed.2d at 227.

FAMILY USE. Another consideration in determining the extent of the curtilage is the area's use for family purposes in connection with the dwelling. "[C]urtilage has been held to include all buildings in close proximity to a dwelling, which are continually used for carrying on domestic employment; or such place as is necessary and convenient to a dwelling, and is habitually used for family purposes." United States v. Potts, 297 F.2d 68, 69 (6th Cir. 1961).

In the *Patler* case (discussed earlier under "Fences"), the defendant claimed that the field outside the fence was part of the curtilage because it was used for family picnics, it was regularly mowed, and the children played there. The court found that the family picnics were infrequent and that one would expect a nongrazing field to be regularly mowed. The evidence was therefore "insufficient to establish the necessity, convenience and habitual use for family purposes which would be required in order to extend the curtilage to include the field." 177 S.E.2d at 621.

DISTANCE FROM THE DWELLING. Some courts use a rule of thumb that the curtilage ends approximately 75 feet from the main dwelling. See United States ex rel. Saiken v. Bensinger, 546 F.2d 1292 (7th Cir. 1976). Other courts refuse to adopt a per se rule in determining the extent of the curtilage, but use a totality of the circumstances approach with the distance from the dwelling as one of many factors to be weighed in making the determination. For example, in State v. Silva, 509 A.2d 659 (Me. 1986), the court held that a marijuana patch located roughly 250 feet behind the defendant's house was within the curtilage and was entitled to Fourth Amendment protection. The marijuana patch was within a cultivated lawn extending from the house to a tree-studded bog just beyond the patch; a swath of trees stood between the patch and the house but was not long enough to cut the back lawn completely in half; and the lawn was dotted with fruit trees, fruit bushes, two gardens, a shed, and flowers.

MULTIPLE-OCCUPANCY DWELLINGS. Multiple-occupancy dwellings are treated differently from single-occupancy dwellings for purposes of determining the extent of curtilage. Some courts have held that the shared areas of multiple-occupancy buildings, such as common corridors, passageways, and yards, are not entitled to the protection of the Fourth Amendment because many people have access to them. Nevertheless, there are many different types of multiple-occupancy dwellings, and courts will examine all the facts and circumstances in determining the curtilage. In Fixel v. Wainwright, 492 F.2d 480 (5th Cir. 1974), two law enforcement officers who had been informed that narcotics were being sold on the defendant's premises observed the defendant's behavior at his residence in a four-unit apartment building. Over a forty-five-minute period, several people entered the defendant's apartment, and each time the defendant would go into his backyard and remove a shaving kit from beneath some rubbish under a tree. One officer then went into the backyard and seized the shaving kit while the other officer arrested the defendant. Chemical analysis revealed that the shaving kit contained heroin.

The government argued that the defendant's backyard was an area common to or shared with other tenants and should not be entitled to the protection usually afforded the curtilage of a purely private residence. The court held, however, that the backyard was a protected area and that the seizure and search of the shaving kit were illegal:

> The backyard of Fixel's home was not a common passageway normally used by the building's tenants for gaining access to the apartments. . . . Nor is the backyard an area open as a corridor to salesmen or other businessmen who might approach the tenants in the course of their trade. . . . This apartment was Fixel's home, he lived there and the backyard of the building was completely removed from the street and surrounded by a chain link fence. . . . While the enjoyment of his backyard is not as exclusive as the backyard of a purely private residence, this area is not as public or shared as the corridors, yards or other common areas of a large apartment complex or motel. Contemporary concepts of living such as multi-unit dwellings must not dilute Fixel's right to privacy anymore than is absolutely required. We believe that the backyard area of Fixel's home is sufficiently removed and private in character that he could reasonably expect privacy. 492 F.2d at 484.

Porches and fire escapes outside a person's apartment or unit in a multiple-occupancy dwelling also fall within the curtilage of the apartment or unit.

> Unlike public halls or stairs which are public areas used in common by tenants and their guests or others lawfully on the property, a fire escape in a non-fireproof building is required outside of each apartment as a secondary means of egress for the occupants of that apartment. While it is true that in the event of fire others might have occasion to lawfully pass over the fire escape of another, this would be the only time that one might be lawfully on the fire escape of another. People v. Terrell, 277 N.Y.S.2d 926, 933 (N.Y. Sup. Ct. 1967).

GARAGES. Garages are usually held to be part of the curtilage, especially if they are near or attached to the dwelling house and used in connection with it. Therefore, in Commonwealth v. Murphy, 233 N.E.2d 5 (Mass. 1968), a case in which a garage and a house were surrounded on three sides by a fence and the garage was close to the house, fifty to seventy-five feet from the street, the garage was held to be within the curtilage. A garage not used by its owner in connection with the owner's residence, however, was held to be outside the curtilage. People v. Swanberg, 255 N.Y.S.2d 267 (N.Y.App.Div. 1964). In addition, a garage used in connection with a multi-unit dwelling was held to be outside the curtilage because it was used in common by many tenants of the dwelling. People v. Terry, 77 Cal.Rptr. 460, 454 P.2d 36 (Cal. 1969).

OTHER OUTBUILDINGS. In determining whether an outbuilding is part of the curtilage, courts consider factors such as distance from the dwelling house, presence and location of fences, family use of the building, and attempts to protect the area from observation. In United States v. Dunn, 480 U.S. 294, 107 S.Ct.

1134, 94 L.Ed.2d 326 (1987), a barn located fifty yards from a fence surrounding a house and sixty yards from the house itself was held to be outside the curtilage. The U.S. Supreme Court found that the owner had done little to protect the barn area from observation by those standing in the open fields. The Court also found it especially significant that law enforcement officials possessed objective data indicating that the barn was not being used for intimate activities of the home. A truck containing a container of phenylacetic acid was backed up to the barn, a strong odor of the acid emanated from the barn, and the sound of a pumplike motor could be heard from within the barn.

In another case, a barn was held to be within the curtilage where a driveway ran between the house and the barn, tracks of vehicles and footprints were visible in the snow leading to both the house and the barn, and no barriers separated the house and the barn. Rosencranz v. United States, 356 F.2d 310 (1st Cir. 1966). A whiskey still located 250 yards from the back of a house on open land was held to be in the open fields. Atwell v. United States, 414 F.2d 136 (5th Cir. 1969). And a concrete outbuilding located only 150 to 180 feet from the nearest residence was held to be outside the curtilage of the residence, because it was separated by a fence and a gate. Brock v. United States, 256 F.2d 55 (5th Cir. 1958).

UNOCCUPIED TRACTS. An unoccupied, uncultivated, remote tract of land is almost always held to be outside the curtilage and in the open fields. The U.S. Supreme Court stated that "the term 'open fields' may include any unoccupied or undeveloped area outside of the curtilage. An open field need be neither 'open' nor a 'field' as those terms are used in common speech. For example . . . a thickly wooded area nonetheless may be an open field as that term is used in construing the Fourth Amendment." Oliver v. United States, 466 U.S. 170, 180 n. 11, 104 S.Ct. 1735, 1742 n. 11, 80 L.Ed.2d 214, 225 n. 11 (1984).

In People v. LaRosa, 267 N.Y.S.2d 235 (N.Y.App.Div. 1966), police investigating a shooting incident obtained admissions from the defendant that he had left two guns in a vacant wooded area that he owned. The area was about one-half mile from the scene of the shooting incident and was remote from human habitation. The police searched the area without a warrant and found the guns. The court held that the search was not constitutionally unreasonable because the area was an open field. In another case, the Wisconsin Supreme Court held that the Fourth Amendment did not even apply to a local sheriff's warrantless digging in a field about 450 feet from the defendant's house in order to find the body of the defendant's wife, who had disappeared.

> Under the "open fields" doctrine, the fact that evidence is concealed or hidden is immaterial. The area [the open field] is simply not within the protection of the Fourth Amendment. If the field where the body was found does not have constitutional protection, the fact that the sheriff, rather than observing the evidence that might have been in plain view, dug into the earth to find the body and committed a trespass in so doing does not confer protection. Conrad v. State, 218 N.W.2d 252, 257 (Wis. 1974).

In a case involving an observation from an airplane of the defendant's open marijuana field surrounded by forests, the court said that the Fourth Amendment guards the privacy of human activity from aerial no less than terrestrial invasion. The court held, however, that one who establishes a three-quarter-acre tract of cultivation surrounded by forests exhibits no reasonable expectation of immunity from overflight.

> The contraband character of his crop doubtless arouses an internal, uncommunicated need for secrecy; the need is not exhibited, entirely subjective, highly personalized, and not consistent with the common habits of mankind in the use of agricultural and woodland areas. Aside from an uncommunicated need to hide his clandestine activity the occupant exhibits no reasonable expectation of privacy consistent with the common habits of persons engaged in agriculture. The aerial overflights which revealed petitioners's open marijuana field did not violate Fourth Amendment restrictions. Dean v. Superior Court, 110 Cal.Rptr. 585, 589–90 (Cal. App. 1973).

A difficult question is presented if the unoccupied area searched is not completely vacant but is being used as a building lot. In People v. Grundeis, 108 N.E.2d 483 (Ill. 1952), law enforcement officers received a complaint that lumber, sacks of cement, and a cart had been stolen. Investigation led the officers to suspect the defendant. They went to the defendant's property, where the defendant was laying the foundation for a house, searched the property without a warrant, and found some of the stolen items.

The court held that the area searched came within the category of open fields, even though a house was in the process of construction on it:

> If the lot had been left completely untouched, there could be no doubt that it would fall within the ruling of the *Hester* case. That a large quantity of building material has been brought upon the lot and a foundation for a house dug out, or even completely laid, does not change the nature of the place. Not even the broad policy of protection against "invasion of 'the sanctity of a man's home and the privacies of life'," . . . is infringed by what took place here. Defendant's constitutional rights were not violated. 108 N.E.2d at 487.

Reasonable Expectation of Privacy

In determining the legality of the search in many of the cases discussed previously, courts have considered whether the person owning or inhabiting the premises had a reasonable expectation of privacy in the area searched. In this sense, reasonable expectation of privacy could be considered just another one of the facts and circumstances used to determine the extent of the curtilage. Since the U.S. Supreme Court decision in Katz v. United States, 389 U.S. 347, 88 S.Ct. 507, 19 L.Ed.2d 576 (1967), however, a person's reasonable expectation of privacy has taken on a whole new meaning and importance in the law of search and seizure.

In the *Katz* case, a landmark opinion involving electronic eavesdropping, the U.S. Supreme Court stated that "the Fourth Amendment protects people, not places." 389 U.S. at 351, 88 S.Ct. at 511, 19 L.Ed.2d at 582. A later court decision said that *Katz* "shifts the focus of the Fourth Amendment from 'protected areas' to the individual's expectations of privacy. Whether the government's activity is considered a 'search' depends upon whether the individual's reasonable expectations of privacy are disturbed." Davis v. United States, 413 F.2d 1226, 1232 (5th Cir. 1969).

In Oliver v. United States, a case involving a police seizure of marijuana from a secluded plot of land surrounded by fences and No Trespassing signs, the U.S. Supreme Court stated that "an individual may not legitimately demand privacy for activities conducted out of doors in fields, except in the area immediately surrounding the home." 466 U.S. at 178, 104 S.Ct. at 1741, 80 L.Ed.2d at 224. The Court went on to say:

> [O]pen fields do not provide the setting for those intimate activities that the [Fourth] Amendment is intended to shelter from government interference or surveillance. There is no societal interest in protecting the privacy of those activities such as the cultivation of crops, that occur in open fields. Moreover, as a practical matter these lands usually are accessible to the public and the police in ways that a home, an office or commercial structure would not be. It is not generally true that fences or "No Trespassing" signs effectively bar the public from viewing open fields in rural areas. And . . . the public and police lawfully may survey lands from the air. For these reasons, the asserted expectation of privacy in open fields is not an expectation that "society recognizes as reasonable." 466 U.S. at 179, 104 S.Ct. at 1741, 80 L.Ed.2d at 224.

Plain View, Open Fields, and Observations into Constitutionally Protected Areas

The open fields and plain view doctrines are often confused by law enforcement officers. The plain view doctrine states that if a law enforcement officer, as the result of a prior valid intrusion into a constitutionally protected area, is in a position in which he or she has a legal right to be, items of evidence lying open to view may be seized (see Chapter 9). Under the open fields doctrine, a law enforcement officer need not be concerned with the validity of the prior intrusion into a constitutionally protected area. Open fields are not a constitutionally protected area, and therefore the officer may not only seize items that are open to view, but may search for items hidden from view and seize them.

In addition, from a vantage point in the open fields or a public place, an officer may, without a warrant, make observations into constitutionally protected areas and illuminate those areas with a flashlight, if necessary. United States v. Dunn, 480 U.S. 294, 107 S.Ct. 1134, 94 L.Ed.2d 326 (1987). These observations may be used as a basis for probable cause to make an arrest or to obtain a search warrant. However, these observations may not violate the reasonable expectation of privacy of the person whose premises or activities are being observed. In California v. Ciraolo, 476 U.S. 207, 106 S.Ct. 1809, 90 L.Ed.2d 210 (1986), the U.S. Supreme Court held that the Fourth Amendment was not violated by a warrantless aerial observation from an altitude of one-thousand feet of a fenced-in backyard within the curtilage of a home. The Court, relying on Katz v. United States, 389 U.S. 347, 88 S.Ct. 507, 19 L.Ed.2d 576 (1967), analyzed the case by means of a two-part inquiry: First, has the individual manifested a subjective expectation of privacy in the object of the challenged search? Second, is society willing to recognize that expectation as reasonable?

The Court found that the defendant clearly manifested his own subjective intent and desire to maintain privacy by placing a ten-foot fence around his backyard. His expectation of privacy from observation from the air was found not to be reasonable, however.

> That the area is within the curtilage does not itself bar all police observation. The Fourth Amendment protection of the home has never been extended to require law enforcement officers to a shield their eyes when passing by a home on public thoroughfares. Nor does the mere fact that an individual has taken measures to restrict some views of his activities preclude an officer's observations from a public vantage point where he has a right to be and which renders the activities clearly visible. 476 U.S. at 213, 106 S.Ct. at 1812, 90 L.Ed.2d 216.

Since the observations took place from a public navigable airspace, from which any member of the public flying in that airspace could have observed everything the officers observed, the defendant's expectation that his backyard was protected from observation was not an expectation that society was prepared to honor.

In a case reaching a contrary conclusion, a narcotics officer investigating a tip about heroin dealing went to the place where the dealing was said to be occurring. The place was a single-family dwelling, seventy feet from the sidewalk, with access from the west. There were no doorways or defined pathways on the east side of the house, and a strip of land covered with grass and dirt separated the east side of the house from the driveway of the apartment next door. The officer went to the east side of the house, peeked through a two-inch gap under the partially drawn shade of a closed window, and observed indications of criminal activity.

The court held that the officer's observations constituted an illegal search. The court initially analyzed the problem in terms of whether the officer was standing upon a part of the property surrounding the house that had been opened, expressly or impliedly, to public use. Under the facts, the officer was found to have made his observations from a position in which he had no right to be. Since neither a warrant nor one of the established exceptions to the warrant requirement justified the intrusion, the intrusion was unlawful.

The court went on to discuss the officer's actions at length, in terms of the defendant's reasonable expectation of privacy:

> [T]he generic *Katz* rule permits the resident of a house to rely justifiably upon the privacy of the surrounding areas as a protection from the peering of the officer unless such residences is "exposed" to that intrusion by the existence of public pathways or other invitations to the public to enter upon the property. This justifiable reliance on the privacy of the property surrounding one's residence thus leads to the *particular* rule that searches conducted without a warrant from such parts of the property *always* are unconstitutional unless an exception to the warrant requirement applies....
>
> Pursuant to the principles of *Katz*, therefore, we do not rest our analysis exclusively upon such abstractions as "trespass" or "constitutionally protected areas" or upon the physical differences between a telephone booth and the land surrounding a residence; we do, however, look to the conduct of people in regard to these elements. Taking into account the nature of the area surrounding a private residence, we ask whether that area has been opened to public use; if so, the occupant cannot claim he expected privacy from all observations of the officer who stands upon that ground; if not, the occupant does deserve that privacy. Since the eavesdropping officer in the case before us stood upon private property and since such property exhibited no invitation to

public use, we find that the officer violated petitioner Lorenzana's expectations of privacy, and hence his constitutional rights. Lorenzana v. Superior Court of Los Angeles County, 108 Cal.Rptr. 585, 594, 511 P.2d 33, 42 (Cal. 1973).

In general, if an officer gathers information while situated in a public place or in a place where an ordinary citizen with legitimate business might be expected to be, the officer will not be invading anyone's reasonable expectation of privacy. Therefore, an officer's observations from an ordinary means of access to a dwelling, such as a front porch or side door, will not ordinarily violate a person's reasonable expectation of privacy. People v. Willard, 47 Cal.Rptr. 734 (Cal.App. 1966). Once officers are in a place in which they have a legitimate right to be, they may look around and peer through windows or other openings.

> Peering through a window or a crack in the door or a keyhole is not, in the abstract, genteel behavior, but the Fourth Amendment does not protect against all conduct unworthy of a good neighbor. . . . [I]t is the duty of a policeman to investigate, and *we cannot say that . . . the Fourth Amendment itself draws the blinds the occupant could have drawn and did not.* People v. Berutko, 77 Cal.Rptr. 217, 222, 453 P.2d 721, 726 (Cal. 1969).

Furthermore, so long as officers are where they have a right to be, they may listen at doors or gather evidence with their other senses. In United States v. Perry, 339 F.Supp. 209 (S.D.Cal. 1972), the court said:

> The general rule is that information obtained by an officer using his natural senses, where the officer has a right to be where he is, is admissible evidence. The fact that the information is in the form of conversations emanating from a private space, such as a hotel room, is not a bar to its admissibility. 339 F.Supp. at 213.

Regardless of which sense an officer is using to detect criminal activity occurring in a constitutionally protected area, the officer does not have authority to enter into the constitutionally protected area to make a search or seizure without a warrant. Only a search warrant gives this authority, unless there is an emergency or the situation falls within one of the other recognized exceptions to the search warrant requirement.

ABANDONED PROPERTY

The meaning of the term *abandoned property* depends upon the interpretation given to the word *searches* in the Fourth Amendment. Courts have held that no search occurs when a law enforcement officer observes property voluntarily discarded by a person. And it is not an illegal seizure to pick up the property and use it as evidence against the person in court. The Fourth Amendment's protection does not extend to abandoned property because a person who abandons property brings to an end any right to privacy in that property. A person cannot complain about the seizure of property no longer in that person's possession or about the property's use as evidence in court.

Abandoned property is treated by the courts similarly to seizable property found lying in plain view. Since there is no search under the Fourth Amendment, officers may lawfully seize the property without a warrant or probable cause. The main difference between the abandonment doctrine and the plain view doctrine turns on the nature of the place from which the officer seizes an object. Under the plain view doctrine, if a law enforcement officer, as the result of a prior valid intrusion into a constitutionally protected area, is in a position in which he or she has a legal right to be, items of evidence lying open to view may be seized. The plain view doctrine is applicable only after the law enforcement officer has lawfully entered into a *constitutionally protected area*. On the other hand, if a law enforcement officer, acting lawfully, seizes objects that have been discarded on the street, in a public park, or in some other *place not protected by the Fourth Amendment to the Constitution*, the seizure is legal under the abandonment doctrine. Note that the abandonment doctrine, unlike the plain view doctrine, involves no intrusion into a constitutionally protected area. Law enforcement officers must learn this distinction because for officers to lawfully seize items that have been discarded within a constitutionally protected area, all elements of the plain view doctrine must be satisfied or any item of evidence seized will be inadmissible in court. When law enforcement officers attempt to justify a seizure of property on the ground that it was abandoned, they must be prepared to prove abandonment. Abandonment is never presumed by the courts but must be established by the prosecution.

The remainder of this chapter is devoted to a discussion of specific facts and circumstances bearing upon the issue of abandonment, as illustrated by decisions of courts throughout the United States.

Factors Determining Abandonment

The factors that the courts consider in determining whether property has been abandoned can be classified into four broad categories:

1. Nature of the place in which the property was left
2. Indications of intent to abandon property
3. Lawfulness of police behavior
4. Reasonable expectation of privacy in the property

Most cases dealing with the issue of abandonment will involve circumstances falling into more than one of the four categories. For example, the nature of the place in which an object is left is usually a strong indication of a person's intent to abandon the property and also of the person's expectation of privacy in the property. Nevertheless, usually one or two circumstances in each case provide the primary basis for a court's decision on the issue of abandonment. These are the circumstances that are emphasized in the cases discussed under each category here.

NATURE OF THE PLACE IN WHICH PROPERTY WAS LEFT. The nature of the place in which property was left is an important determinant of whether or not the property has been abandoned. In *Hester v. United States*, summarized earlier, the U.S. Supreme Court held that it was proper for law enforcement officers to retrieve property discarded by the defendant in an open field. The court said that the protection of the Fourth Amendment did not extend to the open fields. Although it is not clear whether the primary basis for the Court's decision in *Hester* was abandonment or the open fields doctrine, it is clear that the place of discard had a bearing on the Court's determination of abandonment. The Court specifically noted that the evidence was not obtained by entry into the house.

It follows logically that if an object discarded in the open fields of a person's private property is considered abandoned, an object discarded in a public place will also be considered abandoned. In Vincent v. United States, 337 F.2d 891 (8th Cir. 1964), law enforcement officers had the defendant under surveillance for violation of federal narcotics laws. As the defendant disembarked from an airplane at a public airport, he apparently recognized one of the officers, and he discarded contraband narcotics. The officers retrieved the narcotics and immediately arrested the defendant. The court held that the discarded narcotics were admissible in court. There had been no illegal search because the narcotics were abandoned.

In United States v. Lewis, 227 F.Supp. 433 (S.D.N.Y. 1964), the defendant threw a package of heroin into the courtyard of a six-story apartment building. The defendant's only rights in the courtyard were to use it in common with other tenants and with members of the public who had business there. The court held that the warrantless seizure of the abandoned package from the courtyard was legal.

When, however, an object is discarded in response to illegal police activity, and falls within the curtilage of a person's home or business, a warrantless seizure of the object will be illegal. In Hobson v. United States, 226 F.2d 890 (8th Cir. 1955), officers went to a woman's residence to arrest her without a warrant for a narcotics violation. Her husband, the defendant, came to the door but retreated without opening it. The defendant's wife then came to the door, clad only in a slip, and asked the officer to wait until she dressed. Meanwhile, the defendant ran upstairs and threw a package out of the window into an enclosed backyard. The officers then broke into the house, allegedly to arrest the defendant's wife, and without knowing the contents of the thrown package. The package was seized by another officer stationed outside and was found to contain heroin. The court held that the seizure of the package was illegal, stating that the enclosed backyard in which the thrown package landed was part of the curtilage of the defendant's home and was entitled to the same protection as the home itself. A major reason for the court's holding the seizure illegal was the court's finding that the officers entered the residence illegally. If the police had entered legally, the seizure of the package would probably have been upheld under the plain view doctrine.

To summarize, if an object is voluntarily discarded outside the curtilage of a house, it will be considered abandoned; if an object is discarded inside the curtilage, the legality of its seizure will be governed by the plain view doctrine.

When a person has abandoned or vacated premises, officers may search for and seize items of evidence or any other items left on the premises, without a warrant or probable cause and without satisfying any of the exceptions to the warrant requirement. In Abel v. United States, 362 U.S. 217, 80 S.Ct. 683, 4 L.Ed.2d 668 (1960), officers of the Immigration and Naturalization Service arrested the defendant in his hotel room, under an administrative arrest warrant, and charged him with being illegally in the United States. Before he was escorted out of his room, the defendant was permitted to pack his personal belongings. He packed nearly everything in the room except for a few things that he left on a windowsill and that he put in a wastebasket. He then checked out of the hotel, turned in his keys, and paid his bill. Shortly thereafter, an FBI agent, with the permission of the hotel management, searched the defendant's room without a warrant. In the wastebasket, the FBI agent found a hollow pencil containing microfilm and a block of wood containing a "cipher pad."

The Court held that the search for and seizure of the pencil and block of wood were legal:

> These two items were found by an agent of the F.B.I. in the course of a search he undertook of petitioner's hotel room, immediately after petitioner had paid his bill and vacated the room. They were found in the room's wastepaper basket, where petitioner had put them while packing his belongings and preparing to leave. No pretense is made that this search by the F.B.I. was for any purpose other than to gather evidence of crime, that is, evidence of petitioner's espionage. As such, however, it was entirely lawful, although undertaken without a warrant. This is so for the reason that at the time of the the search petitioner had vacated the room. The hotel then had the exclusive right to its possession, and the hotel management freely gave its consent that the search be made. Nor was it unlawful to seize the entire contents of the wastepaper basket, even though some of its contents had no connection with crime. So far as the record shows, petitioner had abandoned these articles. He had thrown them away. So far as he was concerned, they were bona vacantia. There can be nothing unlawful in the Government's appropriation of such abandoned property.... The two items which were eventually introduced in evidence were assertedly means for the commission of espionage, and were themselves seizable as such. These two items having been lawfully seized by the Government in connection with an investigation of crime, we encounter no basis for discussing further their admissibility as evidence. 362 U.S. at 241, 80 S.Ct. at 698, 4 L.Ed.2d at 687–88.

If the defendant in the *Abel* case had not vacated his room, the hotel management could not have given consent to search the room. (See Chapter 8 on consent searches.) The key question for the law enforcement officer who wants to search premises without a warrant, probable cause, or other justification is whether the person residing there intended to abandon the premises. Various indications of intent to abandon, relied upon by the courts, are discussed in the following material.

INDICATIONS OF INTENT TO ABANDON PROPERTY.   An important consideration of courts in determining whether property has been abandoned is the *intent* of the person vacating or discarding property to relinquish all title, possession, or claim to that property. Sometimes intent to abandon is easy to establish, such as when a person voluntarily throws an object away, without any inducement by the police. In many situations, however, a person's intent to abandon property is not so easily established. The following discussion highlights the various indications of intent relied upon by the courts in determining abandonment. The discussion is divided into three parts—premises, objects, and motor vehicles—because intent to abandon is determined in different ways for each kind of property.

Premises.   In *Abel v. United States*, summarized earlier, the Court found that a hotel room had been abandoned when the person moved his personal belongings out of the room, paid his bill, checked out, and turned in his key. In another case involving a hotel room, a court fund that the defendant had abandoned a room he had rented on March 23, when he failed to pay his bill on March 28 and did not return to or communicate with the hotel before his arrest on April 8. At the time he rented the room, the defendant said he intended to stay only one night. A search of the defendant's baggage left in the room was therefore held not to violate his property rights. United States v. Cowan, 396 F.2d 83 (2d Cir. 1968).

In a case involving abandonment of an *apartment*, law enforcement officers were allowed to search the defendant's apartment without a warrant, even though the defendant had three days to go on his lease period. The court said:

> What were the circumstances showing abandonment? Baggett quit his job, received pay for one day's work, told several people that he was going to New Orleans to get a job, paid all bills that he owed except one, told his friends in Little Rock good-bye on the 11th, turned the apartment keys over to the owner, and took all personal belongings to New Orleans with him. Of course, had he returned within the two days before his rent came due, he could not have gone into his apartment for Ballard [the landlord] had the keys. The fact that the rent was paid up for three days after Baggett left does not mean that the apartment had not been abandoned. Baggett v. State, 494 S.W.2d 717, 719 (Ark. 1973).

The following quotation from a case involving a warrantless search of a house illustrates other indications of intent to abandon:

> [I]t was clearly established that even though the Mannings had rented the . . . house for thirty days, they departed after the first day leaving no personal belongings. The door was unlocked, food was on the table, and dishwater was in the sink. Thirty days later the same condition prevailed. Moreover, the decayed food created a stench, the grass was uncut, and the weeds had grown high.
> These circumstances strongly indicate that the Mannings had abandoned the house. . . . United States v. Manning, 440 F.2d 1105, 1111 (5th Cir. 1971).

The non-public areas of a business office come within the Fourth Amendment's protection against unreasonable searches and seizures. If the office is abandoned by its occupant, however, it no longer has this protection. The indications of intent to abandon for an office are similar to those for a room or house. In Mullins v. United States, 487 F.2d 581 (8th Cir. 1973), U.S. postal inspectors, without a warrant, searched for and seized business records from an office that had previously been rented by the defendant. The defendant claimed that the search and seizure were illegal because he did not intend to abandon the office and the records kept there. The court found that the facts indicated an intent to abandon. The search and seizure were made on June 12, 1972. The defendant had rented the office from May 1, 1971, through October 31, 1971, but had left the state in August 1971. No rent had been paid for the office beginning November 1, 1971, nor did the defendant, his wife, or any business associate or employee visit the office after November 1, 1971. Finally, the office had been padlocked by the U.S. District Attorney during February 1972.

The mere absence of a person from premises does not make the premises abandoned, unless the person had an *intent* to abandon the premises. Therefore, in a case in which the defendant's absence from his apartment was involuntary because of his arrest and incarceration, the court held that the prosecution should bear an especially heavy burden of showing that he intended to abandon it. The prosecution did not satisfy this burden by merely showing the defendant's absence without showing any other indications of intent to abandon. United States v. Robinson, 430 F.2d 1141 (6th Cir. 1970).

Objects. Intent to abandon objects involves many of the same considerations as intent to abandon premises. For example, a strong indication of a person's intent to abandon an object is leaving the object unattended and unclaimed for a long period of time. In United States v. Gulledge, 469 F.2d 713 (5th Cir. 1972), two men left a U-Haul trailer at a service station, asking permission to leave it there for two or three days. The men stated that "everything we own is in the trailer." Ten days later, the men not having returned, the service station attendant called law enforcement authorities. The trailer was searched without a warrant and stolen whiskey was found. The court held that the search was legal because the property had been abandoned. In addition, a person "who disclaims any interest in luggage thereby disclaims any concern about whether or not the contents of the luggage remain private." United States v. Tolbert, 692 F.2d 1041, 1045 (6th Cir. 1982).

In other cases involving warrantless searches and seizures of objects, the object is often picked up by a law enforcement officer immediately after it is dropped, thrown away, or otherwise discarded by a person. In these cases, courts cannot rely on the length of time the object has been left unattended to determine whether the object has been abandoned. Courts must look to other circumstances such as the conduct of the defendant and the manner of disposal of the object. In People v. Anderson, 298 N.Y.S.2d 698, 246 N.E.2d 508 (N.Y. 1969), a police officer approached the defendant without probable cause to make an arrest, and the defendant dropped a tin box to the ground. The officer immediately picked up the box, opened it, and found heroin. The court held that the evidence was insufficient to constitute an abandonment:

> There is no proof that the defendant threw it away or attempted to dispose of it in any manner which might have manifested the requisite intention to abandon. Moreover, the police officer's testimony reveals that he picked up the box so soon after it had been dropped that it is impossible to determine whether or not the defendant, if given the opportunity, would have picked up the box himself. Absent any such proof, the seizure of the tin box under the circumstances of this case cannot be sustained. People v. Anderson, 298 N.Y.S.2d 698, 699, 246 N.E.2d 508, 509 (N.Y. 1969).

When, however, the manner of disposal indicates that a defendant intended to permanently relinquish possession of property because of consciousness of guilt or fear of potential apprehension, the courts usually find abandonment. In Stack v. United States, 368 F.2d 788 (1st Cir. 1966), the defendant threw packages out of an automobile he was driving when he noticed that he was being pursued by a car with flashing lights and a siren. Law enforcement officers were lawfully chasing the defendant's auto because they had seen it entered by a man whom the officers had probable cause to arrest. The packages were recovered and were found to be stolen goods. The court held the seizure legal and allowed the introduction of the packages in evidence against the defendant. There was no illegal activity on the part of law enforcement officers.

When there is evidence that an object was intentionally concealed, courts will usually find there was no intent to abandon the object and therefore no abandonment. In State v. Chapman, 250 A.2d 203 (Me. 1969), officers seized a bottle in a barrel located in a garage underneath the defendant's residence. The prosecution claimed the bottle had been abandoned. The court disagreed, saying that "[t]he position of the bottle well down in the barrel and covered with trash and paper strongly suggests that it was intentionally hidden and concealed there." 250 A.2d at 212.

Some courts find an intent to abandon property when the defendant fails to object or take any other affirmative action, but merely allows evidence to be seized in the ordinary course of events. In United States v. Cox, 428 F.2d 683 (7th Cir. 1970), the defendant was in jail after being arrested for bank robbery. He was given a haircut pursuant to routine jail procedures, and the hair clippings were turned over to the FBI, at their request, and used as evidence. In response to the defendant's claim of an illegal search and seizure, the court said:

> At no time has defendant objected to the legality of the prison procedures under which he received his haircut. He has never claimed that the haircut was illegally or improperly given. The thrust of his contention is rather that a warrant should have been obtained before the shorn locks were appropriated by the state officer for analysis. Cox, however, never indicated any desire or intention to retain possession of the hair after it had been scissored from his head. Clippings such as those preserved in the instant case are ordinarily abandoned after being cut. Cox in fact left his hair and has never claimed otherwise. The deputy sheriff was not obliged to inform him that, if abandoned, his hair would be taken and analyzed. Having voluntarily abandoned his property, in this case his hair, Cox may not object to its appropriation by the government. 428 F.2d at 687–88.

Motor Vehicles. Motor vehicles are unique for purposes of the discussion of abandonment in that they are treated both as premises and as objects. In Thom v. State, 450 S.W.2d 550 (Ark. 1970), the defendant, who was tampering with a cigarette machine, left his car in the street and fled on foot to avoid apprehension by an officer. The court said:

> Sometimes an automobile takes on the characteristics of a man's castle. Other times an automobile takes on the characteristic of an overcoat—that is, it is movable and can be discarded by the possessor at will. If appellant in his endeavors to avoid the clutches of the law had discarded his overcoat to make his flight more speedy, no one would think that an officer was unreasonably invading his privacy or security in picking up the overcoat and searching it thoroughly. In that situation most people would agree that the fleeing suspect had abandoned his coat as a matter of expediency as well as any rights relative to its search and seizure. What difference can there be when a fleeing burglar abandons his automobile to escape the clutches of the law? We can see no distinction and consequently hold that when property is abandoned officers in making a search thereof do not violate any rights or security of a citizen guaranteed under the Fourth Amendment. 450 S.W.2d at 552.

If an officer has probable cause to search a motor vehicle, he or she may also be able to justify a search of the vehicle under the *Carroll* doctrine (see Chapter 10).

LAWFULNESS OF POLICE BEHAVIOR. In many of the cases just discussed, property was left or discarded in response to either the presence or the activities of law enforcement officers. In determining whether property is abandoned in these situations, courts examine very closely the lawfulness of the law enforcement officer's role in each incident. If a person discards evidence as a direct result of the unlawful presence or activity of a law enforcement officer, the courts will not consider the act a voluntary abandonment, but rather a forced response to the unlawful police behavior.

The following are examples of cases in which a person discarded an object in response to the lawful activities of the police, and courts considered the object abandoned and therefore seizable without a warrant or other justification:

1. Officers arrested the defendant on authority of a warrant, and while they were escorting him to the police car, the defendant threw away a marijuana cigarette. Oliver v. State, 449 P.2d 252 (Nev. 1969).

2. An officer with probable cause to arrest the defendant was pursuing the defendant's car, and contraband was thrown from the car. Capitoli v. Wainwright, 426 F.2d 868 (5th Cir. 1970).

3. Officers were lawfully approaching the defendant for questioning, and the defendant dropped a bundle of marijuana cigarettes. People v. Blackmon, 80 Cal.Rptr. 862 (Cal.App. 1969).

4. Officers, attempting to execute a valid search warrant, temporarily detained the defendant at the scene of the search, and the defendant discarded a package containing incriminating evidence. State v. Romeo, 203 A.2d 23 (N.J. 1964).

In a case involving unlawful police activity, a law enforcement officer received an anonymous phone call informing him that the defendant could be apprehended at a given place and time with narcotics in his possession. Officers went to the designated place and observed the defendant in his car. The officers told him he was under arrest and to get out of his car and place his hands on top of it. As the defendant did this, he flipped into the street a plastic vial containing narcotics, which the officers retrieved.

The court held that the arrest was unlawful for lack of probable cause. The court also refused to find that the plastic vial was abandoned, because it was thrown away as a result of a *threat* of an illegal search:

> Had the appellant here thrown the item away before the search had been threatened the argument of abandonment might well be persuasive. Here however he threw the vial away only after being told to turn and place his hands atop his vehicle, the position commonly know to be employed by police in searching a suspect for weapons. The vial, as evidenced by the record, was not seen by the officers until it was thrown by appellant. Had it been seen before the threat of an illegal search had been made, even in appellant's hand, the plain view doctrine *may* have applied. But that is not this case. The vial was seen and secured only as a result of the threat of a search, an illegal search. Clearly it was the fruit of illegal activity by the police and ought to have been excluded. Bowles v. State, 267 N.E.2d 56, 59 (Ind. 1971).

In Fletcher v. Wainwright, 399 F.2d 62 (5th Cir. 1968), an officer was investigating a window-smashing incident at a hotel. He spotted, at another hotel, a car believed to have been involved in the incident, and he went to the room occupied by the car's owner in order to interview the owner. The officer had neither a warrant nor probable cause to arrest, and he did not intend to make an arrest. After knocking twice and receiving no response, the officer kicked in the door only to find that the defendants had escaped through a window. They were apprehended shortly thereafter. Stolen jewelry was found beneath the window, where it had been thrown when the officer began kicking down the door.

The court held that there was no voluntary abandonment of the jewelry: "[S]ince the initial entry was improper and the items were thrown out of the window as a direct result of that illegality, the police were not entitled to the fruits and the admission of the jewelry in evidence was reversible error." 399 F.2d at 64–65.

REASONABLE EXPECTATION OF PRIVACY IN THE PROPERTY. As shown in the discussion of the open fields doctrine, since the U.S. Supreme Court decision in *Katz v. United States*, the courts increasingly have analyzed the legality of warrantless searches and seizures in terms of their intrusion upon the defendant's reasonable expectation of privacy. This trend has extended also to cases involving vacated or discarded property. The Minnesota Supreme Court explained:

> In the law of property, the question . . . is whether the owner has voluntarily, intentionally, and unconditionally relinquished his interest in the property so that another, having acquired possession, may successfully assert his superior interest. In the law of search and seizure, however, the question is whether the defendant has, in discarding the property, relinquished his reasonable expectation of privacy so that its seizure and search is reasonable within the limits of the Fourth Amendment. In essence, what is abandoned is not necessarily the defendant's property, but his reasonable expectation of privacy therein. City of St. Paul v. Vaughn, 237 N.W.2d 365, 370–71 (Minn. 1975).

In a case involving supposedly vacated premises, law enforcement officers were investigating a possible arson in a building gutted by fire. The fire occurred on April 14, 1968, and the officers entered the building, made observations, and took photographs on April 24, 1968. Evidence showed that the house had been boarded up on April 14. Thereafter the owner went to the house every day, and both she and the defendant kept some of their personal effects in the house. The defendant claimed that the observations and photographs of the officers were a product of an illegal search and seizure.

The court said:

> The uncontradicted evidence before the court was that the building was not abandoned. On April 24, 1968, it still contained personal effects and had been boarded up to keep the public out.
>
> The test to be used in determining whether a place is a constitutionally protected area within the meaning of the Fourth Amendment is . . . "whether the person has exhibited a reasonable expectation of privacy, and, if so, whether that expectation has been violated by unreasonable governmental intrusion." In the instant matter the owner of the dwelling house clearly demonstrated her expectation of privacy as to the interior of the house and its contents by boarding up the doorways, which were damaged by fire. That expectation was violated by the intrusion of the police on April 24, 1968. Swan v. Superior Court, County of Los Angeles, 87 Cal.Rptr. 280, 282 (Cal. 1970).

Courts differ on the extent of a person's reasonable expectation of privacy in discarded *objects*. The controversy has centered around the search and seizure of trash or garbage by law enforcement officers. In a leading case in this area, law enforcement officers, acting without a warrant, found marijuana in a trash can in the open backyard area of the defendant's residence. The court held that the marijuana in the trash can was not abandoned for the following reasons:

> As we have seen, the trash can was within a few feet of the back door of defendants' home and required trespass for its inspection. It was an adjunct to the domestic economy.... Placing the marijuana in the trash can, so situated and used, was not an abandonment unless as to persons authorized to remove the receptacle's contents, such as trashmen.... The marijuana itself was not visible without "rummaging" in the receptacle. So far as appears defendants alone resided at the house. In the light of the combined facts and circumstances it appears that defendants exhibited an expectation of privacy, and we believe that expectation was reasonable under the circumstances of the case. We can readily ascribe many reasons why residents would not want their castaway clothing, letters, medicine bottlers or other telltale refuse and trash to be examined by neighbors or others, at least not until the trash has lost its identity and meaning by becoming part of a large conglomeration of trash elsewhere. Half truths leading to rumor and gossip may readily flow from an attempt to "read" the contents of another's trash. People v. Edwards, 80 Cal.Rptr. 633, 638, 458 P.2d 713, 718 (Cal. 1969).

Other courts have generally agreed with the holding in the *Edwards* case, and have found a violation of a defendant's reasonable expectation of privacy where the trash can was located within the curtilage of the defendant's house. Ball v. State, 205 N.W.2d 353 (Wis. 1973).

Where garbage is left outside the curtilage of the home, however, the U.S. Supreme Court held that the Fourth Amendment does not prohibit the warrantless search and seizure of the garbage. In California v. Greenwood, ___ U.S. ___,108 S.Ct. 1625, 100 L.Ed.2d 30 (1988), police suspected the defendant of narcotics trafficking, but did not have probable cause to search the defendant's house. Police obtained from the regular trash collector garbage bags left in front of the defendant's house. On the basis of items found in the bags, police obtained a search warrant for the home and discovered controlled substances.

The defendants claimed an expectation of privacy with respect to their trash, but the Court held that even if they had an expectation of privacy, it was not one that society was prepared to accept as reasonable.

> [R]espondents exposed their garbage to the public sufficiently to defeat their claim to Fourth Amendment protection. It is common knowledge that plastic garbage bags left on or at the side of a public street are readily accessible to animals, children, scavengers, snoops, and other members of the public.... Moreover, respondents placed their refuse at the curb for the express purpose of conveying it to a third party, the trash collector, who might himself have sorted through respondent's trash or permitted others, such as the police, to do so. Accordingly, having deposited their garbage "in an area particularly suited for public inspection and, in a manner of speaking, public consumption, for the express purpose of having strangers take it,"... respondents could have had no reasonable expectation of privacy in the inculpatory items that they discarded.... [T]he police cannot reasonably be expected to avert

their eyes from evidence of criminal activity that could have been observed by any member of the public. ___, U.S. at ___, 108 S.Ct. at 1628–29, 100 L.Ed.2d at 36–37.

In United States v. Walker, 624 F.Supp. 99 (D.Md. 1985), law enforcement officers found a paper shopping bag out in the open alongside a road in a sparsely populated rural setting. No attempt had been made to protect the bag from damage from the elements, from removal by a passerby, or from disturbance by an animal. The court held that despite the defendant's claim that he did not intend to abandon the bag, by leaving the bag in the manner he did, the defendant was no longer retaining a reasonable expectation of privacy.

SUMMARY

A law enforcement officer may search for and seize items of evidence lying in the open fields without probable cause, search warrant, or other legal justification without violating a person's Fourth Amendment rights. An officer may also legally make observations from a vantage point in the open fields into constitutionally protected areas, in order to detect criminal activity or evidence.

The open fields are the area lying outside the curtilage of a person's home or business. Whether or not a piece of land or building falls within the curtilage can be determined by consideration of the following factors: the proximity of the area claimed to be curtilage to the home, the inclusion of the area within an enclosure surrounding the home, the nature of the uses to which the area is put, and the steps taken by the resident to protect the area from observation by people passing by.

Since the 1967 U.S. Supreme Court decision in *Katz v. United States*, which held that "the Fourth Amendment protects people, not places," courts have increasingly analyzed the legality of warrantless searches in terms of the defendants' reasonable expectation of privacy, in addition to the concepts of curtilage and open fields. Law enforcement officers, therefore, must be careful to avoid warrantless intrusions not only into the curtilage of a person's house, but also into any area that the person reasonably seeks to preserve as private.

A law enforcement officer, without probable cause, warrant, or other legal justification, may retrieve items of evidence that have been abandoned by their owners without violating Fourth Amendment rights. Property has been abandoned when the owner has voluntarily relinquished all title, possession, or claim to it. Among the factors that the courts rely on in determining whether a given object has been abandoned by its owner are the following:

1. *Nature of the place in which property was left.* As a general rule, if an object is voluntarily discarded inside the curtilage, it will not be considered abandoned; if an object is discarded outside the curtilage, it will be considered abandoned. Objects left on premises, however, may be considered abandoned if the premises themselves have been voluntarily vacated or abandoned.

2. *Indications of intent to abandon property.* Indications of intent to abandon *premises* can be divided into positive acts and omissions. Positive indications of intent to abandon include removing personal belongings, paying final rent and other bills, turning in keys, quitting local employment, and taking leave of

friends. Omissions indicating intent to abandon include failing to pay rent for a long time, long absence from premises, failure to communicate with anyone regarding premises, and failure to attend to or care for premises. Intent to abandon an *object* is indicated by leaving the object unattended for an unreasonable period of time, discarding the object out of consciousness of guilt or fear of apprehension, and allowing the object to be taken away in the ordinary course of events, without objection. Intentional concealment of an object is not considered an indication of intent to abandon. Intent to abandon *vehicles* is determined by the same considerations as those for premises and objects.

3. Lawfulness of police behavior.   Objects discarded as a direct result of the unlawful presence or activity of a law enforcement officer will not be considered voluntarily abandoned.

4. Reasonable expectation of privacy in the property.   Even though property has been vacated or thrown away, under certain circumstances, a person may reasonably retain an expectation of privacy with respect to the property. Such property is not considered abandoned and a search and seizure of it, without a warrant or probable cause, will be illegal.

Determining whether property is abandoned is similar to determining whether it is in the open fields, in that both require a consideration not only of a person's property rights, but also of the person's rights of privacy. Such determinations will always be difficult for the courts as well as for law enforcement officers. In the absence of an emergency, officers should obtain a search warrant whenever possible.

REVIEW AND DISCUSSION QUESTIONS

1. Does the term *open fields* include any place that is public, including forests, lakes, city streets, and stadiums?

2. Which of the following, if any, would be considered a house for purposes of the Fourth Amendment?
   a. Tent
   b. Lean-to
   c. Motor home
   d. Sailboat
   e. Cave

3. Would an aerial observation of marijuana plants growing in a green house on a defendant's roof violate the defendant's reasonable expectation of privacy?

4. Would a person's Fourth Amendment rights be violated by law enforcement officers who, after illegally arresting the person, entered the person's fenced and posted rural property to observe a marijuana field surrounded by a forest?

5. Compare the plain view doctrine, the open fields doctrine, and the abandonment doctrine with respect to the reasonable expectation of privacy.

6. If a person abandons property inside the curtilage of someone else's property, may a law enforcement officer seize the abandoned property?

7. Is observing activities inside a house in the country by looking into a window with binoculars from a field or forest any different from observing activities in a tenth-story apartment from a window in an adjacent apartment building?

8. Does the value of an object have any bearing on the question of whether a person abandoned it? Can a person who runs away from his or her automobile to avoid apprehension by the police be said to give up all reasonable expectations of privacy in the vehicle? What if the person locks the vehicle before fleeing?

9. For each place listed in question 2, what indications of intent to abandon would give a law enforcement officer authority to search for and seize items left at that place?

10. If a person seeks medical attention after being shot while driving an automobile, which of the following, if any, has the person abandoned?

    a. Clothing worn at the time of the shooting

    b. Wallets and other items in the pockets of the clothing

    c. Bullets surgically removed

    d. The automobile

Chapter 12
Stop and Frisk

In Chapter 4, a formal arrest was defined as "the apprehension or detention of the person of another in order that he may be forthcoming to answer for an alleged or supposed crime." Also discussed were seizures tantamount to arrest, in which, although an officer has no intention to take a person into custody and charge the person with a crime, the circumstances surrounding the detention are indistinguishable from an arrest in important respects. Stop and frisk also involves a seizure of a person, but a much briefer and less intrusive seizure.

As a preliminary definition, *stop and frisk* is a police practice involving the temporary detention, questioning, and limited search of a person suspected of criminal activity. It is initiated on a reasonable suspicion of crime amounting to less than probable cause for the purposes of crime prevention and investigation and for the protection of the law enforcement officer carrying out the investigation. A stop and frisk that is initially justifiable may become a seizure tantamount to arrest if the detention and search exceed their allowable purposes or if the extent of the intrusion goes beyond what is reasonably necessary.

Stop and frisk is also distinguished from the common situation, also described in Chapter 4, in which the law enforcement officer approaches a person in a public place and asks if the person is willing to answer questions. In this situation, the officer needs no justification or level of suspicion to approach the person and the officer has no authority to detain the person even momentarily, whether or not the person agrees to cooperate. However, if an initially friendly and neutral encounter somehow provides the officer with reason to suspect criminal activity, the officer may be justified in making the more significant intrusion of a stop and frisk.

The definition of stop and frisk is refined throughout this chapter through discussions of Terry v. Ohio, 392 U.S. 1, 88 S.Ct. 1868, 20 L.Ed.2d 889 (1968); *Terry's* companion cases, Sibron v. New York and Peters v. New York, 392 U.S. 40, 88 S.Ct. 1889, 20 L.Ed.2d 917 (1968); and other cases.

TERRY, SIBRON, AND PETERS

Terry v. Ohio

In the *Terry* case, a police detective with thirty-nine years' experience observed two men alternately pacing back and forth five or six times in front of a store window, each time peering into the store and returning to a corner to confer. The two men were joined briefly by a third man. When he walked away, the first two resumed their pacing, peering, and conferring. When the third man rejoined them again, the detective, suspecting that the men were casing the store for an armed robbery, approached them, identified himself, and asked their names. When the men "mumbled something," the detective grabbed Terry, spun him around in order to place him between the other two suspects and himself, and patted down the outside of his clothing. Feeling a pistol in Terry's coat pocket, the officer seized it. He patted down the outer clothing of the other two men, and one more weapon was found. Terry and the other man were arrested and convicted of carrying concealed weapons. They appealed, claiming that the weapons were obtained by means of an unreasonable search and should not have been admitted into evidence at their trial.

The U.S. Supreme Court affirmed the convictions. The Court said that even though *stop and frisk* represented a lesser restraint than a traditional *arrest and search*, the procedure is still governed by the Fourth Amendment. However, stop and frisk is not subject to as stringent a limitation as is a traditional full arrest and search. Instead of applying the *probable cause* standard to stop and frisk, the Court applied the fundamental test of the Fourth Amendment: the *reasonableness* in all the circumstances of the particular governmental invasion of a citizen's personal security.

In discussing the reasonableness of the officer's actions in this case, the Court first mentioned the long tradition of armed violence of American criminals and the number of law enforcement officers killed or wounded in action. In light of this, the Court recognized law enforcement officers' need to protect themselves when suspicious circumstances indicate possible criminal activity by potentially dangerous persons, but when probable cause for an arrest is lacking. In these situations, the Court felt it would be unreasonable to deny an officer the authority to take necessary steps to determine whether a suspected person is armed and to neutralize the threat of harm. The Court concluded that "where a police officer observes unusual conduct which leads him reasonably to conclude in light of his experience that criminal activity may be afoot and that the persons with whom he is dealing may be armed and presently dangerous, where in the course of investigating this behavior he identifies himself as a policeman and makes reasonable inquiries, and where nothing in the initial stages of the encounter serves to dispel his reasonable fear for his own or other's safety, he is entitled for the protection of himself and others in the area to conduct a carefully limited search of the outer clothing of such persons in an attempt to discover weapons which might be used to assault him." 392 U.S. at 30, 88 S.Ct. at 1884–85, 20 L.Ed.2d at 911.

Sibron v. New York

In the *Sibron* case, a uniformed patrolman observed Sibron in the company of several known drug addicts during an eight-hour period. The officer did not see anything pass between Sibron and the others, nor did he hear any of their conversation. Sibron later entered a restaurant where he spoke to three other known addicts but again nothing was observed to pass between them.

On the basis of these actions alone, the policeman accosted Sibron with the remark, "You know what I am after." Sibron mumbled a reply and began to reach into his pocket. The policeman intercepted his hand, reached into the same pocket, and discovered envelopes containing heroin. Sibron was convicted of unauthorized possession of narcotics and appealed on the basis that the seizure was made in violation of his Fourth Amendment rights.

The Supreme Court found that the policeman in the *Sibron* case did not have probable cause to make an arrest and therefore could not justify the search as incident to arrest. The officer knew nothing of the conversations between Sibron and the others, and saw nothing pass between them. All he had to go on was the fact that the others were addicts. This was not enough. "The inference that persons who talk to narcotics addicts are engaged in criminal traffic in narcotics is simply not the sort of reasonable inference required to support an intrusion by the police upon an individual's personal security." 392 U.S. at 62, 88 S.Ct. at 1902, 20 L.Ed.2d at 934. There was no basis to arrest until after the unlawful search.

Moreover, nothing in the record gave the slightest indication that the officer thought Sibron might be armed. The officer, therefore, could not justify his actions on the grounds of self-protection. The *Terry* case did not authorize a routine frisk of everyone seen on the street or encountered by an officer. The officer in *Sibron* was apparently after narcotics and nothing else. His search was therefore unreasonable under the standards announced in the *Terry* case. Since there was neither probable cause to arrest nor sufficient justification to frisk, the heroin seized by the officer was not admissible in evidence and the conviction of Sibron was reversed.

Peters v. New York

In the *Peters* case, an off-duty patrolman heard a noise outside his apartment door. He saw two men tiptoeing furtively about the hallway, neither of whom he recognized although he had lived in the building for twelve years. After telephoning the police, he entered the hallway with his gun drawn, slamming the door behind him. The two suspects fled down the stairs and the patrolman gave chase. He caught up with the defendant, questioned him, and patted down his clothing. In the course of the frisk, the officer discovered a hard object that he believed could be a weapon. The object was an envelope containing burglar's tools. Peters was convicted of possessing burglar's tools.

The Supreme Court affirmed the conviction of Peters. The Court did not examine the officer's actions from a stop and frisk standpoint, but rather found probable cause to arrest and sufficient authority to search incident to the arrest. The Court's decision emphasized defendant's furtive action and his flight in establishing probable cause.

> It is difficult to conceive of stronger grounds for an arrest, short of actual eyewitness observation of criminal activity.... [D]eliberately furtive actions and flight at the approach of strangers or law officers are strong indicia of *mens rea*, and when coupled with specific knowledge on the part of the officer relating the suspect to the evidence of crime, they are proper factors to be considered

in the decision to make an arrest. 392 U.S. at 66–67, 88 S.Ct. at 1904, 20 L.Ed.2d at 937.

The remainder of this chapter discusses in detail the powers of and limitations on a law enforcement officer in conducting a stop and frisk.

THE REASONABLENESS STANDARD

Stop and frisk procedures are serious intrusions upon an individual's privacy and are governed by the Fourth Amendment to the Constitution prohibiting unreasonable searches and seizures.

> It is quite plain that the Fourth Amendment governs "seizures" of the person which do not eventuate in a trip to the station house and prosecution for crime—"arrests" in traditional terminology. It must be recognized that whenever a police officer accosts an individual and restrains his freedom to walk away, he has "seized" that person. And it is nothing less than sheer torture of the English language to suggest that a careful exploration of the outer surfaces of a person's clothing all over his or her body in an attempt to find weapons is not a "search." Moreover, it is simply fantastic to urge that such a procedure performed in public by a policeman while the citizen stands helpless, perhaps facing a wall with his hands raised, is a "petty indignity." It is a serious intrusion upon the sanctity of the person, which may inflict great indignity and arouse strong resentment, and it is not to be undertaken lightly. 392 U.S. at 16–17, 88 S.Ct. at 1877, 20 L.Ed.2d at 903.

Nevertheless, because a stop is more limited in scope than an arrest and because a frisk is more limited in scope than a full search, a stop and frisk may be judged by a less rigid standard than the probable cause standard applicable to an arrest and search. The *Terry* case made clear that stop and frisk is governed not by the warrant clause of the Fourth Amendment, but by the reasonableness clause. In the stop and frisk situation, the law enforcement officer must necessarily take swift action based upon on-the-spot observations. This type of police conduct has not historically been, and as a practical matter could not be, subjected to the warrant procedure. Instead, the police conduct in the stop and frisk situation must be tested by the Fourth Amendment's general proscription against unreasonable searches and seizures. The question for the law enforcement officer then becomes whether or not it is reasonable, in a particular set of circumstances, for the officer to seize a person and subject the person to a limited search when there is no probable cause to arrest.

Competing Interests

The determination of reasonableness involves a consideration of the competing interests involved in a stop and frisk situation. On one side are the individual's right to privacy and the individual's right to be free from unreasonable searches and seizures. "Even a limited search of the outer clothing for weapons constitutes a severe, though brief, intrusion upon cherished personal security, and it must surely be an annoying, frightening, and perhaps humiliating experience." 392 U.S. at 24–25, 88 S.Ct. at 1881–82, 20 L.Ed.2d at 908.

On the other side are the governmental interests involved. One of these is effective crime prevention and detection. The other governmental interest, with which the Court in *Terry* was most concerned, is the interest of police officers in taking steps to assure themselves that the person with whom they are dealing is not armed with a weapon that could unexpectedly be used against them:

> Certainly it would be unreasonable to require that police officers take unnecessary risks in the performance of their duties. American criminals have a long tradition of armed violence, and every year in this country many law enforcement officers are killed in the line of duty, and thousands more are wounded. 392 U.S. at 23, 88 S.Ct. at 1881, 20 L.Ed.2d at 907.

Balancing these competing interests in a particular situation requires a consideration of

1. whether *any* police interference at all is justified by the circumstances; and

2. if so, *how extensive* an interference those circumstances justify.

In the following discussion, the stop aspect and the frisk aspect are considered separately because the stop and the frisk each have different purposes, different sets of circumstances that will justify them, and different consequences for the person who is subjected to the procedure.

DETERMINATION OF WHETHER TO STOP

The U.S. Supreme Court recognized that stopping persons for the purpose of investigating possible criminal activity is necessary to the government's interest in effective crime prevention and detection: "[I]t is this interest which underlies the recognition that a police officer may in appropriate circumstances and in an appropriate manner approach a person for purposes of investigating possibly criminal behavior even though there is no probable cause to make an arrest." 392 U.S. at 22, 88 S.Ct. at 1880, 20 L.Ed.2d. at 906–7.

What Is a Stop?

Not every approach of a person by a law enforcement officer for purposes of investigating possible criminal activity will be considered a stop. In the *Terry* case, the U.S. Supreme Court noted:

> Obviously not all personal intercourse between policemen and citizens involves "seizures" of persons. Only when the officer, by means of physical force or show of authority, has in some way restrained the liberty of a citizen may we conclude that a "seizure" has occurred. 392 U.S. at 19 n. 16, 88 S.Ct. at 1879 n. 16, 20 L.Ed.2d at 905 n. 16.

A stop is the least intrusive type of seizure of the person governed by the Fourth Amendment. (More intrusive types of seizures—formal arrests and seizures tantamount to arrest—are discussed in Chapter 4.)

In United States v. Mendenhall, 446 U.S. 544, 100 S.Ct. 1870, 64 L.Ed.2d 497 (1980), the U.S. Supreme Court developed a test to be applied in determining whether a person has been seized within the meaning of the Fourth Amendment.

> [A] person has been "seized" within the meaning of the Fourth Amendment only if, in view of all of the circumstances surrounding the incident, a reasonable person would have believed that he was not free to leave. Examples of circumstances that might indicate a seizure even where the person did not attempt to leave, would be the threatening presence of several officers, the display of a weapon by an officer, some physical touching of the person of the citizen, or the use of language or tone of voice indicating that compliance with the officer's request might be compelled. . . . In the absence of some such evidence, otherwise inoffensive contact between a member of the public and the police cannot, as a matter of law, amount to a seizure of that person. 446 U.S. at 554–55, 100 S.Ct. at 1877, 64 L.Ed.2d at 509.

In the *Mendenhall* case, the Court found no seizure (and therefore no stop) where Drug Enforcement Administration (DEA) agents, wearing no uniforms and displaying no weapons, approached the defendant on the public concourse of an airport, identified themselves as federal agents, and asked to see the defendant's identification and airline ticket. Furthermore, the defendant's voluntarily accompanying the agents to a DEA office upon their request was not a seizure (or stop), there being no threats or show of force.

In Michigan v. Chesternut, ___ U.S. ___, 108 S.Ct. 1975, 100 L.Ed.2d 565 (1988), the U.S. Supreme Court said:

> The [*Mendenhall*] test is necessarily imprecise, because it is designed to assess the coercive effect of police conduct, taken as a whole, rather than to focus on particular details of that conduct in isolation. Moreover, what constitutes a restraint on liberty prompting a person to conclude that he is not free to "leave" will vary, not only with the particular police conduct at issue, but also with the setting in which the conduct occurs. ___ U.S. at ___, 108 S.Ct. at 1979, 100 L.Ed.2d at 572.

In the *Chesternut* case, officers in a patrol car chased the defendant after they observed the defendant run when he saw the patrol car. The chase consisted of a brief acceleration to catch up with the defendant followed by a short drive alongside the defendant. The Court held that there was no stop because the defendant could not have reasonably believed that he was not free to disregard the police presence and go about his business. The Court noted that the police did not activate a siren or flashes; did not command the defendant to halt; did not display any weapons; and did not operate the patrol car in an aggressive manner to block the defendant's course or otherwise control the direction or speed of the defendant's movement. The Court recognized that "[w]hile the very presence of a police car driving parallel to a running pedestrian could be somewhat intimidating, this kind of police presence does not, standing alone, constitute a seizure." ___ U.S. at ___, 108 S.Ct. at 1980, 100 L.Ed.2d at 573.

Authority to Stop

Before an officer stops a person, the officer must be able to justify the stop with concrete facts and circumstances indicating possibly criminal behavior. (Indications of criminal activity are discussed in Chapter 6.) As the Supreme Court said in *Terry*: "[I]n justifying the particular intrusion the police officer must be able to point to specific and articulable facts which, taken together with rational inferences from those facts, reasonably warrant that intrusion." 392 U.S.

at 21, 88 S.Ct. at 1880, 20 L.Ed.2d at 906. This means that a court will not accept an officer's mere statement or conclusion that criminal activity was suspected. The officer must be able to back up the conclusion by reciting the specific facts that led to that conclusion. For example, in United States v. Pavelski, 789 F.2d 485 (7th Cir. 1986), the court held that an officer who testified to a "gut feeling that things were really wrong" failed to articulate any objective facts indicative of criminal activity.

Furthermore, the officer's decision to initiate a stop will be judged against the following objective standard: "[W]ould the facts available to the officer at the moment of the seizure or the search 'warrant a man of reasonable caution in the belief' that the action taken was appropriate?" 392 U.S. at 21–22, 88 S.Ct. at 1880, 20 L.Ed.2d at 906. This objective standard is similar to the standard imposed upon law enforcement officers in traditional search and seizure or arrest situations. For example, assume that an officer is attempting to obtain a warrant for a person's arrest. Since probable cause is required to obtain the warrant, the officer must produce specific facts sufficient to support a reasonable belief *that a specific crime has been or is being committed*. In the stop and frisk situation, no crime has been committed—there is only a possibility that criminal activity is under way, perhaps only in the planning stage. However, the officer must still have specific facts indicating a *possibility of impending criminal activity* to justify the initial intrusion. The common element in the two situations is that officers must be able to justify their action with specific facts. The only difference is in the nature of the information to be given, and for an investigative stop, the officer need only show facts indicating the possibility that criminal behavior is afoot.

The officer's authority to stop is not limited to crimes about to be committed or crimes in the process of being committed. The U.S. Supreme Court has authorized the stop of a person whom officers suspected of being involved in a *completed* felony. The Court said:

> [W]here police have been unable to locate a person suspected of involvement in a past crime, the ability to briefly stop that person, ask questions, or check identification in the absence of probable cause promotes the strong government interest in solving crimes and bringing offenders to justice. Restraining police action until after probable cause is obtained would not only hinder the investigation, but might also enable the suspect to flee in the interim and to remain at large. Particularly in the context of felonies or crimes involving a threat to public safety, it is in the public interest that the crime be solved and the suspect detained as promptly as possible. The law enforcement interests at stake in these circumstances outweigh the individual's interest to be free of a stop and detention that is no more extensive than permissible in the investigation of imminent or ongoing crimes. United States v. Hensley, 469 U.S. 221, 229, 105 S.Ct. 675, 681, 83 L.Ed.2d 604, 612 (1985).

Note that an officer has the duty to discontinue the investigation and to not make a *Terry*-type stop of a person when, by the time of the intended stop, justification for the initial suspicion has disappeared.

> The scope of a policeman's inquiry and the permissibility of continuing to press the on-going investigation necessarily depend upon the continuing flow of information coming to the officer's attention after the start of the originally undertaken investigation. If the officer discovers additional evidence of possible

wrongdoing, he may expand his inquiry as suggested by this new information. . . . The converse proposition also holds true. An officer cannot continue to press his investigation when he discovers new evidence demonstrating that his original interpretation of his suspect's actions was mistaken. State v. Garland, 482 A.2d 139, 144 (Me. 1984).

Extent of Stop

Once an officer determines that the circumstances justify stopping an individual to investigate possible criminal activity, to what extent do those circumstances allow the officer to interfere? In other words, how long may the person be detained, how much force may be used, and how much questioning may the person be subjected to?

In Florida v. Royer, 460 U.S. 491, 500, 103 S.Ct. 1319, 1325, 75 L.Ed.2d 229, 238 (1983), the U.S. Supreme Court said:

> The predicate permitting seizures on suspicion short of probable cause is that law enforcement interests warrant a limited intrusion on the personal security of the suspect. The scope of the intrusion permitted will vary to some extent with the particular facts and circumstances of each case. This much, however is clear: an investigative detention must be temporary and last no longer than is necessary to effectuate the purpose of the stop. Similarly, the investigative methods employed should be the least intrusive means reasonably available to verify or dispel the officer's suspicion in a short period of time. . . . It is the State's burden to demonstrate that the seizure it seeks to justify on the basis of a reasonable suspicion was sufficiently limited in scope and duration to satisfy the conditions of an investigative seizure.

An investigative stop can range from a friendly encounter with minimal intrusion to an angry confrontation accompanied by the use of force. Officers must be able to point to specific facts and circumstances to indicate that the extent of the interference with an individual was reasonable.

An officer's initial questioning of a suspect may assure the officer that no further investigation is necessary. For example, a law enforcement officer observed a young man carrying a flashlight and a small box walking on the sidewalk of a residential street at 2:40 A.M. The officer passed the young man in the patrol car and then stopped to ask him what he was doing. The young man replied that he was collecting night crawlers for fishing bait. The officer wished him luck and drove on.

On the other hand, the answers given by the stopped person may cause the officer to believe more strongly that something is amiss. In this situation, the officer is permitted to investigate further or, if probable cause exists, to arrest the person. For example, an officer saw the defendant wearing one topcoat and carrying another. The defendant seemed to be attempting to hide something under the coat he carried. Considering this behavior suspicious, the officer stopped the defendant and asked him what he had under his coat. The defendant replied that he had a tape recorder. When the officer asked him to identify himself, the defendant handed the officer a driver's license describing an older person of a different race. The officer then arrested the defendant.

The court held that the initial suspicious circumstances justified at least the mere questioning of the defendant by the officer. Then, when the officer checked the license, he had "probable cause not only to investigate further but to place the appellant under arrest with the very reasonable belief that the appellant's possession indicated, at the least, receiving stolen goods." Commonwealth v. Howell, 245 A.2d 680, 684 (Pa.Super. 1968).

An investigative stop is not subject to any rigid time limitation, but at some point an extended stop can no longer be justified as reasonable. In determining the reasonableness of the duration of a stop, courts consider the law enforcement purposes to be served by the stop as well as the time reasonably needed to effectuate those purposes. The U.S. Supreme Court said:

> In assessing whether a detention is too long in duration to be justified as an investigative stop, we consider it appropriate to examine whether the police diligently pursued a means of investigation that was likely to confirm or dispel their suspicions quickly, during which time it was necessary to detain the defendant. . . . A court making this assessment should take care to consider whether the police are acting in a swiftly developing situation and in such cases the court should not indulge in unrealistic second-guessing. . . . The question is not simply whether some other alternative was available, but whether the police acted unreasonably in failing to recognize or to pursue it. United States v. Sharpe, 470 U.S. 675, 686–87, 105 S.Ct. 1568, 1575–76, 84 L.Ed.2d 605, 615–16 (1985).

Some reasons that might justify an officer in prolonging the detention of a suspect are that the officer is attempting to obtain further information over the police radio or from other persons, summoning assistance, traveling to the scene of suspected criminal activity, caring for injured persons or responding to other emergency circumstances, and dealing with evasive tactics or other delays caused by the suspect.

Under ordinary circumstances, an officer who has a reasonable suspicion that a person may be engaged in criminal activity should *initiate* a stop of the person immediately. Nevertheless, a short delay in making the stop may be justified in certain situations. For example, in State v. Cyr, 501 A.2d 1303 (Me. 1985), an officer had grounds to stop a truck parked in an area of recent burglaries after observing the person in the driver's seat duck down to avoid detection. However, because the officer was transporting an arrested person, he continued driving slowly past the truck. In his rearview mirror, the officer observed the truck leave its parking place and follow his cruiser. After being informed that no other police unit was available to intercept the truck, the officer stopped the truck some two to three minutes after the first observation.

The court held that the suspicion had not evaporated because of the delay, since the truck remained within the officer's sight at all times and the delay resulted from the presence of an arrested person in the officer's vehicle. A longer delay, however, may cause a stop to be held illegal. For example, in United States v. Posey, 663 F.2d 37 (7th Cir. 1981), the court held that suspicion had evaporated where the defendant was stopped fifteen minutes after suspicion arose and fifteen miles away from the place where the defendant was originally seen.

DETERMINATION OF WHETHER TO FRISK

The law enforcement officer's determination of whether or not to frisk a suspect is a separate issue from the determination of whether or not to stop. It involves a different governmental interest to be served and a different set of factors to be considered by the officer. The governmental interest served by giving police the authority to frisk is that of protecting the officer and others from possible violence by persons being investigated for crime. "[W]e cannot blind ourselves to the need for law enforcement officers to protect themselves and other prospective victims of violence in situations where they may lack probable cause for an arrest." 392 U.S. at 24, 88 S.Ct. at 1881, 20 L.Ed.2d at 907–8.

Balanced against this interest is the citizen's right to privacy, which would necessarily be invaded by giving police the right to frisk suspects. The Supreme Court said: "We must still consider, however, the nature and quality of the intrusion on individual rights which must be accepted if police officers are to be conceded the right to search for weapons in situations where probable cause to arrest for crime is lacking." 392 U.S. at 24, 88 S.Ct. at 1881, 20 L.Ed.2d at 908. As noted earlier, the Court considers the stop and frisk procedure to be a serious intrusion on a person's rights, possibly inflicting great indignity and arousing strong resentment.

The Court considered these competing interests and set out a limited authority for a protective frisk by law enforcement officers in the following terms: "Our evaluation of the proper balance that has to be struck in this type of case leads us to conclude that there must be a narrowly drawn authority to permit a reasonable search for weapons for the protection of the police officer, where he has reason to believe that he is dealing with an armed and dangerous individual, regardless of whether he has probable cause to arrest the individual for a crime." 392 U.S. at 27, 88 S.Ct. at 1883, 20 L.Ed.2d at 909.

Limited Authority

The law enforcement officer's authority to frisk is a limited and narrowly drawn authority. An officer may not frisk everyone that is stopped for an investigation of the possibility of criminal activity. Before deciding to conduct any frisk, an officer must have "reason to believe that he is dealing with an armed and dangerous individual." The officer need not be absolutely certain that the individual is armed. Rather the issue is "whether a reasonably prudent man in the circumstances would be warranted in the belief that his safety or that of others was in danger. . . ." 392 U.S. at 27, 88 S.Ct. at 1883, 20 L.Ed.2d at 909.

Thus, frisks are governed by an objective standard similar to the standard governing stops. An officer must be able to justify a search or frisk of a person by pointing to specific facts and "specific reasonable inferences which he is entitled to draw from the facts in light of his experience." 392 U.S. at 27, 88 S.Ct. at 1883, 20 L.Ed.2d at 909.

Many factors may be taken into consideration in deciding whether or not it is appropriate to frisk a person. Some factors will carry more weight with one officer than with another because of differences in the officers' experience and knowledge. The following is a partial list of things to consider in deciding to frisk a person.

1. The suspected crime involves the use of weapons.
2. The suspect is nervous or edgy about being stopped.
3. There is a bulge in the suspect's clothing.

4. The suspect's hand is concealed in a pocket.

5. The suspect does not present satisfactory identification or an adequate explanation for suspicious behavior.

6. The area the officer is operating in is known to contain armed persons.

7. The suspect exhibits belligerent behavior upon being stopped.

8. The officer believes that the defendant may have been armed on a previous occasion.

Justification to frisk will usually require a combination of one or more of these factors or others, evaluated in the light of an officer's experience and knowledge.

Scope of Search

The Supreme Court requires a frisk to be "a *reasonable* search for weapons for the protection of the police officer." (emphasis supplied) 392 U.S. at 27, 88 S.Ct. at 1883, 20 L.Ed.2d at 909. Since the *only* justifiable purpose of a frisk is the protection of the officer and others, the search must be limited to what is minimally necessary for this protection. Therefore, the frisk must initially be limited to a pat-down of the *outer* clothing. There is no authority to reach inside clothing or into pockets in the *initial* stages of a frisk. During the pat-down, if the officer detects an object that feels like a weapon, the officer may then reach inside the clothing or pocket and seize it. If the object is not a weapon but is some other implement of crime (such as a burglar's tool), that implement is admissible in evidence for the crime to which it relates (e.g., attempted burglary). However, if the officer feels an object that cannot be a weapon but could be evidence of some other crime (such as possession of narcotics or lottery tickets), the officer may not seize the object. The search must end at this point because the only authorized purpose for a frisk is to protect the officer and others, *not* to obtain evidence for use at a subsequent trial. If the officer feels no weapon-like object during the course of the pat-down, the officer can no longer have a reasonable fear that the person is armed. Any further search without probable cause would exceed the purpose of the frisk—namely, the protection of the officer and others—and would be unreasonable under the Fourth Amendment. Any evidence obtained from the search would be inadmissible.

The U.S. Supreme Court has approved an extension of the permissible scope of a protective search for weapons beyond the person of the suspect to include the passenger compartment of an automobile. "[T]he search of the passenger compartment of an automobile, limited to those areas in which a weapon may be placed or hidden, is permissible if the police officer possesses a reasonable belief based on "specific and articulable facts which, taken together with the rational inferences from those facts, reasonably warrant" the officers in believing that the suspect is dangerous and the suspect may gain immediate control of weapons." Michigan v. Long, 463 U.S. 1032, 1049, 103 S.Ct. 3469, 3480, 77 L.Ed.2d 1201, 1220 (1983). In reaching this decision, the Court recognized that roadside encounters between police and suspects are especially hazardous, and that danger may arise from the possible presence of weapons in the area surrounding a suspect. The Court emphasized, however, that its decision does not mean that the police may conduct automobile searches whenever they conduct an investigative stop. Since the sole justification for a *Terry* search is the protection of police officers and others nearby, officers may conduct such a search only when they have a reasonable suspicion that the suspect is dangerous. Unlike a warrantless search incident to a lawful arrest, a *Terry* search is not justified by any need to prevent the disappearance or destruction of evidence of crime.

SPECIFIC CIRCUMSTANCES IN STOP AND FRISK

Stop and frisk encompasses an infinite variety of possible situations. A mere statement of general guidelines may not be sufficient to clearly indicate what behavior is or is not appropriate for a law enforcement officer in a given situation. Therefore, specific situations involving stop and frisk are presented here to show how courts throughout the United States deal with stop and frisk. Actual court decisions are discussed, and emphasis is placed on analyzing the courts' evaluations of the reasonableness of the actions of law enforcement officers. The cases are grouped under various headings indicating major factors influencing the courts' decisions.

Bulge in Clothing

In United States v. Lee, 271 A.2d 566 (D.C.App. 1970), two law enforcement officers in plain clothes approached the entrance of a delicatessen to investigate a robbery of an earlier date. On their way into the store the officers passed the defendant, who was standing outside. Inside the store, the officers overheard the store owner and others mention that the defendant and a companion, who was concealed behind a truck nearby, were acting in a suspicious manner. The owner went outside and told the defendant that everyone was watching him and that he had better leave.

The officers approached the defendant, identified themselves, and asked for his identification. The defendant said, "Why? My name is Lee." When the officers again requested some identification, the defendant reached back with his left hand into his left rear pocket to get his wallet. One of the officers observed a bulge in the waistband of the defendant's pants. An immediate seizure of the object causing the bulge revealed a loaded pistol.

The court found the stop and frisk to be reasonable. With respect to the stop, the court said the action of the officers "is the kind of momentary contact which is and must be recognized as necessary to a sound police-community relationship and its commensurate effective law enforcement. It cannot be said that the accused was so inconvenienced or restricted that the delicate balance between individual freedom and legitimate police activity has been unduly weighted against him." 271 A.2d at 567–68.

In approving the seizure of the gun, the court stated that the officer "had no other choice. He was justifiably concerned for his own safety when the accused revealed that he had something concealed under his waistband. . . .Surely then, under the considerations discussed in Terry v. Ohio, supra, the in-depth search for and seizure of the gun was reasonable—clearly as reasonable as the in-depth search for and seizure of Terry's gun when its presence was discovered by Officer McFadden's sense of touch during the so-called 'frisk.'" 271 A.2d at 568.

Hand Concealed in Pocket

During a routine investigation for a traffic violation, an officer was informed by police radio that the car and driver he was investigating were carrying forged prescriptions for narcotic drugs. The defendant, a passenger in the car, voluntarily got out of the car with his right hand concealed in his coat pocket. The officer asked the defendant to remove his hand from his pocket. Upon the defendant's refusal, the officer removed the hand and frisked the defendant. At no time did the officer go into any hidden places upon the defendant's person. However, clutched in the removed hand was a small yellow envelope, which the officer seized. Upon observing its contents, the officer arrested the defendant for the possession of heroin.

The court held that the initial stop was reasonable. The information received over the police radio during a routine traffic investigation gave the officer good reason at least to investigate further. With respect to the reasonableness of the frisk, the court said:

> A person does not ordinarily alight from an automobile with a hand inserted in a pocket. When the hands are free such person has better maneuverability to accomplish this task. Thus when the hand didn't come out after one or more routine questions by the officer, he certainly by this time had probable cause to initiate reasonable precaution for his own safety. Under such facts and circumstances the frisk for weapons was not unreasonable. State v. Henry, 256 N.E.2d 269, 270 (Ohio Misc. 1969).

Based upon all the facts and circumstances, the court found that the officer had reasonable grounds to believe that the defendant was armed and dangerous. Furthermore, the court held that the heroin taken from the defendant was admissible in evidence against him because, as a result of a reasonable frisk, the defendant *himself* brought the envelope containing the heroin from his pocket, after which it was then in plain view.

Innocent Conduct

A series of individual lawful acts may provide reasonable suspicion of criminal activity sufficient to justify a stop, if the overall pattern of those acts is indicative of criminal activity. In United States v. Martinez, 808 F.2d 1050 (5th Cir. 1987), the defendant purchased several chemicals, each with a legitimate use other than the manufacture of illegal drugs. A Drug Enforcement Administration (DEA) officer stopped the defendant's car based on the officer's knowledge that there was no legitimate use for the particular *combination* of chemicals.

The court held that the stop of the vehicle was justified and that when the officer smelled an odor he recognized as characteristic of illegal drug manufacture, his temporary detention of the occupants of the car for further investigation was also justified. Therefore, the perception of totally innocent activity may provide to an officer with experience and knowledge about a particular type of crime a reasonable and articulable suspicion of criminal activity sufficient to justify a stop.

Admission by Defendant

The defendant's vehicle was stopped by a police officer for speeding. After stopping the vehicle, the officer walked up to it and the defendant got out, holding his right hand in the pocket of his knee-length coat. The pocket was baggy and sagging. The officer grabbed the defendant's arm and asked him if he had a gun. The defendant answered "Yes." The officer then removed the gun and arrested the defendant.

The court assumed without discussion that the stop was reasonable because it was a routine traffic stop. In dealing with the frisk, the court cited *Terry v. Ohio*:

> Terry v. Ohio . . . tells us that when a police officer has reason to believe that he is dealing with an armed individual he has a right to search for weapons regardless of whether he has probable cause to arrest that individual for a crime. Here the officer did not merely think he was dealing with an armed person—he knew he was. State v. Hall, 476 P.2d 930, 931 (Or. App. 1970).

Information from Informants

In Adams v. Williams, 407 U.S. 143, 92 S.Ct. 1921, 32 L.Ed.2d 612 (1972), a law enforcement officer on patrol in his cruiser was approached by a person known to him and was told that a man seated in a nearby vehicle had a gun at his waist and was carrying narcotics. The officer approached the vehicle, tapped on the window, and asked the occupant (the defendant) to open the door. When the defendant rolled down the window instead, the officer reached in, removed a pistol from the defendant's waistband, and then arrested the defendant.

The Court held that the officer acted justifiably in responding to the informant's tip:

> The informant was known to him personally and had provided him with information in the past. This is a stronger case than obtains in the case of an anonymous telephone tip. The informant here came forward personally to give information that was immediately verifiable at the scene. Indeed, under Connecticut law, the informant herself might have been subject to immediate arrest for making a false complaint had Sgt. Connolly's investigation proven the tip incorrect. Thus, while the Court's decisions indicate that this informant's unverified tip may have been insufficient for a narcotics arrest or search warrant, the information carried enough indicia of reliability to justify the officer's forcible stop of Williams.
>
> In reaching this conclusion, we reject respondent's argument that reasonable cause for a stop and frisk can only be based on the officer's personal observation, rather than on information supplied by another person. Informants' tips, like all other clues and evidence coming to a policeman on the scene, may vary greatly in their value and reliability. One simple rule will not cover every situation. Some tips, completely lacking in indicia of reliability, would either warrant no police response or require further investigation before a forcible stop of a suspect would be authorized. But in some situations—for example,

when the victim of a street crime seeks immediate police aid and gives a description of his assailant, or when a credible informant warns of a specific impending crime—the subtleties of the hearsay rule should not thwart an appropriate police response. 407 U.S. at 146–47, 92 S.Ct. at 1923–24, 32 L.Ed.2d at 617–18.

Under *Adams v. Williams*, an officer may stop a person suspected of possible criminal activity based on an informant's tip if the tip carries "enough indicia of reliability." This standard is less than the probable cause standard discussed in Chapter 6. Nevertheless, the officer must be able to give specific reasons why the tip was believed to be reliable. As the quoted material indicates, an anonymous telephone tip might not be sufficiently reliable without corroboration.

Officers may rely upon a police radio dispatch to obtain facts to justify the stop of a person or vehicle. If, however, it is later determined that the person relaying the information over the radio had no factual foundation for the message, the stop will be ruled illegal. In United States v. Robinson, 536 F.2d 1298 (9th Cir. 1976), the court said:

> We recognize that effective law enforcement cannot be conducted unless police officers can act on directions and information transmitted by one officer to another and that officers, who must often act swiftly, cannot be expected to cross-examine their fellow officers about the foundation for the transmitted information. The fact that an officer does not have to have personal knowledge of the evidence supplying good cause for a stop before he can obey a direction to detain a person or a vehicle does not mean that the Government need not produce evidence at trial showing good cause to legitimate the detention when the legality of the stop is challenged. If the dispatcher himself had had founded suspicion, or if he had relied on information from a reliable informant who supplied him with adequate facts to establish founded suspicion, the dispatcher could properly have delegated the stopping function to Officer Holland. But if the dispatcher did not have such cause, he could not create justification simply by relaying a direction to a fellow officer to make the stop. 536 F.2d at 1299–1300.

Frisk of Traffic Offender's Passengers

When an officer makes a stop for a traffic offense and has sufficient specific facts to support a belief that there is a dangerous situation, he or she may frisk the traffic offender's passengers for weapons. In United States v. Tharpe, 536 F.2d 1098 (5th Cir. 1976), the court found sufficient facts to justify such a frisk under the following circumstances: (1) the driver showed the officer a false license; (2) the driver admitted being the "bad check" suspect of whom the officer had just been informed by radio; (3) the officer recognized the two passengers as burglary suspects; (4) the officer was alone; and (5) the encounter occurred late at night.

Routine Vehicle Checks and Roadblocks

In Delaware v. Prouse, 440 U.S. 648, 663, 99 S.Ct. 1391, 1401, 59 L.Ed.2d 660, 673 (1979), the U.S. Supreme Court held "that except in those situations in which there is at least articulable and reasonable suspicion that a motorist is unlicensed or that an automobile is not registered, or that either the vehicle or an occupant is otherwise subject to seizure for violation of law, stopping an automobile and detaining the driver in order to check his driver's license and the registration of the automobile are unreasonable under the Fourth Amendment." The Court expressed its concern that random vehicle checks presented a potential danger of arbitrary or discriminatory enforcement of the law.

Nevertheless, the Court's holding specifically did not preclude states from developing methods for spot checks that involve less intrusion or that do not involve the unconstrained exercise of discretion. The Court suggested as one possible alternative the questioning of all oncoming traffic at roadblock-type stops.

Although motorists have challenged the police practice of establishing roadblocks for routine license and registration checks, courts have approved such roadblocks if they are conducted with proper safeguards to ensure that the individual's reasonable expectation of privacy is not subjected to the unbridled discretion of police officers. Among the factors considered by the courts in determining whether a roadblock is constitutional are the following:

> (1) The degree of discretion, if any, left to the officer in the field; (2) the location designated for the roadblock; (3) the time and duration of the roadblock; (4) standards set by superior officers; (5) advance notice to the public at large; (6) advance warning to the individual approaching motorist; (7) maintenance of safety conditions; (8) degree of fear or anxiety generated by the mode of operation; (9) average length of time each motorist is detained; (10) physical factors surrounding the location, type and method of operation; (11) the availability of less intrusive methods for combating the problem; (12) the degree of effectiveness of the procedure; and (13) any other relevant circumstances which might bear upon the test. State v. Deskins, 673 P.2d 1174, 1185 (Kan. 1983).

None of these factors, considered alone, is necessarily controlling. For example, in State v. Cloukey, 486 A.2d 143 (Me. 1985), a roadblock set up by a deputy sheriff and a state police officer had only modest supervisory involvement. (The sheriff's permission was requested and he was informed of the location of the roadblock by the deputy.) The court held that although written policy and involvement by supervisory personnel in planning the roadblock were preferable, they were not essential, where the roadblock was otherwise conducted for a proper purpose and in a proper manner.

A properly conducted roadblock does not violate an automobile driver's constitutional right to privacy nor does it amount to an illegal search and seizure or an invasion of the right to use the public ways. Inconvenience to drivers who are stopped at roadblocks is not unreasonable when balanced against the necessity to protect the general public against unsafe motor vehicles and against unqualified or incompetent drivers. Furthermore, a systematic roadblock-type stop of all vehicles is often the only practical method of enforcing the law.

Ordering of Driver Out of Vehicle

An officer who has lawfully stopped a motor vehicle for a traffic violation may, for personal safety reasons, order the driver out of the vehicle, even though there is no reason to suspect foul play from the particular driver at the time of the stop. The U.S. Supreme Court said:

> We think this additional intrusion can only be described as de minimis. The driver is being asked to expose to view very little more of his person than is already exposed. The police have already lawfully decided that the driver shall be briefly detained; the only question is whether he shall spend that period sitting in the driver's seat of his car or standing alongside it. Not only is the insistence of the police on the latter choice not a "serious intrusion upon the sanctity of the person," but it hardly rises to the level of a "'petty indignity.'" . . . What is at most a mere inconvenience cannot prevail when balanced against legitimate concerns for the officer's safety. Pennsylvania v. Mimms, 434 U.S. 106, 111, 98 S.Ct. 330, 333 54 L.Ed.2d 331, 337 (1977).

Once the driver is out of the car, the officer may conduct a frisk, if the officer has reason to believe that the person is armed and dangerous.

In State v. Wentworth, 480 A.2d 751 (Me. 1984), the court allowed an officer to request that passengers other than the driver exit the vehicle where the officer had a concern for safety. In that case, while another officer was escorting the driver from the car, a passenger inside the car was observed moving in such a way as to suggest an effort to remove or conceal an unidentified object.

Violent Crime

In People v. Anthony, 86 Cal.Rptr. 767 (Cal.App. 1970), police officers on patrol received a radio report of an armed robbery in their vicinity. The report came in at about 3:30 A.M., minutes after the robbery happened. The officers had seen only one moving car in the vicinity. They approached the car and noticed that one of the passengers fit the description of the robber given to them over the radio. The car was stopped and the two occupants were instructed to get out. No questions were asked, but one of the officers immediately began a pat-down search of the defendant for weapons. Bullets were found and the defendant was arrested.

The court held that both the stop and the frisk were justified.

> It is well established that circumstances short of probable cause to make an arrest may justify an officer's stopping motorists for questioning, and if the circumstances warrant it, the officer may in self-protection request a suspect to alight from an automobile and to submit to a superficial search for concealed weapons. . . . If the reason for the stop is an articulate suspicion of a crime of violence, and the officer has reason to fear for his personal safety, he may immediately proceed to make a pat-down search for weapons without asking any prior questions . . . "'There is no reason why an officer, rightfully but forcibly confronting a person suspected of a serious crime, *should have to ask one question and take the risk that the answer might be a bullet.*'" 86 Cal.Rptr. at 773.

To summarize, an officer is not required to ask questions before frisking a suspect if the nature of the crime being investigated is violent and if the officer has a reasonable fear for his or her own safety.

Objects Felt in Frisk

In People v. Navran, 483 P.2d 228 (Colo. 1971), police had a certain residence under surveillance as a receiving point for marijuana shipments and had probable cause to arrest the occupant of the residence, although he was absent at the time. The defendants entered the driveway of the residence in a car, proceeded up the driveway, and were attempting to back out when the police stopped them. The officers knew that the defendants were not occupants of the residence nor were they subjects of the investigation. Nevertheless, the officers caused the defendants to be spread-eagled against their car and searched. One of the officers patted down the defendants' outer and inner clothing. During the frisk of one defendant, the officer felt a lump in a shirt pocket. This lump was later disclosed to be a plastic bag containing marijuana seeds and a package of roll-your-own cigarette papers.

The court approved the stop:

> Admittedly the police officers would have been derelict in their duty had they not stopped the defendants' vehicle to determine whether the occupant of the residence, or any other known subject of the investigation, was in the car. Likewise, the officers could have detained the defendants long enough to ascertain why they were on the premises. 483 P.2d at 230.

However, the court found the *frisk* unreasonable:

> It is apparent that the search conducted herein was not the "reasonable search of weapons" contemplated by the *Terry* case. . . . The right to "stop and frisk" is not an open invitation to conduct an unlimited search incident to arrest or a means to effect a search to provide grounds for an arrest. Rather, it is a right to conduct a limited search for weapons. . . . The seeds and cigarette papers seized were not shown by any evidence produced at the hearing to have been taken from the defendants under circumstances which would permit a search for weapons. 483 P.2d at 232.

In another case involving objects felt in a frisk, an officer received a radio report that a murder had just been committed. The officer proceeded to the scene of the crime and observed the defendant, who fit the description that the officer had received on the radio. The officer stopped the defendant and conducted a frisk for weapons. Just after the officer started the search around the defendant's waistband, the defendant abruptly grabbed his outside upper jacket pocket. The officer moved the defendant's hand away from the pocket and from the outside felt a round cylindrical object that the officer surmised was a 12 gauge shotgun shell. He reached into the pocket and removed the object, at the same time pulling out a marijuana cigarette. The cylindrical object was revealed to be a lipstick container. The defendant was convicted of unauthorized possession of marijuana.

The reasonableness of the stop was not in question. The officer clearly had a duty to investigate the defendant on the basis of the description given over the police radio. With respect to the reasonableness of the frisk, the court found that the officer could have reasonably believed that his safety was in danger and that the frisk was justified:

> Though there is some confusion in the record it is susceptible of the inference that at the moment the officer had not yet eliminated the possibility that defendant was hiding a relatively short shotgun under his jacket. In any event a shotgun was not necessarily the only object which, in combination with a shell, could be used as a weapon. The officer could reasonably believe that any sharp object could be used as a detonator. . . . Hindsight may suggest that, in order to combine maximum personal safety for the officer with a minimum invasion of

defendant's privacy, the officer should first have ascertained what else defendant was carrying. We do not believe, however, that under the circumstances the officer was required to proceed in the coldly logical sequence which may suggest itself after the event. It appears from the record that his reaching into the pocket was almost a reflexive motion, provoked by defendant's sudden gesture toward the pocket and his own feeling of the contents. We cannot say that under all of the circumstances defendant's constitutional rights were violated. People v. Atmore, 91 Cal.Rptr. 311, 313–14 (Cal.App. 1970).

Collective Knowledge of Police

A law enforcement officer may stop a person on the basis of a wanted flyer indicating that another law enforcement agency has a reasonable suspicion that the person is or was involved in a crime. In United States v. Hensley, 469 U.S. 221, 232, 105 S.Ct. 675, 683–84, 83 L.Ed.2d 604, 614 (1985), the U.S. Supreme Court said: "[I]f a flyer or bulletin has been issued on the basis of articulable facts supporting a reasonable suspicion that the wanted person has committed an offense, then reliance on that flyer or bulletin justifies a stop to check identification . . . to pose questions to the person, or to detain the person briefly while attempting to obtain further information."

The *Hensley* case emphasized that since criminal suspects are increasingly mobile and increasingly likely to flee across jurisdictional boundaries, police in one jurisdiction should be able to act promptly in reliance on information from another jurisdiction. If a flyer has been issued in the absence of a reasonable suspicion, however, a stop in objective reliance upon it would violate the Fourth Amendment, although the officers making the stop would have a good-faith defense to any civil suit arising from the incident. Moreover, a stop made in reliance on a wanted flyer must not be significantly more intrusive than would have been permitted the agency that issued the flyer.

In United States v. Rodriquez, 831 F.2d 162 (7th Cir. 1987), the Drug Enforcement Administration (DEA) was investigating a drug distribution network and had adequate suspicion to stop the defendant's car to check his identification. A DEA agent asked the state police to conduct the stop, and a state police officer did so. The defendant claimed that the state police officer who stopped his car had inadequate information to justify the stop. The court held as follows:

> [T]he officer making the investigatory stop might reasonably rely on the request of another investigator. The requesting DEA agent had good grounds for articulable suspicion and the detaining officer had a reasonable basis for believing the request to be well-founded—even though she did not personally know the facts giving rise to the suspicion. Unlike *Hensley*, here the automobile to be stopped with its occupant was pointed out specifically by the requesting officer, and the detaining officer knew the requesting officer was coordinating a large investigation with local agencies. The state trooper was therefore merely acting as an "extension" or agent of the DEA agent and she could act on the DEA agent's suspicions. 831 F.2d at 166.

Other Unusual Circumstances

In Modesto v. State, 258 A.2d 287 (Del.Super. 1969), after a high-speed chase, a law enforcement officer stopped the defendant's vehicle for speeding. The officer asked the defendant to get out of the vehicle. The defendant turned toward the officer and proceeded to take off his coat while he was still seated in the car. As he got out of the car he dropped the coat on the passenger seat where he had been sitting. The officer thought it was peculiar for the defendant to remove his coat on a cold November night, so the officer grabbed the coat as the defendant was getting out. The officer noticed a pistol on the passenger seat, which had been covered by the coat, and the officer seized the pistol.

The court analyzed the reasonableness of both the stop and the frisk:

> The question then becomes whether or not the policeman acted legally when he reached into the car and picked up the defendant's coat. It should be noted that this case involves an incident where the police had a duty to act in stopping the vehicle. It is not a case of general exploratory investigation. Since the police had a duty to act, they also had a right to take reasonable measures to see that their safety was not endangered. . . . In view of the lateness of the hour, the high speed chase, the number of men in the car [3], the fact that the men had been drinking, the police acted reasonably in self protection in asking the gentlemen to get out of the car. Moreover, under these facts, it was reasonable for the police to conduct a limited pat-down search for weapons. A person cannot avoid such a search of his clothing by removing his clothing when it necessarily remains in the general vicinity where he is to remain. The police do not have to risk watching three men to make sure that they did not at any time go back to the clothing left in the car. And the mere fact that the coat was removed is another circumstance justifying a self protection frisk search. 258 A.2d at 288.

In another case, two police officers received information over the police radio that a shooting had occurred. The suspects were described as two black men in dark clothing and one Puerto Rican in light clothing. The officers proceeded to the scene of the shooting and spotted a black man in dark clothing and a Puerto Rican in light clothing, walking together near the scene, acting normally. The only reasons the police had to connect the two men with the reported shooting were that they were walking in the general area and they fit the limited description police had been given. The police had no information about the physical makeups or characteristics of the men they were seeking. The officers stopped the two men, frisked them on the spot, and found a gun in the defendant's belt.

The court discussed the stop and frisk aspects of the case together:

> A policeman may legally stop a person and question him. But he may not without a warrant restrain that person from walking away and "search" his clothing, unless he has "probable cause" to arrest that person or he observes such unusual and suspicious conduct on the part of the person who is stopped and searched that the policeman may reasonably conclude that criminal activity may be afoot, and that the person with whom he is dealing may be armed and dangerous. Commonwealth v. Berrios, 263 A.2d 342, 343 (Pa. 1970).

The court found that the circumstances of this case would *not* warrant a reasonably prudent man in the belief that his safety or the safety of others was in danger:

> If the policemen were constitutionally justified in searching Berrios under these circumstances, then every Puerto Rican wearing light clothing and walking with a negro in this area could likewise be validly searched. This, we cannot accept. 263 A.2d at 344.

MISCELLANEOUS ISSUES IN STOP AND FRISK

Stop and Frisk and Miranda

As discussed in Chapter 13, the *Miranda* warnings must be given before any questioning of a person in custody or otherwise deprived of freedom of action in any significant way. Are the warnings required to be given before questioning in connection with a stop and frisk?

Most courts agree that a short period of on-the-scene questioning pursuant to a stop and frisk does not require the *Miranda* warnings because the *Miranda* decision was designed to protect against the dangers of compulsion arising when a suspect is swept from familiar surroundings and questioned in a coercive, police-dominated atmosphere. This compelling atmosphere is usually not present in a stop and frisk situation. First, the questions in a stop and frisk situation are not considered to be interrogative but rather are usually neutral and brief. Second, an ordinary stop and frisk situation does not involve taking a person into custody, nor does it involve a significant deprivation of the person's freedom of action.

The key word is *significant*. Although there is definitely a deprivation of a person's freedom of action, because the detention and questioning is brief, casual, and limited in scope, courts have usually not considered it significant enough to require the *Miranda* warnings. If, however, circumstances develop that create a coercive and compelling atmosphere resulting in a significant deprivation of a person's freedom of action, *Miranda* warnings are required. For example, if the police outnumber the suspects, questioning is sustained and accusatory, force is used, or other coercive factors are present, alone or in combination, then very likely the warnings will be required. In other words, in determining custody for *Miranda* purposes, "the ultimate inquiry is simply whether there is a 'formal arrest or restraint on freedom of movement' of the degree associated with a formal arrest." California v. Beheler, 463 U.S. 1121, 1125, 103 S.Ct. 3517, 3520, 77 L.Ed.2d 1275, 1279 (1983).

In Utsler v. State, 171 N.W.2d 739 (S.D. 1969), police officers were alerted by radio to be on the lookout for a white Mustang with California license plates believed to be driven by a person involved in a robbery in a nearby town. When the officers spotted a car fitting that description, they stopped the driver (the defendant), asked him for identification, and asked if he had been in the town where the robbery occurred. The defendant replied that he had. No *Miranda* warnings had been given before the questions.

The court found nothing in the circumstances surrounding the questioning that amounted to an in-custody interrogation calling for *Miranda* warnings:

> Miranda does not bar all inquiry by authorities without previous warnings. . . . In our opinion Miranda was not intended to prohibit police officers from asking suspicious persons such things as their names and recent whereabouts without fully informing them of their constitutional rights. 171 N.W.2d at 743.

State v. Lane, 467 P.2d 304 (Wash. 1970), held that law enforcement officers need not give the *Miranda* warnings before asking questions related to the officers' immediate physical protection. In that case, police were looking for the defendant, who was suspected of robbing a store at gunpoint. Several days after the robbery, eyewitnesses to the robbery recognized the defendant in public and informed police of his whereabouts. Police then broke into the defendant's apartment and placed him under arrest. One officer handcuffed the defendant while the other proceeded to give the defendant *Miranda* warnings. A third officer interrupted, asking, "Do you have the gun?" The defendant replied "I don't have the gun. I wouldn't be dumb enough to have it here."

The defendant claimed on appeal that this potentially incriminating statement should not have been admitted in court because he had not been given the *Miranda* warnings. The court found, however, that the questions were not designed to elicit incriminating information but were apparently for one reason only—the physical protection of the police. The police had good reason to believe the defendant was armed and dangerous because the defendant had an extensive past history of robbery and burglary. The court discussed a quotation from *Terry v. Ohio*:

> "[I]t would appear to be clearly unreasonable to deny the officer the power to take necessary measures to determine whether the person is in fact carrying a weapon and to neutralize the threat of physical harm." Although Terry v. Ohio involved a "stop and frisk" situation which was tested by the reasonableness standard of the Fourth Amendment, we believe the concern there expressed is equally applicable when the Fifth Amendment is involved. Accordingly, we hold that it is not a violation of either the letter or spirit of *Miranda* for police to ask questions which are strictly limited to protecting the immediate physical safety of the police themselves and which could not reasonably be delayed until after warnings are given. 467 P.2d at 306.

Frisking of Persons of the Opposite Sex

The frisking of a person of the opposite sex presents a delicate situation for which there are few specific guidelines. On the one hand, in many situations a law enforcement officer could reasonably fear that a person of the opposite sex presented a danger to the officer or to other persons. On the other hand, if routine frisk procedures are used on a person of the opposite sex, an officer may be subjected to charges of assault or sexual misconduct. Therefore, an examination of the outer clothing of a person of the opposite sex should not be undertaken without some degree of certainty that the person is armed. The officer may ask a person to remove an overcoat or other covering, and the officer may squeeze handbags, shoulder bags, or other containers. Containers should not be opened unless a weaponlike object is felt. If the person is arrested, the search and seizure of clothing, pockets, bags, and bundles is governed by the law of search incident to arrest (see Chapter 7).

Luggage and Other Containers

In United States v. Place, 462 U.S. 696, 103 S.Ct. 2637, 77 L.Ed.2d 110 (1983), the U.S. Supreme Court held that the principles of the *Terry* case apply to the warrantless seizure and limited investigation of personal luggage. In that case, based on information from law enforcement officers in Miami, Drug Enforcement Administration (DEA) agents at a New York airport believed that the defendant might be carrying narcotics. Upon the defendant's arrival at the airport, the agents approached him, informed him of their suspicion, and requested and received identification from him. When the defendant refused to consent to a search of his luggage, one of the agents told him that they were going to take the luggage to a federal judge to try to obtain a search warrant. The agents then took the luggage to another airport where they subjected it to a "sniff test" by a trained narcotics detection dog, and the dog reacted positively to one of the bags. At this point, approximately ninety minutes had elapsed since the seizure of the luggage. The agents later obtained a search warrant for the luggage and, upon opening the luggage, discovered a large quantity of cocaine.

As in the *Terry* case, the Court balanced the nature and quality of the intrusion on the individual's Fourth Amendment interests against the importance of the governmental interests alleged to justify the intrusion. The court found a substantial governmental interest in detecting drug trafficking, a unique problem because it is highly organized and conducted by sophisticated criminal syndicates, the profits are enormous, and drugs are easily concealed. The Court said:

> The context of a particular law enforcement practice, of course, may affect the determination whether a brief intrusion on Fourth Amendment interests on less than probable cause is essential to effective criminal investigation. Because of the inherently transient nature of drug courier activity at airports, allowing police to make brief investigative stops of persons at airports on reasonable suspicion of drug-trafficking substantially enhances the likelihood that police will be able to prevent the flow of narcotics into distribution channels. 462 U.S. at 704, 103 S.Ct. at 2643, 77 L.Ed.2d at 119.

With respect to the intrusion on Fourth Amendment rights, the Court found that seizures of property can vary in intrusiveness and that some brief detentions of personal effects may be so minimally intrusive that strong countervailing governmental interests will justify a seizure based only on specific articulable facts that the property contains contraband or evidence of a crime. The Court held that "when an officer's observations lead him reasonably to believe that a traveler is carrying luggage that contains narcotics, the principles of Terry and its progeny would permit the officer to detain the luggage briefly to investigate the circumstances that aroused his suspicion, provided that the investigative detention is properly limited in scope." 462 U.S. at 706, 103 S.Ct. at 2644, 77 L.Ed.2d at 120.

In addition, the Court specifically found that the brief investigation of the luggage could include a "canine sniff" by a well-trained narcotics detection dog. This procedure was found to be uniquely limited in nature because it does not require opening the luggage, it does not expose noncontraband items to view, and it discloses only the presence or absence of narcotics, a contraband item.

Nevertheless, the Court found that the scope of the investigative detention of the luggage in the *Place* case exceeded the limits established in the *Terry* case, primarily because of the length of the detention. The Court said:

> Although the 90-minute detention of respondent's luggage is sufficient to render the seizure unreasonable, the violation was exacerbated by the failure of the agents to accurately inform respondent of the place to which they were transporting his luggage, of the length of time he might be dispossessed, and of what arrangements would be made for return of the luggage if the investigation

dispelled the suspicion. In short, we hold that the detention of respondent's luggage in this case went beyond the narrow authority possessed by police to detain briefly luggage reasonably suspected to contain narcotics. 462 U.S. at 710, 103 S.Ct. at 2646, 77 L.Ed.2d at 122.

Although the Court did not establish any rigid time limitation on an investigative detention, it clearly indicated that efforts of officers to minimize the intrusion on Fourth Amendment rights would be considered in determining the reasonableness of the detention.

Other types of containers, besides luggage, can also be detained for investigative purposes. In United States v. Van Leeuwen, 397 U.S. 249, 90 S.Ct. 1029, 25 L.Ed.2d 282 (1970), a postal clerk advised a policeman that he was suspicious of two packages of coins that had just been mailed. The policeman immediately noted that the return address was fictitious and that the person who mailed the packages had Canadian license plates. Later investigation disclosed that the addresses on both packages (one in California, the other in Tennessee) were under investigation for trafficking in illegal coins. Upon this basis, a search warrant for both packages was obtained, but not until the packages had been detained for slightly more than a day. The defendants were convicted of trafficking in illegal coins.

The Court upheld the warrantless detention of the packages while the investigation was made, recognizing nevertheless that a detention of mail could at some point become an unreasonable seizure of "papers" or "effects" within the meaning of the Fourth Amendment. The Court emphasized, however, that the investigation was conducted promptly and that most of the delay was attributable to the fact that the Tennessee authorities could not be reached until the following day because of a time zone differential. As in the *Place* case, the length of time of the detention was an important determinant of the detention's reasonableness.

SUMMARY

A law enforcement officer may intrude upon a person's freedom of action and *stop* the person for purposes of investigating possible criminal behavior even though the officer does not have probable cause to arrest the person. A stop is the least intrusive type of seizure of a person governed by the Fourth Amendment. Under that amendment, a person has been seized only if, in view of all the circumstances surrounding the incident, a reasonable person would have believed that he or she was not free to leave.

The officer making a stop must be able to justify the stop with specific circumstances indicating possibly criminal behavior. This investigative detention must last no longer than necessary to achieve its purpose, and the investigative methods used must be the least intrusive means reasonably available to verify or dispel the officer's suspicion.

A law enforcement officer may, upon less than probable cause, intrude upon a person's privacy for purposes of conducting a protective search for weapons, or a *frisk*. A frisk is not automatically authorized whenever there is a stop. The officer must be able to demonstrate that the circumstances reasonably indicated that the person might be armed and dangerous. Furthermore, the frisk must be very strictly limited to a protective purpose. Evidence of crime obtained during a properly conducted frisk will be admissible in court.

The standard to be applied for both the stop and the frisk is whether the action taken by the officer was reasonable at its inception and limited in scope to what was minimally necessary for the accomplishment of the lawful purpose. This standard was developed by the U.S. Supreme Court as a result of a careful balancing of the needs of the police to prevent and investigate crime and to protect themselves and others from danger against the constitutional rights of individuals to their privacy, security, and freedom of action. Achieving an equitable balance in the infinite variety of encounters between police and citizens requires a careful consideration of the totality of the facts and circumstances.

REVIEW AND DISCUSSION QUESTIONS

1. Name some of the factors that might distinguish a *Terry*-type investigative stop from a seizure tantamount to an arrest.

2. In determining whether he or she has a reasonable suspicion that criminal activity is afoot, must an officer have a particular crime in mind?

3. Is less evidence required to support an investigative stop for a suspected serious violent crime than for a minor misdemeanor?

4. If an officer reasonably believes that a person is armed and dangerous, may the officer frisk the person regardless of the circumstances? Will any weapons found be admissible in evidence?

5. How does the indicia of reliability test for evaluating an informant's tip in the stop and frisk situation differ from the totality of the circumstances test of the *Gates* case discussed in Chapter 6? Why should there be different tests?

6. Must there be an *immediate* possibility of criminal activity to justify a *Terry*-type investigative stop, or would a possibility of criminal activity at some time in the future suffice?

7. Assuming that a frisk of a person is warranted, how extensive a search is permitted? Can the officer look for razor blades, nails, vials of acid, or mace containers? Can the officer look into briefcases, shopping bags, purses, hatbands, and other containers?

8. Should an officer conducting a roadblock-type stop to check licenses and registrations be allowed to order every driver stopped out of his or her vehicle? What factors might provide justification to frisk a driver or passengers in this situation?

9. Assuming that a law enforcement officer reasonably believes that a suspect is dangerous and may gain immediate control of weapons from an automobile, how extensive a protective search of the automobile may be made? May the officer look into suitcases and other containers?

10. If law enforcement officers have a reasonable suspicion that a package contains contraband, does the length of time that they may detain the package for investigation depend upon whether a person is carrying the package?

PART FOUR
Confessions, Identification, and Electronic Surveillance

CHAPTER 13
Admissions and Confessions

Since the U.S. Supreme Court decision in Miranda v. Arizona, 384 U.S. 436, 86 S.Ct. 1602, 16 L.Ed.2d 694 (1966), the name *Miranda* has become very familiar to criminal justice personnel throughout the United States. The *Miranda* decision radically changed the course of law enforcement in the area of admissions, confessions, and interrogations. This chapter focuses on the *Miranda* decision and the multitude of other court decisions interpreting *Miranda*. Other aspects of the law governing admissions and confessions are also discussed.

HISTORICAL BACKGROUND

Before 1964, the test for the admissibility of a defendant's admission or confession was its "voluntariness." An involuntary statement was ruled inadmissible because it violated the due process clause of the Fourteenth Amendment to the Constitution. Involuntary statements violate due process for the following reasons: First, an involuntary statement is considered to be inherently untrustworthy or unreliable, and convictions based on unreliable evidence violate due process. Second, coercive police practices are a violation of "fundamental fairness," an essential element of due process. Therefore, a confession coerced by the police violates due process, even if that confession is otherwise reliable. Finally, free choice is an essential aspect of due process, and an involuntary confession cannot be the product of a person's free and rational choice.

The voluntariness test was established in Brown v. Mississippi, 297 U.S. 278, 56 S.Ct. 461, 80 L.Ed. 682 (1936), in which the U.S. Supreme Court held that a confession coerced from a defendant by means of police brutality violated due process of law. Later cases established that various other forms of police coercive conduct, including the more subtle psychological pressures, might render a resulting confession involuntary and thus violative of due process. In addition to outright brutality and violence, the following kinds of police conduct were found to violate due process:

1. Threats of violence. State v. Jennings, 367 So.2d 357 (La. 1979).

2. Confinement of the suspect in a small space until the suspect confessed. United States v. Koch, 552 F.2d 1216 (7th Cir. 1977).

3. Deprivation of food or sleep. Robinson v. Smith, 451 F.Supp. 1278 (W.D.N.Y. 1978).

4. Extended periods of incommunicado interrogation. Ashcraft v. Tennessee, 322 U.S. 143, 64 S.Ct. 921, 88 L.Ed. 1192 (1944); Davis v. North Carolina, 384 U.S. 737, 86 S.Ct. 1761, 16 L.Ed.2d 895 (1966).

5. Promises of leniency. Brady v. United States, 397 U.S. 742, 90 S.Ct. 1463, 25 L.Ed.2d 747 (1970).

6. Trickery or deception. Spano v. New York, 360 U.S. 315, 79 S.Ct. 1202, 3 L.Ed.2d 1265 (1959). However, some courts have adopted the view that "[c]onfessions generally are not vitiated when they are obtained by deception or trickery, as long as the means employed are not calculated to produce an untrue statement." Matter of D.A.S., 391 A.2d 255 (D.C. 1978).

7. Obtaining of a statement during a period of unnecessary delay between arrest and arraignment. McNabb v. United States, 318 U.S. 332, 63 S.Ct. 608, 87 L.Ed. 819 (1943); Mallory v. United States, 354 U.S. 449, 77 S.Ct. 1356, 1 L.Ed.2d 1479 (1957). The *McNabb* and *Mallory* cases apply only to federal courts and hold that any admission or confession obtained during an unreasonable delay between arrest and appearance before a magistrate will be inadmissible in court. The *McNabb-Mallory* rule has been codified in the Federal Criminal Code (18 U.S.C. §3501), and several states have adopted similar provisions.

Courts also examine the personal characteristics of defendants in determining the voluntariness of an admission or confession. Some of the characteristics considered important are age; mental capacity; education level; physical or mental impairment from illness, injury, or intoxication; and prior experience in dealing with the police. The U.S. Supreme Court said that these personal characteristics are "relevant only in establishing a setting in which actual coercion might have been exerted to overcome the will of the suspect." Procunier v. Atchley, 400 U.S. 446, 453–54, 91 S.Ct. 485, 489, 27 L.Ed.2d 524, 531 (1971). The Court elaborated in Colorado v. Connelly, stating that "while mental condition is surely relevant to an individual's susceptibility to police coercion, mere examination of the confessant's state of mind can never conclude the due process inquiry. . . . [C]oercive police activity is a necessary predicate to the finding that a confession is not 'voluntary' within the meaning of the Due Process Clause of the Fourteenth Amendment." 479 U.S. 157, 165–67, 107 S.Ct. 515, 521–22, 93 L.Ed.2d 473, 483–84 (1986). Therefore, absent coercive conduct by the police, even an inexperienced young person with a mental disorder could be found to have made a voluntary confession.

Determination of the voluntariness of an admission or confession can be summarized as follows:

1. If no police coercion occurred, any statement will be considered voluntary, regardless of the mental or physical condition of the suspect.

2. If police coercion occurred, the voluntariness of the statement will be evaluated on the basis of the totality of the circumstances surrounding the giving of the statement. Except for the use of physical violence by the police, no single fact or circumstance will be solely determinative.

In 1964, a major change in the law took place. In the case of Escobedo v. Illinois, 378 U.S. 478, 84 S.Ct. 1758, 12 L.Ed.2d 977 (1964), the U.S. Supreme Court held that "where . . . the investigation is no longer a general inquiry into an unsolved crime but has begun to focus on a particular suspect, the suspect has been taken into police custody, the police carry out a process of interrogations that lends itself to eliciting incriminating statements, the suspect has requested and been denied an opportunity to consult with his lawyer, and the police have not effectively warned him of his absolute constitutional right to remain silent, the accused has been denied 'the Assistance of Counsel' in violation of the Sixth Amendment to the Constitution as 'made obligatory upon the States by the Fourteenth Amendment,' . . . and . . . no statement elicited by the police during the interrogation may be used against him at a criminal trial." 378 U.S. at 491, 84 S.Ct. at 1765, 12 L.Ed.2d at 986.

The *Escobedo* case was significant not only because it shifted the area of inquiry from due process to the Sixth Amendment, but also because it did not follow a totality of the circumstances approach. Instead, the Court took a single circumstance and made it the single determinative factor in all cases in which it occurred. The Court said that "when the process shifts from investigatory to accusatory—when its focus is on the accused and its purpose is to elicit a confession . . . the accused must be permitted to consult with his lawyer." 378 U.S. at 492, 84 S.Ct. at 1766, 12 L.Ed.2d at 987. This has come to be known as the *Escobedo focus of investigation* test.

Miranda v. Arizona, decided two years later in 1966, again rejected a totality of the circumstances approach, extended the *Escobedo* decision, and shifted the area of inquiry to the Fifth Amendment. In short, the *Miranda* case held that "the prosecution may not use statements, whether exculpatory or inculpatory, stemming from custodial interrogation of the defendant unless it demonstrates the use of procedural safeguards effective to secure the privilege against self-incrimination." 384 U.S. at 444, 86 S.Ct. at 1612, 16 L.Ed.2d at 706. Such statements may not be used to prove the case against the defendant even if the statements were otherwise voluntary. If the statements were not voluntary, they will be inadmissible even though the *Miranda* requirements were satisfied.

FACTS AND HOLDINGS OF MIRANDA

The Court's opinion in *Miranda v. Arizona* encompasses three other cases besides *Miranda*, all dealing with the admissibility of statements obtained from a person who is subjected to custodial police interrogation. A brief description of the facts of each case is presented to delineate the scope of the opinion.

In *Miranda v. Arizona*, the defendant was arrested at his home for rape and taken to a police station where he was identified by the complaining witness. The defendant was then interrogated and within two hours signed a written confession. At no time was the defendant informed of his right to consult with an attorney, his right to have an attorney present during the interrogation, or his right not to be compelled to incriminate himself.

In *Vignera v. New York*, the defendant was apprehended in connection with a robbery and was taken to detective squad headquarters. The defendant was interrogated, confessed, and was then locked up. About eight hours later, the defendant was interrogated again and gave a written statement. At no time was the defendant informed of any of his rights.

In *Westover v. United States*, the defendant was arrested by municipal police as a robbery suspect. The municipal police, and later the FBI, interrogated the defendant at the municipal police department. After two hours of questioning, the defendant signed two confessions. The Court noted that the FBI interrogation was conducted following the interrogation by municipal police in the same police station—in the same compelling surroundings.

In *California v. Stewart*, the defendant was arrested at his home where police found proceeds from a robbery. The defendant was then taken to a police station and placed in a cell, where, over a period of five days, he was interrogated nine times. The Court noted that the defendant was isolated with his interrogators at all times except when he was being confronted by an accusing witness.

In each of these cases, the defendant was questioned by police officers, detectives, or a prosecuting attorney in unfamiliar surroundings, cut off from the outside world. In none of the cases was the defendant given a full and effective warning of his rights at the outset of the interrogation process. In all of the cases, the questioning elicited oral statements. In three of the cases, signed statements were also given, and those statements were admitted into evidence at trial. Thus, all the cases shared the features of incommunicado interrogation of a person in a police-dominated atmosphere, resulting in self-incriminating statements without full warnings of constitutional rights.

In *Miranda*, the Court reviewed the facts in each case and then discussed specific police interrogation techniques as prescribed in police manuals. In condemning those techniques, the Court said:

> It is obvious that such an interrogation environment is created for no purpose other than to subjugate the individual to the will of his examiner. This atmosphere carries its own badge of intimidation. To be sure, this is not physical intimidation, but it is equally destructive of human dignity. The current practice of incommunicado interrogation is at odds with one of our Nation's most cherished principles—that the individual may not be compelled to incriminate himself. Unless adequate protective devices are employed to dispel the compulsion inherent in custodial surroundings, no statement obtained from the defendant can truly be the product of his free choice. 384 U.S. at 457–58, 86 S.Ct. at 1619, 16 L.Ed.2d at 714.

The Court then established procedural safeguards to protect the privilege against self-incrimination. Those safeguards are the *Miranda* warnings so familiar to law enforcement personnel.

> [W]hen an individual is taken into custody or otherwise deprived of his freedom by the authorities in any significant way and is subjected to questioning, the privilege against self-incrimination is jeopardized. Procedural safeguards must be employed to protect the privilege and unless other fully effective means are adopted to notify the person of his right of silence and to assure that the exercise of the right will be scrupulously honored, the following measures are required. He must be warned prior to any question that he has the right to remain silent, that anything he says can be used against him in a court of law, that he has the right to the presence of an attorney, and that if he cannot afford

an attorney one will be appointed for him prior to any questioning if he so desires. Opportunity to exercise these rights must be afforded to him throughout the interrogation. After such warnings have been given, and such opportunity afforded him, the individual may knowingly and intelligently waive these rights and agree to answer questions or make a statement. But unless and until such warnings and waiver are demonstrated by the prosecution at trial no evidence obtained as a result of interrogation can be used against him. 384 U.S. at 478–79, 86 S.Ct. at 1630, 16 L.Ed.2d at 726.

ISSUES OF MIRANDA

The *Miranda* decision has raised many questions; in general, the issues can be divided into two categories:

1. The first category is whether *Miranda* requirements apply to the particular case. Under this general heading, the issues are whether the defendant's statements were the result of interrogation, whether the interrogator was a law enforcement officer or agent, and whether the seriousness of the offense has any bearing.

2. The second category is whether *Miranda* requirements have been met in a case in which they apply. Under this general heading, the issues are whether the warnings were adequate, whether rights were clearly waived, whether the suspect was competent to waive the rights, and whether more than one interrogation is allowed under *Miranda*.

In short, the major issues of *Miranda* hinge on the meaning of four terms: *custody, interrogation, warning,* and *waiver*. The remainder of this chapter is devoted to a discussion of the meanings of these terms as well as a discussion of additional miscellaneous issues.

CUSTODY

The warnings required by the *Miranda* case must be given before police question a person who is in custody or deprived of his or her freedom of action in any significant way. "Although the circumstances of each case must certainly influence a determination of whether a suspect is 'in custody' for purposes of receiving *Miranda* protection, the ultimate inquiry is simply whether there is a 'formal arrest or restraint on freedom of movement' of the degree associated with a formal arrest." California v. Beheler, 463 U.S. 1121, 1125, 103 S.Ct. 3517, 3520, 77 L.Ed.2d 1275, 1279 (1983). In other words, has there been a seizure tantamount to arrest? (See Chapter 4.)

The following discussion examines various factors considered by the courts in determining whether a person is in custody for *Miranda* purposes.

Focus of Investigation

The *Miranda* decision is generally understood to have abandoned the focus of investigation test of the *Escobedo* case to determine when an interrogated suspect is entitled to warnings. United States v. Feather, 801 F.2d 157 (4th Cir.

1986). Courts now hold that even though (1) an officer knows the suspect committed the crime, or (2) the officer intends to arrest the suspect at the end of the questioning, or (3) the officer would not allow the suspect to leave if the suspect tried, *Miranda* warnings need not be given if the interview is not otherwise custodial. State v. Hall, 468 P.2d 598 (Ariz. 1970). The U.S. Supreme Court specifically held that, even though a suspect is clearly the focus of a criminal investigation, the suspect need not be given *Miranda* warnings if he or she is not otherwise in custody or deprived of freedom of action in any significant way. Beckwith v. United States, 425 U.S. 341, 96 S.Ct. 1612, 48 L.Ed.2d 1 (1976).

The focus concept may still have some vitality as one of the circumstances to be considered by a court in determining the custody issue. In a case in which three agents interviewed a suspect in his home, the court said that in the absence of actual arrest, something must be said or done by the authorities, either in their manner or approach or in the tone or extent of their questioning, that indicates they would not have heeded a request to depart or have allowed the suspect to do so. The court went on to say:

> This is not to say that the amount of information possessed by the police and the consequent acuity of their "focus," is irrelevant. The more cause for believing the suspect committed the crime, the greater the tendency to bear down in interrogation and to create the kind of atmosphere of significant restraint that triggers Miranda. . . . United States v. Hall, 421 F.2d 540, 545 (2d Cir. 1969).

Therefore, an interview with a suspect could initially be noncustodial in all respects. However, as the questioning became more intense and pointed, a reasonable person might no longer feel free to go about personal and business affairs. A court might decide that, at this point, the person was significantly deprived of freedom of action and thus entitled to *Miranda* warnings.

Place of Interrogation

Court decisions interpreting *Miranda* hold that the place of interrogation is an important, but not conclusive, factor in determining custody. The following discussion analyzes cases that have placed strong reliance on the place of interrogation in determining the question of custody.

POLICE STATIONS. In all four of the cases decided by the *Miranda* opinion, the suspect was questioned in a police station after arrest. There is little question that custody exists in this type of situation. Other courts have held that even if a person is not under arrest but is present at a police station for questioning at the command of the police, the person is in custody for purposes of *Miranda*. United States v. Pierce, 397 F.2d 128 (4th Cir. 1968).

In Oregon v. Mathiason, 429 U.S. 492, 97 S.Ct. 711, 50 L.Ed.2d 714 (1977), however, the U.S. Supreme Court held that a suspect questioned in a police station is not necessarily in custody. In that case, the defendant, a parolee, was a suspect in a burglary. A state police officer asked him to come to the state police offices "to discuss something." When the defendant arrived, the officer took him into a closed office and told him that he was not under arrest. The officer then informed the defendant that he was a suspect in the burglary and falsely stated that the defendant's fingerprints had been found at the scene.

Within five minutes, the defendant confessed to the burglary. He left the office one-half-hour later.

The Court held that the *Miranda* warnings were not required because the defendant was not in custody.

> There is no indication that the questioning took place in a context where respondent's freedom to depart was restricted in any way. He came voluntarily to the police station, where he was immediately informed that he was not under arrest. At the close of a one half-hour interview respondent did in fact leave the police station without hindrance. It is clear from these facts that Mathiason was not in custody "or otherwise deprived of his freedom of action in any significant way." . . . .

> Any interview of one suspected of a crime by a police officer will have coercive aspects to it, simply by virtue of the fact that the police officer is part of a law enforcement system which may ultimately cause the suspect to be charged with a crime. But police officers are not required to administer Miranda warnings to everyone whom they question. Nor is the requirement of warnings imposed simply because the questioning takes place in the station house, or because the questioned person is one whom the police suspect. Miranda warnings are required only where there has been such a restriction on a person's freedom as to render him "in custody." It was that sort of coercive environment to which Miranda by its terms was made applicable, and to which it is limited. 429 U.S. at 495, 97 S.Ct. at 714, 50 L.Ed.2d at 719.

PRISONS AND JAILS. In Mathis v. United States, 391 U.S. 1, 88 S.Ct. 1503, 20 L.Ed.2d 381 (1968), a person who was incarcerated in a penitentiary for one offense was held to be in custody for purposes of an interrogation conducted by IRS (Internal Revenue Service) agents with respect to another offense. However, in United States v. Conley, 779 F.2d 970, 972–73 (4th Cir. 1985), the court said:

> We decline to read *Mathis* as compelling the use of *Miranda* warnings prior to all prisoner interrogations and hold that a prison inmate is not automatically always in "custody" within the meaning of *Miranda*. . . . A different approach to the custody determination is warranted in the paradigmatic custodial prison setting where, by definition, the entire population is under restraint of free movement. The Ninth Circuit has taken the position that "restriction" is a relative concept and that, in this context, it "necessarily implies a change in the surroundings of the prisoner which results in an added imposition on his freedom of movement." . . . We agree that this approach best reconciles *Mathis* and *Miranda* in the unique context of prisons and the problems peculiar to their administration. 779 F.2d at 972–73.

Therefore, in United States v. Cooper, 800 F.2d 412 (4th Cir. 1986), the court found that questioning of a prisoner that took place in a disciplinary boardroom occurred in an inherently less restrictive area than the defendant's cell and that the questioning was therefore noncustodial.

HOMES. Ordinarily, interrogation of a person in that person's home is noncustodial because the person is in the privacy and comfort of the home and there is an absence of a "police-dominated atmosphere." However, in Orozco

v. Texas, 394 U.S. 324, 89 S.Ct. 1095, 22 L.Ed.2d 311 (1969), a suspect was questioned at 4:00 A.M. in his bedroom by four officers, one of whom later testified that the suspect was under arrest. The Court held that even though the questioning was brief and the suspect was in familiar surroundings, the interrogation was custodial. The key reasons for the decision were the time of the interrogation, the number of officers present, and the somewhat unclear evidence of formal arrest.

PLACES OF BUSINESS. Interrogation of a person at his or her place of business is usually held to be noncustodial. Like the home, the place of business represents a familiar surrounding. United States v. Venerable, 807 F.2d 745 (8th Cir. 1986). However, in United States v. Steele, 648 F.Supp. 1375 (N.D. Ind. 1986), a postal employee who was approached at her work station, asked to accompany two postal inspectors to a small room in the post office, and questioned for an hour and forty-five minutes was found to be in custody. The court said:

> The defendant was not subjected to severe restraint on her physical freedom. She was not handcuffed nor locked in any type of detention facility. In addition, she was not faced with a large number of police officers. She was, however, placed in a closely confined area and confronted by two government agents. Because this was an environment in which the defendant had no control, the physical restraint used, and the show of authority made by the inspectors remain significant. 648 F.Supp. at 1379.

The court also noted that the postal inspectors represented not only law enforcement authority, but the authority of the defendant's employer as well. The court found that "a reasonable person would not feel free to rebuff the inspectors out of fear of jeopardizing his or her job as well as encouraging criminal suspicion. Because the interrogators had the power to initiate criminal charges and to terminate the defendant's job, this situation involved coercion greater than the more common situation involving a suspect approached on the street by a police officer." 648 F.Supp. at 1378.

STORES, RESTAURANTS, AND OTHER PUBLIC PLACES. Public places such as stores, restaurants, and bars are considered less familiar to a suspect than a home or office. Nevertheless, courts usually find that an interrogation conducted in these places is noncustodial, because the suspect is in a place of personal choice and is not isolated from the outside world. In addition, there is usually not a police-dominated atmosphere in a public place. Lucas v. United States, 408 F.2d 835 (9th Cir. 1969).

HOSPITALS. Questioning of a suspect who is confined in a hospital as a patient but who is not under arrest is usually held to be a noncustodial interrogation. United States v. Martin, 781 F.2d 671 (9th Cir. 1986). Factors supporting such a holding are a lack of a compelling atmosphere, a routine nature of questioning, and a lack of any deprivation of the defendant's freedom by the police. However, if the questioning is intense and pointed or if the suspect is very sick or highly drugged, a hospital interview could be held custodial. State v. Ross, 157 N.W.2d 860 (Neb. 1968).

CRIME SCENES. In *Miranda*, the Court said that its decision was "not intended to hamper the traditional function of police officers in investigating crime. . . . General on-the-scene questioning as to facts surrounding a crime or other general questioning of citizens in the fact-finding process is not affected by our holding. It is an act of responsible citizenship for individuals to give whatever information they may have to aid in law enforcement. In such situations the compelling atmosphere inherent in the process of in custody interrogation is not necessarily present." 384 U.S. at 477–78, 86 S.Ct. at 1629–30, 16 L.Ed.2d at 725–26.

In general, courts have held that the questioning of a suspect near the scene of a crime before an arrest is made is not custodial interrogation. People v. Schwartz, 30 A.D.2d 385, 292 N.Y.S.2d 518 (N.Y.App.Div. 1968). In State v. Oxentine, 154 S.E.2d 529 (N.C. 1967), for example, the defendant shot the victim in the defendant's home. When the police arrived at the scene and asked what happened, the defendant replied that he shot the victim. The court held that the defendant was not in custody or deprived of his freedom in any significant way and that *Miranda* warnings were not required. "We do not interpret this important decision [*Miranda*] to exclude statements made at the scene of an investigation when nobody has been arrested, detained, or charged." 154 S.E.2d at 531.

BRIEF STREET ENCOUNTERS. The ordinary *Terry*-type investigative stop and the ordinary traffic stop are noncustodial and do not require the administration of *Miranda* warnings. The U.S. Supreme Court said:

> Under the Fourth Amendment . . . a policeman who lacks probable cause but whose "observations lead him reasonably to suspect" that a particular person has committed, is committing, or is about to commit a crime, may detain that person briefly in order to "investigate the circumstances that provoke suspicion." . . . "[T]he stop and inquiry must be 'reasonably related in scope to the justification for their initiation.'" . . . Typically, this means that the officer may ask the detainee a moderate number of questions to determine his identity and to try to obtain information confirming or dispelling the officer's suspicions. But the detainee is not obliged to respond. And, unless the detainee's answers provide the officer with probable cause to arrest him, he must then be released. The comparatively nonthreatening character of detentions of this sort explains the absence of any suggestion in our opinions that *Terry* stops are subject to the dictates of *Miranda*. The similarly noncoercive aspect of ordinary traffic stops prompts us to hold that persons temporarily detained pursuant to such stops are not "in custody" for the purposes of *Miranda*. Berkemer v. McCarty, 468 U.S. 420, 439–40, 104 S.Ct. 3138, 3150, 82 L.Ed.2d 317, 334–35 (1983).

Time of Interrogation

An interrogation conducted during business hours is less likely to be considered custodial than is an interrogation carried out in the late evening or early morning. The time of the interrogation was a significant reason for holding the interrogation at the suspect's home to be custodial in the *Orozco* case (see earlier discussion under "Homes"). Had the questioning of the suspect taken place during business hours, that interrogation might have been held to be noncustodial.

Presence of Other Persons

The *Miranda* decision expressly indicated a concern for the suspect who is "cut off from the outside world." 384 U.S. at 445, 86 S.Ct. at 1612, 16 L.Ed.2d at 707. Courts have interpreted this to mean that the presence of family, friends, or neutral persons during the interrogation of a suspect may render the interrogation noncustodial. People v. Butterfield, 65 Cal.Rptr. 765 (Cal.App. 1968). Correspondingly, the deliberate removal of a suspect from the presence of family and friends is indicative of custody. Commonwealth v. Sites, 235 A.2d 387 (Pa. 1967). Some courts speak of a "balance of power" and find custody to exist where the sheer number of police indicates a police-dominated atmosphere. Orozco v. Texas, 394 U.S. 324, 89 S.Ct. 1095, 22 L.Ed.2d 311 (1969).

Suspect under Arrest or Restraint

A suspect who is told that he or she is under arrest is definitely in custody for *Miranda* purposes. Duckett v. State, 240 A.2d 332 (Md. Spec. App. 1968). Conversely, a suspect who is told that he or she is not under arrest and is free to leave at any time is usually not considered to be in custody for *Miranda* purposes. United States v. Guarno, 819 F.2d 28 (2d Cir. 1987).

Physical restraint of a suspect short of formal arrest is usually indicative of custody. State v. Saunders, 435 P.2d 39 (Ariz. 1967). By the same token, an absence of physical restraint has led courts to conclude that the defendant was not in custody. People v. Merchant, 67 Cal.Rptr. 459 (Cal.App. 1968). The physical restraint of a person must be accomplished by law enforcement officers, however, or the restraint is not custody for *Miranda* purposes. In Wilson v. Coon, 808 F.2d 688 (8th Cir. 1987), a brief restraint of the defendant by a medical technician for medical purposes was held not to constitute custody.

If an officer holds a gun on a suspect, the officer clearly creates a custodial situation. People v. Shivers, 286 N.Y.S.2d 827, 233 N.E.2d 836 (N.Y. 1967). However, if the suspect is also armed, a court is unlikely to find that the suspect was in custody. Yates v. United States, 384 F.2d 586 (5th Cir. 1967).

The absence of other incidents of arrest such as handcuffing, searching, fingerprinting, photographing, and other booking procedures tends to indicate a noncustodial interview. Hicks v. United States, 382 F.2d 158 (D.C. Cir. 1967). The use of these procedures leads to the contrary conclusion. People v. Ellingsen, 65 Cal.Rptr. 744 (Cal.App. 1968).

A probationer, although subject to a number of restrictive conditions governing various aspects of life, is not in custody for purposes of *Miranda* simply by reason of the probationer status. Furthermore, an interview between a probationer and a probation officer, which is noncustodial in all respects, does not become custodial for *Miranda* purposes because the probation officer could compel attendance and truthful answers at the interview. Minnesota v. Murphy, 465 U.S. 420, 104 S.Ct. 1136, 79 L.Ed.2d 409 (1984).

Duration and Nature of Questioning

The duration and nature of an interrogation is significant in determining custody for purposes of *Miranda*. Most courts that allow questioning without *Miranda* warnings at crime scenes and during brief street encounters emphasize that the questioning is of short duration and involves only a few general investigative questions. Such brief, routine police inquiries generally indicate a noncustodial setting.

In Allen v. United States, 390 F.2d 476 (D.C. Cir. 1968), an officer stopped a car being driven in an unusual manner by the defendant. A passenger in the car was injured and bleeding. The defendant gave suspicious answers to the officer's questions. When the officer asked the passenger if he had been beaten and by whom, the passenger mumbled something and pointed at the defendant. The officer then asked the defendant if he had beaten the passenger and the defendant said yes. The court held that the officer acted properly by asking routine questions to clarify the situation. The court found that *Miranda* warnings were unnecessary, pointing out that warnings hamper and perhaps demean routine police investigation and make cooperative citizens nervous.

Psychological Restraints

Even when a person is not physically restrained, psychological restraints may be so powerful as to create an atmosphere of coercion constituting custody for *Miranda* purposes. In United States v. Beraun-Panez, 812 F.2d 578 (9th Cir. 1987), the court said:

> Although not physically bound, Beraun-Panez was subjected to psychological restraints just as binding. Accusing Beraun-Panez repeatedly of lying, confronting him with false or misleading witness statements, employing good guy/bad guy tactics, taking advantage of Beraun-Panez's insecurities about his alien status, keeping him separated from his co-worker in a remote rural location, insisting on the "truth" until he told them what they sought, the officers established a setting from which a reasonable person would believe that he or she was not free to leave. 812 F.2d at 580.

Interview Initiated by Suspect

If a suspect summons the police or initiates the interview, or both, a court is likely to hold that subsequent police interrogation is noncustodial. In United States v. Jonas, 786 F.2d 1019 (11th Cir. 1986), the defendant learned indirectly that an FBI agent wanted to contact him. He called the agent, agreed to talk with the FBI, and appeared voluntarily at FBI offices. The interview was held to be noncustodial.

Statements to Undercover Agents or Informants

Suspects who do not know they are speaking to a law enforcement officer cannot have a reasonable belief that they are in custody. Therefore, questioning by undercover agents or informants is usually considered to be noncustodial.

Hoffa v. United States, 385 U.S. 293, 87 S.Ct. 408, 176 L.Ed.2d 374 (1966); United States v. Jones, 801 F.2d 304 (8th Cir. 1986).

INTERROGATION

The *Miranda* requirements apply only if a person in custody is subjected to interrogation. In Rhode Island v. Innis, 446 U.S. 291, 100 S.Ct. 1682, 64 L.Ed.2d 297 (1980), the U.S. Supreme Court explained the meaning of *interrogation* for purposes of *Miranda*.

> [T]he Miranda safeguards come into play whenever a person in custody is subjected to either express questioning or its functional equivalent. That is to say, the term "interrogation" under Miranda refers not only to express questioning, but also to any words or actions on the part of police (other than those normally attendant to arrest and custody) that the police should know are reasonably likely to elicit an incriminating response from the suspect. 446 U.S. at 300–301, 100 S.Ct. at 1689, 64 L.Ed.2d at 307–8.

The Court further refined the definition by stating that an incriminating response is any response—whether inculpatory or exculpatory—that the prosecution may seek to introduce at trial. Although this definition of interrogation is broad, many situations in which a person converses with or gives information to a law enforcement officer are not considered to be interrogation for *Miranda* purposes and do not require *Miranda* warnings.

Volunteered Statements

The most obvious situation not constituting interrogation is a volunteered statement—a statement made of a person's own volition and not in response to questioning by a law enforcement officer. In the *Miranda* opinion, the Court stated that "[v]olunteered statements of any kind are not barred by the Fifth Amendment and their admissibility is not affected by our holding today." 384 U.S. at 478, 86 S.Ct. at 1630, 16 L.Ed.2d at 726.

Volunteered statements sometimes occur when a person simply walks up to a police officer on the street or walks into a police station and makes incriminating statements. People v. Hines, 57 Cal.Rptr. 757, 425 P.2d 557 (Cal. 1967). Volunteered statements occur more frequently, however, when a person is in custody, either before, during, or after interrogation. Deck v. United States, 395 F.2d 89 (9th Cir. 1968). Volunteered statements may occur during interrogation when the suspect makes an incriminating statement that is not in response to an officer's question. For example, in Parson v. United States, 387 F.2d 944 (10th Cir. 1968), an officer asked the defendant where the key to his car was, so the car could be moved off the street and put in storage. The defendant replied that the car had been stolen. The court held that the statement that the car was stolen was not responsive to the inquiry about the key and was completely voluntary.

Law enforcement officers need not interrupt a volunteered statement in order to warn a suspect of *Miranda* rights. The *Miranda* decision specifically states that "[t]here is no requirement that police stop a person who enters a police station and states that he wishes to confess to a crime, or a person who calls the police to offer a confession or any other statement he desires to make." 384 U.S. at 478, 86 S.Ct. at 1630, 16 L.Ed.2d at 726.

Clarifying Questions

Since many volunteered statements are ambiguous, an officer hearing a statement may try to clarify what is being said. Courts have held that a statement is volunteered even if some questions are asked by police. The questions must not, however, be directed to expand upon what the person originally intended to say, but merely to clear up or explain the original statement. People v. Sunday, 79 Cal.Rptr. 752 (Cal.App. 1969).

In People v. Savage, 242 N.E.2d 446 (Ill. App. 1968), a man walked into a police station and said, "I done it; I done it; arrest me; arrest me." The officer asked him what he had done and the man said he killed his wife. Then the officer asked him how, and the man replied, "With an axe, that's all I had." The court held that the officer's clarifying questions were not interrogation and that no *Miranda* warnings were required.

Brief and Routine Questions

In the determination of custody, a brief and routine nature of questioning is usually indicative of a lack of custody. Courts have also held that brief and routine questioning is not interrogation under *Miranda*, even if the suspect is in custody.

Brief, routine questions are asked by law enforcement officers in a great variety of situations. If the questions are not reasonably likely to elicit an incriminating response, the questions are not interrogation for purposes of *Miranda*. For example, in South Dakota v. Neville, 459 U.S. 553, 565 n. 15, 103 S.Ct. 916, 923 n. 15, 74 L.Ed.2d 748, 759 n.15 (1983), the U.S. Supreme Court held that a police inquiry to determine whether a suspect will take a blood alcohol test is not an interrogation within the meaning of *Miranda*. Nor is police questioning of a suspect to ensure that the suspect understands his or her duty to submit to an alcohol test. State v. Allen, 485 A.2d 953 (Me. 1984). In addition, the routine gathering of background biographical information, such as questioning during routine booking procedures, will not ordinarily constitute interrogation where the questions of identity are not directly related to the facts of the crime being investigated. United States v. Feldman, 788 F.2d 544 (9th Cir. 1986). Therefore, questions about name, age, residence, social security number, and employment are usually not considered to be interrogation.

Spontaneous Questions

When law enforcement officers ask questions spontaneously, impulsively, or in response to an emergency, the questions are usually held not to be interrogation. In People v. Morse, 452 P.2d 607 (Cal. 1969), a jailer and a guard were called to a cell area where they found a prisoner near death from strangling. While tending to the injured prisoner, they asked the defendant, who was also a prisoner, about the incident and received incriminating replies. The court held that this questioning was couched in a context of "stupefied wonder-ment," not one of incisive inquiry, and that the questioning was not interroga-tion for purposes of *Miranda*.

In Turner v. Sullivan, 661 F.Supp. 535 (E.D.N.Y. 1987), a law enforcement of-ficer asked, "What happened to you?" when the arrested defendant complained that his leg was hurting, and the defendant gave an incriminating response. The court held that there was no interrogation.

> [T]he officer's question was a natural response to petitioner's remark that his leg hurt. The statement at issue was part of a colloquy, initiated by petitioner, about his physical condition. . . . The officer's inquiry . . . was not an effort to elicit information, but rather evidenced the appropriate concern about peti-tioner's injuries. The officer could not have foreseen that the response might help the prosecution by placing defendant at the scene of the crime. Accord-ingly, because there was no interrogation and thus no *Miranda* violation, the statement was properly admitted. 661 F.Supp. at 538.

Questions Related to Public Safety

Closely related to spontaneous questions are questions asked by a law enforce-ment officer out of a concern for public safety. In New York v. Quarles, 467 U.S. 649, 104 S.Ct. 2626, 81 L.Ed.2d 550 (1984), two police officers were ap-proached by a woman who told them that she had just been raped and that her assailant had entered a nearby supermarket and was carrying a gun. One of the officers entered the store and observed the defendant, who matched the de-scription given by the woman. The officer pursued the defendant with a drawn gun and ordered the defendant to stop and put his hands over his head. The offi-cer frisked the defendant and discovered that he was wearing an empty shoul-der holster. After handcuffing the defendant, the officer asked him where the gun was and the defendant nodded toward some empty cartons and responded that "the gun is over there."

Although the defendant was in police custody when he made his statements and the facts fell within the coverage of *Miranda*, the U.S. Supreme Court held that there was a "public safety" exception to the requirement that *Miranda* warnings be given before a suspect's answers may be admitted into evidence. The Court said:

> The police in this case, in the very act of apprehending a suspect, were con-fronted with the immediate necessity of ascertaining the whereabouts of a gun which they had every reason to believe the suspect had just removed from his empty holster and discarded in the supermarket. So long as the gun was con-cealed somewhere in the supermarket, with its actual whereabouts unknown, it obviously posed more than one danger to the public safety: an accomplice might make use of it, a customer or employee might later come upon it. 467 U.S. at 657, 104 S.Ct. at 2632, 81 L.Ed.2d at 557–58.

The Court concluded that the need for answers to questions in a situation pos-ing a threat to the public safety outweighed the need for the prophylactic rule protecting the Fifth Amendment's privilege against self-incrimination. Fur-thermore, the Court held that the availability of the public safety exception does not depend upon the motivation of the individual officers involved. The Court recognized that in a spontaneous, emergency situation like the one in the

Quarles case, most police officers act out of several different, instinctive motives: a concern for their own safety and that of others, and, perhaps, the desire to obtain incriminating evidence from the suspect. A rigid adherence to the *Miranda* rules is not required when police officers ask questions reasonably prompted by a concern for the public safety.

Finally, the Court acknowledged that the public safety exception lessens the clarity of the *Miranda* rule, but expressed confidence that the police would instinctively respond appropriately in situations threatening the public safety.

> [W]e recognize here the importance of a workable rule "to guide police officers, who have only limited time and expertise to reflect on and balance the social and individual interests involved in the specific circumstances they confront." . . . But . . . we believe that the [public safety] exception . . . lessens the necessity of that on-the-scene balancing process. The exception will not be difficult for police officers to apply because in each case it will be circumscribed by the exigency which justifies it. We think police officers can and will distinguish almost instinctively between questions necessary to secure their own safety or the safety of the public and questions designed solely to elicit testimonial evidence from a suspect. 467 U.S. at 658–59, 104 S.Ct. at 2633, 81 L.Ed.2d at 559.

Confrontation of Suspects with Evidence

In general, it is proper for a law enforcement officer to confront a suspect with evidence or other facts in a case being investigated. Often, after such a confrontation, a suspect may make incriminating statements. Are these incriminating statements voluntary or are they the product of a form of "silent interrogation"?

Courts have decided the issue both ways depending on the circumstances of individual cases. When there is no verbal interrogation and the suspect is merely confronted with evidence, an accomplice, scientific reports, and so on, courts have held that incriminating statements made after the confrontation were not the product of interrogation. People v. Doss, 256 N.E.2d 753 (Ill. 1970). When, however, along with such a confrontation, an officer subtly attempts to get the suspect to talk, courts have found interrogation and have suppressed statements obtained without prior warnings. State v. LaFernier, 155 N.W.2d 93 (Wis. 1967). The crucial question under *Rhode Island v. Innis* (discussed earlier) is whether the officer's words or actions are reasonably likely to elicit an incriminating response. Toliver v. Gathright, 501 F.Supp. 148 (E.D.Va 1980).

Statements Responding to Statements by Officers

A law enforcement officer may receive an incriminating reply to a mere comment or statement that is not a question. If the officer did not intend to elicit incriminating information, the suspect's incriminating statement is usually held not to be the product of interrogation. United States v. Pellegrini, 309 F.Supp. 250 (S.D.N.Y. 1970). If, however, the officer's statement is deliberately directed toward eliciting incriminating information, courts will consider the statement as tantamount to interrogation. Brewer v. Williams, 430 U.S. 387, 97 S.Ct. 1232,

51 L.Ed.2d 424 (1977). (The facts of *Brewer v. Williams* are presented later in this chapter under the heading "Attempts after Defendant Is Formally Charged.")

Interrogation by Private Citizens

The *Miranda* warning requirements apply only to custodial interrogations conducted by *law enforcement officers*. Therefore, incriminating statements made by a person in response to custodial interrogation by a private citizen will be admissible in court despite a lack of prior warnings.

In United States v. Pace, 833 F.2d 1307 (9th Cir. 1987), the defendant's cell mate, acting on his own initiative and without prior arrangement with the government, elicited incriminating statements from the defendant. The court held that since the cell mate was not the government's agent, the government did not participate in any custodial interrogation in obtaining the confession, and no *Miranda* warnings were required.

Multiple Attempts at Interrogation

In the *Miranda* opinion, the Court said:

> Once warnings have been given, the subsequent procedure is clear. If the individual indicates in any manner, at any time prior to or during questioning, that he wishes to remain silent, the interrogation must cease. At this point he has shown that he intends to exercise his Fifth Amendment privilege; any statement taken after the person invokes his privilege cannot be other than the product of compulsion, subtle or otherwise. Without the right to cut off questioning, the setting of in custody interrogation operates on the individual to overcome free choice in producing a statement after the privilege has been once invoked. If the individual states that he wants an attorney, the interrogation must cease until an attorney is present. At that time the individual must have an opportunity to confer with the attorney and to have him present during any subsequent questioning. If the individual cannot obtain an attorney and he indicates that he wants one before speaking to police, they must respect his decision to remain silent. 384 U.S. at 473–74, 86 S.Ct. at 1627–28, 16 L.Ed.2d at 723.

The quoted language commands that once a suspect indicates either a desire to remain silent or a desire for an attorney, all questioning must stop, at least until the suspect confers with an attorney. Nevertheless, under certain circumstances, some courts have admitted statements obtained after multiple attempts to question suspects.

ATTEMPTS AFTER RIGHT TO SILENCE IS INVOKED. The U.S. Supreme Court has, under limited conditions, allowed a second interrogation of a suspect who exercised the *Miranda* right of silence after being given warnings. In Michigan v. Mosley, 423 U.S. 96, 96 S.Ct. 321, 46 L.Ed.2d 313 (1975), the defendant was arrested early in the afternoon in connection with certain robberies and was given the *Miranda* warnings by a police detective. After indicating that he understood the warnings, the defendant declined to discuss the robberies, and the detective ceased the interrogation. Shortly after 6:00 P.M. the same day, after giving another set of *Miranda* warnings, a different police detective questioned the defendant about a murder that was unrelated to the robberies. The defendant made an incriminating statement that was used against him at his trial. He was convicted of the murder.

The Court held that admitting the defendant's statement into evidence did not violate *Miranda* principles. Even though the *Miranda* opinion states that the interrogation must cease when the person in custody indicates a desire to remain silent, the Court in the *Mosley* case held that "neither this passage nor any other passage in the *Miranda* opinion can sensibly be read to create a per se proscription of indefinite duration upon any further questioning by any police officer on any subject, once the person in custody has indicated a desire to remain silent." 423 U.S. at 102–3, 96 S.Ct. at 326, 46 L.Ed.2d at 320–21. The Court then gave several reasons why it allowed the second interrogation in the *Mosley* case: The defendant's right to cut off questioning had been "scrupulously honored" by the first detective. The first detective ceased the interrogation when the defendant refused to answer and did not try to wear down his resistance by repeated efforts to make him change his mind. The second interrogation was directed toward a different crime with a different time and place of occurrence. And, the second interrogation began after a significant time lapse and after the defendant had been given a fresh set of warnings.

In United States v. Olof, 527 F.2d 752 (9th Cir. 1975), the court held that a second interrogation by federal agents, conducted three hours after the defendant had refused to make a statement after being given the *Miranda* warnings, violated the defendant's rights. Although the agents gave the defendant fresh warnings, they pressured him to cooperate and they questioned him about the same crime for which the first warnings were given.

These cases suggest the following guidelines for conducting a second custodial interrogation of a person who has exercised the *Miranda* right to remain silent.

1. Scrupulously honor the person's right to terminate questioning at the initial interrogation.

2. Allow a significant amount of time to intervene between the first and second interrogation attempts.

3. Give the person complete *Miranda* warnings again.

4. Do not employ any pressure to cooperate or other illegal tactics.

ATTEMPTS AFTER RIGHT TO COUNSEL IS INVOKED. As the quotation at the beginning of this section indicates, *Miranda* created a rigid rule that an accused's request for an attorney is per se an invocation of Fifth Amendment rights, requiring that all interrogation cease. This rigid rule is based on an attorney's unique ability to protect the Fifth Amendment rights of a client undergoing custodial interrogation. Once an accused person indicates that he or she is not competent to deal with the authorities without legal advice, courts will closely examine any later choice to make a decision without counsel's presence. Therefore, although an accused may waive *Miranda* rights and submit to interrogation, the U.S. Supreme Court has recognized that additional safeguards are necessary after an accused has exercised the right to counsel.

The Court established these safeguards in the case of Edwards v. Arizona, 451 U.S. 477, 101 S.Ct. 1880, 68 L.Ed.2d 378 (1981). In that case, the defendant voluntarily submitted to questioning but later stated that the wanted an attorney before the discussions continued. The following day, detectives accosted the defendant in the county jail, and when the defendant refused to speak with the detectives he was told that "he had" to talk. The Court held that subsequent incriminating statements made without his attorney present violated the rights secured to the defendant by the Fifth and Fourteenth Amendments. The Court stated:

> [W]hen an accused has invoked his right to have counsel present during custodial interrogation, a valid waiver of that right cannot be established by showing only that he responded to further police-initiated custodial interrogation even if he has been advised of his rights. We further hold that an accused, such as [the defendant], having expressed his desire to deal with the police only through counsel, is not subject to further interrogation by the authorities until counsel has been made available to him, unless the accused himself initiates further communication, exchanges, or conversations with the police. 451 U.S. at 484–85, 101 S.Ct. at 1884–85, 68 L.Ed.2d at 386.

Relying on the Sixth Amendment, the U.S. Supreme Court also applied the *Edwards* rule to assertions of the right to counsel made at or after the initiation of adversary judicial proceedings. The Court held that "if police initiate interrogation after a defendant's assertion, at an arraignment or similar proceeding, of his right to counsel, any waiver of the defendant's right to counsel for that police-initiated interrogation is invalid." Michigan v. Jackson, 475 U.S. 625, 636, 106 S.Ct. 1404, 1411, 89 L.Ed.2d 631, 642 (1986). Thus, whether the right to counsel is invoked during custodial interrogation or at an arraignment or similar proceeding, at or after which the defendant's Sixth Amendment right to counsel has attached, police may not further interrogate the defendant without affording him or her counsel, unless the defendant initiates further communication with the police. However, if police action after the suspect has invoked his or her right to counsel is not "interrogation" or the "functional equivalent" of interrogation, then the *Edwards* rule does not apply and the suspect's statements may be admissible.

In Arizona v. Mauro, ___ U.S. ___, 107 S.Ct. 1931, 95 L.Ed.2d 458 (1987), the defendant, who was in custody on suspicion of murdering his son, indicated that he did not wish to be questioned further without a lawyer present, and the questioning then ceased. The defendant's wife, who was being questioned in another room, asked if she could speak to her husband. They were allowed to speak, but an officer was present in the room and the conversation was tape-recorded with the couple's knowledge. The recording was used against the defendant at his trial.

The U.S. Supreme Court held that the actions of the police were not the functional equivalent of police interrogation. There was no evidence indicating that the officers sent the wife in to see her husband for the purpose of eliciting incriminating statements. Nor was the officer's presence in the room improper, since there were legitimate reasons for his presence, including the wife's safety and various security considerations. Furthermore, it is improbable that the defendant would have felt he was being coerced to incriminate himself simply because he was told his wife would be allowed to speak to him.

Even though the police knew there was a possibility that the defendant would incriminate himself, "[o]fficers do not interrogate a suspect simply by hoping that he will incriminate himself." ___ U.S. at ___, 107 S.Ct. at 1936, 95 L.Ed.2d at 468. The Court held that the officers acted reasonably and that the defendant's tape-recorded statements could be used against him at trial. "Police departments need not adopt inflexible rules barring suspects from speaking with their spouses, nor must they ignore legitimate security concerns by allowing spouses to meet in private." ___ U.S. at ___, 107 S.Ct. at 1937, 95 L.Ed.2d at 468.

The following actions by police have been held to be interrogation, or the functional equivalent of interrogation, in violation of the *Edwards* rule prohibiting further interrogation after the defendant's invocation of the right to counsel.

— Resubmitting a waiver of rights form (which the defendant previously refused to sign) accompanied by an announcement that a victim of a shooting had died and that the charge was now murder. (The waiver of rights form is discussed later in this chapter.) State v. Iovino, 524 A.2d 556 (R.I. 1987).

— Offering to explain the operation of the criminal justice system to the defendant. (The court noted that despite their seeming innocence, such explanations are often designed to inform a defendant that cooperation may be beneficial.) United States v. Johnson, 812 F.2d 1329 (11th Cir. 1986).

— Exhibiting an incriminating document to the defendant ten minutes after he had invoked his *Miranda* rights to counsel. United States v. Walker, 624 F.Supp. 103 (D.Md. 1985).

— Calling the defendant by the nickname of the person believed to have committed the particular offense. State v. Dellorfano, 517 A.2d 1163 (N.H. 1986).

— Confronting the defendant with an arrest warrant and photographs of his fingerprints taken at the crime scene. Clark v. Marshall, 600 F.Supp. 1520 (E.D. Ohio 1985).

In Smith v. Illinois, 469 U.S. 91, 105 S.Ct. 490, 83 L.Ed.2d 488 (1984), the Court held that after an accused has requested counsel, courts will not allow an accused's responses to further interrogation to be used to cast retrospective doubt on the clarity of the initial request itself. The Court said, "'No authority, and no logic, permits the interrogator to proceed . . . on his own terms and as if the defendant had requested nothing, in the hope that the defendant might be induced to say something casting retrospective doubt on his initial statement that he wished to speak through an attorney or not at all.'" 469 U.S. at 99, 105 S.Ct. at 495, 83 L.Ed.2d at 496.

In Oregon v. Bradshaw, 462 U.S. 1039, 103 S.Ct. 2830, 77 L.Ed.2d 405 (1983), the U.S. Supreme Court attempted to explain what would constitute the initiation of further communication with the police:

> [T]here are undoubtedly situations where a bare inquiry by either a defendant or by a police officer should not be held to "initiate" any conversation or dialogue. There are some inquiries, such as a request for a drink of water or a request to use a telephone that are so routine that they cannot be fairly said to represent a desire on the part of an accused to open up a more generalized discussion relating directly or indirectly to the investigation. Such inquiries or statements, by either an accused or a police officer, relating to routine inci-

dents of the custodial relationship, will not generally "initiate" a conversation in the sense in which that word was used in *Edwards*. 462 U.S. at 1045, 103 S.Ct. at 2835, 77 L.Ed.2d at 412.

In *Bradshaw,* the Court found that the defendant's question to a police officer, after the defendant had asked for an attorney, as to what was going to happen to him now "evinced a willingness and a desire for a generalized discussion about the investigation; it was not merely a necessary inquiry arising out of the incidents of the custodial relationship." 462 U.S. at 412, 103 S.Ct. at 2835, 77 L.Ed.2d at 412.

The *Edwards* case also established a second prerequisite to police interrogation of an accused who has requested an attorney. Once it is established that the accused "initiated" further conversation or dialogue with the police, the next inquiry is "whether a valid waiver of the right to counsel and the right to silence had occurred, that is, whether the purported waiver was knowing and intelligent and found to be so under the totality of the circumstances, including the necessary fact that the accused, not the police, reopened the dialogue with the authorities." 451 U.S. at 486 n. 9, 101 S.Ct. at 1885 n. 9, 68 L.Ed.2d at 387 n. 9. In the *Bradshaw* case, the Court found a knowing waiver where the police made no threats, promises, or inducements to talk; the defendant was properly advised of his rights and understood them; and within a short time the defendant changed his mind and decided to talk without any impropriety on the part of the police. In Wyrick v. Fields, 459 U.S. 42, 44, 103 S.Ct. 394, 396, 74 L.Ed.2d 214, 218 (1982), the U.S. Supreme Court held that by waiving his right to counsel at a polygraph examination, the accused also validly waived his right to have counsel present at post-test questioning, "unless the circumstances changed so seriously that his answers no longer were voluntary, or unless he no longer was making a 'knowing and intelligent relinquishment or abandonment' of his rights." (See the discussion of waiver later in this chapter.)

To summarize, before a suspect in custody can be subjected to further interrogation after requesting an attorney, there must first be a showing that the suspect initiated communication with the authorities. Once this is established, it is still necessary to establish as a separate matter the existence of a knowing and intelligent waiver of the right to counsel and the right to silence. Once a valid waiver is made, interrogation may continue until the circumstances change so seriously that the answers are no longer voluntary or until the accused revokes the waiver.

ATTEMPTS AFTER RIGHTS ARE WAIVED. Often, a suspect may waive *Miranda* rights and submit to interrogation, and after an interval of time, police may wish to interrogate the suspect again. The general rule is that warnings need not be repeated at the second interrogation. People v. Hill, 58 Cal.Rptr. 340, 426 P.2d 908 (Cal. 1967). However, some courts have required a repetition of the warnings under certain circumstances.

The Supreme Court of Pennsylvania listed five significant factors in determining whether an accused must be reinformed of his or her *Miranda* rights:

> (1) the time lapse between the last *Miranda* warnings and the accused's statement; (2) interruptions in the continuity of the interrogation; (3) whether there was a change of location between the place where the last *Miranda* warnings

were given and the place where the accused's statement was made; (4) whether the same officer who gave the warnings also conducted the interrogation resulting in the accused's statement; and (5) whether the statement elicited during complained of interrogation differed significantly from other statements which had been preceded by *Miranda* warnings. Commonwealth v. Wideman, 334 A.2d 594, 598 (Pa. 1975).

Where *Miranda* warnings are not repeated during an ongoing interrogation, the ultimate question is whether the defendant, with full knowledge of his or her legal rights, knowingly and intentionally relinquished those rights.

ATTEMPTS AFTER AN UNWARNED ADMISSION. In Oregon v. Elstad, 470 U.S. 298, 105 S.Ct. 1285, 84 L.Ed.2d 222 (1985), a law enforcement officer investigating a burglary obtained an admission from the defendant in a custodial setting without first giving the defendant the *Miranda* warnings. Shortly thereafter, at the stationhouse, the defendant was given complete *Miranda* warnings, waived his rights, and gave a written confession.

The U.S. Supreme Court held that, although the initial unwarned admission was inadmissible in court, the written confession was admissible. The Court reasoned that despite the *Miranda* violation before the officer obtained the first admission, there was no *constitutional* violation, since no coercion or other illegal means were used to break the defendant's will. (In other words, a *Miranda* violation is not a constitutional violation unless it is accompanied by other circumstances indicating that the defendant's statement was compelled.) Since the first admission was obtained without a constitutional violation, the "fruit of the poisonous tree" doctrine did not apply to the written confession obtained shortly thereafter. (That doctrine applies only to constitutional violations.)

The Court then evaluated the written statement as follows:

> We must conclude that, absent deliberately coercive or improper tactics in obtaining the initial statement, the mere fact that a suspect has made an unwarned admission does not warrant a presumption of compulsion. A subsequent administration of *Miranda* warnings to a suspect who has given a voluntary but unwarned statement ordinarily should suffice to remove the conditions that precluded admission of the earlier statement. In such circumstances, the finder of fact may reasonably conclude that the suspect made a rational and intelligent choice whether to waive or invoke his rights. 470 U.S. at 314, 105 S.Ct. at 1296, 84 L.Ed.2d at 235.

For the law enforcement officer, the lesson from the *Elstad* case is that after an admission is obtained as a result of interrogating a suspect, the officer should carefully comply with all *Miranda* procedures in all subsequent interrogations, before obtaining further statements, no matter how much time has elapsed between interrogations. This will ensure that even if an earlier statement is ruled inadmissible because of a *Miranda* violation, later statements will have a better chance of being admitted. Furthermore, even if an officer believes that a statement has been obtained in violation of *Miranda*, the officer need not warn that the prior statement cannot be used against the suspect. "Police officers are ill equipped to pinch-hit for counsel, construing the murky and difficult questions of when 'custody' begins or whether a given unwarned statement will ultimately be held inadmissible." 470 U.S. at 316, 105 S.Ct. at 1297, 84 L.Ed.2d at 237.

ATTEMPTS AFTER DEFENDANT IS FORMALLY CHARGED. In Massiah v. United States, 377 U.S. 201, 84 S.Ct. 1199, 12 L.Ed.2d 246 (1964), after the defendant was indicted, federal agents obtained incriminating statements from the defendant in the absence of his counsel. While the defendant was free on bail, his co-defendant, in cooperation with the federal agents, engaged the defendant in conversation in the presence of a hidden radio transmitter. The Court held that the statements were inadmissible because the defendant was denied the basic protection of his Sixth Amendment right to assistance of counsel.

The *Massiah* decision has become less significant in recent years because the *Miranda* decision has resulted in courts shifting their emphasis from the Sixth Amendment to the Fifth Amendment. Nevertheless, as stated by the Fifth Circuit Court of Appeals:

> [I]t [*Massiah*] retains its vitality and stands as a supplement to *Miranda: Massiah* teaches that although the government may properly continue to gather evidence against a defendant after he has been indicted, it may not nullify the protection *Miranda* affords a defendant by using trickery to extract incriminating statements from him that otherwise could not be obtained without first giving the required warnings. Today *Massiah* simply means that after indictment and counsel has been retained the Fifth Amendment prevents law enforcement authorities from deliberately eliciting incriminating statements from a defendant by the surreptitious methods used in that case. United States v. Hayles, 471 F.2d 788,791 (5th Cir. 1973).

The U.S. Supreme Court affirmed the continuing validity of the *Massiah* case in Brewer v. Williams, 430 U.S. 387, 97 S.Ct. 1232, 51 L.Ed.2d 424 (1977). In that case, the defendant had been arrested, arraigned, and jailed in Davenport, Iowa, for abducting a ten-year-old girl in Des Moines, Iowa, and was being transported by police to Des Moines to talk to his lawyer there. Both the defendant's Des Moines lawyer and the lawyer at his Davenport arraignment advised the defendant not to make any statements until after he had consulted with his Des Moines lawyer. The police officers who were to accompany the defendant on the trip agreed not to question him during the trip. Nevertheless, one of the police officers, who knew that the defendant was a former mental patient and was deeply religious, suggested that the defendant reveal the location of the girl's body because her parents were entitled to a Christian burial for the girl, who was taken away from them on Christmas Eve. The defendant eventually made several incriminating statements during the trip and finally directed the police to the girl's body.

The U.S. Supreme Court, citing *Massiah*, held that a person against whom adversary proceedings have commenced has a right to legal representation when the government interrogates him or her. Since the officer's "Christian burial" speech was tantamount to interrogation and the defendant had been formally charged, the defendant was entitled to the assistance of counsel at the time he made the incriminating statements. The Court found that the defendant did not waive his right to counsel, and therefore held any evidence relating to or resulting from his statements inadmissible.

In United States v. Henry, 447 U.S. 264, 100 S.Ct. 2183, 65 L.Ed.2d 115 (1980), the U.S. Supreme Court held inadmissible statements made by an indicted and imprisoned defendant to a paid undisclosed government informant who was in the same cell block. Although the informant did not question the defendant, the informant "stimulated" conversations with the defendant and developed a relationship of trust and confidence with the defendant. As a result, the defendant made incriminating statements without the assistance of counsel. This indirect and surreptitious type of interrogation was an impermissible interference with the defendant's right to the assistance of counsel in violation of *Massiah*. The Court emphasized the potential susceptibility of an incarcerated person to subtle influences of government undercover agents.

Futhermore, even when a confrontation between an accused and a police agent is initiated by the accused, the government may not deliberately attempt to elicit information without counsel being present. In Maine v. Moulton, 474 U.S. 159, 106 S.Ct. 477, 88 L.Ed.2d 481 (1985), the U.S. Supreme Court said that the guarantee of the Sixth Amendment includes the government's affirmative obligation not to act in a manner that circumvents the protections accorded the accused who invokes his or her right to rely on counsel as a "medium" between the accused and the government. The Court continued:

> [T]he Sixth Amendment is not violated whenever—by luck or happenstance—the State obtains incriminating statements from the accused after the right to counsel has attached.... However, knowing exploitation by the State of an opportunity to confront the accused without counsel being present is as much a breach of the State's obligation not to circumvent the right to assistance of counsel as is the intentional creation of such an opportunity. Accordingly, the Sixth Amendment is violated when the State obtains incriminating statements by knowingly circumventing the accused's right to have counsel present in a confrontation between the accused and a state agent. 474 U.S. at 176, 106 S.Ct. at 487, 88 L.Ed.2d at 496.

The *Henry* and *Moulton* cases illustrate that courts will carefully examine any attempts to circumvent the right of any formally charged person to have counsel present at a confrontation between the person and police agents. But, as the first sentence of the preceding quotation indicates, the defendant's Sixth Amendment rights are not violated when an informant, either through prior arrangement or voluntarily, reports the defendant's incriminating statements to the police. "[T]he defendant must demonstrate that the police and their informant took some action, beyond merely listening, that was designed deliberately to elicit incriminating remarks." Kuhlmann v. Wilson, 477 U.S. 436, 106 S.Ct. 2616, 91 L.Ed.2d 364 (1986).

This prohibition against attempts to elicit information in the absence of counsel is not intended to hamper police investigations of crimes other than the crime for which adversary proceedings have already commenced. The police need to investigate crimes for which formal charges have already been filed as well as new or additional crimes. Either type of investigation may require surveillance of persons already indicted. Moreover, police who are investigating a person suspected of committing one crime and formally charged with having committed another crime may seek to discover evidence useful at a trial of either crime. In seeking evidence relating to pending charges, however, police investigative powers are limited by the Sixth Amendment rights of the accused. Therefore, incriminating statements relating to pending charges will be inadmissible at the trial of those charges, even though police were also investigating other crimes, if, in obtaining the evidence, the government violated the Sixth Amendment by knowingly circumventing the accused's right to the assistance of counsel. On the other hand, evidence relating to charges to which the Sixth Amendment right to counsel had not attached at the time the evidence was obtained will not be inadmissible merely because other charges were pending at the time. Maine v. Moulton, 474 U.S. 159, 106 S.Ct. 477, 88 L.Ed.2d 481 (1985).

WARNING

The warnings that must be given by a law enforcement officer before conducting a custodial interrogation are as follows:

1. You have the right to remain silent.

2. Anything you say can and will be used against you in a court of law.

3. You have the right to consult with a lawyer and to have the lawyer present with you while you are being questioned.

4. If you cannot afford to hire a lawyer, a lawyer will be appointed to represent you before any questioning, if you wish.

Manner of Giving Warnings

Miranda warnings must be stated clearly and in an unhurried manner—so that the person warned understands his or her rights and feels free to claim them without fear. The warnings should not be given in a careless, indifferent, and superficial manner.

When warnings are given to an immature, illiterate, or mentally impaired person, the warnings must be given in language that the person can comprehend and on which the person can knowingly act. If necessary, the officer should explain and interpret the warnings. The test is whether the words used by the officer, in view of the age, intelligence, and demeanor of the individual being interrogated, convey a clear understanding of all *Miranda* rights. Anderson v. State, 253 A.2d 387 (Md. Spec. App. 1969).

Does the Suspect Require Warnings?

SUSPECT KNOWS HIS OR HER RIGHTS. The *Miranda* opinion made it clear that law enforcement officers are not to assume that any suspect knows his or her rights:

> The Fifth Amendment privilege is so fundamental to our system of constitutional rule and the expedient of giving an adequate warning as to the availability of the privilege so simple, we will not pause to inquire in individual cases whether the defendant was aware of his rights without a warning being given. Assessments of the knowledge the defendant possessed, based on information as to his age, education, intelligence, or prior contact with authorities, can never be more than speculation: a warning is a clearcut fact. More important, whatever the background of the person interrogated, a warning at the time of the interrogation is indispensable to overcome its pressures and to insure that the individual knows he is free to exercise the privilege at that point in time. 384 U.S. at 468–69, 86 S.Ct. at 1625, 16 L.Ed.2d at 720.

SUSPECT IS NOT INDIGENT. If a suspect is known to be financially able to afford a lawyer, officers need not give the warning that a lawyer will be appointed in case of indigency. However, a law enforcement officer may not always be able to correctly determine a person's financial status, and "the expedient of giving a warning is too simple and the rights involved too important to engage in *ex post facto* inquiries into financial ability when there is any doubt at all on that score." (emphasis supplied) 384 U.S. at 473, 86 S.Ct. at 1627, 16 L.Ed.2d at 723. Therefore, officers should give the complete set of *Miranda* warnings before conducting any custodial interrogation.

SUSPECT HAS AN ATTORNEY PRESENT. The *Miranda* opinion implies that the warnings are not required to be given to persons who have an attorney present with them:

> The presence of counsel . . . would be the adequate protective device necessary to make the process of police interrogation conform to the dictates of the privilege. His presence would insure that statements made in the government-established atmosphere are not the product of compulsion. 384 U.S. at 466, 86 S.Ct. at 1623, 16 L.Ed.2d at 719.

WAIVER

A *waiver* is a voluntary and intentional relinquishment of a known right. The *Miranda* decision held that the defendant may waive the rights conveyed in the *Miranda* warnings "provided the waiver is made voluntarily, knowingly and intelligently." 384 U.S. at 475, 86 S.Ct. at 1628, 16 L.Ed.2d at 724. The inquiry whether the defendant has made a full and effective waiver has two distinct dimensions. As stated by the U.S. Supreme Court:

> First the relinquishment of the right must have been voluntary in the sense that it was the product of a free and deliberate choice rather than intimidation, coercion or deception. Second, the waiver must have been made with a full awareness both of the nature of the right being abandoned and the consequences of the decision to abandon it. Only if the "totality of the circumstances surrounding the interrogation" reveal both an uncoerced choice and the requisite level of comprehension may a court properly conclude that the *Miranda* rights have been waived. Moran v. Burbine, 475 U.S. 412, 421, 106 S.Ct. 1135, 1141, 89 L.Ed.2d 410, 421 (1986).

To satisfy this totality of the circumstances test, law enforcement officers must know what constitutes a waiver and must follow recommended procedures in obtaining the waiver. They also must be aware of the legal concerns involved in the two-dimensional inquiry regarding the validity of a waiver: (1) voluntariness and (2) requisite level of comprehension.

Obtaining a Waiver

After the *Miranda* warnings have been administered, the law enforcement officer should first ask the suspect if he or she understands the rights that have been explained. The officer should then ask the suspect if he or she wishes to talk without first consulting a lawyer or having a lawyer present during questioning. If the officer receives an affirmative answer to both questions, the officer should carefully note the exact language in which the answer was given in order to preserve it for possible future use in court. The officer may then proceed with the interrogation of the suspect.

If possible, the officer should always try to obtain a written waiver of rights from the suspect before questioning. A written waiver is almost always held to be sufficient if the suspect is literate and there is no evidence of police coercion. Menendez v. United States, 393 F.2d 312 (5th Cir. 1968). The following form is suggested for this purpose.

Waiver of Rights

I have had my rights explained to me and I understand what my rights are.

I am willing to answer questions and make a statement.

I do not want a lawyer at this time.

I understand and know what I am doing.

No promises or threats have been made to me and no pressure or coercion of any kind has been used against me.

Signed

Time   Date

Witness

Witness

If a written statement is obtained as a result of questioning, it should also be signed by the suspect and witnesses. The statement should indicate the place, date, and time the taking of the statement began and the place, date, and time the statement was signed by the suspect. As a further substantiation of the validity of the waiver, it is also suggested that the law enforcement officer ask the suspect to sign the form entitled "Reaffirmation of Waiver" after a written statement is obtained.

Law enforcement officers may not always be able to obtain written waivers or unambiguous oral waivers. Suspects may express themselves through an infinite variety of words and actions, which courts may or may not determine to be valid waivers of *Miranda* rights. Some suspects may be indecisive and may never clearly claim or waive their rights. Nevertheless, waiver of *Miranda* rights must be proved by the prosecution by a preponderance of the evidence. Colorado v. Connelly, 479 U.S. 157, 107 S.Ct. 515, 93 L.Ed.2d 473 (1986). Moreover, the absence of any evidence of waiver will result in a finding of no waiver and the exclusion of any statement obtained. Tague v. Louisiana, 444 U.S. 469, 100 S.Ct. 652, 62 L.Ed.2d 622 (1980). Therefore, when no written waiver or unambiguous oral waiver can be obtained, law enforcement officers should write

---

Reaffirmation of Waiver

The entire statement I have just made and signed consisting of _____ pages was made by me after I carefully considered the rights I was giving up in making the statement.

At no time while I was making the statement did I decide to or indicate any desire to reclaim any of those rights.

Signed

Time   Date

Witness

Witness

---

down all circumstances surrounding the attempt to obtain waiver so that the prosecution will have evidence to prove that the waiver was voluntary, knowing, and intelligent.

Some courts require officers to cease all questioning if a suspect's exercise of the right to counsel is ambiguous. These courts allow further questioning only after the suspect's intention is clarified and the right to counsel is unequivocally waived. United States v. Nordling, 804 F.2d 1466 (9th Cir. 1986).

Words and Actions Indicating Waiver

When a defendant has been fully informed of his or her *Miranda* rights, any comprehensible oral statement of understanding and willingness to speak is usually acceptable as a waiver of rights. Examples of valid waivers are cases in which a suspect said, "I might as well tell you about it," United States v. Boykin, 398 F.2d 483, 484 (3d Cir. 1968); "I'll tell you," State v. Kremens, 245 A.2d 313, 315 (N.J. 1968); or, "I know all that," State v. Brown, 202 So.2d 274, 279 (La. 1967). Courts have also approved nonverbal waivers such as nods and shrugs. Mullaney v. State, 246 A.2d 291 (Md. 1968). After receiving a waiver in any of these forms, the law enforcement officer may begin questioning of the suspect.

Often a suspect will indicate an understanding of *Miranda* rights and then simply begin to make a statement without any other verbal or nonverbal indication of waiver. Most courts have held that once the suspect has been informed of *Miranda* rights and indicates an understanding of those rights, choosing to speak without a lawyer present is sufficient evidence of a knowing and voluntary waiver of the rights. United States v. Puig, 810 F.2d 1085 (11th Cir. 1987). However, this rule is probably valid only if the statement of the suspect follows closely after the suspect indicates an understanding of the warnings. Billings v. People, 466 P.2d 474 (Colo. 1970).

A suspect who indicates a desire to talk to a lawyer at some time in the future but who agrees to answer questions without a lawyer has waived the right to counsel. Thompson v. State, 235 So.2d 354 (Fla.Dist.Ct.App. 1970).

A request to see someone other than a lawyer is not considered to be an assertion of rights under *Miranda*, although a denial of such a request may have some bearing on the voluntariness of the statements. For example, in Fare v. Michael C., 442 U.S. 707, 99 S.Ct. 2560, 61 L.Ed.2d 197 (1979), the U.S. Supreme Court held that a juvenile waived his *Miranda* rights even though he had been denied a request to speak to his probation officer. The Court found that the request, made by an experienced older juvenile with an extensive prior record, did not per se constitute a request to remain silent nor was it tantamount to a request for an attorney. However, some states require a parent, guardian, or other interested adult to be notified before a juvenile may be found to have waived *Miranda* rights.

A request for counsel made by a suspect to a friend or relative is not the same as a request to the police. Therefore, even if the police are aware of such a request, the request does not operate as an exercise of *Miranda* rights. People v. Smith, 246 N.E.2d 689 (Ill.App. 1969).

Once a suspect has been given *Miranda* warnings, the suspect's refusal to give a written statement outside the presence of his or her attorney does not render ineffective the suspect's clear waiver of rights for the purpose of giving an oral statement. In Connecticut v. Barrett, 479 U.S. 523, 107 S.Ct. 828, 93 L.Ed.2d 920 (1987), the suspect, who was in custody on a sexual assault charge, was given the *Miranda* warnings and indicated to the police that he would not make a written statement outside the presence of his attorney. He then clearly expressed his willingness to speak with the police without an attorney and made an oral statement admitting his involvement in the sexual assault.

The Court held that the defendant's exercise of his right to counsel was limited by its terms to the making of written statements and did not prohibit further police questioning leading to the oral confession. Although the settled approach to questions of waiver requires giving a broad rather than a narrow interpretation to a defendant's request for counsel, the Court said:

> Interpretation is only required where the defendant's words, understood as ordinary people would understand them, are ambiguous. Here, however, Barrett made clear his intentions, and they were honored by police. To conclude that respondent invoked his right to counsel for all purposes requires not a broad interpretation of an ambiguous statement, but a disregard of the ordinary meaning of respondent's statement. 479 U.S. at 529–30, 107 S.Ct. at 832, 93 L.Ed.2d at 928.

When a suspect indicates, after giving a valid written or oral waiver, a desire not to have any notes taken, this may suggest that the suspect erroneously believes that oral statements cannot be used as evidence in court. The law enforcement officer should explain that oral statements can be used against the suspect in court. Otherwise, a court might invalidate the waiver. Frazier v. United States, 419 F.2d 1161 (D.C. Cir. 1969).

Voluntariness of Waiver

In Colorado v. Connelly, 479 U.S. 157, 107 S.Ct. 515, 93 L.Ed.2d 473 (1986), the U.S. Supreme Court held that the voluntariness inquiry in the *Miranda* waiver context was the same as that in the Fifth Amendment confession context. The Court said:

> The sole concern of the Fifth Amendment, on which *Miranda* was based, is governmental coercion. . . . The voluntariness of a waiver of this privilege has always depended on the absence of police overreaching, not on "free choice" in any broader sense of the word. 479 U.S. at 170, 107 S.Ct. at 523, 93 L.Ed.2d at 486.

Therefore, absent evidence that a suspect's will was overborne and his or her capacity for self-determination critically impaired because of coercive police conduct, the suspect's waiver of *Miranda* rights will be considered voluntary. The *Connelly* case holds that even if a suspect is compelled to waive *Miranda* rights for some psychological or other reason, if the compulsion did not flow from the police, the waiver will not be held involuntary.

Psychological tactics, such as playing on the defendant's sympathies or explaining that honesty is the best policy, have been variously interpreted by courts in determining the voluntariness of a defendant's waiver. Some courts apply a totality of the circumstances test to determine whether the defendant's will was overborne or his or her capacity for self-determination was critically impaired. In United States v. Pelton, 835 F.2d 1067 (4th Cir. 1987), the court said:

> Agents may properly initiate discussions on cooperation, and may indicate that they will make this cooperation known. . . . General encouragement to cooperate is far different from specific promises of leniency. 835 F.2d at 1073.

With respect to the use of psychological tactics, the Third Circuit Court of Appeals said:

> These ploys may play a part in the suspect's decision to confess, but so long as that decision is a product of the suspect's own balancing of competing considerations the confession is voluntary. The question . . . is whether . . . statements were so manipulative or coercive that they deprived [the defendant] of his ability to make an unconstrained, autonomous decision to confess. Miller v. Fenton, 796 F.2d 598, 605 (3d Cir. 1986).

Requisite Level of Comprehension

The requirement that a waiver must be made with full awareness of both the right being abandoned and the consequences of the decision to abandon that right is satisfied by careful administration of the *Miranda* warnings to a suspect. As stated by the U.S. Supreme Court:

> The Constitution does not require that a criminal suspect know and understand every possible consequence of a waiver of the Fifth Amendment privilege. . . . The Fifth Amendment's guarantee is both simpler and more fundamental: A defendant may not be compelled to be a witness against himself in any respect. The *Miranda* warnings protect this privilege by insuring that a suspect knows that he may choose not to talk to law enforcement officers, to talk only with counsel present, or to discontinue talking at any time. The *Miranda* warnings ensure that a waiver of these rights is knowing and intelligent by requiring that the suspect be fully advised of this constitutional privilege, including the critical advice that whatever he chooses to say may be used as evidence against him. Colorado v. Spring, 479 U.S. 564, 574, 107 S.Ct. 851, 857–58, 93 L.Ed.2d 954, 966 (1987).

SUSPECT'S NEED FOR ADDITIONAL USEFUL INFORMATION. Suspects often claim that their waivers of *Miranda* rights were involuntary because police or prosecutors failed to give them enough information upon which to base the decision to waive or not waive the rights. In Moran v. Burbine, 475 U.S. 412, 106 S.Ct. 1135, 89 L.Ed.2d 410 (1986), the U.S. Supreme Court held that the police are not required to inform an uncharged suspect of an attorney's attempts to reach him or her, or to otherwise keep the suspect abreast of the status of his or her legal representation, before giving *Miranda* warnings and obtaining a waiver of *Miranda* rights. In the *Burbine* case, an attorney who was contacted by the suspect's sister without the suspect's knowledge, attempted to telephone the suspect, who was in custody at the police station. The police assured the attorney that the suspect would not be questioned any further that day. Later that evening, however, police informed the suspect of his *Miranda* rights, the suspect executed a series of valid written waivers, and the suspect eventually confessed to a murder. At no point during the course of interrogation, which occurred before arraignment, did the suspect request an attorney.

The Court held that the police's failure to inform the suspect of the attorney's phone call did not deprive the suspect of information essential to his ability to knowingly waive his Fifth Amendment rights. The Court said:

> Events occurring outside the presence of the suspect and entirely unknown to him surely can have no bearing on the capacity to comprehend and knowingly relinquish a constitutional right. . . . Once it is determined that a suspect's decision not to rely on his rights was uncoerced, that he at all times knew he could stand mute and request a lawyer, and that he was aware of the state's intention to use his statements to secure a conviction, the analysis is complete and the waiver is valid as a matter of law. 475 U.S. at 422–23, 106 S.Ct. at 1141–42, 89 L.Ed.2d at 421–22.

Furthermore, whether the police conduct in the case was intentional or inadvertent, the Court held that the state of mind of the police was irrelevant to the question of the intelligence and voluntariness of the suspect's election to abandon his rights. Finally, there was no violation of the suspect's Sixth Amendment right to counsel. The Court reasoned that if that right had attached, the police would have been prohibited from interfering with the attorney's efforts to assist the suspect. But since the interrogation took place *before* the initiation of adversary judicial proceedings, the right to counsel did not attach, and the suspect could not have his confession suppressed for a violation of a right he did not have.

The Court frowned upon the police's deception of the attorney, but found that this conduct was not so offensive as to deprive the defendant of the fundamental fairness guaranteed by the due process clause of the Fourteenth Amendment. The Court specifically warned, however, that a more flagrant violation by the police might rise to the level of a due process violation. Therefore, the *Burbine* case should not be interpreted as generally approving dishonest or shady dealings by the police with defense attorneys in interrogation situations occurring before the initiation of formal charges. In fact, some states have explicitly rejected the ruling in *Moran v. Burbine* based on state constitutional law. The California Supreme Court held as follows:

[W]hether or not a suspect in custody has previously waived his rights to silence and counsel, the police may not deny him the opportunity, before questioning begins or resumes, to meet with his retained or appointed counsel who has taken diligent steps to come to his aid.

If the lawyer comes to the station before interrogation begins or while it is still in progress, the suspect must promptly be told, and if he then wishes to see his counsel, he must be allowed to do so. Moreover, the police may not engage in conduct, intentional or grossly negligent, which is calculated to mislead, delay, or dissuade counsel in his efforts to reach his client. Such conduct constitutes a denial of a California suspect's *Miranda* rights to counsel, and it invalidates any subsequent statements. People v. Houston, 230 Cal.Rptr. 141, 149, 724 P.2d 1166, 1174–75 (Cal. 1986).

In Colorado v. Spring, 479 U.S. 564, 107 S.Ct. 851, 93 L.Ed.2d 954 (1987), the defendant contended that the failure of police to inform him of the potential subjects of interrogation constituted police trickery and deception as condemned in *Miranda*, and rendered his waiver of *Miranda* rights invalid. The U.S. Supreme Court declined to hold that "mere silence by law enforcement officials as to the subject matter of an interrogation is 'trickery' sufficient to invalidate a suspect's waiver of *Miranda* rights. . . ." 479 U.S. at 576, 107 S.Ct. at 858, 93 L.Ed.2d at 967. Citing *Moran v. Burbine*, the Court said that a valid waiver does not require that police supply a suspect with all useful information to help the suspect calibrate his or her self-interest in deciding whether to speak or to stand by his or her rights. The Court concluded as follows:

> This Court's holding in *Miranda* specifically required that the police inform a criminal suspect that he has the right to remain silent and that *anything* he says may be used against him. There is no qualification of this broad and explicit warning. The warning, as formulated in *Miranda*, conveys to a suspect the nature of his constitutional privilege and the consequences of abandoning it. Accordingly, we hold that a suspect's awareness of all the possible subjects of questioning in advance of interrogation is not relevant to determining whether the suspect voluntarily, knowingly, and intelligently waived his Fifth Amendment privilege. 479 U.S. at 577, 107 S.Ct. at 859, 93 L.Ed.2d at 968.

In United States v. Tapp, 812 F.2d 177 (5th Cir. 1987), the court held that the interrogating officer's failure to inform the defendant that he was the target of the investigation did not render the defendant's waiver of *Miranda* rights involuntary.

SUSPECT'S COMPETENCY. The inquiry as to whether the suspect has the requisite level of comprehension to validly waive *Miranda* rights is also directed at the competency of the suspect. Those who might *not* be considered competent to waive their rights are persons who are in pain from injury or illness, Pea v. United States, 397 F.2d 627 (D.C. Cir. 1967); persons who are under the influence of alcohol or drugs, United States v. Guaydacan, 470 F.2d 1173 (9th Cir. 1972); persons who are psychologically or mentally disabled; and persons who are very young or very old. In determining competency to waive *Miranda* rights, courts will examine all the circumstances surrounding the waiver, with no single factor controlling.

In a case involving a juvenile, the U.S. Supreme Court stated:

> This totality of circumstances approach is adequate to determine whether there has been a waiver even where interrogation of juveniles is involved. . . . The totality approach permits—indeed, it mandates—inquiry into all the circumstances surrounding the interrogation. This includes evaluation of the juvenile's age, experience, education, background, and intelligence, and into whether he had the capacity to understand the warnings given him, the nature of his Fifth Amendment rights, and the consequences of waiving those rights. Fare v. Michael C., 442 U.S. 707, 725, 99 S.Ct. 2560, 2572, 61 L.Ed.2d 197, 212 (1979).

Additional circumstances to be considered in determining a waiver of a juvenile's rights are as follows: (1) knowledge of the accused as to the substance of the charge, if any has been filed; (2) whether the accused is held incommunicado or allowed to consult with relatives, friends or an attorney; (3) whether the accused was interrogated before or after formal charges had been filed; (4) method used in interrogation; (5) length of interrogations; and (6) whether or not the accused refused to voluntarily give statements on prior occasions. West v. United States, 399 F.2d 467 (5th Cir. 1968).

In general, the officer should carefully observe the suspect and take notes on all indications of the suspect's competence or incompetence to waive *Miranda* rights. In State v. Addington, 518 A.2d 449 (Me. 1986), the court found that the suspect's refusal to talk to officers and refusal to undergo certain tests were supportive of the conclusion that his waiver of *Miranda* rights was voluntary, knowing, and intelligent.

Generally, unless an officer is positive that the suspect is incapable of understanding and waiving *Miranda* rights, the officer should not refrain from trying to obtain a lawful confession. It is the duty of the courts, not of the law enforcement officer, to finally determine whether or not there was a voluntary, knowing, and intelligent waiver and a voluntary and trustworthy confession.

OTHER MIRANDA ISSUES

Fourth Amendment Violations

For purposes of this chapter, when a law enforcement officer attempts to obtain a statement from a person, not only must the voluntariness and *Miranda* requirements be satisfied, but the officer must not violate the person's reasonable expectation of privacy. Thus, even though a law enforcement officer has satisfied all the *Miranda* requirements in obtaining a statement from a person, the statement may still be inadmissible in court if it was obtained in violation of the person's Fourth Amendment rights.

The leading case on this subject is Katz v. United States, 389 U.S. 347, 88 S.Ct. 507, 19 L.Ed.2d 576 (1967), in which the defendant, who was in a telephone booth, was eavesdropped on by federal agents, who had attached an electronic listening and recording device to the outside of the booth. The Court held that despite the lack of an intrusion into a constitutionally protected area, the defendant's statements were inadmissible in court because they were taken in violation of his reasonable expectation of privacy. The Court said that "once it is recognized that the Fourth Amendment protects people—and not simply 'areas'—against unreasonable searches and seizures, it becomes clear that the reach of that Amendment cannot turn upon the presence or absence of a physical intrusion into any given enclosure." 389 U.S. at 353, 88 S.Ct. at 512, 19 L.Ed.2d at 583.

In Halpin v. Superior Court, 101 Cal.Rptr. 375, 495 P.2d 1295 (Cal. 1972), the incarcerated defendant's wife visited him at the jail during regular visiting hours. A detective allowed the defendant and his wife to use his office to converse, and the detective left the office. The conversation was secretly taped and was used in court against the defendant. The court ruled the tapes inadmissible, stating that law enforcement officers may not deliberately create an expectation of privacy so that a prisoner and his or her visitor will be "lulled" into believing their conversations will be confidential.

In United States v. Fisch, 474 F.2d 1071 (9th Cir. 1973), law enforcement officers were investigating a narcotics smuggling operation. The officers obtained a motel room adjacent to that of the suspects, and, by listening at the door, the officers heard a discussion of criminal acts. The officers used no electronic devices and committed no trespass. The court ruled that the statements were admissible, holding that the defendants had no justifiable expectation of privacy in their conversations. The court emphasized that a person's interest in privacy must be balanced against the public's interest in the investigation and prosecution of crime:

> Upon balance, appraising the public and private interests here involved, we are satisfied that the expectations of the defendants as to their privacy, even were such expectations to be considered reasonable despite their audible disclosures, must be subordinated to the public interest in law enforcement. In sum, there has been no justifiable reliance, the expectation of privacy not being "one that society is prepared to recognize as 'reasonable.'" 474 F.2d at 1078–79.

Misdemeanors and Other Proceedings

Miranda has been held inapplicable to minor misdemeanors and minor traffic offenses. State v. Pyle, 249 N.E.2d 826 (Ohio 1969). In State v. Macuk, 268 A.2d 1 (N.J. 1970), the New Jersey Supreme Court stated the reasons why *Miranda* rules are inapplicable to motor vehicle violations:

1. The type of police questioning used in motor vehicle violations is not ordinarily the lengthy incommunicado interrogation at which *Miranda* was aimed. Usually the questions are simple, standard, and directed toward filling out routine police reports.

2. Usually traffic violations are not serious enough to warrant the time-consuming inconvenience to the administration of justice.

3. It would be impossible to provide sufficient numbers of lawyers for all the motor vehicle violators who would be likely to request legal advice.

However, where the suspect may be exposed to a substantial term of imprisonment for a misdemeanor, *Miranda* has been held to be applicable. Commonwealth v. Bonser, 258 A.2d 675 (Pa.Super. 1969).

Other proceedings to which *Miranda* has been held inapplicable are customs procedures, civil commitments, extradition proceedings, license revocation proceedings, and field sobriety tests. In general, unless the suspect is subject to a possible substantial criminal penalty, *Miranda* warnings are not necessary.

EFFECT OF MIRANDA IN COURT

Statements taken in violation of *Miranda* requirements will be inadmissible in court to prove the defendant's guilt of crime. In recent years, however, courts have allowed the use of statements taken in violation of *Miranda* for purposes other than the proof of a defendant's guilt. In Harris v. New York, 401 U.S. 222, 91 S.Ct. 643, 28 L.Ed.2d 1 (1971), and Oregon v. Hass, 420 U.S. 714, 95 S.Ct. 1215, 43 L.Ed.2d 570 (1975), the Court admitted testimony of previous inconsistent statements taken from a defendant in violation of his *Miranda* rights solely for the purpose of impeaching the defendant's testimony at trial. Stressing that the trustworthiness of the defendant's earlier conflicting statements must satisfy legal standards, the Court in *Harris* said:

> The shield provided by *Miranda* cannot be perverted into a license to use perjury by way of a defense, free from the risk of confrontation with prior inconsistent utterances. We hold, therefore, that petitioner's credibility was appropriately impeached by use of his earlier conflicting statements. 401 U.S. at 226, 91 S.Ct. at 646, 28 L.Ed.2d at 5.

Law enforcement officers should not interpret the *Harris* and *Hass* cases as providing an opportunity to evade the requirements of the *Miranda* case. An admission or confession obtained in compliance with *Miranda* is much more valuable to the prosecution than is an illegally obtained statement to be used only for impeachment. In addition, *involuntary* statements obtained from a defendant cannot be used for any purpose in a criminal trial. The U.S. Supreme Court has stated that "*any* criminal trial use against a defendant of his *involuntary* statement is a denial of due process of law, 'even though there is ample evidence aside from the confession to support the conviction.'" Mincey v. Arizona, 437 U.S. 385, 398, 98 S.Ct. 2408, 2416, 57 L.Ed.2d 290, 303 (1978).

In United States v. Hale, 422 U.S. 171, 95 S.Ct. 2133, 45 L.Ed.2d 99 (1975), and Doyle v. Ohio, 426 U.S. 610, 96 S.Ct. 2240, 49 L.Ed.2d 91 (1976), the U.S. Supreme Court held that a defendant's silence after receiving the *Miranda* warnings could not be used against the defendant at trial for the purpose of impeaching his or her trial testimony. The Court quoted the *Hale* case in the *Doyle* case as follows:

> "'[W]hen a person under arrest is informed as *Miranda* requires, that he may remain silent, that anything he says may be used against him, and that he may have an attorney if he wishes, it seems to me that it does not comport with due process to permit the prosecution during the trial to call attention to his silence at the time of arrest and to insist that because he did not speak about the facts of the case at that time, as he was told he need not do, an unfavorable inference might be drawn as to the truth of his trial testimony. . . .'" 426 U.S. at 619, 96 S.Ct. at 2245, 49 L.Ed.2d at 98.

Another effect of a *Miranda* violation is that it may cause evidence obtained in a subsequent search and seizure to be held inadmissible. In People v. Superior Court (Keithley), 118 Cal.Rptr. 617, 530 P.2d 585 (Cal. 1975), the court held that a consent to search obtained after questioning conducted in violation of *Miranda* was the product of illegal conduct. The consent to search was declared invalid. Strict compliance with the *Miranda* requirements will avoid the risk of exclusion not only of statements obtained but also of evidence seized in a subsequent search. United States v. Cassell, 452 F.2d 533 (7th Cir. 1971).

SUMMARY

An admission or confession obtained by a law enforcement officer will be inadmissible in court unless (1) it is voluntary and (2) the requirements of the Supreme Court case of *Miranda v. Arizona* are satisfied. Courts will find a statement involuntary if the statement is a product of police coercion, whether by force or by subtler forms of coercion, and if, in the totality of the circumstances, the statement is not the result of a person's free and rational choice. In making the determination of voluntariness, courts will consider the personal characteristics of the defendant, such as age, mental capacity, physical or mental impairment, and prior experience with the police, in establishing the setting in which coercion might operate to overcome the will of the defendant.

The *Miranda* case held that a statement obtained by police during a custodial interrogation of a defendant is inadmissible unless the police used certain procedural safeguards to secure the defendant's privilege against self-incrimination. Those procedural safeguards are the giving of warnings of rights and the obtaining of a valid waiver of those rights before an interrogation is begun. The major issues of *Miranda* can thus be broken down into four categories: custody, interrogation, warning, and waiver.

A person is in custody if the person is under arrest or is restrained so that he or she is deprived of freedom of action in any significant way. Custody can be equated with an arrest or a seizure tantamount to arrest, as discussed in Chapter 4. Custody is determined by examining the totality of facts and circumstances surrounding an encounter between a person and law enforcement authorities, including the place; the time; the presence of family, friends, or other persons; the nature and duration of questioning; and the conduct and number of police officers. The determination of custody requires a balancing of the needs of effective law enforcement against the need to protect persons from the coercion inherent in a compelling, police-dominated atmosphere.

Interrogation refers not only to express questioning but also to any words or actions on the part of police that the police should know are reasonably likely to elicit an incriminating response. Nevertheless, clarifying questions, spontaneous questions, and other brief and routine questions are not considered to be interrogation for *Miranda* purposes. In addition, volunteered statements are not the product of interrogation and are not subject to the *Miranda* requirements. Multiple attempts at interrogation are permitted after a defendant's invocation of the right to silence, but the defendant's right to cut off questioning must be scrupulously honored, fresh warnings must be given, and no coercion or other pressures may be employed. If the defendant has exercised the right to counsel, further interrogation without counsel may be conducted only upon the initiation of the defendant and the waiver of *Miranda* rights. After a defendant has been formally charged and has retained counsel, law enforcement authorities are prohibited from using any methods, however surreptitious or indirect, to elicit incriminating evidence from the defendant in the absence of counsel.

Before persons in custody may be subjected to interrogation, they must be given the familiar *Miranda* warnings:

1. You have the right to remain silent.

2. Anything you say can and will be used against you in a court of law.

3. You have the right to consult with a lawyer and to have the lawyer present with you while you are being questioned.

4. If you cannot afford to hire a lawyer, a lawyer will be appointed to represent you before any questioning, if you wish.

These warning must be recited clearly and unhurriedly and must be carefully explained to immature, illiterate, or mentally impaired persons.

If a person waives the *Miranda* rights to remain silent and to have an attorney, the person may be questioned. To be effective, a waiver of *Miranda* rights must be voluntary and must be made with a full awareness of both the nature of the right being abandoned and the consequences of the decision to abandon that right. Waiver will not be inferred from mere silence, but may be expressed by a great variety of words and gestures. If possible, an officer should obtain a written waiver of rights, because this provides the best evidence of a voluntary and intentional relinquishment of a known right.

Even though the voluntariness and *Miranda* requirements have been met, a statement may still be inadmissible if the officer violates a person's reasonable expectation of privacy in obtaining the statement. In addition, *Miranda* is inapplicable to minor misdemeanors, traffic offenses, and other proceedings in which the defendant is not potentially subject to a substantial term of imprisonment.

REVIEW AND DISCUSSION QUESTIONS

1. Would any of the following actions cause a statement of a suspect to be involuntary?
   a. Making an appeal to the suspect's moral or religious beliefs
   b. Confronting the suspect with the deceased or seriously injured victim of the crime in question
   c. Starting an argument with, challenging, or baiting the suspect

2. Does a person need a lawyer to help decide whether or not to waive *Miranda* rights? Is the compelling atmosphere of a custodial setting just as likely to influence a person's decision to waive rights as it is to influence the decision to confess?

3. Is a person's giving of consent to search an inculpatory or exculpatory statement? Should a person in custody be given *Miranda* warnings before being asked for a consent to search?

4. Assume that a person has been formally arrested for one crime, and police want to question that person about another, unrelated crime. Are *Miranda* warnings required to be given before the questioning? If the answer is no, what additional circumstances might cause *Miranda* warnings to be required?

5. It is reasonable to assume that a person under investigation for a crime might think that complete silence in the face of an accusation might not look good to a judge or a jury. Should the *Miranda* warnings include a statement that a person's silence may not be used against the person in any way?

6. Should suspects be told the nature and seriousness of the offense for which they are being interrogated? What if a person believes that he is being investigated for an accident caused by his driving while intoxicated, but he does not know that a person in the other vehicle has died?

7. What would be the advantages and disadvantages of requiring law enforcement officers to tape-record the entire process of administration of *Miranda* warnings and the suspect's invocation or waiver of rights?

8. Is it proper for a law enforcement officer to inform a suspect who has just invoked the *Miranda* right to counsel that the case against the suspect is strong and that immediate cooperation with the authorities would be beneficial in the long run? If the suspect says, "What do you mean?" would this be considered an initiation of further communication by the suspect and a waiver of the right to counsel?

9. Considering the confusion and pressures associated with being arrested and transported to a police station, should arrested persons be advised, in addition to the *Miranda* warnings, of where they are being taken, what is going to happen to them, how long they will be held, and with whom they may communicate?

10. Would the *Massiah* rule be violated if conversations of an indicted and imprisoned person were obtained by means of a listening device installed in that person's cell?

CHAPTER 14
Pre-trial Identification Procedures

Pre-trial confrontation of a suspected criminal with witnesses to or victims of a crime has long been an accepted law enforcement technique to identify perpetrators of crime and also to clear from suspicion those who are innocent. In 1967, the U.S. Supreme Court decided three major cases governing this area of the law: United States v. Wade, 388 U.S. 218, 87 S.Ct. 1926, 18 L.Ed.2d 1149; Gilbert v. California, 388 U.S. 263, 87 S.Ct. 1951, 18 L.Ed.2d 1178; and Stovall v. Denno, 388 U.S. 293, 87 S.Ct. 1967, 18 L.Ed.2d 1199. These decisions provide the groundwork for most of the law applicable to pre-trial identification procedures today.

The discussion of the *Wade, Gilbert,* and *Stovall* cases will use the terms *showup, lineup,* and *confrontation* throughout. A *showup* is the presentation of a single suspect to a victim or witness of a crime for the purpose of identifying the perpetrator of the crime. A *lineup* is the presentation at one time of several persons, including a suspect, to a victim or witness of a crime for the purpose of identifying the perpetrator of the crime. A lineup gives the victim or witness several alternative choices. A *confrontation* includes both showups and lineups and is any presentation of a suspect to a victim or witness of a crime for the purpose of identifying the perpetrator of the crime. These terms are also sometimes used in connection with photographic or voice identifications. Thus, for example, a photographic showup would be a presentation of a single photograph of a suspect to a victim or witness of a crime.

REQUIREMENT OF COUNSEL—THE WADE-GILBERT RULE

In the *Wade* and *Gilbert* decisions, the Supreme Court decided that a pre-trial confrontation of a suspect of a crime with witnesses or victims of the crime is a critical stage in the legal proceedings against the suspect and that the suspect has a right to the presence of a lawyer at the confrontation if he or she so desires. Furthermore, if the suspect is unable to afford a lawyer, he or she is entitled to have one appointed by the court. This ruling is an extension of the right of all accused persons to have the assistance of counsel for their defense at all critical stages of their criminal prosecution as guaranteed by the Sixth Amendment to the Constitution.

Basis of Court's Decision

The Supreme Court's reasoning in the *Wade* and *Gilbert* cases was based on (1) the inherent unreliability of eyewitness identifications and (2) the possibility of improper suggestions being made to witnesses during the confrontation procedure. The court said:

> The vagaries of eyewitness identification are well-known; the annals of criminal law are rife with instances of mistaken identification. . . . The identification of strangers is proverbially untrustworthy. . . . A major factor contributing to the high incidence of miscarriage of justice from mistaken identification has been the degree of suggestion inherent in the manner in which the prosecution presents the suspect to witnesses for pretrial identification. A commentator has observed that "[t]he influence of improper suggestion upon identifying witnesses probably accounts for more miscarriages of justice than any other single factor—perhaps it is responsible for more such errors than all other factors combined." . . . Suggestion can be created intentionally or unintentionally in many subtle ways. And the dangers for the suspect are particularly grave when the witness's opportunity for observation was insubstantial, and thus his susceptibility to suggestion the greatest. 388 U.S. at 228–29, 87 S.Ct. at 1933, 18 L.Ed.2d at 1158–59.

The Court believed that the presence of counsel at the pre-trial confrontation with witnesses would prevent misconduct by those conducting the confrontation. In addition, counsel would have firsthand knowledge of events at the confrontation and could, therefore, conduct an intelligent cross-examination of witnesses at a later suppression hearing or trial and point out any improprieties that might have occurred. The Court said:

> Since it appears that there is grave potential for prejudice, intentional or not, in the pretrial lineup, which may not be capable of reconstruction at trial, and since presence of counsel itself can often avert prejudice and assure a meaningful confrontation at trial, there can be little doubt that for Wade the post-indictment lineup was a critical stage of the prosecution at which he was "as much entitled to such aid [of counsel] . . . as at the trial itself." . . . Thus both Wade and his counsel should have been notified of the impending lineup, and counsel's presence should have been a requisite to conduct of the lineup, absent an "intelligent waiver." 388 U.S. at 236–37, 87 S.Ct. at 1937, 18 L.Ed.2d at 1162–63.

Waiver of Right to Counsel

As the preceding quotation indicates, suspects may waive their right to the presence of counsel at a pre-trial confrontation. Before suspects can intelligently and understandingly waive their right to presence of counsel, they should be clearly advised of their rights. The "Pre-trial Identification Warning and Waiver" form on page 336 is suggested for this purpose.

Substitute Counsel

If a suspect requests the advice and presence of his or her own lawyer and that lawyer is not immediately available, a substitute lawyer may sometimes be called for the purpose of the confrontation. Zamora v. Guam, 394 F.2d 815 (9th Cir. 1968). As stated in United States v. Wade, "Although the right to counsel usually means a right to the suspect's own counsel, provision for substitute counsel may be justified on the ground that the substitute counsel's presence may eliminate the hazards which render the lineup a critical stage for the presence of the suspect's *own* counsel." 388 U.S. at 237 n. 9, 87 S.Ct. at 1938 n. 9, 18 L.Ed.2d at 1163–64 n. 27.

GUIDELINES FOR LINEUP IDENTIFICATIONS

As a general rule, the decision to conduct a lineup is made at the discretion of the police or prosecution. Although the police, the prosecution, or the court may grant a suspect's request for a lineup, there is no requirement that such a request be granted. United States v. Harvey, 756 F.2d 636 (8th Cir. 1985).

The following material presents guidelines for the law enforcement officer in conducting a lineup identification after the suspect has been advised of the right to counsel and counsel has been retained or waived.

Before the Lineup

1. No lineup identification should be conducted by a law enforcement officer without the officer discussing with the prosecuting attorney the legal advisability of the lineup.

2. A person in custody may be compelled to participate in a lineup without there being a violation of Fourth or Fifth Amendment rights. Most courts hold that once a person is in custody, his or her liberty is not further infringed by that person's being presented in a lineup for witnesses to view. People v. Hodge, 526 P.2d 309 (Colo. 1974). In addition, the right against compulsory self-incrimination is not violated by a lineup, because no one is compelled to utter any words of a testimonial or communicative nature.

Compelling persons who are not in custody to appear in a lineup involves a much greater intrusion on liberty and is usually done only by order of a court or grand jury, or by authority of statute in some states. Some courts have upheld the ordering of a person not in custody to appear in a lineup in serious cases in which the public interest in law enforcement outweighed the privacy interests of the person. Wise v. Murphy, 275 A.2d 205 (D.C. App. 1971). Other courts have held that a person not in custody cannot be ordered to participate in a lineup without there being probable cause to arrest. Alphonso C. v. Morgenthau, 376 N.Y.S.2d 126 (N.Y.App.Div. 1975).

Pre-Trial Identification Warning and Waiver

Name   Address

Age   Place

Date   Time

Warning

Before appearing at any confrontation with any witnesses being conducted by (Name of Police Department) in relation to (Description of Offense), you are entitled to be informed of your legal rights.

The results of the confrontation can and will be used against you in court.

You have the right to the presence and advice of an attorney of your choice at any such confrontation.

If you cannot afford an attorney and you want one, an attorney will be appointed for you at no expense, before any confrontation is held.

Waiver

I have been advised of my right to the advice of an attorney and to have an attorney present at any confrontation with witnesses, and that if I cannot afford a lawyer, one will be appointed for me before any such confrontation occurs. I understand these rights.

I do not want a lawyer and I understand and know what I am doing.

No promises have been made to me and no pressures of any kind have been used against me.

_____

Signature of Suspect

Certification

I, (Name of Officer), hereby certify that I read the above warning to (Name of Suspect) on (Date), that this person indicated an understanding of the rights, and that this person signed the WAIVER form in my presence.

_____

Signature of Officer

_____

Witness

3. A record should be made of the suspect's waiver of the right to counsel and voluntary participation in the lineup. If counsel is present, counsel's name should be recorded.

4. If the suspect has chosen to have an attorney present at the lineup proceedings, the attorney should be given every opportunity to observe all the proceedings, to take notes, and to tape-record the identification process in whole or in part. If the attorney has any suggestions that might improve the fairness of the proceedings, the officer in charge may follow them if they are reasonable and practicable. However, the attorney should not be allowed to control the proceedings in any way.

The suspect's attorney must be made aware that an identification is taking place. The attorney's mere presence will not satisfy the *Wade-Gilbert* rule. In a case in which the suspect and his attorney were unaware that witnesses had identified the suspect during his arraignment, the suspect's right to counsel was held to be violated. Mason v. United States, 414 F.2d 1176 (D.C. Cir. 1969). Counsel's purpose is to ensure that the identification is conducted fairly and to reconstruct the procedures at trial. Counsel can do neither if he or she is unaware that an identification is taking place.

5. Even when the suspect's counsel is not required at a lineup (see the following section entitled "Exceptions to the Wade-Gilbert Rule"), officers should allow counsel to be present in order to minimize subsequent challenges to the fairness of the lineup. State v. Taylor, 210 N.W.2d 873 (Wis. 1973).

6. The names of all persons participating in the lineup and the names of the officers conducting the lineup should be recorded and preserved.

7. The witness or victim viewing the lineup should be advised of the purpose for which the lineup is being conducted, but the officer should not suggest that the suspect is one of those in the lineup or even that the suspect is in police custody.

8. All witnesses who are to view the lineup should be prevented from seeing the suspect in custody, particularly in handcuffs, or in any other circumstances that would indicate the identity of the suspect in question.

9. If possible, witnesses should not be allowed to view photographs of the suspect before the lineup. If a witness has viewed photographs before the lineup, the officer conducting the lineup should inform the suspect's counsel and the court of any identification of the suspect's photograph, any failure to identify the suspect's photograph, and any identification of a photograph of someone other than the suspect.

10. Before viewing the lineup, each witness should be required to give to the officer in charge of the lineup a written description of the perpetrator of the crime. A copy should be made available to the suspect's counsel.

During the Lineup

1. Insofar as possible, all persons in the lineup should be of the same general weight, height, age, and race; should have the same general physical characteristics; and should be dressed similarly. A suspect may be required to wear distinctive clothing at the lineup. United States v. King, 433 F.2d 937 (9th Cir.

1970). In addition, a suspect may be required to shave, trim his or her hair, or even grow a beard before participating in a lineup. United States v. O'Neal, 349 F.Supp. 572 (N.D. Ohio 1972). If a suspect fails to cooperate with identification procedures or attempts to change his or her appearance, the officer conducting the lineup should keep a careful record of this behavior.

2. If any body movement, gesture, or verbal statement is necessary, it should be made one time only by each person in the lineup, and repeated only at the express request of the observing witness or victim. Again, the officer conducting the lineup should keep a careful record of a suspect's failure to cooperate.

3. A color photograph of the lineup should be taken and developed as soon as possible. A copy of the photograph should be made available immediately to the suspect's counsel.

4. If more than one witness is called to view a lineup, the persons who have already viewed the lineup should not be allowed to converse with the persons who have not yet viewed the lineup. It is good practice to keep witnesses who have viewed the lineup in a room separate from witnesses who have not yet viewed the lineup. Furthermore, only one witness at a time should be present in the room where the lineup is being conducted.

5. The officer in charge of the lineup should not engage in unnecessary conversation with witnesses.

6. The officer in charge of the lineup should not allow unnecessary persons in the lineup room. A suggested group of people to include is the witness, the officer conducting the lineup, the prosecuting attorney, the suspect's attorney, and an investigator.

7. Upon entering the room in which the lineup is being conducted, each witness should be handed a form for use in the identification. The form should be signed by the witness, the defense attorney, and the law enforcement officer conducting the lineup. A suggested form appears on page 339.

8. A copy of the identification form should be given to the suspect's attorney at the time each witness completes his or her viewing of the lineup.

9. Use of a one-way mirror in a lineup, so that the suspect is unable to know what occurs on the other side of the mirror, has been held to be a prima facie violation of constitutional due process. This means that a lineup identification in which a one-way mirror is so used will be illegal, unless the officer in charge of the lineup can show that particularly compelling or exigent circumstances made the use of the mirror necessary. State v. Northup, 303 A.2d 1, 5 (Me. 1973). When the suspect's counsel is present, however, one-way mirrors may be permitted because counsel can observe the conduct of the lineup and preserve the suspect's rights. A one-way mirror may also be used to protect witnesses who fear retaliation. Commonwealth v. Lopes, 287 N.E.2d 118 (Mass. 1972).

After the Lineup

1. The officer in charge of a lineup should take complete notes of everything that takes place at the lineup and should prepare an official report of all the proceedings, to be filed in the department's permanent records. A copy should be made available to the suspect's attorney.

Witness Lineup Identification Form

The positions of the persons in the lineup will be numbered left to right, beginning with 1 on your left.

A. If you have previously seen one or more of the persons in the lineup, place an X in the appropriate square (or squares) corresponding to the number of the person in the lineup.

B. Then sign your name and fill in the date.

C. When completed, hand this sheet to the officer.

1	2	3	4	5	6	7
☐	☐	☐	☐	☐	☐	☐

_____

Signature of Witness

_____

Date and Time

_____

Signature of Law Enforcement Officer

_____

Signature of Attorney for Suspect

---

2. Any officer who observed a lineup must disclose to the court that reviews the lineup any evidence that might affect the accuracy of the identification, whether the evidence was observed before, during, or after the lineup. Failure to do so may be a violation of the suspect's due process rights.

EXCEPTIONS TO THE WADE-GILBERT RULE

The *Wade* and *Gilbert* decisions have caused much controversy and have generated many conflicting opinions in subsequent court decisions. Some lower courts have limited *Wade* and *Gilbert* to their particular facts. Others have created exceptions to the broad holdings implicit in the decisions. Several of those exceptions are discussed here.

Identifications Conducted before the Initiation of Adversary Judicial Proceedings

KIRBY v. ILLINOIS.   The *Wade* and *Gilbert* decisions generated various lower-court interpretations on the following issue: At what stage of a criminal proceeding does a suspect have a right to counsel at an identification procedure? Both the *Wade* and *Gilbert* decisions dealt with identification procedures that took place after the suspect had already been indicted. Some lower courts, interpreting these decisions literally, restricted the right to counsel only to lineups and showups occurring after the formal filing of charges. People v. Palmer, 244 N.E.2d 173 (Ill. 1969). Other courts reasoned that since the purpose of counsel's presence is to prevent prejudice to the suspect and ensure meaningful cross-examination of witnesses at trial on the issue of identification, counsel should be required whether the lineup or showup occurs before or after the formal filing of criminal charges. People v. Fowler, 82 Cal.Rptr. 363, 461 P.2d 643 (Cal. 1969).

The U.S. Supreme Court decided the issue in Kirby v. Illinois, 406 U.S. 682, 92 S.Ct. 1877, 32 L.Ed.2d 411 (1972). In the *Kirby* case, the Court held that the right to counsel attaches to lineups and showups held "at or after the initiation of adversary judicial criminal proceedings—whether by way of formal charge, preliminary hearing, indictment, information or arraignment." 406 U.S. at 689, 92 S.Ct. at 1882, 32 L.Ed.2d at 417. Therefore, a law enforcement officer need not warn a suspect of the right to counsel at a confrontation, if the suspect has not been formally charged with a crime.

Courts differ in their interpretations of when a suspect has been formally charged with a crime. The Supreme Court of Pennsylvania, for example, affords an accused a right to counsel at all lineups held after arrest. Commonwealth v. Richman, 320 A.2d 351 (Pa. 1974). In People v. Blake, 361 N.Y.S.2d 881, 320 N.E.2d 625 (N.Y. 1974), the court concluded that a complaint for an arrest warrant triggers the right to counsel since it is an "accusatory instrument." Other courts have held that the issuance of an arrest warrant triggers the right to counsel. United States ex rel. Robinson v. Zelker, 468 F.2d 159 (2d Cir. 1972). And in Ellis v. Grammer, 664 F.Supp. 1292 (D. Neb. 1987), the court held that a defendant who has been formally charged for one offense does not have a right to counsel at a lineup conducted for a different offense of which the defendant is suspected. An officer conducting a confrontation with witnesses must determine at what point in the criminal justice process the right to counsel at pretrial identification procedures attaches under the law applicable to the officer's jurisdiction.

Even though a suspect has no right to counsel at a confrontation with witnesses held before the initiation of adversary judicial criminal proceedings, the suspect retains the right to have the identification procedure conducted in a fair and impartial manner. In the *Kirby* case, the Court said:

> What has been said is not to suggest that there may not be occasions during the course of a criminal investigation when the police do abuse identification procedures. Such abuses are not beyond the reach of the Constitution. As the Court pointed out in *Wade* itself, it is always necessary to "scrutinize *any* pretrial confrontation. . . ." 388 U.S. at 227, 87 S.Ct. at 1932. The Due Process Clause of the Fifth and Fourteenth Amendments forbids a lineup that is unnecessarily suggestive and conducive to irreparable mistaken identification. Stovall v. Denno, 388 U.S. 293, 87 S.Ct. 1967, 18 L.Ed.2d 1199; Foster v. California, 394 U.S. 440, 89 S.Ct. 1127, 22 L.Ed.2d 402. When a person has not been formally charged with a criminal offense, *Stovall* strikes the appropriate constitutional balance between the right of a suspect to be protected from prejudicial procedures and the interest of society in the prompt and purposeful investigation of an unsolved crime. 406 U.S. at 690–91, S.Ct. at 1883, 32 L.Ed.2d at 418–19.

STOVALL v. DENNO. The case of Stovall v. Denno, 388 U.S. 293, 87 S.Ct. 1967, 18 L.Ed.2d 1199 (1967), mentioned in the previous quote from the *Kirby* case, held that the due process clause of the Fifth and Fourteenth Amendments to the Constitution forbids any pre-trial identification procedure that is unnecessarily suggestive and conducive to irreparable mistaken identification. For the law enforcement officer, this simply means that *all* lineups and showups must be conducted in a fair and impartial manner. The word *all* is emphasized because the *Stovall* test applies whether or not a suspect is represented by an attorney at the identification procedure.

The *Stovall* case is particularly important with respect to confrontations occurring *before* the initiation of adversary judicial criminal proceedings against a suspect. Courts will carefully scrutinize identification procedures for fairness and impartiality in these instances because suspects are without the benefit of an attorney to protect their rights. Therefore, when a law enforcement officer conducts a *lineup* to identify a suspect, before the suspect has been formally charged, the officer should follow carefully the recommended procedures in the section of this chapter entitled "Guidelines for Lineup Identifications."

When a *showup* rather than a lineup is used, the officer must exercise great care to ensure that identification procedures are fair and impartial. A common type of showup is the on-the-scene showup in which a suspect is arrested or apprehended at or near the scene of a crime and is immediately brought before victims or witnesses by a law enforcement officer for identification purposes. Clearly, so long as adversary judicial criminal proceedings have not been initiated, the suspect has no right to counsel at this type of confrontation. But does an on-the-scene showup satisfy the *Stovall* requirements of fairness and impartiality?

Although courts differ on this question, the prevailing view is that practical considerations may justify a prompt on-the-scene showup under the *Stovall* test. In Russell v. United States, 408 F.2d 1280 (D.C. Cir. 1969), the court said that the delay required to assemble a lineup "may not only cause the detention of an innocent suspect; it may also diminish the reliability of any identification obtained." 480 F.2d at 1284. The court also suggested that only "fresh" on-the-scene identifications that occur within minutes of the witnessed crime would satisfy the *Stovall* standard. In Johnson v. Dugger, 817 F.2d 726 (11th Cir. 1987), the court said:

> Although show-ups are widely condemned . . . immediate confrontations allow identification before the suspect has altered his appearance and while the witness' memory is fresh, and permit the quick release of innocent persons. . . . Therefore, show-ups are not unnecessarily suggestive unless the police aggravate the suggestiveness of the confrontation.

In Bates v. United States, 405 F.2d 1104 (D.C. Cir. 1968), the court said:

> There is no prohibition against a viewing of a suspect alone in what is called a "one-man showup" when this occurs near the time of the alleged criminal act; such a course does not tend to bring about misidentification but rather in some circumstances to insure accuracy. The rationale underlying this is in some respects not unlike that which the law relies on to make an exception to the hearsay rule, allowing spontaneous utterances a standing which they would not be given if uttered at a later point in time. An early identification is not error. Of course, proof of infirmities and subjective factors, such as hysteria of a witness,

can be explored on cross-examination and in argument. Prudent police work would confine these on-the-spot identifications to situations in which possible doubts as to identification needed to be resolved promptly; absent such need the conventional lineup viewing is the appropriate procedure. 405 F.2d at 1106.

Therefore, law enforcement officers should use on-the-scene showups only when a suspect can be shown to a witness minutes after the crime has occurred. Furthermore, officers should not coach the witness or add in any way to the already inherent suggestiveness of the on-the-scene identification. If there is a significant delay between the commission of the crime and the confrontation, officers should take the suspect to the station and conduct a lineup in accordance with suggested procedures in the section of this chapter entitled "Guidelines for Lineup Identifications."

NEIL v. BIGGERS. Despite the advice in the previous paragraph, law enforcement officers have often conducted showups several days, weeks, or even months after a crime has occurred. Before 1972, most courts, applying the standards of *Stovall v. Denno*, held that delayed one-on-one confrontations were impermissibly suggestive and violative of due process. Evidence obtained from identifications made under these circumstances was held inadmissible in court.

In 1972, however, the U.S. Supreme Court decided the case of Neil v. Biggers, 409 U.S. 188, 93 S.Ct. 375, 34 L.Ed.2d 401, focusing on whether the identification was accurate or reliable despite the suggestiveness of the identification procedure. *Neil v. Biggers* involved a defendant who had been convicted of rape on evidence consisting, in part, of the victim's visual and voice identification of the defendant at a stationhouse showup seven months after the crime. At the time of the crime, the victim was in her assailant's presence for nearly one-half-hour and the victim directly observed her assailant indoors and under a full moon outdoors. The victim testified at trial that she had no doubt that the defendant was her assailant. Immediately after the crime, she gave the police a thorough description of the assailant that matched the description of the defendant. The victim had also made no identification of others presented at previous showups or lineups, or through photographs.

Despite its concern about the seven-month delay between the crime and the confrontation, the Court held that the central question was "whether under the 'totality of the circumstances' the identification was reliable even though the confrontation procedure was suggestive." 409 U.S. at 199, 93 S.Ct. at 382, 34 L.Ed.2d at 411. The Court listed the following five factors to be considered in evaluating the likelihood of misidentification:

1. Witness's opportunity to view the criminal at the time of the crime

2. Witness's degree of attention

3. Accuracy of the witness's prior description of the criminal

4. Level of certainty demonstrated by the witness at the confrontation

5. Length of time between the crime and the confrontation

Applying these considerations to the facts of the case, the Court found no substantial likelihood of misidentification and held the evidence of the identification to be admissible in court.

MANSON v. BRATHWAITE. In the case of Manson v. Brathwaite, 432 U.S. 98, 97 S.Ct. 2243, 53 L.Ed.2d 140 (1977), the Court added an additional factor to be considered by courts in determining the admissibility of identification evidence: the corrupting effect of the suggestive identification itself. The *Brathwaite* case involved an undercover drug officer's viewing of a single photograph of a drug crime suspect that had been left in his office by a fellow officer. Two days had elapsed between the crime and the viewing of the photograph. After finding that the single photographic display was unnecessarily suggestive, the Court considered the five factors affecting the reliability of an identification set out in *Neil v. Biggers*. The Court found that the undercover officer was no casual observer, but a trained police officer; that the officer had sufficient opportunity to view the suspect for two or three minutes in natural light; that the officer accurately described the suspect in detail within minutes of the crime; that the officer positively identified the photograph in court as that of the drug seller; and that the officer made the photographic identification only two days after the crime.

The Court's analysis of the five factors indicated that the undercover drug officer was able to make an accurate identification of the defendant. The Court did not end its discussion at this stage as it did in the *Biggers* case, however. Instead, the Court took the additional step of analyzing the corrupting effect of the suggestive identification and then weighing that against the factors indicating reliability. The Court said:

> Although identifications arising from single-photograph displays may be viewed in general with suspicion, . . . we find in the instant case little pressure on the witness to acquiesce in the suggestion that such a display entails. D'Onofrio had left the photograph at Glover's office and was not present when Glover first viewed it two days after the event. There thus was little urgency and Glover could view the photograph at his leisure. And since Glover examined the photograph alone, there was no coercive pressure to make an identification arising from the presence of another. The identification was made in circumstances allowing care and reflection. 432 U.S. at 116, 97 S.Ct. at 2254, 53 L.Ed.2d at 155.

Under the totality of the circumstances, the Court held that the identification was reliable and that evidence of the identification was admissible in court.

The following quotation from the *Brathwaite* case sets out the basic test for determining the admissibility of evidence of identifications that take place before the initiation of adversary judicial criminal proceedings.

> We therefore conclude that reliability is the linchpin in determining the admissibility of identification testimony for both pre- and post-*Stovall* confrontations. The factors to be considered are set out in *Biggers*. 409 U.S. at 199–200, 93 S.Ct. at 382. These include the opportunity of the witness to view the criminal at the time of the crime, the witness' degree of attention, the accuracy of his prior description of the criminal, the level of certainty demonstrated at the confrontation, and the time between the crime and the confrontation. Against these factors is to be weighed the corrupting effect of the suggestive identification itself. 432 U.S. at 114, 97 S.Ct. at 2253, 53 L.Ed.2d at 154.

The lesson of the *Biggers* and *Brathwaite* cases is that even though an officer conducts an unnecessarily suggestive identification procedure, the evidence is not necessarily lost because it may still be admitted in court if the identification was otherwise reliable. However, these cases should not be interpreted as evidencing a lack of concern about conducting fair and impartial identification procedures. As the Court stated in the *Brathwaite* case:

> [I]t would have been better had D'Onofrio presented Glover with a photographic array including "so far as practicable . . . a reasonable number of persons similar to any person then suspected whose likeness is included in the array." . . . The use of that procedure would have enhanced the force of the identification at trial and would have avoided the risk that the evidence would be excluded as unreliable. 432 U.S. at 117, 97 S.Ct. at 2254, 53 L.Ed.2d at 155.

Law enforcement officers have control over the conduct of the identification procedures, but they have little or no control over the five factors determining the reliability of the identification. Therefore, officers should conduct all identification procedures fairly and impartially. To avoid the risk that identification evidence will be excluded as unreliable, officers should follow the guidelines for lineup identifications set out earlier in this chapter. When photographs are used, officers should follow the guidelines on photographic identifications appearing later in this chapter.

Emergency Identifications

In an emergency (e.g., if a witness is believed to be dying), a relaxation of the right to counsel rule and the *Stovall* "fairness" rule may be allowed when necessary to prevent the loss of vital evidence. In Trask v. Robbins, 421 F.2d 773 (1st Cir. 1970), for example, a defendant who was being held in jail on a charge of robbing a store was presented to a hospitalized victim of a separate assault and robbery offense that was under investigation. There was uncertainty as to whether the defendant had retained a lawyer on the store robbery charge, and no lawyer was contacted for the identification proceeding in the separate assault and robbery crime. The defendant was transported to the hospital by a deputy sheriff. The victim spontaneously and positively identified the defendant as his assailant. The defendant claimed that he should have been represented by a lawyer at this pre-trial confrontation with the victim.

The court applied the *Stovall* test and decided that a claimed violation of constitutional rights in the conduct of a confrontation with a witness depends on the totality of the circumstances surrounding the confrontation. In this case, the circumstances surrounding the identification were not unnecessarily suggestive and conducive to irreparable mistaken identification: (1) no preliminary statements were made to the victim; (2) the victim's words of identification were spontaneous and positive; (3) the defendant said nothing in the presence of the victim; (4) the case was merely in the investigatory stage; and (5) the critically injured victim (thought to be dying) was about to be moved to a distant hospital. Under these emergency conditions, the fact that a lawyer was not present did not void the identification.

PHOTOGRAPHIC IDENTIFICATIONS

A common and accepted method of police investigation is the showing of mug shots or photographs to witnesses to aid in identifying or eliminating criminal suspects. In *Simmons v. United States*, 390 U.S. 377, 88 S.Ct. 967, 19 L.Ed.2d 1247 (1968), the U.S. Supreme Court approved this procedure, subject to the same standards of fairness set out in *Stovall v. Denno*. Furthermore, the U.S. Supreme Court held that there is no right to counsel at any photographic identification procedure, whether that procedure is held before or after the initiation of adversary judicial criminal proceedings. *United States v. Ash*, 413 U.S. 300, 93 S.Ct. 2568, 37 L.Ed.2d 619 (1973).

Each case, therefore, must be decided on the totality of the circumstances surrounding it, and the identification evidence will be excluded in court "only if the photographic identification procedure was so impermissibly suggestive as to give rise to a very substantial likelihood of irreparable misidentification." 390 U.S. at 384, 88 S.Ct. at 971, 19 L.Ed.2d at 1253.

The following guidelines, based on the *Simmons* case, are suggested for photographic identifications.

1. More than one photograph should be shown to a witness. In the *Simmons* case, six photographs were shown to several witnesses, and the Supreme Court suggested that even more than six would be preferable. "In the absence of exigent circumstances, presentation of a single photograph to the victim of a crime amounts to an unnecessarily suggestive photographic identification procedure." *United States v. Jones*, 652 F.Supp. 1561, 1570 (S.D.N.Y. 1986).

2. The people appearing in the photographs should be of the same general age, height, weight, hair color, and skin color.

3. No group of photographs should be arranged in such a way that the photograph of a single person recurs or is in any way emphasized. Furthermore, the officer conducting the identification should do nothing to indicate which picture is that of the suspect. *Cikora v. Wainwright*, 661 F.Supp. 813 (S.D. Fla. 1987).

4. If there are two or more suspects, no two should appear together in a group photo.

5. Witnesses should be handled in a manner similar to that suggested in the guidelines for lineup identifications.

6. If there are several witnesses, only some of them should be shown the photographs to obtain an initial identification. Then the suspect should be displayed to the remaining witnesses in a more reliable lineup. By following this procedure, the officer helps ensure that the perceptions of the witnesses at the lineup are not influenced by a viewing of the photographs.

7. The officer in charge should take careful notes of all remarks made by witnesses while viewing photos, and of all identifications of and failures to identify the suspect.

8. After the photographs have been shown to the witnesses, they should be numbered and preserved as evidence.

9. After a witness selects a photograph from a photographic display, that witness should not be shown the same photograph in later photographic displays. Such a procedure would tend to fix the image of the photograph in the witness's mind and blur the image actually perceived at the crime. *United States v. Eatherton*, 519 F.2d 603 (1st Cir. 1975).

10. Photographs of suspects in the act of committing the crime (such as bank robbery surveillance photographs) do not present any problems of suggestiveness and mistaken identification. Courts have held that presenting such photographs to witnesses shows the actual perpetrator of the crime in the act rather than suggesting a number of possible perpetrators. The photographs refresh the witness's memory of the actual crime and thereby strengthen the reliability of the witness's in-court identification. United States v. Browne, 829 F.2d 760 (9th Cir. 1987).

11. Mug shots should not be used together with other photographs for identification purposes. Mug shots may prejudice the pictured persons by implying that they have criminal records.

12. A photograph in a photographic display may be altered (to show what the person would look like with a beard or a hat, for example) so long as all other photographs in the display are altered in the same way. United States v. Dunbar, 767 F.2d 72 (3d Cir. 1985).

13. "Once law enforcement officers obtain from a witness a photographic identification of a suspect which is both untainted and positive, they may show other pictures of that properly and positively identified suspect to the witness without implicating the concerns of *Simmons* and its progeny." United States v. Jones, 652 F.Supp. 1561 (S.D.N.Y. 1986).

14. Photographic identification should not be used once a suspect's identity is known and the suspect is in police custody. A lineup should be used in these circumstances because lineups are more accurate than photographic identifications. State v. Wallace, 285 So.2d 796 (La. 1973).

These guidelines are only suggested; different circumstances may require different identification procedures. The law requires that the totality of the circumstances surrounding an identification must not be so overly suggestive as to cause a substantial likelihood of irreparable misidentification. As discussed earlier, courts will look beyond the mere fact of a suggestive photographic identification procedure in determining whether there was a substantial likelihood of irreparable misidentification. Courts will analyze each case with respect to the five factors determining the reliability of the identification as set out in *Neil v. Biggers*. Courts will then weigh those factors against the corrupting effect of the suggestive identification, as was done in *Manson v. Brathwaite*. Law enforcement officers should follow the guidelines for photographic identifications set out in this section to minimize the suggestiveness of identification procedures and to help ensure that identification evidence will not be excluded as unreliable.

EFFECT OF AN IMPROPER IDENTIFICATION PROCEDURE

To enforce the standards set out by the U.S. Supreme Court with respect to pretrial identifications, certain rules have been established for the admission of identification evidence in court. If a pre-trial identification is made in violation of a defendant's right to counsel or if the identification is unreliable and thereby violates a defendant's due process rights, the court must exclude at trial

1. any evidence of the pre-trial identification presented as a part of the prosecution's direct case; and

2. any identification of the perpetrator of the crime made by a witness in court.

If, however, the prosecution can establish by clear and convincing evidence that a witness has a source independent from the illegal confrontation for identifying the perpetrator of the crime, the court may allow in-court identification testimony. A court will find that an in-court identification has an independent source when the court is convinced that the identifying witness, by drawing on personal memory of the crime and observations of the defendant during the crime, has such a clear and definite image of the defendant that the witness can make an identification unaffected by the illegal confrontation. Some factors considered by judges in determining an independent source are as follows:

1. Opportunity for observation during the crime

2. Prior knowledge of the identity of the perpetrator of the crime

3. Accuracy of the witness's description of the perpetrator given to the police

4. Failure of the witness to identity the defendant at prior confrontations

5. Identification of a person other than the defendant before the confrontation

6. Lapse of time between the crime and the confrontation

7. Differences of opinion among witnesses

Law enforcement officers should obtain information on these factors from witnesses and record the information in their reports. Officers should obtain as much detail as possible because strong evidence of an independent source for identification of a criminal can salvage an improperly conducted identification procedure.

SUMMARY

A criminal suspect has a right to counsel at all lineups and showups conducted *at or after* the initiation of adversary judicial criminal proceedings against the suspect. The emergency showup is the only possible exception to this rule. In every other case, the suspect should be warned of the right to counsel in accordance with the form provided in this chapter. All formal confrontations should be conducted in accordance with the guidelines for lineup identifications provided in this chapter.

If a lineup or showup is conducted *before* adversary judicial proceedings are initiated against a suspect, the suspect is *not* entitled to the presence or advice of counsel. Nevertheless, *all* pre-trial identification procedures, whether lineups or showups, must be conducted in accordance with due process, which forbids any pre-trial identification procedure that is unnecessarily suggestive and conducive to irreparable mistaken identification. As further interpreted by the U.S. Supreme Court, due process simply requires that all pre-trial identifications be reliable in the totality of the circumstances, or evidence of the identification will be inadmissible in court. Factors to be considered in determining reliability are the witness's opportunity to view the criminal at the time of the crime, the witness's degree of attention, the accuracy of the witness's prior description, the level of certainty demonstrated by the witness at the confrontation, and the length of time between the crime and the confrontation. These factors are to be weighed against the corrupting effect of any suggestive identification. Officers conducting lineups are again advised to follow the guidelines for lineup identifications presented in this chapter.

A criminal suspect is *not* entitled to the presence or advice of counsel at *photographic* identification procedures no matter when those procedures are held. Nevertheless, such procedures must be conducted as fairly and impartially as possible. Officers are advised to follow the guidelines for photographic identifications provided in this chapter.

REVIEW AND DISCUSSION QUESTIONS

1. What circumstances might justify the use of a one-way mirror during a lineup procedure? What if a witness or victim refuses to participate in a lineup unless a one-way mirror is used?

2. Why should a person not have a right to demand an immediate lineup to clear himself or herself and avoid the many inconveniences associated with being arrested?

3. State three ways in which a law enforcement officer conducting a lineup can decrease the suggestibility of the lineup. State three ways in which a law enforcement officer can decrease the suggestibility of a one-man showup.

4. Assume that a suspect is about to be placed in a lineup and is told by a law enforcement officer that she has a right to counsel at the lineup. If the suspect asks, "Why do I need a lawyer?" what should the officer tell her?

5. Why should photographic identification procedures not be used when a physical lineup is contemplated? What arguments would a defense attorney make at a suppression hearing under each of the following circumstances?

   a. The witness identified the defendant's photograph at a pre-trial photographic display, but failed to identify the defendant at a later physical lineup.

   b. The witness failed to identify the defendant's photograph at a pre-trial photographic display, but identified the defendant at a later physical lineup.

   c. The witness identified the defendant's photograph at a pre-trial photographic display and also identified the defendant at a later physical lineup.

6. Is it possible to conduct a fair lineup when the suspect is unusually tall or short or has very distinctive features or deformities?

7. Would an emergency one-person showup be justified if the suspect and not the victim were seriously injured? In what ways could the suggestibility of the showup be decreased?

8. Would certain suggestive pre-trial identification procedures be excusable in a small rural police department as opposed to a large urban police department? What procedures might be excusable and why?

9. Discuss the following quotation from Justice William J. Brennan's dissenting opinion in United States v. Ash, 413 U.S. 300, 344, 93 S.Ct. 2568, 2591, 37

L.Ed.2d 619, 646–47 (1973), in which the U.S. Supreme Court held that there is no right to counsel at any photographic identification procedure: "There is something ironic about the Court's conclusion today that a pretrial lineup identification is a "critical stage" of the prosecution because counsel's presence can help to compensate for the accused's deficiencies as an observer, but that a pretrial photographic identification is not a "critical stage" of the prosecution because the accused is not able to observe at all."

10. Would there be any need for counsel at a lineup if the entire lineup procedure were recorded on both audiotape and videotape?

CHAPTER 15
Electronic Surveillance

Electronic surveillance through the use of wiretaps, bugs, or other devices to overhear conversations or obtain other kinds of information is a relatively recent concern of criminal and constitutional law. Certainly the Founding Fathers could not have even imagined the possibilities for gathering information on crime created by the marvels of twentieth-century technology. Nor could they, when they drafted the Constitution, have contemplated the potential invasions of privacy brought about by the new technology. It is not surprising, then, that the Constitution gives little guidance for balancing privacy interests against the need for effective law enforcement in the area of electronic surveillance.

On the one hand, electronic listening, tracking, and recording devices provide a very powerful tool for law enforcement officials in investigating and prosecuting crime. On the other hand, the potential for the abuse of individual rights can be far greater with electronic surveillance than with any ordinary search or seizure. The task of resolving these competing interests has fallen on state legislatures, the United States Congress, and, ultimately, the courts. This chapter traces the early development of the law of electronic surveillance, examines legislative responses to the problem, and analyzes court decisions in this area.

HISTORY

Although electronic eavesdropping has been used as an information-gathering technique since the mid-1800s, the U.S. Supreme Court did not decide its first electronic eavesdropping case until 1928. In Olmstead v. United States, 277 U.S. 438, 48 S.Ct. 564, 72 L.Ed. 944 (1928), a case involving interception of telephone conversations by means of a wiretap, the Court held that wiretapping was not covered by the Fourth Amendment. One reason for this decision, as discussed in Chapter 3 under "Privacy," was that there was no search so long as there was no physical trespass into the defendant's premises. The other reason was that all the evidence had been obtained by hearing only, and since the Fourth Amendment referred only to the seizure of tangible items, the interception of a conversation could not qualify as a seizure. As shown in Chapter 3, the *Katz* case rendered invalid the first rationale of the *Olmstead* decision by changing the focus of Fourth Amendment analysis from a "property" approach to a "privacy" approach. The second rationale of the *Olmstead* decision has been disposed of by Berger v. New York, 388 U.S. 41, 87 S.Ct. 1873, 18 L.Ed.2d 1040 (1967), which is discussed later in this chapter.

In the *Olmstead* opinion, the Court noted that "Congress may of course protect the secrecy of telephone messages by making them when intercepted, inadmissible in evidence in federal criminal trials, by direct legislation, and thus depart from the common law of evidence." 277 U.S. at 465–66, 48 S.Ct. at 568, 72 L.Ed. at 951. Six years later, Congress did just that with the passage of Section 605 of the Federal Communications Act of 1934, which read, in part: "[N]o person not being authorized by the sender shall intercept any communication and divulge or publish the existence, contents, substance, purport, effect, or meaning of such intercepted communication to any person. . . ."

In Nardone v. United States, 302 U.S. 379, 58 S.Ct. 275, 82 L.Ed. 314 (1937), the U.S. Supreme Court held that Section 605 applied to federal law enforcement officers and that testimony of federal officers in court about the contents of intercepted conversations was a form of divulgence prohibited by the act and was therefore inadmissible. Wiretapping was not illegal under the Court's interpretation, however, if the information was not used outside the governmental agency. Weiss v. United States, 308 U.S. 321, 60 S.Ct. 269, 84 L.Ed. 298 (1939), held that Section 605 applied to intrastate as well as interstate communications. Therefore, wiretap evidence obtained by state law enforcement officers was inadmissible in a federal prosecution, but, under the decision in Schwartz v. Texas, 344 U.S. 199, 73 S.Ct. 232, 97 L.Ed. 231 (1952), was admissible in a state prosecution because the exclusionary rule had not yet been applied to the states. It was not until 1968, seven years after *Mapp v. Ohio* and after wiretapping itself had been made subject to the Fourth Amendment, that the *Schwartz* decision was overruled by Lee v. Florida, 392 U.S. 378, 88 S.Ct. 2096, 20 L.Ed.2d 1166 (1968), and wiretap evidence obtained by state officials was made inadmissible in state prosecutions.

The *Lee* case was decided just two days before the enactment by Congress of Title III of the Omnibus Crime Control and Safe Streets Act of 1968, 18 U.S.C.A. §§ 2510–20, which superceded Section 605 of the 1934 act. Most of the rest of this chapter deals with the enactment, content, and interpretation of Title III. But first the following section provides some background on the constitutionality of electronic surveillance to set the stage for the discussion of Title III.

THE CONSTITUTIONALITY OF ELECTRONIC SURVEILLANCE

As discussed earlier, in the 60s, the U.S. Supreme Court clearly established that electronic surveillance is a search and seizure within the meaning of the Fourth Amendment. Given that premise, it became necessary for the Court to decide what kinds of electronic surveillance the Fourth Amendment allows, to what extent electronic surveillance is allowed, and what kinds of electronic surveillance are prohibited, if any. The guidelines for these constitutional limits on electronic surveillance were worked out in a series of decisions in the mid-60s.

This discussion begins with Justice William J. Brennan's dissent in Lopez v. United States, 373 U.S. 427, 83 S.Ct. 1381, 10 L.Ed.2d 462 (1963). In that dissent, Justice Brennan echoed the fears of law enforcement officials that if wiretaps were subjected to Fourth Amendment analysis, they would be completely prohibited, because they would be seen as inherently unreasonable searches. Brennan stated, "For one thing, electronic surveillance is almost inherently indiscriminate, so that compliance with the requirement of particularity in the Fourth Amendment would be difficult." 373 U.S. at 463, 83 S.Ct. at 1401, 10 L.Ed.2d at 485. He continued:

> If in fact no warrant could be devised for electronic searches, that would be a compelling reason for forbidding them altogether. The requirements of the Fourth Amendment . . . are the bedrock rules without which there would be no effective protection of the right to personal liberty. . . . Electronic searches cannot be tolerated in the name of law enforcement if they are inherently unconstitutional. 373 U.S. at 464, 83 S.Ct. at 1401, 10 L.Ed.2d at 485.

Despite his strong language, it is clear that Brennan left open the possibility that some forms of electronic surveillance might be constitutionally permissible.

The U.S. Supreme Court first explicitly considered the constitutionality of electronic surveillance conducted under authority of a warrant three years later in Osborn v. United States, 385 U.S. 323, 87 S.Ct. 429, 17 L.Ed.2d 394 (1966). In that case, federal law enforcement officials had information that labor leader Jimmy Hoffa's attorney was trying to bribe a prospective juror. The officials obtained a warrant authorizing an undercover agent with a concealed tape recorder to record a specific conversation with the attorney. The tape of the conversation was admitted at trial and the attorney was convicted of attempting to bribe a juror. The U.S. Supreme Court upheld the conviction, emphasizing that "[t]he issue here is . . . the permissibility of using such a device under the most precise and discriminate circumstances. . . ." 385 U.S. at 329, 87 S.Ct. at 432–33, 17 L.Ed.2d at 399.

The Court's limited grant of constitutional permissibility for electronic surveillance was tested again the next year in Berger v. New York, 388 U.S. 41, 87 S.Ct. 1873, 18 L.Ed.2d 1040 (1967). In *Berger*, the issue was the constitutionality of a New York statute that authorized electronic surveillance pursuant to a judicial warrant. The New York law provided as follows:

> An ex parte order for eavesdropping . . . may be issued by any justice . . . or judge . . . upon oath or affirmation of a district attorney, or of the attorney-general or of an officer above the rank of sergeant of any police department of the state . . . that there is reasonable ground to believe that evidence of crime may be thus obtained, and particularly describing the person or persons whose communications or discussions are to be overheard or recorded and the purpose thereof, and, in the case of a telegraphic or telephonic communication, identifying the particular telephone number or telegraph line involved. In connection with the issuance of such an order the justice or judge may examine on oath the applicant and any other witness he may produce and shall satisfy himself of the existence of reasonable grounds for the granting of such application. Any such order shall be effective for the time specified therein but not for a period of more than two months unless extended or renewed by the justice or judge

who signed and issued the original order upon satisfying himself that such an extension or renewal is in the public interest. . . . N.Y. Code Crim. Proc. § 813-a.

The U.S. Supreme Court first held that conversations were protected by the Fourth Amendment and that the use of electronic devices to capture conversations was a search within the meaning of the Fourth Amendment. The Court then held the New York statute unconstitutional, primarily because it did not properly limit the nature, scope, or duration of the electronic surveillance. In so holding, the Court emphasized that the availability of an initial two-month surveillance period was "the equivalent of a series of intrusions, searches, and seizures pursuant to a single showing of probable cause." 388 U.S. at 59, 87 S.Ct. at 1883, 18 L.Ed.2d at 1052. The Court also stressed that the statute placed no termination requirement on the eavesdrop, even after the desired conversation had been obtained. Furthermore, the statute had two major deficiencies with respect to probable cause. First, an eavesdropping warrant could be issued without probable cause that a particular crime had been committed and without a particular description of the "property" (conversations in this context) to be seized. Second, an eavesdropping order could be extended or renewed without a showing of probable cause for continuation of the eavesdrop. Finally, in contrast to conventional search warrant procedures, the statute permitted electronic eavesdropping without prior notice or a showing of exigency excusing notice.

The Court's concern with the overbroad authorization of the New York statute is reflected in its comparison of the electronic search in the *Berger* case with the search in the *Osborn* case discussed earlier:

> The invasion [in *Osborn*] was lawful because there was sufficient proof to obtain a search warrant to make the search for the limited purpose outlined in the order of the judges. Through these "precise and discriminate" procedures the order authorizing the use of the electronic device afforded similar protections to those that are present in the use of conventional warrants authorizing the seizure of tangible evidence. Among other safeguards, the order described the type of conversation sought with particularity, thus indicating the specific objective of the Government in entering the constitutionally protected areas and the limitations placed upon the officer executing the warrant. Under it the officer could not search unauthorized areas; likewise, once the property sought, and for which the order was issued, was found the officer could not use the order as a passkey to further search. In addition, the order authorized one limited intrusion rather than a series or a continuous surveillance. And, we note that a new order was issued when the officer sought to resume the search and probable cause was shown for the succeeding one. Moreover, the order was executed by the officer with dispatch, not over a prolonged and extended period. In this manner no greater invasion of privacy was permitted than was necessary under the circumstances. Finally the officer was required to and did make a return on the order showing how it was executed and what was seized. Through these strict precautions the danger of an unlawful search and seizure was minimized. 388 U.S. at 57, 87 S.Ct. at 1882–83, 18 L.Ed.2d at 1051.

Despite the Court's disapproval of the New York statute in the *Berger* case, the possibility that a properly circumscribed warrant procedure for electronic surveillance could be created was left open. This possibility was given further credence by the landmark case of *Katz v. United States* (discussed in Chapter 3). In that case, FBI agents attached an electronic listening device to a public telephone booth and recorded the defendant's calls. The Court held that the interception was an unlawful search and seizure because there was no warrant. In discussing the warrant requirement, the Court said:

> [T]he surveillance was limited, both in scope and in duration, to the specific purpose of establishing the contents of the petitioner's unlawful telephonic communications. The agents confined their surveillance to the brief periods during which he [Katz] used the telephone booth, and they took great care to overhear only the conversation of the petitioner himself.
>
> Accepting this account of the Government's actions as accurate, it is clear that this surveillance was so narrowly circumscribed that a duly authorized magistrate, properly notified of the need for such investigation, specifically informed of the basis on which is was to proceed, and clearly apprised of the precise intrusion it would entail, could constitutionally have authorized, with appropriate safeguards, the very limited search and seizure that the Government asserts in fact took place. 389 U.S.374, 354, 88 S.Ct. 507, 512–13, 19 L.Ed.2d 576, 583–84 (1967).

The possibility that a constitutionally permissible warrant procedure for electronic surveillance could be set up paved the way for congressional action in this area. In the year following the *Berger* and *Katz* opinions, Congress enacted the Omnibus Crime Control and Safe Streets Act of 1968. Title III of that act superceded the prohibition against wiretapping in Section 605 of the Federal Communications Act of 1934 and provided authorization for electronic surveillance pursuant to warrant.

As a background for discussion of Title III, the constitutional principles established by the *Lopez, Osborn, Berger*, and *Katz* cases are summarized here. First, electronic surveillance by agents of the government is a search and seizure governed by the Fourth Amendment. Second, electronic surveillance is permissible only if conducted pursuant to the authority of a warrant affording protections similar to those present in the use of conventional warrants authorizing the seizure of tangible evidence. Finally, a warrant procedure authorizing electronic surveillance must carefully circumscribe the search in nature, scope, and duration and must not permit "a trespassory invasion of the home or office, by general warrant, contrary to the command of the Fourth Amendment." 388 U.S. at 64, 87 S.Ct. at 1886, 18 L.Ed.2d at 1055.

TITLE III OF THE OMNIBUS CRIME CONTROL AND SAFE STREETS ACT OF 1968

The passage of Title III of the Omnibus Crime Control and Safe Streets Act of 1968, following so closely on the heels of the *Berger* and *Katz* decisions, was not simply a result of Congress enacting legislation in response to the constitutional guidelines set out in those decisions. There had long been concern about the inadequacy of existing electronic surveillance legislation. Besides the issues raised in various Supreme Court cases, defense lawyers and civil libertarians complained of Justice Department abuses under Section 605 of the Federal Communications Act of 1934 and other violations of the privacy rights of American citizens. On the other side, proponents of electronic surveillance argued that wiretapping and bugging were essential tools for law enforcement officials to combat the modern sophisticated criminal, especially in the area of organized crime. In fact, the belief that electronic surveillance was the only way to deal with the unique problems of investigating and prosecuting organized crime prompted the President's Crime Commission to recommend legislation authorizing electronic surveillance. Another impetus leading to the passage of Title III in 1968 was the political pressures that were exerted in the context of a national climate of fear brought about by intense social unrest and the assassinations of Martin Luther King, Jr. and Robert F. Kennedy and exemplified by the "law and order" presidential campaign of Richard M. Nixon. The result was a bipartisan effort to balance modern society's conflicting demands for privacy and for more effective law enforcement.

The discussion now turns to a detailed examination of Title III and cases interpreting it. Because of the length of the law, it is not possible to reproduce Title III's provisions verbatim. Therefore, the discussion is necessarily general in nature.

Judicial Supervision

One important characteristic of Title III, designed to protect against governmental abuses of citizens' privacy rights, is the law's provision for judicial supervision of all aspects of electronic surveillance. Federal law enforcement officials may not intercept wire, oral, or electronic communications without prior judicial approval. (The 1986 amendments to Title III extended the law's coverage to include all forms of electronic communications and not just spoken conversations transmitted by telephone or overheard electronically.)

A court may issue an interception order only for specified crimes including espionage, treason, labor racketeering, murder, kidnapping, robbery, extortion, bribery of public officials, gambling, drug trafficking, escape, and counterfeiting. Before issuing an interception order, the court must find all of of the following:

1. Probable cause to believe that the person whose communication is to be intercepted has committed, is committing, or is about to commit one of the specified crimes

2. Probable cause to believe that particular communications concerning that offense will be obtained through the interception

3. That normal investigative procedures have been tried and have failed or reasonably appear to be unlikely to succeed if tried or reasonably appear to be too dangerous

4. Probable cause to believe that the facility from which, or the place where, the wire, oral, or electronic communications are to be intercepted is being used or is about to be used in connection with the commission of the specified offense, or is leased to, listed in the name of, or commonly used by the suspect

Other aspects of judicial supervision of electronic surveillance are the court's power to require, at any time, reports on the progress of the interception toward the achievement of authorized objectives; the requirement of court approval for any extension of the surveillance; and the requirement that the recordings of any communications be sealed under directions of the court immediately upon the expiration of the order.

Judicial sanctions for violations of Title III include criminal penalties, penalties for contempt of court, and awards of civil damages. In addition, 18 U.S.C.A. § 2515 provides for the exclusion of evidence obtained in violation of Title III. In United States v. Spadaccino, 800 F.2d 292 (2d Cir. 1986), the court held that the good faith exception to the exclusionary rule did not apply to violations of Title III. The court said that where the legislature has spoken clearly on the issue, "it is appropriate to look to the terms of the statute and the intentions of the legislature, rather than to invoke judge-made exceptions to judge-made rules." 800 F.2d at 296.

Procedures

Title III establishes specific procedures for the application for, the issuance of, and the execution of court orders for the interception of wire, oral, or electronic communications.

APPLICATION. Application procedures for interception orders are governed by 18 U.S.C.A. § 2518(1), which is quoted here:

§ 2518. Procedure for interception of wire, oral, or electronic communications

(1) Each application for an order authorizing or approving the interception of a wire, oral, or electronic communication under this chapter shall be made in writing upon oath or affirmation to a judge of competent jurisdiction and shall state the applicant's authority to make such application. Each application shall include the following information:

(a) the identity of the investigative or law enforcement officer making the application, and the officer authorizing the application;

(b) a full and complete statement of the facts and circumstances relied upon by the applicant, to justify his belief that an order should be issued, including (i) details as to the particular offense that has been, is being, or is about to be committed, (ii) except as provided in subsection (11), a particular description of the nature and location of the facilities from which or the place where the communication is to be intercepted, (iii) a particular description of the type of communications sought to be intercepted, (iv) the identity of the person, if known, committing the offense and whose communications are to be intercepted;

(c) a full and complete statement as to whether or not other investigative procedures have been tried and failed or why they reasonably appear to be unlikely to succeed if tried or to be too dangerous;

(d) a statement of the period of time for which the interception is required to be maintained. If the nature of the investigation is such that the authorization for interception should not automatically terminate when the described type of communication has been first obtained, a particular description of facts establishing probable cause to believe that additional communications of the same type will occur thereafter;

(e) a full and complete statement of the facts concerning all previous applications known to the individual authorizing and making the application, made to any judge for authorization to intercept, or for approval of interceptions of, wire, oral, or electronic communications involving any of the same persons, facilities or places specified in the application, and the action taken by the judge on each such application; and

(f) where the application is for the extension of an order, a statement setting forth the results thus far obtained from the interception, or a reasonable explanation of the failure to obtain such results.

Only the U.S. attorney general or other federal attorneys specified by Title III may authorize an application for a federal interception order. Only a federal investigative or law enforcement officer, as defined by Title III, or an attorney authorized to prosecute Title III offenses, may make an application for a federal interception order. With respect to the requirement of identifying the person whose communications are to be intercepted, the U.S. Supreme Court held that the applicant must name all persons who the government has probable cause to believe are committing the offense for which the application is made. United States v. Donovan, 429 U.S. 413, 97 S.Ct. 658, 50 L.Ed.2d 652 (1977). The *Donovan* case also held, however, that failure to comply with this identification requirement did not require the exclusion of evidence obtained by the interception.

ISSUANCE. If, on the basis of the application, the judge makes the required findings, the judge may issue an order authorizing or approving the interception of wire, oral, or electronic communications. Each order must specify all of the following:

1. The identity, if known, of the person whose communications are to be intercepted

2. The nature and location of the communications facilities as to which, or the place where, authority to intercept is granted

3. A particular description of the type of communications sought to be intercepted, and a statement of the particular offense to which the communication relates

4. The identity of the agency authorized to intercept the communications, and the identity of the person authorizing the application

5. The period of time during which the interception is authorized, including a statement as to whether or not the interception shall automatically terminate when the described communication has been first obtained

EXECUTION. Every order to intercept wire, oral, or electronic communications must be executed "as soon as practicable." In United States v. Martino, 664 F.2d 860 (2d Cir. 1981), however, the court held that delay in the execution of an interception order did not require the suppression of evidence obtained if the delay was not willful and if the information upon which probable cause was based had not become stale.

Title III requires that authorized interceptions be conducted in such a way as to minimize the interception of communications not otherwise subject to interception under Title III. This minimization effort must be objectively reasonable under the circumstances. In Scott v. United States, 436 U.S. 128, 98 S.Ct. 1717, 56 L.Ed.2d 168 (1978), the U.S. Supreme Court held an interception reasonable although only 40 percent of the intercepted conversations related to crimes specified in the order because the remaining conversations were ambiguous and were of brief duration.

When a law enforcement officer intercepts communications relating to offenses other than those specified in the interception order, the officer must apply as soon as possible for judicial approval to disclose the evidence in court. Without judicial approval, the evidence may not be disclosed. In United States v. Van Horn, 789 F.2d 1492 (11th Cir. 1986), the court held that the judicial approval could take the form of the judge's granting of an extension order after receiving progress reports and applications for extensions describing the nature of the conversations being intercepted.

Authorized interceptions must terminate upon attainment of the authorized objective, or in any event in thirty days. Extensions of an interception order may be granted, but only upon reapplication in accordance with the same procedures as for an original application.

Immediately upon the expiration of an interception order, recordings are required to be delivered to the judge issuing the order and to be sealed under the judge's directions. The purposes of this requirement are to prevent tampering, to aid in establishing the chain of custody, to protect confidentiality, and to establish judicial control over the surveillance. The statutory term *immediately* has been interpreted to mean without unnecessary or unreasonable delay. Failure to deliver the recordings or unjustifiable or unexplained late delivery may cause the recordings to be excluded from evidence. Before ordering suppression, however, courts will examine all the circumstances, including whether the defendant has been prejudiced by tampering or other governmental misconduct. United States v. Rodriguez, 786 F.2d 472 (2d Cir. 1986).

Finally, within a reasonable time, but not later than 90 days after the termination of the period of an order, an *inventory* must be served upon the persons named in the order and upon such other parties to intercepted communications as the judge may determine in the interest of justice. This inventory must also be served after emergency interceptions are carried out. It must include a notice of the fact of the order, the date of approval of the application, the period of the authorized interception, and a statement of whether or not wire, oral, or electronic communications were intercepted during the period. Failure to serve the inventory is not grounds for suppression unless the failure causes actual, incurable prejudice. United States v. Harrigan, 586 F.2d 860, 865 (1st Cir. 1978).

If requested by the applicant, an interception order may require providers of wire or electronic communication services, landlords, custodians, or other persons to furnish the applicant with "all information, facilities, and technical assistance necessary to accomplish the interception unobtrusively and with a minimum of interference with the services" provided by those persons. 18 U.S.C.A. § 2518 (4). The applicant is required to provide reasonable compensation for the facilities or assistance.

Individual Rights

As stated earlier, Title III was the result of a bipartisan congressional effort to balance the need for more effective law enforcement against the need to protect constitutional rights. Examples of specific ways in which Title III provides for the protection of individual rights are given in this section.

First, a person who was a party to any intercepted communication or against whom the interception was directed has a limited right to inspect such portions of the intercepted communications, applications, and orders as the judge determines to be in the interest of justice. The prosecution may not use as evidence the contents of an intercepted communication unless each party has been furnished with a copy of the application and a copy of the interception order not less than ten days before the trial, hearing, or proceeding. This ten-day notice period is designed to provide a person with the opportunity to make a motion to suppress.

Second, a person's privacy rights are protected by the provision that applications and orders granted under Title III may be disclosed only upon a showing of good cause before a judge. In In re Applications of Kansas City Star, 666 F.2d 1168 (8th Cir. 1981), the court held that in determining whether there is good cause for disclosure, courts must consider what effect disclosure of applications and orders has on a person's privacy when there is no suppression hearing and no governmental need to disclose the documents. The court held that there was not good cause to disclose to the news media affidavits relating to wiretaps on third parties that had been released to the defendant. In addition, the First Circuit Court of Appeals held that the Freedom of Information Act (5 U.S.C.A. § 552) could not be used to gain access to records of electronic surveillance made in violation of the Fourth Amendment. Providence Journal Company v. Federal Bureau of Investigation, 602 F.2d 1010 (1st Cir. 1979).

A third individual right under Title III arises when the victim of an illegal interception is called as a witness before a grand jury and is asked questions based upon that interception. In Gelbard v. United States, 408 U.S. 41, 92 S.Ct. 2357, 33 L.Ed.2d 179 (1972), the U.S. Supreme Court held that a grand jury witness may invoke a violation of Title III as a defense to charges of contempt for refusing to answer questions. Generally, if the witness makes a preliminary showing that the government's questions were based on illegally obtained information, the burden shifts to the government to prove otherwise. If the government fails, the witness may refuse to testify without penalty.

Another individual right under Title III is the right of a person whose communications have been intercepted, disclosed, or used in violation of Title III to bring a civil action against the person who caused the violation. Defendants in such an action may avoid liability by establishing that they relied in good faith on a court order or legislative authorization and that their actions were objectively reasonable. In Kilgore v. Mitchell, 623 F.2d 631 (9th Cir. 1980), the court held that the actions of governmental investigators were objectively reasonable where the surveillance was conducted pursuant to a court order, was consistent with Department of Justice policies, and was conducted before Title III was interpreted by the courts.

Finally, Title III permits any person who was a party to any intercepted communication or a person against whom an interception was directed to move to suppress the contents of the communication or evidence derived from it. In Alderman v. United States, 394 U.S. 165, 89 S.Ct. 961, 22 L.Ed.2d 176 (1969), the U.S. Supreme Court held that the owner of premises where allegedly illegal electronic surveillance occurred also may move to suppress such evidence on Fourth Amendment grounds. Grounds for suppression under Title III are that

1. the communication was unlawfully intercepted;
2. the order of authorization or approval under which the communication was intercepted is insufficient on its face; or
3. the interception was not made in conformity with the order of authorization or approval.

Generally, courts have been reluctant to suppress evidence for a violation of Title III unless the violation was central to the statutory scheme. For example, in United States v. Giordano, 416 U.S. 505, 94 S.Ct. 1820, 40 L.Ed.2d 341 (1974), the U.S. Supreme Court ordered suppression where an executive assistant of the U.S. attorney general, rather than the attorney general himself or a specially designated assistant, had authorized an application for an interception order. The Court considered authorization by the attorney general or a specially designated assistant central to the statutory scheme of promoting restraint by centralizing eavesdropping responsibility in a politically accountable government official. In United States v. Chavez, 416 U.S. 562, 94 S.Ct. 1849, 40 L.Ed.2d 380 (1974), however, the Justice Department contended that the attorney general had in fact personally approved the surveillance request, but the application had misrepresented the authorizing official to be his executive assistant. Despite the technical violation, the Court denied suppression because the violation was not considered central to the statutory scheme. The Court said, "No role more significant than a reporting function designed to establish on paper that one of the major procedural protections of Title III had been properly accomplished is apparent." 416 U.S. at 579, 94 S.Ct. at 1858, 40 L.Ed.2d at 394.

Applicability to the States

Title III specifically authorizes state law enforcement officials to apply for, obtain, and execute orders authorizing or approving the interception of wire, oral, or electronic communications. The procedures are similar to those governing federal interception orders. The primary difference is that the state procedure must be authorized by a separate state statute. If a state statute so authorizes, the principal prosecuting attorney of the state, or of a political subdivision of the state, may apply to a state court judge of competent jurisdiction for an interception order. In granting the order, the judge must comply with both the applicable state statute and Title III. The interception order may be granted only when the interception may provide "evidence of the commission of the offense of murder, kidnapping, gambling, robbery, bribery, extortion, or dealing in narcotic drugs, marihuana or other dangerous drugs, or other crime dangerous to life, limb, or property, and punishable by imprisonment for more than one year, designated in any applicable State statute authorizing such interception, or any conspiracy to commit any of the foregoing offenses." 18 U.S.C.A. § 2516(2).

State legislation may not authorize interceptions that fall short of the requirements of Title III. On the other hand, states may enact laws that place stricter
limits on electronic surveillance than those in Title III. Federal courts are not
obliged to adhere to more restrictive state laws, however, and will generally
admit evidence that violates such a law, so long as the evidence was not obtained in violation of Title III. For example, in United States v. Daniel, 667 F.2d
783 (9th Cir. 1982), an interception of a conversation without a search warrant
violated state law. Nevertheless, the evidence was held admissible in federal
court because Title III does not require a warrant when one of the parties to the
intercepted conversation consents to the interception.

Exceptions to Title III

Many types of interceptions of wire, oral, or electronic communications either
are not covered by provisions of Title III or are specifically excepted from coverage. Because these exceptions are numerous, they are discussed here in general terms only.

A party to an oral communication who has no reasonable expectation of privacy with respect to the communication is not protected either by Title III or
by the Fourth Amendment. In Title III, the term *oral communication* is defined
as "any oral communication uttered by a person exhibiting an expectation that
such communication is not subject to interception under circumstances justifying such expectation but such term does not include any electronic communication." 18 U.S.C.A. § 2510(2). In State v. Salisbury, 662 F.2d 738 (11th Cir.
1981), the court held that a party to a conversation has no legitimate expectation that another party to the conversation will not record the conversation or
reveal its contents to authorities. In United States v. Harrelson, 754 F.2d 1153
(5th Cir. 1985), the court held that surreptitiously recorded conversations between a prison inmate and his wife did not qualify as oral conversations. The
court found that the couple suspected eavesdropping and therefore could have
had no reasonable expectation of privacy. "Mistaking the degree of intrusion of
which probable eavesdroppers are capable is not at all the same thing as believing there are no eavesdroppers." 754 F.2d at 1170.

Sections 2511(2)(c) and 2511(2)(d) exclude consent surveillance from the
regulatory scheme established by Title III for court-ordered surveillance.
Therefore, when one party to a communication consents to the interception of
the communication, neither Title III nor the Fourth Amendment prevents the
use of the communication in court against another party to the communication. Thus, a law enforcement officer or a private citizen who is a party to a communication may intercept the communication or permit a law enforcement official to intercept the communication without violating Title III of the Fourth
Amendment. For example, in United States v. Capo, 693 F.2d 1330 (11th Cir.
1982), the government's interception of a conversation between a consenting
informant and the defendant was held not to be a violation of the Fourth
Amendment since the defendant willingly projected his voice outside the privacy of his home and his voice was intercepted at the other end. A private citizen, however, may not intercept a communication "for the purpose of committing any criminal or tortious act in violation of the Constitution or laws of the
United States or of any state." The absence of federal regulation or preemption

regarding consent surveillance has left the states free to fashion their own approaches by statute or court decision.

Under Title III, an operator of a switchboard or an officer, employee, or agent of any communication common carrier may intercept, disclose, or use a wire communication in the normal course of business if necessary to the rendition of service or the protection of the rights or property of the carrier. Communication common carriers may not, however, use service observing or random monitoring except for mechanical or service quality control checks. Furthermore, under Title III, an employee of the Federal Communications Commission (FCC) may intercept, disclose, or use radio communications if he or she does so in the normal course of employment and pursuant to FCC monitoring responsibilities.

Title III exempts from its coverage any interception conducted by investigative or law enforcement officers using telephone or telegraph facilities in the ordinary course of their duties. In Campiti v. Walonis, 611 F.2d 387 (1st Cir. 1979), the court held that this exemption did not apply when an unusual method of surveillance was used to monitor a prison inmate's telephone conversations. In that case, an officer's listening to an inmate's conversation on an extension phone without the inmate's knowledge was found not to be within the ordinary course of the officer's duties, since the usual method of monitoring conversations was to stand close enough to hear the inmate's part of the conversation.

Another exception to Title III states that "it shall not be unlawful for an officer, employee, or agent of the United States in the normal course of his official duty to conduct electronic surveillance, as defined in section 101 of the Foreign Intelligence Surveillance Act of 1978 (FISA), as authorized by that Act." 18 U.S.C.A. § 2511(2)(e). Title III also generally leaves the overseeing of all foreign intelligence to the FISA and other applicable federal statutes (the FISA provides for judicial supervision of surveillance undertaken in furtherance of national security).

Title III does not apply to electronic surveillance conducted outside the territorial jurisdiction of the United States. For example, Stowe v. Devoy, 588 F.2d 336 (2d 1978), held that neither Title III nor the Fourth Amendment applied to evidence obtained in Canada by Canadian officials in compliance with Canadian law.

Title III does not apply to the use of electronic devices emitting signals that enable law enforcement officials to track the location of objects and persons. Use of these devices, sometimes called transmitters or beepers, is governed solely by the Fourth Amendment. Since most of the legal issues involving these devices relate to the attachment of the devices to vehicles and containers, discussion of these issues appear in Chapter 10 dealing with the warrantless search of vehicles and containers.

Similarly, Title III does not apply to trap and trace devices and pen registers. A trap and trace device traces the source of calls made to a particular telephone number. A pen register records all numbers dialed from a particular telephone number. In Smith v. Maryland, 442 U.S. 735, 99 S.Ct. 2577, 61 L.Ed.2d 220 (1979), the U.S. Supreme Court held that the installation and use of a pen register is not a search and is therefore not subject to the Fourth Amendment. The Court reasoned that the defendant had no reasonable expectation of privacy in the destination of his outgoing phone calls because the telephone company routinely monitors these calls to check billing, to detect fraud, and to prevent other violations of law. Federal courts have not yet addressed the Fourth Amendment implications of the use of trap and trace devices. Because telephone companies do not routinely monitor incoming calls, the rationale of the *Smith* case may not apply to the use of those devices. Since the *Smith* decision, Congress has enacted legislation (18 U.S.C.A. §§ 3121–26) prohibiting the installation or use of a pen register or a trap and trace device except by court order.

Although law enforcement officials must obtain a judicial order to intercept wire, oral, or electronic communications, neither Title III nor the Fourth Amendment requires them to obtain judicial authorization to covertly enter premises to install a listening device. In Dalia v. United States, 441 U.S. 238, 99 S.Ct. 1682, 60 L.Ed.2d 177 (1979), a federal court authorized the interception of all oral communications concerning an interstate stolen goods conspiracy at the defendant's office. Although the interception order did not explicitly authorize entry into the defendant's office, FBI agents secretly entered the office and installed a listening device in the ceiling. Six weeks later, after the surveillance had terminated, the agents reentered the office and removed the device. The defendant was convicted, partly on the basis of intercepted conversations. The U.S. Supreme Court considered the legislative history of Title III and concluded as follows:

> [O]ne simply cannot assume that Congress, aware that most bugging requires covert entry, nonetheless wished to except surveillance requiring such entries from the broad authorization of Title III, and that it resolved to do so by remaining silent on the subject. On the contrary, the language and history of Title III convey quite a different explanation for Congress' failure to distinguish between surveillance that requires convert entry and that which does not. Those considering the surveillance legislation understood that, by authorizing electronic interception of oral communications in addition to wire communications, they were necessarily authorizing surreptitious entries. 441 U.S. at 252, 99 S.Ct. at 1691, 60 L.Ed.2d at 189.

With respect to the Fourth Amendment, the Court found that nothing in the language of the Fourth Amendment or the Court's decisions suggested that search warrants must include a specification of the precise manner in which those warrants must be executed. "On the contrary, it is generally left to the discretion of the executing officers to determine the details of how best to proceed with the performance of a search authorized by warrant—subject of course to the general Fourth Amendment protection 'against unreasonable searches and seizures.'" 441 U.S. at 257, 99 S.Ct. at 1693, 60 L.Ed.2d at 192.

Finally, Title III provides authority for designated federal or state officials to intercept wire, oral, or electronic communications without a prior interception order if (1) an emergency situation exists that involves immediate danger of death or serious physical injury to any person, that involves conspiratorial activities threatening the national security interest, or that involves conspiratorial activities characteristic of organized crime; and (2) an interception order cannot be obtained in sufficient time. The determination of emergency must be made by the U.S. attorney general or other governmental official specified in Title III. The law enforcement officer carrying out the emergency surveillance must apply for an interception order under § 2518 within forty-eight hours after the interception has occurred or begins to occur. If an order is not obtained, the interception must immediately terminate when the sought-after communication is obtained or when the application is denied, whichever is earlier.

Constitutionality of Title III

This discussion of Title III of the Omnibus Crime Control and Safe Streets Act of 1968 has centered around the specific provisions of the act and court interpretation of those provisions. By and large, these decisions have eroded the limited protections provided by the act and have provided little support for the constitutional principles established in the *Osborn, Berger,* and *Katz* decisions discussed earlier. Although Title III has survived constitutional challenges in several lower federal courts and similar statutes have survived constitutional challenges in state courts, the U.S. Supreme Court has yet to decide on the constitutionality of Title III. It remains to be seen whether Title III, as interpreted, can withstand a challenge based upon the Fourth Amendment's prohibition against general searches.

SUMMARY

Electronic surveillance was originally considered beyond the coverage of the Fourth Amendment because it involved no trespass into the defendant's premises and because it involved no seizure of tangible items. In a series of U.S. Supreme Court decisions in the mid-sixties, the Court reversed this approach and held that electronic surveillance by agents of the government is a search and seizure governed by the Fourth Amendment. The leading case adopting this new approach was *Katz v. United States*, which held that the Fourth Amendment protects people not places, thereby shifting the focus of the Fourth Amendment from property to privacy. In addition, the Court held that electronic surveillance is permissible only if conducted pursuant to a warrant that carefully limits the surveillance in nature, scope, and duration.

In 1968, Congress enacted Title III of the Omnibus Crime Control and Safe Streets Act, which attempts to balance the need to use electronic surveillance for more effective law enforcement against the need to protect the privacy rights of individuals. Title III provides for judicial supervision of all aspects of electronic surveillance and establishes warrant procedures similar to those required for the search and seizure of tangible objects. These procedures are designed to limit who can authorize an application for an interception order, who can apply for an order, the duration of electronic surveillance allowed, and various aspects of the execution of an interception order. Individual rights provided under Title III include a limited right to inspect intercepted communications, restrictions on the disclosure of applications and orders, and rights to bring civil actions and motions to suppress for violations. Title III also specifically provides that state law enforcement officials may apply for, obtain, and execute electronic surveillance orders if authorized by a separate state statute.

There are many exceptions to the coverage of Title III. Title III does not protect a party to a conversation who has no reasonable expectation of privacy with respect to that conversation. Furthermore, if one party to a conversation consents to the interception of that conversation, the conversation may be used against the other party. Any interception conducted by investigative or law enforcement officers using telephone or telegraph facilities in the ordinary course of their duties is exempted. And electronic surveillance related to national security and foreign intelligence is governed primarily by the Foreign Intelligence Surveillance Act of 1978. Finally, Title III does not apply to the use of electronic devices such as beepers, trap and trace devices, and pen registers.

Although a warrant is required to intercept wire, oral, or electronic communications, judicial approval is not required to covertly enter premises to install a listening device. Neither is a warrant required to intercept wire, oral, or electronic communications in emergencies involving immediate danger of death or serious physical injury, or conspiracies threatening national security or involving organized crime, although an interception order must be applied for within forty-eight hours of the interception.

In general, court decisions interpreting the specific provisions of Title III have tended to erode the limited protections to individual rights provided in the act by refusing to suppress evidence for a violation of Title III unless the violation was central to the statutory scheme or unless there was incurable prejudice to the defendant. The constitutionality of Title III has yet to be determined by the U.S. Supreme Court.

REVIEW AND DISCUSSION QUESTIONS

1. Would an amendment to the Constitution dealing with modern-day intrusions on privacy have been a better way to deal with the problems posed by electronic surveillance than was stretching the interpretation of the Fourth Amendment? Draft such an amendment.

2. Describe three ways in which court decisions have eroded the limited protections to individual rights provided in Title III of the Omnibus Crime Control and Safe Streets Act of 1968.

3. A physical trespass to property is no longer required to invoke the protections of the Fourth Amendment in electronic eavesdropping cases, but is it safe to say that if there is a physical trespass, the Fourth Amendment's protections are automatically invoked?

4. Is installing a listening device in someone's home the same as hiding a police officer in a closet in the home? How does the police officer's ability to look through a keyhole in the closet affect the comparison?

5. Since Title III does not require judicial authority to covertly enter premises to install a listening device, is it correct to say that a person's conversations are no more protected in his or her home than they are in a telephone booth?

6. Under Title III, should the allowable duration of an interception order depend on the nature of the crime? Give examples.

7. How can a law enforcement officer ensure that authorized interceptions are conducted in such a way as to minimize the interception of communications not otherwise subject to interception under Title III? Should compliance

with this requirement of Title III depend on the subjective intention of the officers conducting the surveillance?

8. Give some examples of ways in which a law enforcement official applying for an interception order might indicate that normal investigative procedures have failed, appear unlikely to succeed, or would be too dangerous.

9. What are some potential problems in determining when the authorized objective of an interception order under Title III has been attained?

10. Give some examples of conversations that would not be protected by Title III or by the Fourth Amendment because a party to the conversation has no reasonable expectation of privacy with respect to the conversation.

TABLE OF CASES

INDEX

References are to Pages